SEX AND HARM IN
THE AGE OF CONSENT

SEX AND HARM IN THE AGE OF CONSENT

JOSEPH J. FISCHEL

UNIVERSITY OF MINNESOTA PRESS
MINNEAPOLIS • LONDON

The University of Minnesota Press gratefully acknowledges financial assistance for the publication of this book from the Frederick W. Hilles Publication Fund of Yale University.

A different version of chapter 2 was published as "Transcendent Homosexuals and Dangerous Sex Offenders: Sexual Harm and Freedom in the Judicial Imaginary," *Duke Journal of Gender Law and Policy* 17, no. 2 (2010): 277–312. A different version of chapter 3 was published as "*Per Se* or Power? Age and Sexual Consent," *Yale Journal of Law and Feminism* 22, no. 2 (2010): 279–341.

Published by the University of Minnesota Press
111 Third Avenue South, Suite 290
Minneapolis, MN 55401-2520
http://www.upress.umn.edu

Printed in the United States of America on acid-free paper

The University of Minnesota is an equal-opportunity educator and employer.

22 21 20 19 18 17 16   10 9 8 7 6 5 4 3 2 1

Library of Congress Cataloging-in-Publication Data
Names: Fischel, Joseph J., author.
Title: Sex and harm in the age of consent / Joseph J. Fischel.
Description: Minneapolis : University of Minnesota Press, 2016. | Includes bibliographical references and index.
Identifiers: LCCN 2015042584 | ISBN 978-0-8166-9475-4 (hc) | ISBN 978-0-8166-9476-1 (pb)
Subjects: LCSH: Sex crimes—United States | Consent (Law)—United States. | Sex customs—United States. | Sex offenders—United States.
Classification: LCC KF9325 .F57 2016 | DDC 345.73/0253—dc23
LC record available at http://lccn.loc.gov/2015042584

Contents

Acknowledgments

As this project unfolded and its queries around sex, age, and harm congealed, I anticipated from readers righteous resistance, reactionary misunderstanding, or the absolute worst, indifference. I found instead unending support, compassionate critique, and a most rewarding community of thinkers, activists, and friends whose contributions to the book have been nothing less than astounding.

I started assembling *Sex and Harm in the Age of Consent* as a doctoral student at the University of Chicago. There I had the unparalleled fortune of working with Lauren Berlant, who advised this project, and me, for many years. My writing, thinking, and teaching benefited incalculably from all her guidance and interlocution. Patchen Markell and Bernard Harcourt provided critical coaching as well. I am particularly grateful to Patchen for his help reconstructing the Introduction and final chapter of the book, and to Bernard for calling me out when I drifted into boring. At the University of Chicago, the project received generous intellectual and financial support from the Department of Political Science, the Center for the Study of Gender and Sexuality, and the Office of the Provost. Many thanks to all those who conversed with me over coffee, workshops, office hours, e-mails, conferences, and slow rides up Lake Shore Drive: Kathy Anderson, Scott Anderson, Cathy Cohen, Julie Cooper, Rose Corrigan, Andrew Dilts, Samuel Galloway, Rachel Goodman, Daragh Grant, Marissa Guerrero, Eric Hundman, Theo Kuhnlohe, Don Kulick, Ainsley LeSure, Gabriel Mares, Stuart Michaels, Martha Nussbaum, Gina Olson, Laurie Jo Reynolds, Scott Richmond, Nathan Tarcov, Lisa Wedeen, Aaron Welo, Richard Wright, and Linda Zerilli. Thank you to Kathryn Bond Stockton for helping my queer thoughts grow (up?) into queerer arguments. Infinite gratitude to Diana Kim and Jon Rogowksi for hugs, cocktails, and everything else important.

The project has been deeply textured by the many places and people it has encountered over the past six years. Thank you to the staff of the *Duke Journal of Gender Law and Policy*; to the indefatigable Zach Herz and the staff of the *Yale Journal of Law and Feminism*; to Katherine Franke, Beth Povinelli, Kendall Thomas, Carole Vance, and Beck Witt at the Center for Gender and Sexuality Law at Columbia Law School; to Tim Dean, Lisa Downing, and the Consent Workshop crew at the Institute of Advanced Studies, University of Birmingham; and to Adrienne Davis, Deborah Dinner, Amber Jamilla Musser, and Anca Parvulescu at Washington University in St. Louis.

In 2011–12, I was a postdoctoral fellow at the Pembroke Center for Teaching and Research on Women, where I had the privilege of adventuring with the very best littermates, Crystal Biruk and Poulomi Saha. Thank you, too, to the folks in and around the Pembroke consent seminar, from whom I learned so much: Denise Davis, Donna Goodnow, Jane Gordon, Hunter Hargraves, Lynne Joyrich, Suzanne Stewart-Steinberg, Elizabeth Weed, Debbie Weinstein, and many others.

During the past few years working at Yale University, I have been blessed with colleagues and students who are as engaged as they are encyclopedic: Melanie Boyd, Jill Campbell, Craig Canfield, George Chauncey, Inderpal Grewal, Linda Hase, Greta Toe Pick LaFleur, Katie Lofton, Vida Maralani, Joanne Meyerowitz, Ali Miller, John Palmer, Gabe Rosenberg, and Linn Tonstad. The Yale Office of the Provost generously brought Elizabeth Bernstein to campus for a twenty-four-hour mentor-a-thon, and her insights were precise and transformative.

A special shout-out to two bitingly brilliant, former-student comrades, Hilary O'Connell and Chamonix Adams Porter. As the book neared final approach, Hilary worked miracles as a research and editorial assistant.

The book was caffeinated by Saugatuck Coffee, Caribou Coffee, and Argo Tea in Chicago, Blue State Coffee in Providence and New Haven, and Joe's in Provincetown; it was balanced by Yoga East and Will Coons in Provincetown, CorePower and Noah Powell in Chicago, Breathing Time in Providence, and Fresh Yoga in New Haven.

This project would never have been completed without the help of family. My mother, Shelley Fischel, taught me how to write. She has been my most steadfast editor, critic, and friend. My father, Bob Fischel, taught me not to hate Freud, which meant I learned to sit with latency in its many dimensions. The years when *Sex and Harm in the Age of Consent* crystallized were the same years my sister Eliana Fischel and I became best friends: her care and carefulness infuse the book throughout (even if she might disagree with some of its arguments). Elva Neyra continues to be a most necessary source of love, support, and counsel. My partner, Igor Souza, has anchored this project and its occasionally flighty author. I thank him for all his love, but even more for his patience.

A final thank you to the editors and staff at the University of Minnesota Press, especially to Pieter Martin for seeing promise in the project and steering it along, and to Kristian Tvedten for his assistance. Julie Novkov, David Richards, and Carlos Ball gave precise, superb feedback.

This book is dedicated to my late friend Sam Kasoff, defender of all us kids, a virtuoso of bravery and bigheartedness.

Whatever is worth retaining here is a collaborative achievement. Whatever is wanting is my responsibility. All polemics my own, all puns intended.

Introduction

Sex and the Ends of Consent

I know that homosexuals cannot biologically reproduce children;
therefore, they must recruit our children.

—Anita Bryant

[Public signs let] everybody in that community know *exactly* where
that pervert lives in the community.

—Sheriff Gordon Smith, Bradford County, Florida

INFORMAL PROVOCATION 1:
"EXACTLY WHERE THAT PERVERT LIVES"

In April 2013, at the direction of local sheriff Gordon Smith, Bradford
County, Florida, erected red signs in front of the homes of "sex predators"—
a subspecies of those persons Florida designates "sex offenders." The signs
read, "[Name] is a convicted sexual predator and lives at this location"
(Figure 1). This policy has been implemented on top of and as a way to
toughen the sex offender registration and notification (SORN) requirements already in place (and federally mandated) in Florida and across the
nation. "Registration" typically compels the sex offender to periodically
confirm his[1] whereabouts to local authorities, and "notification" almost
always requires dissemination of the sex offender's personal information
(his photograph, bodily characteristics, address, conviction, and much
more) through the Internet as well as through other methods of public
notice—for example, postcards to nearby residents and schools.

When Sheriff Smith tells us it is important, vital even, that the community knows "exactly" where the "pervert" resides, he relays a host of almost
unimpeachable assumptions shared by legislators, judges, and much of the
American public about sex offenders: (1) that whomever the law designates a "predator" is necessarily a "pervert"—that the statutory term tells
us something, perhaps everything, about the organization of the predator's desires and the compulsivity of his behaviors; (2) that sex offenders

Figure 1. In April 2013, the Bradford County, Florida, police department installed signs in front of the residences of "sex predators." Courtesy of the Bradford County Sheriff's Office.

will undoubtedly recidivate, if unchecked by regulatory measures, like public signs and online registries; (3) that sex offenders offend in close proximity to their residences; and (4) that the signs will make the Bradford County community safer from sexual harm.

All four assumptions are wrong.[2] The signs, like the sex offender laws they metaphorize and magnify, misperceive and then mischaracterize sources of and solutions to sexual harm. Equally important, these assumptions increasingly structure our very comprehension of sexual harm: as locatable (*"exactly"* locatable) in bad persons; fixable by criminal law and police power; and, less explicitly but no less powerfully, demarcated by the absence of consent. The chain of equivalence runs thus: a "sexual predator" = a sex pervert = a person who violates the dictate of consent, either against an unwilling woman or, in our contemporary, collective imaginary, against an incompetent and innocent child.

Sheriff Smith, like many local authorities, national politicians, and pundits, talks about sex offenders as if they are addicted to sexual violence, as if their sexual acts are uncontrollable, as if their errant desires are fully constitutive of who they are, and as if they are always already coming after the children.[3] This sort of rhetoric has a much longer history, one that predates but was popularized by Anita Bryant and has been deployed mainly against gay men.[4] As will become evident over the course of the book, I will not insist that sex offenders are simply the latest sexual outcast, recipients of redirected phobia. Rather, I will gesture to the ways in which the sex offender is culturally and legally produced, how that linguistic production bears a striking resemblance to the historical vilification of the homosexual, how the fiction of the sex offender disqualifies him from equal treatment under the law, and how, finally, this fictional character helps functionalize consent as the metric that matters for late modern sexual ethics. The stranger sex offender is a distorted, distorting figure, not simply a scapegoat, but also an organizing, palliative character that compromises better critical thinking and legal regulation around sex, age, age difference, and gender inequality.

INFORMAL PROVOCATION 2: TOO FAR . . . ?

According to a 2012 report in *The Daily Beast*, Francie Baldino is part of a "surprising rebellion" to repeal current sex offender laws as applied to teenagers. Baldino's son Ken was arrested in 2004 for having sex with his girlfriend, when he was eighteen and she was fourteen. Until 2011, Ken was listed on the Michigan Public Sex Offender Registry, was required to wear a GPS tracking device, and, among other restrictions, had to remain one thousand feet from schools and childcare centers.[5] Baldino, along with mothers-cum-activists nationwide, protests that sex offender regulations are unjustly enforced against teenagers. Baldino's objections are echoed by law journal authors, bloggers, and mainstream news commentators. These critics contend that young people are not pedophiles and predators, that they are less likely to recidivate than adult sex offenders, that these laws hurt those whom they are designed to protect.[6] Indeed, haven't the laws gone too far?

We should be cautious of the "too far" argument for at least two reasons. First, "too far" presupposes a "just right," as if SORN laws as currently codified and enforced would be appropriate mechanisms to curtail sexual violence, if only a select group of young people were removed from the online registries and exempted from additional requirements. To the extent that the predicate of the too-far argument is *the law should treat teenage lovers differently from pedophiles or violent sexual predators,* it naturalizes the social and statutory constructs of the pedophile and the violent sexual predator, takes for granted their preeminence as perpetrators of sexual harm, and assumes that extant SORN laws work. Even if we assume that young sex offenders are categorically different from adult sex offenders—less likely to recidivate, less culpable, less "hardened"—why would we assume that state systems of registration, online notification, residency restrictions, GPS tracking, and so on effectively deter the "truly" predatory?[7] And if the most common SORN regulations fail to make the nation sexually safer, why should only young people be exempted? The too-far argument reiterates predation, rather than relation, as the problem of sexual violence.

Second, "too far" potentially precludes young people from being envisioned either as competent sexual agents or as sexual aggressors. Baldino says of her son, "he was just a dumb kid," and he "did stupid things."[8] The age-appropriate idiocy (or immaturity, more generously) of youth is a recurring theme among those who call for the declassification of young persons as sex offenders. But by making adolescents "stupid" and "dumb," activists rescript them as innocent and incompetent children.

The rhetorical equivalence of youthfulness and dumbness risks not only rendering young people's sexual agency unintelligible, but also eclipses the fact that young people, particularly boys, do sexually pressure, coerce, and assault. By all accounts, the sexual encounters between Ken and his then girlfriend were wanted and welcomed. Nonetheless, journalistic, progressive, and activist insistence on young people's immaturity, inexperience, and underdevelopment may discredit young people's sexual decision making, but also convert sexually coercive or impermissible behavior into "boys will be boys" triviality.[9]

INFORMAL PROVOCATION 3: . . . OR NOT ENOUGH?

In March 2013, two teenage boys, football players from Steubenville, Ohio, were convicted of raping a teenage girl.[10] The story became a national scandal when, seven months earlier, it was revealed by crime blogger Alexandria Goddard that the boys and their friends callously broadcast incriminating pictures and comments over cell phones and social media. Goddard, who claimed that the local veneration of football hamstrung a more timely investigation, asked her readers, "What *normal* person would even consider that posting the brutal rape of a young girl is something that should be shared with their peers?"[11]

After the "delinquent" verdict against the boys had been announced, CNN and other newscasters lamented the fate of these so-called misbehaving boys, who might face a lifetime of SORN requirements and thus ruined futures.[12] The newscasters were widely lambasted for their complicity in victim blaming and their insensitivity to the gravity of sexual violence.[13] These were not boys who made terrible mistakes, but predators by constitution.[14] In this carceral-feminist register,[15] the verdict and attendant SORN requirements were overdue remedy against a high-school-football-infused culture that does not do enough to check, and even tacitly condones, the preternaturally violent boys in its midst.

But must these teenagers be predatory rapists (or foolhardy, undeveloped youth)[16] for their conduct to qualify (or disqualify) as sexual injury in our national consciousness? And must the gravity of sexual injury be indexed and recompensed by the severity of SORN requirements?

The sentencing in the Steubenville case exposes another upshot of legally codifying young sexual actors as either strictly predatory or strictly victimized. One of the boys received an extra year of juvenile detention because he photographed and disseminated nude pictures of the sixteen-year-old girl.[17] We might agree that the boy should be penalized for taking pictures of this unconscious, exposed girl from his cell phone. But why? The strict liability offense bars anyone from photographing nude teenagers, whether or not the teenager would like to be photographed, and whether the minor is ten or seventeen.[18] Is the harm here the same kind of harm as teenagers willfully exchanging revealing pictures of themselves? Is there even an identifiable harm in the latter scenario? If there is, is it a harm to be redressed by criminal law? What kind of young girl is imagined by law, and by law's addressees (all of us), when the gravamen of the offense is her nudity, rather than constraints on her decision making? Child pornography law, a "not enough" remonstration, makes innocence, rather than the autonomous young subject, the victim of sexual violence.[19]

When the repercussions to (some) acts of sexual misconduct are life-crushing penalties and regulatory injunctions, it is no wonder children are remade to be innocent by news anchors, community activists, and law scholars. Both the "too far" and "not enough" critics reiterate the logic that underpins sex offender law and saturates U.S. public opinion:[20] the story of sexual harm is the story of predatory male desire and victimized innocent youth (victimized by predators or alternatively by predatory law).

Nonconsent both constitutes and may be read off of these characters: the child cannot meaningfully consent, the predator overrides nonconsent.

I recall the stories of Sheriff Smith and his signage, Francie Baldino and her son, and the Steubenville rape case not, primarily, to carry a brief for the ostracized sex offender. *Sex and Harm in the Age of Consent* is less concerned with the legal and cultural maltreatment of the sex offender than with how the sex offender, the child, and consent (mis)shape our understanding of sexual harm. As a feminist project committed to the minimization of sexual violence, this book wonders how else the story of sexual harm might be told, were we unglued from our dominant sociolegal tropes and terms.[21] To that end, it initiates its inquiry with an uncomfortable, maybe indecorous question.

A MORE FORMAL SCHEMATIZATION

What if our nationally privileged sexuality were no longer heterosexuality but adult consensuality?[22] If this is the case, or if it is unevenly becoming so in life and law, why would it be a problem, and what kind of problem would it be? Surely, the age line and the consent line—and the age line often stands in for the consent line—tell us something truer about sexual right and wrong than does the gender line. We late moderns are no dupes of presentism, blinded by liberal *doxa*: age and consent are just better principles than gender to morally and legally adjudicate sex.

This book does not challenge these commonplace suppositions, in part because I mostly agree with them. Rather, it proposes that age and/as consent, as typically understood and legislated in the arena of sex, carry unexpected and unjust consequences. The first half of the book exposits some of those consequences. The second half presents other concepts for our cultural and juridical lexicon that might minimize those consequences. Both the diagnostic and normative sides of this argument—what age and consent do with sex and what else we could do with sex—are elaborated in the following pages.

In a different but equally epidemic context, canvassing the hyperbolic ways obesity registers in national political and legal discourse, Lauren Berlant writes, "the case is not a thing, but a cluster of factors that only looks solid at a certain distance."[23] *Sex and Harm in the Age of Consent* tracks a "cluster of factors," a contemporary, shifting, multidimensional, multidiscursive problem. It does not track a singular literature, law, theory, or history.[24] There are, in what follows, a series of overlapping, conflicting phenomena, sets of questions, some severe statutes, some less severe statutes, a few movies, and a popular but now cancelled television show. Schematized below are parts of the case-in-motion this project aims to illuminate and then better adjudicate. I begin with the constelling components, provide an outline of the book, address the question (hinted at by the epigraphs) *are sex offenders the new queers,* and then explain some absences.

CONSTELLATING COMPONENTS: THE CHILD, THE SEX OFFENDER, CONSENT, PEREMPTION

Sex and Harm in the Age of Consent interrogates the figures of the child and the sex offender, and the figuration of consent, in U.S. law and popular culture. It diagnoses how some dominant understandings of sexual harm and danger are mediated through and against the child and the offender. I argue that consent purchases its normative force as a primary ethical metric through the symbolic production of the sex offender and the child as its characterological bookends. That's a mouthful, so more simply: consent cannot do the kinds of things we want it to do, cannot divide good sex from bad, harm from freedom, or respond to the kinds of sexual/sexualized inequalities and injustices that pervade late modern life in the United States. Under the dominance of the consent paradigm, the child becomes a person defined through her inability to consent, and the sex offender, assumed uncontrollable and recidivistic, becomes a person defined as consent's transgressor. I suggest displacing (non)consent as the gravamen adjudicating sexual harm, so that we might analyze more precisely problems of sexual inequality and injustice, while we unload the injurious cultural baggage borne by the child and the sex offender.

In the past two decades, laws prohibiting sodomy have been found unconstitutional, and lesbian and gay couples are increasingly getting married and having children. It is unlawful to harass women (and men) in the workplace or in educational institutions, and it is increasingly unlawful to discriminate against some sexual and gender minorities. If HBO's *Sex and the City* and *Girls* are portents for anything, certain demographics of women have more sexual scripts and sexual options available to them than in the past, sexual roles are less predestined by gender identity, and sex toys, sex talk, sex imagery, and sex therapy circulate more freewheelingly in public channels. Pornography and other sexually explicit materials are more widely available and accessible than they have ever historically been.

Although not infused with the revolutionary headiness of the late 1960s, there seems to be some national consensus, at least among progressives, that sex—for the consenting adult, a positively profound qualifier—is alright, possibly good, despite or because of its benign variations.[25] This is not, however, to imply that sex does not still scandalize or cannot be weaponized to take down a politician or public figure. (The scandalized, weaponized sex usually involves some form of apparent nonconsent, say, in the form of the third-party nonpermitting wife, the compromised prostitute, or the underage congressional page.)

Incremental acceptance of sexual pluralism and gender equality does not exhaust our national contemporary story. *Sex and Harm in the Age of Consent* asks what other parts of the tale (the historical present) would become intelligible if our exemplary characters mapping the cartography of sexual justice were not the woman and the homosexual, but instead the young subject and the sex offender. Temporarily substituting the woman and the homosexual with the young subject and the sex offender does not jettison gender and sexuality from the analyses but recalculates their organizing force. Once we make the substitution, we witness other emergent but not altogether new phenomena. At the same historical moment in which U.S. LGBT people achieved unprecedented representational legitimacy in media and significant legal protections—from the 1990s to the present—a new wave of statutory and federal sex offender registration, notification, and civil commitment laws emerged, as did national anxieties over sexual threats from online, predatory strangers. Courts affirmed the constitutionality of severe public regulation and police supervision of released sex offenders. State and federal child pornography laws broadened their coverage and (for the most part) received judicial sanction.[26]

This is one pressing puzzle: in law, sexual minorities notionally comprised of consenting adults, namely gays and lesbians, are increasingly protected while sex offenders are increasingly pilloried.[27] Meanwhile, after an unending cast of LGBT characters parade through televisual and filmic form post-*Ellen*, we then witness the emergence of popular shows like *To Catch a Predator* and *Law and Order: Special Victims Unit*, and films like *The Woodsman, Doubt, Mysterious Skin, Capturing the Friedmans, Happiness, Hard Candy, Little Children,* and *The Girl with the Dragon Tattoo* (maybe even *The Reader* and *An Education*), not to mention images of abducted children and predatory men regularly broadcast in nightly news programs. All of these texts, in highly different approaches, reflect on or reproduce the narrative power of the adult, presumptively male, sexual predator and the presumptively innocent, unaware, but sexualized child. This observation segues another puzzle: while consenting adults are juridically granted sexual carte blanche (or something symbolically like it),[28] the child is offered ever fewer legal affordances. Although age of sexual consent laws have tended to liberalize over the twentieth and twenty-first centuries, new child pornography provisions and the dominance of abstinence-only or abstinence-plus sex education cramps the sexual autonomy of the young subject. While two same-age teenagers may be legally permitted to have sex, for example, they are likely to know little about methods of contraception and STI prevention, and to learn far less or even nothing about sexual harassment, mass-mediated gender norms, or sexual pleasure (from sex ed, that is).[29] Should they film or photograph their sex or themselves naked, they could be convicted for the production or distribution of child pornography or similar charges (as was one of the Steubenville teenagers discussed earlier, although we likely and rightly do not extend the same sympathies to him that we do to Romeos and Juliets).[30]

But let's not panic, because panic makes for hasty interpretation: that is, as the gay is no longer a tenable projection for social and sexual anxiety, the sex offender is the new queer. While one camp of politicians, concerned parents, and district attorneys seeking reelection call for more stringent ways to penalize sex offenders and immunize children from sex, another camp of liberal critics—as we saw above—bemoan that sex offender laws have gone "too far," that prosecuting teenagers who have sex or who exchange nude pictures of themselves signals puritanical overreach. Underlying both approaches is a collectively shared assumption that U.S. national culture is antisex, erotophobic, or generally freaked out, in some Christian-rooted way, by sex. If it can no longer be gays who bear the brunt of social sexual anxieties, it might as well be the newly reminted sex offender; after all, he is the *real* bad guy. Clearly, I do not reside in the first camp (the trigger-happy district attorneys), and while I share many sympathies with the second camp (liberal skeptics), I am less interested in protest than in inquiry, for there is more to the story of how and why the child and the sex offender have taken up key positions in our legal and cultural sexual landscape. At the center of this inquiry is consent.

Consent, a legal metric, is first a moral concept. It names a state of affairs (someone either has or has not consented) that has moral significance: the absence and presence of consent cleanly divides sexual harm from freedom

the *right* way, without, it seems, demonizing or demoralizing nonnormative but nonharmful sex practices. Consent gives liberals reason to embrace
a pluralism of sexual practices up to the limit marked by the presence
of coercion. It signals individual contract rather than hierarchy of status,
and therefore better respects individual decision making and better tracks
individual flourishing. Under the ambit of consent, gay is great, (adult)
pornography is permissible, and other private sexual arrangements are just
not your business.

Yet, consent is flimsy. It cannot do all the work of sexual adjudication
assigned for it by law or by the social. Sex that is regretted, unpleasant, or
even harmful occurs in legally consensual relations. And some of the sex
that occurs in legally nonconsensual relations, between minors or between
adults and minors, is formative, transformative, good, great, OK, or non-
momentous. Perhaps more importantly, sex between minors and between
minors and adults may in some instances be unjust or impermissible
whether or not the sex is wanted or consented to, in which case we, and
the law, require another vocabulary for thinking sexual harm as meaning
something other than consent's violation.[31]

The book is not, nor could it be, a polemic against consent; instead,
it inquires about consent's cultural and legal collateral. Consent as a structuring abstraction, whether for sex or political life, is not analogous to a
policy. One is not for or against consent the way one may be for or against
gun control, tax increases, or same-sex marriage. Or rather, if one is against
consent, one is a beast. Such a person, if a person, is unfit for the obliga-
tions of the democratic polity, and unfit for sex. Why? As for governance,
in the constellation of modern political thought, consent is a guarantor
of legitimate subordination to sovereign power; it underwrites civic and
political obligation. In the absence of consent, sovereign power is tyranni-
cal, and participation is unjustly compelled.[32] As for sex, in the history of
liberal legal theory and feminist scholarship, and in contemporary feminist
activism, consent is an imperfect but critical guarantor of sexual integrity
and autonomy. To countenance consent is to understand rape not as a
violation of one man's property (daughter or wife) by another man, but as
an assault against a rights-bearing person with her own set of plans, sexual
or otherwise. In the absence of consent, sex is assaultive, and participation
is unjustly compelled.[33]

Given consent's ethical primacy for modern political discourse and for
(late) modern sexual relations, an objective of the book is not to upend

consent but rather to deprioritize its juridical claim as a metric for permissible sex and to demagnetize its cultural appeal as a slogan for good sex. This endeavor is important because consent can only do the sex work we want it to do, can only perform so successfully, if subtended by other fictions: the incompetent child, the recidivistic sex offender, and the decriminalized and de-moralized homosexual. And these fictions organize apprehensions of sex and sexual violence that are at best misleading and at worst oppressive.

I am not the first to raise objections to the consent paradigm. Neither the political theoretic idealization of consent nor the transformative force of consent for sex (and these stories imbricate in ways not specified here) is without its critics. From Karl Marx to Antonio Gramsci to Louis Althusser to Martha Nussbaum, philosophers and activists have countered that the consent of the governed may be secured through ideological forces, material scarcities, and/or "adaptive preferences" to the constraints of social order, cultural aesthetics, and public discourse.[34] From John Stuart Mill to Simone de Beauvoir to Carole Pateman to Catharine MacKinnon, feminist philosophers and activists have countered that the sexual consent of the woman, or the otherwise vulnerable subject, may be engineered or extracted by socially imposed ignorance, enculturated submission, and/or financial/emotional dependency.[35] Where consent implies a plainly demarcated line between impermissible and permissible sex, authors like Stephen Schulhofer, Martha Chamallas, Susan Caringella, Nicola Gavey, and Michelle Oberman have drawn attention to the spectrum of scenarios that may qualify as unwanted or exploitive sex without meeting the threshold of nonconsensual, coercive sex.[36] Others, like Gayle Rubin, William Eskridge, and Judith Butler, have observed that only some sex practices and sexual subjects are elevated to the privilege of a consent inquiry.[37] In the United States, historically, same-sex sex, sadomasochistic sex, and sex across certain age divides, for example, have been criminalized to some degree or another, and consent is often immaterial to the criminality. An endeavor of *Sex and Harm in the Age of Consent* is to track the elevation of some same-sex sex into the realm of respectability with the simultaneous reamplification of sex offenders and sex offenses as imminent threats to the national order and the national child.

Of course no critics of consent—feminist or materialist—prefer compulsion to consensus, or sexual violence to consent. But in a variety of forms, these critics press upon the operations of consent in our visions of political freedom and our regulations of sexual relations. *Sex and Harm in the Age of Consent* takes these criticisms as points of departure to consider what sorts of sexual inequalities and misconduct consent obscures, what forms of sexual order and subjectivity consent produces, and what ethical and legal frameworks are undersold as a consequence of consent's preeminence.

Consent's flimsiness is both camouflaged and shored up by the juridical and social construction of the child and the sex offender; these characters provide consent's alibi. When, by way of cultural representation and juridical pronouncement, the child is rendered incapable of consent and the sex offender is rendered as consent's unrelenting transgressor, sexual harm comes to look like a dummy variable. This operation comes at too high a cost: sexual harm is perceived as a problem of predation rather than relation; violations of young people are perceived as violations of innocence rather than sexual autonomy; consent crowds out other terms and modes of thinking that might make for more sexually just worlds.

Under the reigning sociolegal tableaus, the decriminalized homosexual emerges, intermittently, as the figure of sexual freedom par excellence, the "consenting adult" whose raison d'être (or at the very least, whose liberty-entitlement wager) is not marriage, baby making, or abortion, but simply the pleasure of sex itself. These figures—the child, the sex offender, and the homosexual—project a picture of a world in which consent really could do all the moral work with which it is burdened; they make consent not moral, but moralized.[38]

Consent, then, is moralized. As a moralized concept, it churns out figures for its own normativity and forecloses a more capacious, multifactored understanding of sexual harm and freedom. Such an understanding requires principles and considerations besides consent—principles and considerations that will undoubtedly generate their own juridical and discursive collateral fallout. But my aspiration is to minimize rather than eliminate costs. Working in the realms of law, sex, power, and discourse, propositional theory always subordinates (or minimally, undervalues) someone or something.

I admit that it is doubtful Wendy Brown would endorse the way I have appropriated her distinction between morality in politics and political moralism.[39] For her, the latter describes an unreflective tendency of leftists and liberals to channel frustrated energies and failed efforts to reorganize economic and political arrangement into remonstrations and prosecutions of persons, speech, and bad manners. Enraged but devastated by the apparently unalterable, unjust, and deadening conditions of late capitalism, progressives too often turn to state power and the punishment of chimeric bad guys as compensatory substitutions for world building. Applied to the case of sexual harm, we might understand cultural and legislative preoccupations with the sex offender as national neuroses—unrealizable desires for a socially and sexually just world rechanneled as vengefulness. So far, so good. But for Brown, it sometimes seems that any call or longing for legal codification or state-enforced prohibition invariably falls prey to this sort of depoliticizing, ahistorical moralism. My contention is that if sexual harm is to be codified and statutorily regulated anyhow, progressives have a moral, not just moralistic, stake in normatively defensible law and adjudication. So while a more sexually just, less harmful world requires all sorts of investments, interventions, new thinking, and social transformations, a good chunk of this book insists that state-enforced prohibitions and prosecutions could be part of that vision rather than hostile to it, if extant prohibitions and prosecutions are rethought, revised, and sometimes replaced, with a particular eye toward the propulsive power of consent.

Sexual threat, freedom, and injury are not best thought of as embodied in persons (the sex offender, the consenting adult-cum-homosexual, and the child, respectively). Rather than aim to detect sex harm in the particular person and then relocate, confine, castigate, or castrate him, we should instead more carefully regulate and protect young sexual subjectivity and more critically examine how forms of coercion and constraint against the young sexual subject are variegated by social axes of inequality.

To these ends, I propose that sexual autonomy, "peremption," and vulnerability surpass consent, predation, and innocence as conceptual guideposts for thinking sex, and regulating sex, between young people and between young people and adults. As I shall demonstrate from the selected textual and visual materials, such an ethical and legal reorientation is already germinating in national discourses.

The book adopts its definition of "sexual autonomy" from Stephen Schulhofer and modifies the concept through feminist theoretic reconstructions of autonomy as relational rather than individualistic.[40] I ask what sexual autonomy entails when applied to the young subject (Schulhofer applies sexual autonomy mostly to heterosexual adult relations and for purposes of better protecting women) and provisionally answer that

sexual autonomy impels, inter alia, the holding open of intimate and relational options, resources for comprehensive sex education, attentiveness
to queer marginality, and restrictions on sex in relations of dependence.
While age of consent statutes tend to figure the young subject as someone on whom is conferred, all at once, on a birthday in her late teens,
powers of fully willed sexual decision making, sexual autonomy allows us
to acknowledge the young person as a vulnerable and desiring person
whose sexual and intimate choices are particularly prone to interference.

"Peremption" gets full conceptual parsing in the last chapter. As the
book proceeds, it makes the case that if we were less culturally and legally
preoccupied with the sexualized child and more concerned with conditions of gendered adolescence, we might have a more forgiving, but also
more generative, approach for conceptualizing sex and sexualized injury.
To move from predation to peremption as a locus of sexual harm is, once
again, to make relations, rather than bad persons, the object of intervention. Peremption refers to the way forces—people, education, sex education, cultural and commodity messaging, normative gender and sexual
expectations—constrain the young subject and disqualify possibilities for
more successful, less damaged, modes of intimacy. The films examined
in the fourth chapter illuminate that one upshot of gender difference is
the way some boys, even proto-queer boys, are asymmetrically conferred
forms of cultural capital to better navigate themselves out of crowded,
potentially injurious conditions.

"Vulnerability" does less structuring work for the arguments of the
book than autonomy and peremption, but "vulnerability" courses throughout the text to offset the discursive and political power of "innocence."
Cultural narratives (media coverage of child sex abuse; television shows
like *To Catch a Predator* and *Law & Order: Special Victims Unit*) and criminal law (age of consent statutes) envision children and young people as
a special class, deserving particularistic protections and moral attention.
Sex and Harm in the Age of Consent also makes the case that young people
be considered as a separate class under (sex) law, but on account of vulnerability, not innocence. Such a classification is attuned to asymmetric
susceptibility, to the ways young people are disproportionately prone to
imposition and interference.[41] Heightened protections are tailored to the
promotion of sexual autonomy rather than unilateral prohibitions against
sex. Therefore, while I resist narratives of innocence, I am also pushing
back against certain strands of progressive scholarship and activism that

either equate innocence with vulnerability and/or assume that narratives of innocence and vulnerability are only rhetorical maneuvers to preserve traditional gender and sexual norms.[42]

The set of shifts from consent to sexual autonomy, from the predator to peremption, from innocence to vulnerability, and from the child to the adolescent points us toward a wider, less simplistic set of ethical dilemmas presently eclipsed by mass-mediated stories of predatory pedophiles and lost innocence on the one hand (Jerry Sandusky, Jimmy Savile) or stories of prosecutorial overreach on the other ("sexting," the Duke lacrosse team scandal).[43] Among other consequences of this shift, we are positioned to consider how law produces sexual personae; how consent may be a necessary but not sufficient metric for the realization of sexual autonomy; how protecting the sexual autonomy of young subjects may carry fewer perverse consequences than protecting innocence; how intergenerational sexual relations are both precarious and formative, especially for same-sex partners; and how some young people are made more vulnerable, and their sexual autonomy more perempted, by institutional constraints, skewed conferrals of privilege, and systemic patterns of inequality.

Toward the end of the book, as the narrative transitions from the child and the sex offender to adolescent boys and girls, an alternative paradigm of sexual regulation emerges, attentive to differential distributions of vulnerability and autonomy. This encounter with adolescents encourages thinking incompetence not as the opposite of sexual subjectivity, but as a necessary (and always only partially surmountable) condition of possibility for sexual autonomy. Incompetence is a place from which to grow—or to get stuck, depending on the circumstances. By encountering adolescence as exemplary of sexual subjectivity *tout court*—its own sexual orientation—sexual harm is given greater dimension too, marked not only by the violation of consent, but also by less spectacular and less individualized threats to or disqualifications of sexual possibility.

Once we observe that the child and the sex offender are standing in to substantiate consent, that they are constructs to help recognize and relieve sexual harm, we are called upon to think and regulate sex better. For the most part, the scholarly literature critiquing contemporary manifestations of the sexualized child and the sex offender hail from moral panic scholarship, cultural studies of sex and gender, or a hybrid of the two. In general though (and I admit to generalizing), these texts aim to diagnose anxiogenic phenomena surrounding the child and the offender: we learn, for example, that sexual panics erupt during social or political crises; or that sexual scapegoating occurs in the face of upended gendered mores; or that the cultural propping up of the innocent child operates to eroticize the child, to scrub out its polymorphous sexuality, or to advance conservative political policy.[44] These are important, necessary lessons to learn, but in overlooking the extent to which the child and the offender symbolize flawed sociolegal efforts to manage sexual harm and freedom, this literature overlooks too the possibility of alternatives. The sex predator is not only a "metaphor for *other* conditions of injury in the body politic," but also a metonymy, a character who constellates through identification and simplification the feared fact of sexual harm.[45] By proposing alternatives to reigning conceptions of sexual harm, the last half of the book begins where Roger Lancaster ends. In *Sex Panic and the Punitive State* (2011), Lancaster brilliantly tracks how perceived sexual threats to the innocence of the child have constructed and bulwarked U.S. neoliberal carceral, punitive, and surveillance practices. Unloading our presumptions of youthful innocence, he suggests, would militate against excessive punishment and deflate public fear. In a concluding appendix, "Notes on Method," he writes:

> No doubt my starting with a denial of adolescent sexlessness and my refusal of a strictly hygienic view of sexuality imply complications for policy, which no longer would be about "protecting innocence" but then could be oriented around other principles: calibrated harm reduction, perhaps, or nurturing well-being. . . . I do not minimize the suffering involved in genuine acts of harm; *I am simply calling for more rigor and less hysteria in defining terms, calibrating distinctions, and investigating claims* (some of which will be false). I have tried to show how hypertrophied conceptions of harm have harmful effects.[46]

One goal of this book then, spelled out now in a chapter outline, is to marshal contemporary concerns for the young subject and the sex offender alike in order to (re)define terms and calibrate distinctions.

The structure of the book is mirrored, and presented in four chapters. The first chapter focuses on cultural representation, the next two chapters centralize law, and the final chapter returns to cultural representation, after a theoretical interlude. The first two chapters are more diagnostic, describing how the figures of the child and the sex offender produce dominant understandings of sexual harm, freedom, and consent. The second two chapters are more normative: How might we better theorize sexual harm through the concepts of sexual autonomy, vulnerability, and peremption? How are age and age difference inflected by queerness and sexual difference, among other axes of social stratification?

The first chapter critiques and builds on existing literature that diagnoses and responds to "moral panics," "sex panics," and "child sex panics." By investigating NBC's now cancelled *To Catch a Predator,* I suggest that extant cultural-constructivist literature is necessary but insufficient in understanding and therefore redressing nationalized affective attachment to the child. The child and the predator, I argue, must be considered political, not just sexual-social, constructs, who generate meanings of consent, capacity, and control as organizational points for the political self-understanding of the contemporary American subject.[47] This theoretical intervention allows for a sympathetic consideration of the kinds of gendered, sexualized inequalities that may animate contemporary social concern. It affords too a more careful canvassing of the perceived risk, vulnerability, dependence, and desire ascribed to girls, boys, and offenders.

The second chapter exposits late twentieth- and early twenty-first-century SORN laws by comparing the changes in rhetoric and judicial argument from *Bowers v. Hardwick* to *Lawrence v. Texas* against the rhetoric and argument of the 2003 sex offender Supreme Court cases, *Smith v. Doe* (2003) and *Connecticut Department of Public Safety v. Doe* (2003). *Bowers* (1986) held a Georgia antisodomy law constitutional, *Lawrence* (2003) overturned *Bowers,* and *Smith* and *Connecticut* rejected several constitutional challenges to SORN regulations.

I claim that the "sex offender" has been juridically codified as the exhaustive figure of sexual amorality and dangerousness, a position vacated by the once homophobic but now more dignified juridical construction of the homosexual. From this perspective, "recidivism," invariably uttered in the same breath as "sex offender," is not simply a question of fact but a trope that schematizes sexual harm in gothic form.[48] The pervasiveness of the recidivism trope is propelled, counterintuitively, by the juridical construction of the "consenting adult" as the paragon of sexual freedom, celebrated in *Lawrence.* In combination, the trope of recidivism and the norm of the free consenting adult paralyzingly position the young sexual subject and overlook how gender asymmetry and queerness may inform sexual experience. As a matter for theory, the reigning juridical tableau of sexual harm is gothic and individualistic, pointing our ethical gaze too acutely. As a matter for people's lives, this tableau induces the demonization of some adults, hastens the criminalization or condemnation of many young sexual subjects, and stymies sexual autonomy.

The third chapter shifts legal focus from SORN laws to age of consent statutes. Partially on account of a reigning legal positivism, age of consent statutes are often taken for granted as betraying a true, right, and transhistorical division between adults and youth, between consensual competency and incapacity. Here, I assert that the concept of sexual autonomy ought to govern legal regulations around age, age difference, and sexual activity. A conceptual commitment to sexual autonomy envisions young people as volitional but vulnerable subjects, rather than innocent incompetents. A practical commitment to sexual autonomy portends, in slightly more specific terms than outlined above, a lowered age of sexual consent in several jurisdictions, decriminalization of sex between minors, heightened legal supervision on age difference and relations of dependence, and a more robust standard of consent (more like affirmation than acquiescence) for sex between minors and between minors and adults. What also surfaces through the analyses is that concerns around age, age difference, and sex both reflect and displace more normatively apt questions around gender, gendered power and submission, and queer sexuality. U.S. criminal law, ostensibly neutral and primarily prohibitory, is ultimately an inadequate forum to adjudicate problems of power and coercion that arise across gender and sexuality difference at the interface of age and age difference. Therefore, not only ought age of consent law to be reformed and its principles be rethought, but law itself ought to be deemphasized, refigured as a way to help better frame the problems of age and sex rather than as a way to resolve them.

The fourth and final chapter contends that to more fully apprehend and ethically respond to problems of sexual relations across age difference, we need to interrogate how gendered socialization, queer identification, and the coerciveness of heterosexuality play out in the process of growing up. Investigating *Doubt* (2008), *Thirteen* (2003), and *Superbad* (2007), I propose that these films help us understand that neither sexual difference (girls are socialized to be wounded sexualized subjects, boys are socialized to be sexual adventurers) nor "gay exceptionalism" (boys' sexual experiences with older men are allegedly normatively acceptable because of homophobia or the need to sustain the transmission of gay cultural life) explains away normative differences regarding intergenerational sexual encounters. Rather, the relation between sexual difference and gay excep- tionalism is recursive. The sexual and the homosocial mark boys' path to adult citizenship and often freeze girls as the raw material over which that perilous path to masculine citizenship is forged or failed. And yet, these films also navigate (or in *Doubt*'s case, circumnavigates) the pleasures and perils of young sex, visually and narratively supposing that what makes the young, gendered subject vulnerable and prone to disproportionate impo- sition is not sex per se, but structures in proximity to sex. Through these filmic explorations, I call attention to (1) the way peremption is a perva- sive feature of adolescence but gender asymmetrical and (2) how such gender-skewed peremption is relieved or exacerbated by other social axes of inequality.

The conclusion summarizes key contributions of the book and specu- lates, briefly and broadly, how those contributions might inform two zones of progressive politics (gay rights and anti–sexual violence campaigns) and two zones of theory (legal theoretic critiques of "autonomy" and queer- theoretic critiques of "the child"). Along the way, the conclusion wonders about other sex scandals, or the sex that is not-yet scandalous.[49] What harms are more perceivable, what political and sexual relations possible, probable, or problematic, when our thinking and regulating sex are gov- erned not—exhaustively—by consent, innocence, and predation, but by sexual autonomy, vulnerability, and peremption?

ARE SEX OFFENDERS THE NEW QUEERS?

The pedophile and the homosexual have always been in bed together, yet their preferred or prefixed relational positions have changed over time. Sometimes public anxiety about pedophiles masquerades homophobia; sometimes homophobic political leaders or opportunists affiliate homo- sexuals with pedophiles or child recruiters; sometimes self-proclaimed pedophiles liken their social and political struggles to those of homosexu- als. In response to political impugnation and/or pedophilic association, mainstream gay rights organizations, gay scholars, and gay media charac- ters loudly disavow any and all connections to pedophilic desire, insisting that the pedophile is an altogether different species than the homosex- ual, or that "heterosexual" men are more likely than "homosexual" men to sexually abuse children. The ghost of gayness haunts this project.

For Lancaster, "homosexuality" sits at the "murky core" of both "sex panics" and his critical work on them.[50] He notes that U.S. sex panics of yesteryear (the postwar sex crime panic,[51] the late 1970s antipornography crusades, and the Anita Bryant–led "Save Our Children" campaigns) were more "overtly homophobic" than current national anxieties around the child, innocence, and sexual threat. Where once homosexuals found themselves explicit targets of police, prosecutorial, and public harassment, current campaigns to protect children and persecute sex offenders are not, on the face of it, antigay. This development brooks two possibilities for Lancaster. First, he is suspicious that social anxiety around sex predators rearticulates resonant homophobia that is now politically bad table manners. Evidence for this is growing concern with the young white *boy* as the paradigmatically threatened subject. Second, if social cohesion and communal solidarity structurally require an Other, an outcast, gays and lesbians are too tolerated, assimilated, celebrated, etc., to play the constituting Other any longer.[52] In that case, the sex offender is the new queer, another folk devil, fungible to the requirements of historical circumstance.

I find less evidence for the first possibility, although homophobia certainly still fuels many a local or national outbreak of fear around sexually predatory teachers, priests, or congressmen. Nevertheless, that boys since the late 1970s are more consistently considered potential victims of sex threat seems less to do (now, not in the 1970s) with the wolf of homophobia hiding in sex offender sheepskin and more to do with the production of the child as a gender-neutralized figure of innocence, and the production of the sex offender as another taxonomic type of sexual identity, albeit a malignant one.

As for the second possibility—sex offenders are the new queers—I agree, and say so in the second chapter.[53] But as I also comment there, this does not tell us everything and leaves out two critical features.

First, it overlooks how the cultural and legal valorization of consent is partially what operationalizes the substitution of our latest folk devil. It is not simply the case that someone or some group just always gets the short end of the stick, and it is the sex offender's turn.[54] Rather, because the *consenting adult* has emerged in our late modern democratic population as the symbol of both the sexually moral agent and the free citizen, the child and the sex offender are consent's, and therefore the polity's, outsiders. In the celebratory (juridical, social) language of consent, the homosexual is no longer as available for demonizing projection. The sex offender is.

Second, and as important, gay people as a class do not harm people. Many sex offenders, but not all, do. Sometimes that harm takes the form of nonconsent, and sometimes it does not. The harm might also be the exploitation of vulnerability or the crowding out of sexual autonomy. My contention is that more precise moral and legal theorizing, theorizing that specifies forms of sexual vulnerability and tracks encroachments on sexual autonomy, is necessary to neutralize the juridical personification of sexual evil or the social demonization of sexual persons.

THE EMBARRASSED ETC.:
ADULT WOMEN AND PREDATORY PRIESTS

In presenting components of this project to various readers and at academic conferences, I am often asked some version of these two questions: What about female sex offenders? What about priests?[55] I comment below on both these characters and their relative absences from this project, knowing fully that they are not the only characters or intersected identities receiving short shrift.[56]

The (Elusive) Female Sex Offender

In interrogating the ways sex harm and threat are determined in U.S. law and media through figures of the sex offender, the child, and consent, I am hoping to show as well how predatory male desire and the gender-neutral child are determinative of the contemporary national narrative. Insofar as the homosexual has slid from the embodiment of threat to the embodiment of freedom (as the consenting adult), insofar as children are positioned as uniformly vulnerable to risk and harm, and insofar as the predator palliates as the pathologically recidivistic *man* whose object choice is both gender indiscriminate and then—often, contemporarily—irrelevant, male predatory desire and the gender-neutral child saturate the juridical and popular cultural landscape of sexual danger. It is for this reason foremost that the adult woman, the female sex offender, is not a fundamental concern of the project.

There are indeed women who are convicted of sex offenses, women who admit to sex offending, and children and adults who report being sexually abused by women. That, though, is the point: by parsing the tropes of recidivism and pathology that attach to adult male offenders, by centralizing sexual relations rather than personae as loci of coercion, and by theorizing circumstantial and structural constraints that perempt the young sexual subject, forms of sexual injustice that span across genders and ages may become more identifiable, more visible to theoretic and political scrutiny.

Currently, very, very few female sex offenders are reported to authorities, and there is significant discrepancy between the smaller number of convicted female sex offenders and the larger number of people who report being victimized by women.[57] In some jurisdictions, women are ineligible to be certain kinds of sex offenders, because the sex offense requires penetration with a penis.[58] Of the few women who are convicted, many of those are charged with acting as an accomplice to their male partners.[59] Police and prosecutors are not as likely to pursue sexual abuse claims made against women.[60] Sex abuse by women may even be more underreported than sex abuse by men because victims are potentially embarrassed that the offender was female.[61] Studies of sex offender recidivism mainly sample men.[62]

In media accounts, tropes of recidivism, evilness, and dangerousness are almost entirely disconnected to women offenders, who are instead reported as delusional, love-sick, and depressed;[63] often they are school teachers, presented as hopeless young women who fell in love with an unlikely (but not traumatized) male object choice.[64] As CBS reports of one such teacher, "many were baffled that the twenty-three-year-old newlywed threw it all away for her underage victim."[65] Although the teachers are legally charged with the same offenses as their male counterparts (child rape, sexual abuse of a child, etc.), they are presented not as threats but as emotionally driven oddities, as disturbed but not too disturbing.

It will not be any more accurate (or any more just) to simply assert that women offend just like men, to protest that victims of female sexual abuse are as traumatized as victims of male sexual abuse, or to naively claim that sexual abuse is not patterned by gender asymmetry. The more challenging dilemma is to rethink what sexual abuse means, what sexual autonomy entails, and how gender inflects national understandings of—and personal encounters with—intergenerational sex.

In the beginning of 2011, on NBC's *Today Show,* Meredith Vieira asked the infamous Mary Kay Letourneau if she would approve of her thirteen-year-old daughter having sexual relations with her teacher (Letourneau first initiated sex with her now husband when he was thirteen). She answered "no" because of the physiological differences between girls and boys, which put her in an easy bind for Vieira to exploit: she asks if Letourneau would approve sex with a teacher if her daughter were instead a son. No, stumbles Letourneau, kids of all genders should get to have kid fun when they're kids (I paraphrase).[66] Letourneau collapses the possibility of gender difference into science and anatomy, and she need not. It may be that the genders of the participants in age-discordant sex matters in the distribution of its pleasurable or painful dynamics, but this may have more to do with boys' and girls' skewed socialization into sexual subjectivity and less to do with their genitals and their neurological development, a hypothesis that initiates at the end of the third chapter and extends into the fourth.

The Predatory Priest

Female sex offenders are a rare breed in popularized accounts of sexual threat, and even rarer in criminal law. The predatory priest, although perhaps also underrepresented legally, is a ubiquitous staple in news media and has been episodically since at least 1984.[67]

The phenomenon of sex abuse in the Catholic Church might be (and has been) read as one installation of patterned, diffused popular fears around the sexual threat posed by adult men toward children. Understood as such, there will be a story of the causes, the displaced anxieties, the hyperbolized anecdotes, the incongruences between the evidence and the narration of evidence, that will be parallel to and share conceptual coordinates with other diagnoses of sex panics. Indeed, the popular assumption of rampant, institutionally sanctioned sexual abuse of young boys supposedly particular and endemic to priests, priesthood, and the Catholic Church has been challenged, although not vocally. There is evidence that far fewer priests have sexually abused children than is reported, that girls as well as boys are abused, that adolescents are more commonly approached than children, that sexual abuse in other religious, cloistered environments may be neither more nor less prevalent than in the Catholic Church.[68] The media presentation of abuse in the church, the amplification of numbers, the literary and editorial diatribes, and the singling out of "folk devils" have led Philip Jenkins and others to conclude that this cultural phenomenon has the structure of a moral panic. The popular preoccupation of sex abuse in the church may result from conceptions of adult male desire as necessarily predatory, from homophobia refracted in the guise of hostility to the church, and most of all, from a deep, historically persistent anticlericalism that has long—since medieval pogroms—utilized priests' alleged sexual disorderliness as fuel for its political power. Indeed, the sex of the church sex abuse scandal is less central in media attention than is the clerical and papist hypocrisy of which that sex seems to be an unalterably seamless sign.[69] The elitism, sexual mysteriousness, moral self-aggrandizement, and comparative wealth and privilege of Catholic leadership may have helped make the church an object of widespread resentment.

The predatory priest, then, and his gravitational pull, is a book unto himself. While he receives a brief consideration in the fourth chapter, when I look at *Doubt,* I am ultimately more concerned there with the way the narrative of sex scandal suffocates young queer desire than with any particularities of the priest imago.

As detailed later on, I advocate for the creation of adolescents as a discrete sex class under law and I argue for tighter regulations around sex in relations of dependence and authority. I also ask readers to consider how axes of social stratification differentiate young subjects' relation to sexuality. It strikes me that in combination, these proposals would work to de-dramatize the church as the locale of sexual abuse (as a corollary to de-dramatizing the sex offender as the persona non grata inflicting sex harm), to disaggregate otherwise monolithic accounts of abuse, and to de-eroticize by disputing the innocence of the young person, while still drawing attention to the relational constraints between priest and young subject that make this sex legally impermissible.[70]

Whether the ordination of women into the priesthood or the removal of the celibacy requirement would reduce sexual abuse in the church are important questions, but not mine—although such initiatives might in turn work to open out spaces of sexual autonomy for the young subject, as would, most likely, a more liberalized clerical engagement with eros and bodies.[71] Meanwhile, Jenkins is probably correct: there is something homophobic and something anticlerical attendant to the media and popular targeting of the church.[72] But neither fact should detract from first, identifying and mitigating forms of sexual coercion inside the church and out, and second, theorizing the consequences and blind spots of localizing sex harm to disliked persons and institutions. Whereas Jenkins appeals to his audience to disaggregate *pedophilic* abuse by clergy from abuses of authority evidenced in what he calls "consensual relationships with older boys or young men," I am unconvinced that the latter is not itself a form of *sexual* constraint.[73] A relation between a priest and a boy in his late teens is still an infraction of his, the teen's, sexual autonomy.[74] We can and should differentiate degrees of sexual offense without demonizing offenders as uniform regarding their motivations, their object choices, and the impact of their harmful conduct.

1 "Especially Heinous"

Politics, Predation, Sex Panics

But what wrestling is above all meant to portray is a purely moral concept: that of justice. The idea of "paying" is essential to wrestling, and the crowd's "Give it to him" means above all else "Make him pay." This is therefore, needless to say, an immanent justice. . . . The nearer the good luck of a contestant to his downfall, the more satisfying the dramatic mime is felt to be. Justice is therefore the embodiment of a possible transgression; it is from the fact that there is a Law that the spectacle of the passions which infringe it derives its value.

—Roland Barthes

At one point, he tells her his hobby is taking pictures of himself masturbating, and then sends the decoy some of those shots. He doesn't stop there. Later, he sends her child pornography.

—Chris Hansen

Since child sexual abuse and sexual predators are perhaps the only topics as politically volatile as terrorism, certain caveats seem appropriate. This chapter will not do two things. First, it will not suggest that rates of sexual violence are interminably rising, that persons who commit sexual crimes are unstoppably evil and uncontrollably recidivistic, that one political party or another is administratively lax on sex offenders, nor allege any other similarly positivist claim that is empirically inaccurate but morally self-satisfying and politically manipulative.[1]

Second, however, this chapter will not insist that collective concerns over child sexual abuse and children's sexual vulnerability are only irrational projections, transmuted latent hostilities, erotophobic, homophobic, or reflective of traditional gender mores.[2] The cultural fascination with child abductions, sexting, and *Law and Order: Special Victims Unit* (*SVU*) are not best explained by collapsed recourse to law-and-order ideology, patriarchy, or any other totalizing -ism. Although I ambivalently understand contemporary anxieties over sexually threatened youth as a "moral panic," I do so to explore, not ridicule, nationalized affective attachments— mediated through media, and mediated through law—to the sexualized child and its problematic suitors.

To paraphrase Foucault, the problem is not that nobody is talking about children, sexuality, and sex offenders, that such things are impossible to talk about, or that they have been suppressed from the public lexicon. To the contrary, we cannot not talk about child sexual abuse and sex predators, and we cannot not watch the latest television drama series or live news report on the sex offender, the priest, or their victims. American football coach Jerry Sandusky and British entertainer Jimmy Savile are, as of this writing, the most recent, inglorious additions to the long line of sex villains that parade through print, televisual, and online media. As feminists have pointed out since the 1970s (or the 1890s), lots of talk (or lots of laws) may obscure from view routine patterns of sexual violence, the coerciveness of everyday heterosexuality, and the primary perpetrators of sexual abuse. And, as James Kincaid has pointed out since 1998, counternarratives, countertalk, suggest not that we have discovered some truth, but that we are caught in a story, in this instance a gothic story in which good and evil are characteristics rarely diluted with distinction:[3] either the child is the victim or the incipient irredeemable abuser, recovered memory is salvation or slanderous, sex offender laws are grossly overbroad or disappointingly underinclusive.[4]

Since there exists a "veritable discursive explosion" around children, sex, and sexual predation, this chapter talks about talk, and in two parts.[5] I am interested in exploring the national response to sexual violence against children and young people and the way that response is reflected, molded, amplified, or vindicated in representational media form and legal codification.[6] To initiate this pursuit, the first section of this chapter explicates the television series *To Catch a Predator* (*TCAP*). I do so to capture prescient tropes around sexual predation, but also to evidence the importance of supplementing what I am calling "cultural constructivist literature" with a more delicate account of law, harm, and sex.

In the second section, I read *TCAP* through the lens of scholarship on moral panic, sex panic, and child sex panic to develop my argument against and alongside these literatures. Of course, the collected works of these combined literatures are substantial, and so I nonarbitrarily but not at all scientifically centralize three texts for theorizing through questions of children, sex, and sexual harm: Stanley Cohen's *Folk Devils and Moral Panics: The Creation of the Mods and Rockers* (1972; 3rd ed. 2002), Gayle Rubin's "Thinking Sex: Notes for a Radical Theory of the Politics of Sexuality" (1984; repr. 1993), and Gail Hawkes and R. Danielle Egan's "Landscapes of Erotophobia: The Sexual(ized) Child in the Postmodern Anglophone West" (2008).

In their respective contributions, these authors criticize the construction, moralization, and amplification of sociolegal problems (problems identical with or similar to the concerns of this book). Analyzing their proposed diagnoses and solutions allows us to more carefully trace the nationalized anxiety circulating around the sexual vulnerability of the child. At the same time, their arguments mystify or leave unaddressed certain aspects of sociolegal moralization. I therefore extract these authors' best insights for theorizing contemporary national representations of the sexually threatened child, but I point as well to their conceptual shortcomings: particularly, to Cohen's impoverished account of law, Rubin's underspecified account of harm, and Hawkes and Egan's myopic account of gender and sexuality.

Interpreting *TCAP* against these works, I propose the following: (1) law ought to be more explicitly theorized as a productive, anatomizing force in the creation of sexual subjects and the constitution of (what is recognizable as) sexual violence, rather than as a final, unfortunate episode or effect of moral panic;[7] (2) critical scholarship must identify the kinds of sexual harm that do or should concern a democratic citizenry in order to more effectively understand and deflate sexual hyperbole; and (3) both the agents provocateurs of "child sex panics" and their scholarly critics neglect or misunderstand the ways concern over age and sex are at once proxies for and displacements of more complicated problems of gendered power and queer sexuality.

PANIC, PREDATORS, PLEASURES, AND PAINS

To Catch a Predator offers a primer for reading the ways law, fears of harm and danger, and dominant constructs of sexuality and gender inform national "child sex panics" or what we might more sympathetically call national affect around the sexually threatened and vulnerable child.

TCAP aired from 2004 to 2007 on NBC's *Dateline* news show and was its most popular series.[8] It was a "ratings bonanza," "a major force in public policy," and specifically referenced by legislators as a pivotal inspiration for the enactment of the Adam Walsh Act, which updated and intensified federalized sex offender regulations.[9] The show was hosted by Chris Hansen and developed in collaboration with an online watchdog group, Perverted Justice (PJ). PJ entered social-networking sites and chat rooms posing as young teens, engaging in sexual conversations with older men. Once the men were lured in—and PJ members often repeatedly and seductively reassured the men that, yes, they want to have sex with the underage girl (or sometimes boy), and, no, they would not be caught—the "child" arranges to meet at her "home" for sex.[10] The home is equipped with *Dateline*'s hidden video cameras and microphones. After flirtatious exchange between the young but legal "decoy" and the "predator," the decoy disappears offscreen and Hansen enters, excoriates the man, and asks him what he is doing and why he is doing it, the performance replete with graphic, indulgent readings of the predator's online courting ("you asked him in your chat if he was top or bottom. What does that mean?"; see Figures 2 and 3).[11] After the man profusely apologizes, cries, becomes defensive, becomes furious, or expresses some other expected, cyclically predictable emotion, Hansen tells him he "is free to go," at which point he is greeted by a swarm of police who usually tackle him and then arrest him (law enforcement was a later addition to the show; see Figure 4). Let's bracket common criticism the show received (it is dehumanizing, entrapping, disgusting; it is shock TV posing as investigative journalism)[12] and instead draw preliminary attention to how the show creates and contains sexual violence and sexual subjects.

The following is a typical transcript:

DECOY: Did you bring condoms?

LORNE ARMSTRONG: Yes, I did.

DECOY: Where are they?

ARMSTRONG: Out in the truck.

DECOY: Well, what good are they going to do in the truck, if we're in here?

ARMSTRONG (*laughing*): Well, yell at me, why don't you. I haven't had a kiss yet.

DECOY: Oh, OK. Well, then, what did you want to do?

ARMSTRONG: I want to kiss, first.

. . .

CHRIS HANSEN: . . . You want to explain yourself?

ARMSTRONG: Not really, I'd never, really, was going to do anything.

Figure 2. "Predator" John Elliot exposes himself to the "decoy" (and to us).

Figure 3. Elliot meets the "decoy," Kacie.

Figure 4. Elliot is arrested by several officers of the Bowling Green, Kentucky, police department.

HANSEN: You weren't really going to do anything?

. . .

HANSEN: And she is how old?

ARMSTRONG: Supposed to be thirteen.

HANSEN: And how old are you?

ARMSTRONG: Thirty-seven.

. . .

HANSEN: . . . What do you think ought to happen to you?

ARMSTRONG: I think I should go to counseling to get off the Internet. I've got to do something, because I can't do thi—oh my God (*crying*).

HANSEN: Well, there is something I've got to tell you. I'm Chris Hansen, of *Dateline NBC*, and we're doing a story on—

ARMSTRONG: Oh, God (*crying*).

HANSEN: Now, you're free to walk out of this house right now. But if there's anything else you want to say, now would be the time to say it.

He has nothing further to say and tries to make a quick exit, apparently not
knowing what's in store for him outside.

COPS: Sheriff's office! Down! Get down! On the ground, on the ground.

Hands behind your back, put your hands behind your back.

He's taken to the local police station where his car is searched.[13]

This scene is hyperbolic, sensationalist, and vigilante but captures something about contemporary cultural anxieties in the United States around
questions of sex, vulnerability, and power as they materialize in relations
between adults and youth. At the same time, the social panic around sex
offenders and children impedes unpacking the very intuition that something is wrong. Panic and outrage debilitate and sometimes vilify critical
analyses.

The show performs the pedophilia it purportedly condemns.[14] It offers
its audience the language and imagery of sexual perversion under the veneer
of repulsion.[15] The viewer experiences the pleasure of prurient transgression as voyeur, peeking into the world of the predator through the lens of
the hidden camera, listening to the illicit chat, anticipating the scene's
exposed and depraved culmination:[16] the penalized subject is delivered
as a commodity constructed for communal solidarity and consumed for
customer satisfaction.[17] The domestic intimacy visually arranged among
participants—audience and child, child and predator, predator and audience, predator and Hansen, audience and Hansen—is sacralized by being
invasively sexualized, opening itself to the feel goodness of a spectacular,
vigilante resolution (like Barthes's wrestlers). The only relation not cine-
matographically staged, left absent, is one between the fatherly Hansen
and the unnamed decoy, who silently walks offstage as Hansen enters. Not
incidentally, *that* is the relation most commonly sexually abusive, a relation
choreographed as unimaginable and therefore unproblematic. "Stranger
danger" is resonant vernacular of both media and media audiences, but
familial sexual abuse is approached with more discomfort, more shame,
and, presently, less talk.[18]

The vigilantism circumnavigates the erotics of the scene—the lust for
blood neutralizes the lust for the girl. At precisely the moment the sex act
ought to occur in this narrative, the audience instead witnesses, and therefore participates in, the public shaming of the predator, his moral behead-
ing. This climax promises pleasure with justice, disidentifies the viewer
from the predator, or perhaps anesthetizes and partitions that identification

by cordoning off the predator, and predatory desire, as desperate, criminal, foreign, locatable, and perverted. The problem of sexual harm is condensed into a perverted body and a perverted choice, thus extracted from structural loci like the family, everyday sexual exchange, and commodity capitalism.[19] Sexual violence is imagined as the result of a bad personal decision and then spectacularized through individualized confession: "many processes collaborate to make structural conditions of existence seem like properties of the body and of the person."[20]

The performance of righteous comeuppance, meanwhile, does double duty—it realizes the desire for vengeance and retroactively transforms the voyeuristic pleasure into a defensible yearning that the bad guys (out there, on TV, online, not in our homes) get it in the end. The decoy is actually nineteen or twenty (posing as thirteen online), a college coed, a notionally normal and prized object of male heterosexual desire. She initiates the conversations and playfully asks about condoms, problematizing her status as prey.[21] She is the only one unnamed in the online transcript, known as the "decoy," a term generally associated with duck hunting. She is objectified, but by the network.

This, then, is *reading #1* of *TCAP*, from which we can extract some baseline insights: getting just feels like getting off; potentially structural problems and prevalent features surrounding sexual violence are rerouted onto one presumptively predatory person; the figure of the genderless (that is, interchangeably male or female) child at risk, needing paternal and political protection, is at the onset troubled by the sexualized girl (and sometimes boy) on-screen, literally marginalized offscreen by Chris Hansen and NBC; and law resolves.

Holding these conclusions in mind, let's turn to selective cultural constructivist literature, to benefit from its interpretive purchase as well as to signal and supplement its conceptual misgivings.

PANIC LIT, OR HOW TO READ AND NOT READ
TO CATCH A PREDATOR

How can we better understand a show like *To Catch a Predator* and the national affect it reflects by reading it through the lens of cultural constructivist literature? Below are limited synopses of selected, important "panic" texts: Stanley Cohen's *Folk Devils and Moral Panics*, Gayle Rubin's "Thinking Sex," and Gail Hawkes and R. Danielle Egan's "Landscapes of

Erotophobia." After each synopsis, I reread *TCAP* through the text, and then reread the text through *TCAP.*

Stanley Cohen, *Folk Devils and Moral Panics: The Creation of the Mods and Rockers*

In 2002, Stanley Cohen published the third edition of *Folk Devils and Moral Panics*. There, he maintains that a moral panic model still holds explanatory power over three decades of social problems, by locating the actors, moral entrepreneurs, claims makers, and media manipulators that figure (or disfigure) problems, amplify anxieties, and create and control deviants and deviance. The original text compellingly illustrates how iso-lated, localized events may or may not be amplified by media actors, may or may not be rhetorically or politically linked to other or broader societal ills, and may be leveraged for profit motives, regressive political agendas, or the restoration of traditional morality. The model goes some way toward explaining episodic social concerns over recreational drugs, immigrants, sexually dangerous persons, and epidemics over the past thirty years in Western nations. For the purposes of parsing the phenomena of moral/ media panic around children and sex in the early twenty-first-century United States, I want to focus on two issues Cohen raises: media and the production of cultural meaning, and law and the moralization of social problems.

Media and the Production of Cultural Meaning

Responding to criticism of the moral panic framework as outdated and therefore atrophied, Cohen concedes that scholars

> are correct that today's more sophisticated, self-aware and fragmented media make the original notion of spasmodic ("every now and then") panic out of date. "Panic" is rather a mode of representation in which daily events are regularly brought to the public's attention . . . moral panics have their own internal trajectory—a microphysics of outrage—which, however, is initiated and sustained by wider social and political forces.[22]

Cohen thus attenuates his oft-cited claim that "societies appear to be sub-ject, every now and then, to periods of moral panic."[23] Clearly influenced by poststructuralism and media studies, *societies* are no longer passively subject to panic periods ex nihilo, but "wider social and political forces" provide the dynamic undercurrent to moments of heightened social hysteria. On this account, media are credited with more than the amplification of deviance in the interests of profit maximization or the maintenance of reactionary conservative politics. Rather, media continually shape and re-shape the social problem, represent and re-present it in forms that potentially resonate with broader social sentiment.[24] Implicitly, the divide between "media" and the "public" collapses as well with the diffusion of media and their agents across communication technologies—it is difficult to hold on to a conception of a unidirectional causal arrow where "media" influence "society" with the rapid emergence of social media.[25]

In the realm of media and social power then, we should retain two insights from Cohen (and the critics who influenced him) in comprehending the portrayal and national reception of children and sexual threat. First, the development of a moral panic and the construction of its attendant folk devils arise in part from sociopolitical dynamics that are not only *latent* (concealed or disfigured), but also *diachronic* and *deeper.* In this sense, perhaps panics are better thought of as superficial points of condensation rather than substitutive points of displacement.[26] Second, media matter: not only in the distribution and amplification of a perceived problem, but also in the social organization of the problem.

Applying Cohen's analysis of media to *TCAP*, we notice that the material harm—child sexual abuse—is distributed, amplified, and organized by the show, which stokes and channels social frenzy. The use of social media to ensnare the predators, and the interaction between *Dateline,* PJ, and local law enforcement, troubles the divide between "media" and "culture": part of the show's appeal is that it makes its audience feel political, engaged, and participatory in meting out justice through the semblance of civic involvement. The citizen power emblematized by PJ and the sense of presence (in two senses of the term—the audience is *there,* and *there* is a recurrent *now*) engendered by hidden cameras offer hooked audiences the opportunity to catch the predator they are transfixed on watching, enabling a "panic" feedback loop that demands a new predator for every installment.[27]

TCAP, like many influential reality and reality crime programs preceding and succeeding it, blurs news and entertainment to the point where the genres themselves dissolve,[28] where reality is created through the visual production of domestic intimacy, an intimacy that is threatened and brokered on the sexualized body of the girl or boy decoy and the uncomfortable, shifty body of the predator. The cameras welcome the audience into their home and infuse that home with an anticipation of bodily pain, sex, and retribution. It is the appeal to the real through pain that obscures the show's performance of sexual violence as performative. The punished predator absorbs the pain reserved for the child; he generates collective viewer identity and communal affect; he brings into being a just, vigilant, civic, and politically participatory audience.[29]

And then law ends the orgiastic, organizing media scene, mirroring and motivating[30] legislation as a desired goal of community agitation (and mirroring law as a popular motif in conventional pornography). Law is good—violent—but good, important, conclusive. The bad guy is captured, the problem momentarily solved, until the next episode. But is that all for law?

Law and the Social Problem

While Cohen revised his theorization of media influence, the role of law in the moral panic analysis remained mostly stagnant. The end of that oft-cited passage reads: "Sometimes the panic passes over and is forgotten, except in folklore ... other times it has more serious and long-lasting repercussions and might produce such changes as those in the legal and social policy or even in the way the society conceives itself."[31] Note that law is only an endpoint in this story and that society's changed self-conception is juxtaposed to legal reform ("or even ...").

As for the Mods and Rockers in the 1960s, Cohen reports that while some politicians and local activists attempted to pass legislation to restrict the mobility and influence of young men, efforts mostly failed. Nonetheless, as he modeled the story, the "diffusion" of a concern "produces a generalized belief system—mythologies, stigmas, stereotypes—but it also produces or tries to produce new methods of control. The informal societal reaction can be extended and formalized, *the ultimate formalization being achieved when new laws are actually created.*"[32] Law then is ultimate, formalizing, and final. Cohen does not allow the possibility that not only do mythologies, stigmas, and stereotypes come to influence law, but that law also shapes prevailing mythologies, stigmas, and stereotypes. Although such multidirectional influence may not have been the case with the Mods and Rockers, neither should the single case study be granted too much explanatory purchase for other social turned sociolegal problems.

While critical, critical race, and feminist legal scholars as well as soci-
ologists working in law have long comprehended the symbolic, synthetic
functions of law, such theorization has never quite held traction in the
archive of writings on moral panics, sex panics, and child sex panics. Law
in this literature is often thought as overbroad, belated, and bad.[33]

A deeper account of law and its symbolic, synthetic power here may
begin with the paternalist, Chris Hansen. As Amy Adler convincingly suggests, Hansen may substitute for the class of fathers, abusing the abuser in
a televised rendition of Freud's famous sadomasochistic case study, *A
Child Is Being Beaten*.[34] The show eroticizes the witnessing of humiliation.
The voyeuristic engagement with *TCAP* is transmuted into a scripted
sadomasochistic, juridical scene wherein the audience discovers pleasure
both in its televisual aggression (*the predator is being beaten, and I like
watching it*) and in an imaginative substitution with the predator (*a pleasuring of the shaming pain one receives for seeking pleasure from the father—I
am a predator, bad me, I am being beaten, now I like being beaten*). The audience tacks between both wells of pleasure as a third-party observer on the
family room couch, like the child bystander in the third stage of Freud's
dream sequence.[35]

But Hansen is not the only representative of the class of fathers in this
ritualized scene, and so analysis of law as a transmutation of pain (of the
predator) into pleasure (watching the predator) and pleasure (I am predatory) into erotic pain (I luxuriate in being shamed) is partial. There are
also, in addition to Hansen, the functionaries of the state, the law enforcement, the army of police at the edge of ensuing brutalization. In *A Child Is
Being Beaten*, the violence is all in fantasy, and that is the point—fantasy
channels violence, unlocks its enmeshment with pleasure, but keeps it
somewhere in the head. Hansen's violence in the domesticated interior of
the NBC home set is still fantastical—a reprimand for fantasy, for wish-
fulfillment, for talking dirty and "bringing condoms" (that the "predator"
brings condoms is a recurring evidentiary sticking point for Hansen and
the show; would we rather the predator hadn't brought condoms?). The
predator is morally shamed for his imagination and intention. However,
once the predator steps outside the domestic, beyond the realm of a containable family drama in which shame and paternal authority can be marshaled to charge the sexual currents of the moment, the violence of the
scene is no longer fantastic or metaphoric. The predator steps outside, and
law kicks the shit out of him.

Now, one might take the expected route: law and its enforcers are bad, oppressive, patriarchal, the final stage of sexualized moral panic. I want to pursue a different question: What is law doing in the final scene, in this show, in the national imagination—if such a unitary imagination exists, and it might not[36]—of sexual harm, children, and predators? How does law work to frame the problem, to identify the kind of harm sex harm is, what to do about it, and how it operates across bodies?

The presence of law makes the problem of sexual violence one of criminal justice, rather than, say, public health,[37] social structure, inequality, or gender enculturation. Violence is individuated, pathological, and most importantly, punitively fixable through the juridical arm of the state, and by extension, the juridical view of the audience.[38] When law tackles the predator, the problem is literally surrounded, grounded, and dissolved.[39] Sexual harm is embodied by and exhausted in the man on-screen, made visible by the hidden cameras and knowable by Hansen's battery of questions ("what are you doing here?") and his staged reading of the online transcripts. (Hansen immediately discredits any gestures of moral reservation on the part of the "predator," for such gestures undermine the making of the predator into a predator.)[40] As Hansen, the media crew, and the coterie of police assume positions of father and state, sexual harm is anthropomorphized in the body of the predator, now a criminological type, and imagined as a threat extinguished by the paternalistic power of adult men. It may be more useful to think of *TCAP* less as a reflection and stimulant of moral panic and more as a hybrid genre of reality crime television and pornography. As reality crime, it breeds "law-and-order ideology" that evacuates any structural account of social violence and disorder by pinning the problem of crime onto the delinquent and defective criminal.[41] As pornography, it insists on visibility, on relentless epistemological revelation through seeing and surfacing that becomes an erotic placeholder for what cannot be known through representation.[42] *TCAP*, then, eroticizes criminal justice, eroticizes law, and aggrandizes its efficacy. That final moment, the arrest of the beaten down predator, grants its audience political efficacy, epistemological certainty, and pleasure.[43]

Cohen importantly denaturalizes—in case such denaturalization is still necessary—affective and media reactions to societal ills, interjecting that these reactions are not just overreactions but politicized reactions, stoked and shaped for purposes that often contravene objectives to minimize or eradicate harm and danger.[44] However, Cohen's theorization of law as the occasional last, unfortunate step of a moral panic obscures law's power to materialize scenes of sexual violence, to attribute accountability, to create good and bad characters, and to provide frames of reference and frames of justice for television audiences and anxious citizens and parents.

Gayle S. Rubin, "Thinking Sex: Notes for a Radical Theory of the Politics of Sexuality"

Rubin's explosive essay was first published in 1984. A major progenitor of third-wave academic feminism and queer studies, it makes sexuality an object of political import and argues that sexuality in its contemporary, Western form is an axis of social stratification irreducible to gender hierarchy. Borrowing from the moral panic framework, she proposes—amid the conservative political climate of the 1980s, the rollback of earlier social welfare reforms, revitalized homophobia, and an ascendant feminism hostile to graphic representations of sex—that "it is precisely at times such as these, when we live the possibility of unthinkable destruction, that people are likely to become dangerously crazy about sexuality."[45] Rubin suggests that sexual subjects marked different are politically and legally demonized to still social anxieties or allay fears that are un- or only partially related to sexuality. Importantly, but perhaps too strongly,[46] she makes the case that sex is unique, potent, and prevalent raw material for the escalation of moral panics and the instantiation of social hierarchy in the United States. Her trenchant and sympathetic attention to the wrath incurred by "boy-lovers," her polemic account of sex law, and her consequent underdeveloped definition of sexual harm both depart from but also fortify the difficulties of Cohen's original moral panic model.

Cross-generational Sex: The "lowliest of all"

Rubin writes, resonantly,

> For over a century, no tactic for stirring up erotic hysteria has been as reliable as the appeal to protect children. . . . Like communists and homosexuals in the 1950s, boy-lovers are so stigmatized that it is difficult to find defenders of their civil liberties, let alone their erotic orientation. Consequently, the police have feasted on them . . . the most despised sexual castes currently include transsexuals, transvestites, fetishists, sadomasochists, sex workers such as prostitutes and porn models, and the *lowliest of all, those whose eroticism transgresses generational boundaries.*[47]

It is hard to disagree, even if you despise "those" people too. Whether it is neoliberal or neoconservative politicians hoping to expand surveillance or punitive power,[48] religious conservatives attempting to neutralize gay civil rights,[49] secular liberals attempting to discredit religious righteousness,[50] or gay political organizations seeking social legitimacy,[51] the specter of the pedophile is an always available foil, abject, morally worthless, and morally endangering. Whether a figure to be ridiculed, juxtaposed, or demonized, the child-lover is the worst of the worst in the ranks of sexual identities. It is necessary—and more possible, with Rubin's intervention—to keep this malleable and maligned figure in mind when considering the media and social dynamics of "child sex panics." Moral repugnance at the pedophile–cum-sex offender–cum-predator functions to map out the problem of sex and youth in its particular and popular form.[52]

How might Rubin's analysis of sexual demonization and social repulsion against intergenerational sex help us view the drama of the endangered child? The men of *TCAP* are characterized by Hansen and PJ as sick, perverted, and predatory. The antidote is a retreat to the hetero nuclear home, to proper sexual objects, to staying far from the Internet and the publicity, sexuality, and nonnormative connections the Internet makes available.

The *thou shalt nots* of Hansen's book *To Catch a Predator: Protecting Your Kids from Online Enemies Already in Your Home* (Figure 5) perfectly emblematize everything Rubin takes to be wrong with dominant, Anglo-American, sociopolitical responses to sex and harm: parents should better regulate and restrict their children, kids are sexless, strangers are sick, the home is haven, the Internet is terrifying.[53]

But then we might watch TV a little closer. Is the harm, or the feared danger, really the "predator"? The show's title says so, and Hansen has claimed these men are better thought of as "predators" rather than "pedophiles," as the former more rightly connotes violence and danger.[54] Journalistic criticism of the show largely accepts this characterization—their truck is with the treatment of predators, not the appellation.

The men on *TCAP*, though, are more pathetic than predatory. Racially diverse, they are more often than not overweight, frumpy, painfully unattractive (against any norm of American masculinity), and socially dysfunctional. Their fleshiness, sweatiness, and twitching comportments mark them as politically unfit and socially deadweight, but not imminently sexually dangerous.[55] They are divorced, single and lonely, or having marriage

to catch a predator

Protecting Your
Kids from Online
Enemies Already
in Your Home

CHRIS HANSEN
Correspondent for
DATELINE NBC'S "TO CATCH A PREDATOR" SERIES

Figure 5. Chris Hansen confronts the reel of predatory men in his book *To Catch a Predator: Protecting Your Kids from Online Enemies Already in Your Home.*

trouble.[56] Some are evidently mentally disabled. Some equivocate upon arrival. None of these qualifiers necessarily makes men searching for sex with a young teenager online any less culpable, but they do impact what we take to be the problem. Rubin admonishes that men who look for younger love and sex are swiftly demonized, that such men are retrograde personified, easy targets for misplaced aggression. But when one observes the men of *TCAP* break down, cry uncontrollably, deferentially call Hansen "sir,"[57] and get assaulted by gleeful law enforcement, the nominal premise of the show is troubled. Reading Rubin and watching *TCAP*, one realizes that the problem of sex across generations is not, or not always, evil, animalistic men online who ruthlessly search out prey.[58] There may be some serious problems *TCAP* and intergenerational sex present, questions that people who care about sex, freedom, and harm need to seriously grapple with, but *TCAP* does not successfully make the case that the problem is predators. Rubin, on the other hand, does not successfully make the case that there is no problem at all, or that predators are nothing other than foils for bulwarking sexual normativity. While her exposition of sex law and her reconstruction of sex harm shift the terms of the conversation away from predation, she retains consent as a comprehensive (although not purified) metric for sexual adjudication, leaving us only partially equipped to more capaciously theorize sexually coercive relations.

Rubin's Sex Law

Before critiquing Rubin's account of sex law, a moment of context is in order: She wrote "Thinking Sex" in the early 1980s in San Francisco, shortly after child pornography exposés were leveraged to police gay men and gay youth, and in the middle of the AIDS pandemic, growing homophobia, and a political assault on affirmative action, abortion rights, and welfare programs. Her fierce condemnation of sex law responded to this national rightward movement, but the ferocity blunted more analytic precision.

Asserting first that "sex law is the most adamantine instrument of sexual stratification and erotic persecution" and that "sex law is harsh,"[59] Rubin then makes a distinction between two kinds of sex law: those against coercion and forced sex, and those perpetuating "erotic injustice."

> Only rape law contains such a distinction [between consent and coercion].
> Rape law is based on the assumption, correct in my view, that heterosexual

activity may be freely chosen or forcibly coerced. One has the legal right to engage in heterosexual behavior as long as it does not gall under the purview of other statutes and as long as it is agreeable to both parties.[60]

The law is especially ferocious in maintaining the boundary between childhood "innocence" and "adult" sexuality. Rather than recognizing the sexuality of the young, and attempting to provide for it in a caring and responsible manner, our culture denies and punishes erotic interest and activity by anyone under the local age of consent. . . . These laws make no distinction between the most brutal rape and the most gentle romance.[61]

Rubin acknowledges that "consent" as both a legal construct and social ideal is inattentive to structural inequalities that trouble women's bargaining power, but she nonetheless defends laws that allegedly address "actual" coercion and condemns laws that allegedly sexually stratify, for instance, by age or sex act.[62]

There are two critical and related problems with her reading of sex law. First, like Cohen's moral panic model, law is imagined only as the last stop, a juridical top-down finale to an otherwise more socially interactive, multiply influenced set of sexual practices and experiences. That law may shape problems, inflect the continuing and dynamic social understandings of a problem, and produce sexual subjects it then regulates are underexamined possibilities. Second, the distinction between "good" sex law and "bad" sex law is too clean-cut.

Rubin's descriptions of rape law and age of consent law misinform. As for rape law, sex need not be "agreeable to both parties" for it to be legal. Standards of consent vary from state to state (and not all states utilize a consent standard), but the threshold for consent is most often nonresistance, so a lot of sex takes place legally that is, if not coerced, far from mutual and less than agreeable.[63] So too, "rape law" is barely a cohesive unit for analysis. By 1984, about half of states codified an array of sexual assault laws that differentiated according to several criteria: levels of force, form of conduct (penetration or molestation, for example), with or without a weapon, and so forth.[64] As for age of consent statutes, Rubin reiterates the misperception that age of consent laws are per se proscriptions that equally penalize any and all sex between persons on either side of an age line. Again, by 1984, the law was disaggregated, partially as a result of 1970s feminist-led reforms. Most age of consent laws were gender neutralized, many age-span provisions replaced per se proscriptions, and the laws did (and do) differentiate between "the most brutal rape" and "the most gentle romance." Degrees of force, age difference, types of conduct, and some-times the relations of the persons involved all inform the criminal legal response to cross-generational sex (and did so in 1984, although not to the same extent as now).[65] In particular, age-span provisions were enacted in part to refocus law toward the presumptive power differential between the parties, rather than punish young people for having sex. Although it is nonetheless still true that engaging in sexual acts with someone below a certain age or outside a set age-span is usually a strict liability offense, and although it was true that criminal laws targeted same-sex sexual activity regardless of the presence or absence of consent, other factors also calibrate(d) the severity of the crime and therefore the sentencing.

The concern here is not so much the finer points of criminal statutes Rubin overlooks. Rather, it is that such inattention invites a dichotomous understanding of the state apparatus and its legal power: law is "good" (rape law) or "bad" (age of consent and other status-based sex law); it cleanly routes coercion or it indefensibly reiterates sexual normativity. Under this rubric, law can neither be thought in its more productive, complex, constitutive capacity, nor be politically harnessed to advance sexual justice. For Rubin, there are two possibilities: enforce existing rape laws against coercive sex and/or repeal everything else. Such a representation of criminal law disallows a more textured cartography of sexual violence, its legal coordinates and (partial) remedies. Rubin insists that the problem of sex is forcible coercion, that this problem alone should concern sexually democratic citizenry and democratic law. On this account, the only ethical concerns one should legitimately hold toward *TCAP* are the disqualification of youthful desire and the criminalization of what appears to be an interest in consensual sex with a teenager.

But is there nothing impermissible or at least questionable about an older man seeking out a younger teenager for a sexual encounter? Is the only critical problem here that the relation is itself regarded as a problem? Is the preservation of (hetero)sexual normativity the only contestable issue?[66]

Rubin's Sex Harm

For Rubin, what sexual injustice entails is the social segregation and scape-goating of sexual subjects, the political organization of sexuality that values up some against the degradation of others. Sexual justice and injustice is in this instance about groups. Individually, what should separate good sex from bad, legal from criminal, is coercion:

> A democratic morality should judge sexual acts by the way partners treat one another, the level of mutual consideration, the presence or absence of coercion, and the quantity and quality of pleasure they provide . . . whether sex acts are gay or straight, couples or in groups . . . commercial or free . . . should not be ethical concerns.[67]

A telling omission occurs in this passage. While Rubin begins her description of the moral atrocity of sex law by spelling out the inanity and severity of laws around age, she shifts her attention to nonnormative consensual sex acts between adults to arrive at her conclusion that sex law persecutes and violates the desires and bodies of minoritized sexual subjects. Indeed, throughout the essay, when she pushes up against state or social excess, the sympathetic subject is often the boy-lover.[68] But when she pushes up against the question of ethics, law, and consent, the sympathetic subject is often the consenting homosexual.[69]

I want to suggest that this is because the question of sex and the child starkly throws into relief that "consent" and "coercion" cannot and should not be the only metrics that define sexual harm, and too, that "consent" and "coercion" are not so easily read off sexual experience.[70] Rubin wants to steer away from a moralistic feminism that detects any power dynamic in sexual exchange and representation as patriarchal and damaging. But we need not indict all power asymmetry in sex to suggest that the relations between younger and older persons may rightly—from a sexually democratic perspective—raise different sorts of ethical concerns than gay sex, prostitution, and cross-dressing. Indeed, it may be ethical concerns around vulnerability, pleasure, and dependence, and not simply child innocence and adult predation, that partially animate social anxieties around sex and youth. Such anxieties are not necessarily stoked only to squash youthful sexuality, to enforce sexual norms, or to demonize categories of persons.[71] In other words, that those who cross generational boundaries are the "lowliest of all" may reflect more than phobic or disavowing disgust. What if sex across generational divides is morally distinguishable from other nonnormative sexual activity, such as gay sex or sex for money? In that case, a more attuned diagnosis of what counts as sexual harm and threat may be necessary both to restrain the sexual demonizing of "predators" and to articulate a more robust account of sexual ethics that moves beyond coercion and consent as morally determinative. At a generational remove from the political conditions that urged "Thinking Sex," we are better able to resist Rubin's staging of coercion and consent as the only material suitable for ethical discussion, and intergenerational sex, gay sex, sex for money, and sex in groups as unsuitable. Holding such sexual activities to ethical scrutiny need not be moralistic or condemnatory; rather, it suggests that both coercion and consent are variably contoured, compromised, complemented, and even sometimes supplanted by factors like gender, money, dependency, age and age difference, and sexuality.

In 2011, Rubin authored a retrospective on "Thinking Sex" in response to a conference celebrating the original essay's import and influence in the field of gender and sexuality studies. "Blood under the Bridge: Reflections on 'Thinking Sex'" reminds the reader of the resolutely hostile climate Rubin and like-minded scholars encountered in their defenses of sexual pluralism. Antipornography feminist groups continually attempted to boycott and/or blacklist Rubin from conferences and speaking engagements, condemning her interrogations of sexual stratification as themselves misogynistic. "Blood under the Bridge" recalls that the primary objective of "Thinking Sex" was not to deliver a competing model of sexual ethics out of whole cloth, but rather to make discernible how moral discomfort and sexual normativity translate into unjust political practices and repressive law. My critique above and below, then, is not that Rubin wrote an essay she had no interest in writing; the critique is an exploration of the limits and possibilities that Rubin's remapping of sexuality proffers.

Rubin returns to the problem of intergenerational sex her original essay posed, admitting that her gestures there were "far too sketchy" and underdeveloped.[72] Still, she countermands that moral panic around the sexuality of both the young and the men who desire them has exponentially exploded since the early 1980s, making it ever more difficult to diligently inquire about intergenerational sexual contact and intimacy. Rubin asks several open-ended questions that could sharpen our reading of *TCAP* (both as infotainment and as metonymic):

> what constitutes sexual abuse and how can it be prevented and minimized; how should young people learn about sex; what are the appropriate roles of adults in the sexual lives and learning of children; . . . what is pedophilia, and

what is child molestation; who abuses children; . . . and for what offenses is
someone labeled a "sex offender"?[73]

These are questions we tend not to ask because we think we know the
answers to them. The "self-evident" powerfully norms and contains the
discourse of youth sexuality. The very verbalization of these questions is
therefore politically energizing, unsettling collective assurances that we
know sex harm or sex abuse when we see it. However, because Rubin never
detaches from the magnetism of the consent/coercion paradigm, "Thinking Sex" and "Blood under the Bridge" provide neither the terms nor the
theory that might begin to answer the questions she so courageously pos-
tulates. In the retrospective essay, Rubin documents how antipornography
feminists mobilized disgust to conflate "some things that are clearly horrible, such as rape, with some other things that might be pleasurable, such
as being spanked."[74] Rubin is not wrong, but like "Thinking Sex," the only
remaining, relevant moral distinction here is between pleasure as signaled
by consent (what transforms hitting into erotic spanking) and horror as
indexed by coercion (rape).

Intergenerational sex distinctly complicates the consent/coercion, plea-
sure/horror paradigm of sexual harm, and not because youth are categorically unable (or able) to consent. As I elaborate over the next two
chapters, age differences are often proxies for other morally significant
differences too—of development, experience, gender, sexuality, and dependence—that matter when it comes to sex. These differences must be
attended to by thought—and sometimes by law—that does not revolve
exclusively around consent and coercion, or presumptive innocence and
presumptive predation. Rubin invests so heavily in the consent/coercion
framework because she is rightly dubious of arguments to false consciousness (women's consent as manufactured) and asymmetrical gendered
socialization (women's consent as adaptive) that would deny sexual freedom to women in defense of their protection.[75] Yet we can canvass the
complications that sex across age differences presents to the sexual autonomy of young subjects without liquidating consent of all value whatsoever.
Consent matters, but not comprehensively.[76]

At one level of critique, the liberal seductiveness of the consent/coercion
paradigm prohibits Rubin from exploring a broader set of terms and factors to assess intergenerational sex. At another, more stringent level of critique, the attachment to the consent/coercion paradigm may redouble the

problem Rubin wishes to diagnose. If, in our contemporary, collective, national imagination, sex across age difference is so seamlessly interpreted as an unsolicited imposition upon the incompetent child, then holding the consent/coercion line confirms what we already know: adults can consent, young people cannot, and the problem *TCAP* presents is the problem of the coerced child (a redundancy, in fact). By objecting to contemporary considerations of child sexuality while primarily banking on consent and coercion for sexual ethics, we very well might remain where we started if, when it comes to sex, youth are culturally defined by consent's absence and men who desire young people are culturally defined as coercers.

Insofar as "Thinking Sex" and "Blood under the Bridge" demonstrate how easily normative outsiders (whether queer-minded feminists or boy-lovers) become moral outcasts, reading Rubin's essays against *TCAP* reconfronts our complacency with the "ick" factor of the man who appears wanting sex with a teen. But there is something about that "ick" that is not just aversion to sexual deviants, or to sexual children. And while we interrogate the way media, law, and media representation of law function to individualize and externalize sexual violence, we can nevertheless appreciate that *TCAP* (in a sensationalist, self-righteous way) tells its audience that consent and coercion do not fully capture sex that is harmful, dangerous, or just bad. It may tell its audience too that the desiring young subject is disproportionately exposed to risk and pain. The source of anxiety may not be that predators or *TCAP* sexualize young people whom a duped audience otherwise believe are innocent; rather, the source of anxiety may be instead that we know young people are sexual but are positioned more vulnerably than adults, on account of differences in capacity, knowledge, and relations of dependence.[77] These questions of vulnerability, risk, sex, and youth are taken up by Hawkes and Egan's "Landscapes of Erotophobia."

Gail Hawkes and R. Danielle Egan, "Landscapes of Erotophobia: The Sexual(ized) Child in the Postmodern Anglophone West"

Let's jump ahead about twenty-five years, skipping over different kinds of panic and anxieties around children and sex, symptomized in concerns from incest to allegedly rampant satanic daycare centers to stranger predators lurking in playgrounds and websites. Let's skip over a considerable amount of literature that wedded the insights of Cohen with those of

Rubin to understand changing national affects to sexually endangered children and sexually dangerous adults.[78] I examine here a relatively recent example of work on children, sex, and threat, to pinpoint both the productive and stagnant lines of contemporary inquiry, while squaring this analysis with the pleasures and pains *TCAP* elevates and eclipses.

Hawkes and Egan's "Landscapes of Erotophobia" introduces a special issue of *Sexuality and Culture* focused on representations and regulations of children and sexuality in public institutions, literature and film, and social scientific study. Hawkes and Egan's concept of "proper sexualization" as a critical explanatory variable is promising for their cultural diagnosis, yet their fallback to girls' subordination as the lynchpin for decoding sociolegal renditions of sexual threat impedes a more careful consideration of the issues they identify.

Proper and Improper Sexualization

Hawkes and Egan suggest that a central underlying cause of fear in the "Anglophone West" around children's sexuality may have less to do with preserving a mythic sexualized innocence of children and more to do with concern that children are "properly" sexualized, according to dominant understandings of "correct" temporal development, proper timeline of sexual experiences, the right gender of object choice, and the appropriate (same) age of partner. "Proper sexualization," they posit, is the "imperative that . . . undergirds both erotophobia and the sexualization panic."[79] This sort of explanation squares better with, well, the world than the insinuation that social panic demands or desires an outright erasure of childhood sexuality.[80] Concerns over safer-sex education, gay teachers, the appropriate amount of flesh to air on MTV or YouTube, the right age to air that flesh, suggest an incessant predilection with propriety and with guiding developing sexuality into "heteronormative adulthood."[81] On this account, "erotic agency" is not wholesale denied or discounted, but fretted over and governed. Its susceptibility to dangerous detour is the substance of moral preoccupation. Whereas for Rubin, law and social conservatives were in the business of suppression, for Egan and Hawkes, moral entrepreneurs, anxious parents, and politicians may be more in the business of sexual risk management.

TCAP posits that its nameless child is sexual ("did you bring condoms?"), but about-to-be sexualized in all the wrong ways, by adults with no best interests of the child in mind. The problem of "proper sexualization" begins to explain the figuring of both sexual threat and the state in the show. The child and its bodily borders assume center stage at the cultural nexus between a popularized psychoanalytic sexuality—polymorphous perversity—and the late modern redirection of criminal law toward preemption and risk containment. If psychoanalysis "as a theory of erotic accidents . . . incites a wish for risk management,"[82] so too do state and federal policies aimed to curb dangerousness. The preventive neoliberal state,[83] together with a psychoanalytic account of "normal" sexuality as antiteleogical, moldable, constructed, and endangered, discursively threatens the child from every side: terrorists, homosexuals (waning), pedophiles (waxing), violent video games, and toys from China. The very crime for which *TCAP*'s predators are often charged is "*attempting* lewd behavior on a minor," emblematizing perfectly the conjunction of the state's focus on preemption with the social focus on the child's not-quite but nonetheless highly malleable and reversible heterosexuality.[84] In a landscape of ubiquitous risk and nationalized prevention, the child stands for—or is sterilized as—a stabilization point for nostalgic return to life before *all that,* a prop through which adults envision life as safe, simple, and manageable.[85]

Still though, for Hawkes and Egan, there is a running implication that all anxiety around youthful sexuality is about securing a stable adult heterosexual identity; discomfort with erotic agency is discomfort with an exploratory sexuality that may not fall under hetero tutelage. For Cohen, the "harm" of the Mods and Rockers materially exists, but disproportionate social response and media amplification distort its severity and pervasiveness. For Rubin, the only sexual harm that counts is coercion, and moral panic around sex fortifies repressive norms and sexual standards, ostracizes sexual subjects, and figures children as sexless. For Hawkes and Egan, there is a harm to which the social responds, the harm of "improper sexualization"; youth are indeed sexual, but their sexuality must be disciplined and governed toward proper objects. Hawkes and Egan allow that "youth sexuality" may be not just a latent substitute for other anxieties (although they say this too) but may be, transparently, a source of discontent sui generis. Unfortunately, they do not allow for an interpretation of adults' or politicians' concerns for youth sexuality or intergenerational sex as anything other than concerns about channeling young polymorphous perversity into adult heterosexuality. There may in part be a simpler answer: that the desires and vulnerability of youth, along with the social specialization of sex, make the combination of youth and sex ethically demanding and inherently, presently, anxiogenic. These anxieties are moralized and hyperbolized in the age of consent, when adult consensuality begins to outpace heterosexuality as the normative gold star.

Gender Matters

"Gender Matters" promisingly headlines the closing section of Hawkes and Egan's essay. "The phenomena of erotophobia and sexualization panic is," they write, "founded upon naturalized assumptions about gender, that are consistently obscured behind a smokescreen of age."[86] But Hawkes and Egan's elaboration reveals that gender matters only in predictably gendered ways: public outrage over sexualized youth is a smokescreen to curb the erotic agency of girls and reimagine them as passive, treasured objects of male desire. Under these lights, "girl danger" is diagnosed as the risk of "premature sexualization," and "boy danger" is diagnosed as "risk to and the destruction of the future manhood of youth." Panics, then, are differentially gendered, aimed at securing male sex right and reigning in the dangers of unbridled female sexuality.[87] Rubin's concluding comments in "Thinking Sex" about the fixations of certain strands of second-wave feminism come to mind here. Panic might be gendered, anxieties around child sexuality might be gendered, acts of sexual harm may be inflected by both gender and sexuality, but these phenomena are not always or only manifestations of misogyny or the suppression of girls' sexuality.

I want to preliminarily propose that the gender and sexuality of partners cannot be split from age and age difference in discussions of sexual harm and freedom and that the contemporary dynamics of heterosexuality and the remaining cultural constraints on queer sexuality suggest that sex across age means different things for differently gendered and sexual subjects. I am not suggesting that hetero sex across age is unacceptable and homo sex across age is permissible, but I am suggesting that gender and sexuality need to be more thoroughly integrated into conversations around sex and age difference and that Hawkes and Egan do not aptly engage these potent intersections. It may be that sex across age with girls and sex across age with boys raise different questions, and raise different questions because of gender and sexuality difference. To emphasize, such a suggestion need not presuppose that all girls are sexless, that all boys are sexually willing, and that gay sex across age is morally neutral and straight sex morally suspect. But if sexuality is a political arrangement and gender is in part a production of social inequality, then "gender [and sexuality] matter" in the arena of sex and age in ways more complicated than Hawkes and Egan's gloss permits.

To approach the same problem from a contiguous starting point, consider another *TCAP* dialogue:

> ANTHONY PALUMBO: I'm not gay or anything. I'm just saying.
> CHRIS HANSEN: This isn't about gay or straight. Nobody cares what adults do.
> PALUMBO (*interrupting*): No, I'm just saying.
> HANSEN: But when you involve somebody who is fourteen, that's when it becomes an issue.
> PALUMBO (*interrupting*): I thought he was eighteen.[88]

But why is sex across age difference categorically not "about gay or straight"? Shouldn't that be a hypothesis rather than an apriority? Why wouldn't gayness, straightness, or gendered socialization matter "when it becomes an issue"? *TCAP* collapses the problem of sex across age difference to the problem of age alone, and this may be a welcome development for Rubin and other scholars who have observed that campaigns against pedophiles are often thin cover for campaigns against gays. *TCAP* is an equal opportunity exposé. Hansen leverages the libertarian legitimacy of gayness against pedophilia ("nobody cares what adults do"). I want to query the act of legitimizing through discrediting and refuse the premature partitioning of sexuality from normative valuations of intergenerational sex.

Both "improper sexualization" and the centrality of gender in "Landscapes of Erotophobia" bring us closer to the argument I am attempting to articulate, lending itself to a political analytic and not purely a sexual-social one. Yet Hawkes and Egan stall on the foregone conclusion of heteronormativity or at-risk heterosexuality as a singularly significant explanation. They stall as well on the presumption that it is girls and girls alone for whom adult anxieties are accorded, that social fixation on children is exclusively fixation on gender normativity and maintaining girlhood innocence.[89] As *TCAP* would have it, the problem is genderless and about age. As Hawkes and Egan would have it, the problem is not about age, but about gender and about girls. Neither answer is complete: age and gender interface, and sexuality and gendered socialization complicate the normative terrain.

CONCLUSION

What, ultimately, is the harm *TCAP* delivers? It is not exactly sexual violence, as no sexually violent act ever takes place—unless one considers policemen piling up on a now emasculated man an act of sexual violence.

On the other hand, *TCAP* generates domestic, ruptured intimacy-cum-political solidarity through the specter of sexual violence, and it loads its cast of characters with weighty but seemingly simple meanings: Hansen alternates between sovereign adjudicator, pop psychoanalyst ("explain this to me"), and child savior. The predator functions alternatively as pariah, pathetic, and personified (if incomprehensibly incompetent) evil. And the child is innocent if hesitantly precocious ("so, I see you like younger girls").[90] At first blush, the characters are overdrawn, the story line gothic.

But interpretive complications, as we have seen, abound, and those complications turn heavily on gender, embedded in the imperiled masculinity of the predators and the sexual agency of the (usually) female decoy (Figure 6). The figure purported to embody evil is also socially dysfunctional, lonely, scared, and patently frustrated at his failure to achieve any semblance of hegemonic masculinity;[91] likewise, the girl is coy, playful, and pubescent, yet is also only afforded the smallest of speaking roles. Just

Figure 6. Kacie, the "decoy," from "New Jersey." Kacie poses as a thirteen-year-old. "To Catch a Predator—Ocean County, New Jersey," 2015.

as the show's narrative and character presentation challenge its own type-casting of the predator, the child "decoy" is a similarly conflicted subject. The harm here is not about sexualizing an otherwise innocent, incapable child. The "decoys" on the show are nineteen or twenty and ask the predators a host of sexual questions. They flirt. PJ members pose as twelve- and thirteen-year-olds, not eight-year-olds. They are at the pubescent brink of socially and legally acceptable sexual subjectivity. On-screen then is a desiring, "legal," (usually) female subject juxtaposed with a corruptible, asexual, jailbait child conjured by Hansen.

The players' speech acts and bodily performances undermine their scripted roles. The tripartite story of the "good guy," "bad guy," and "damsel in distress" (the story Ummni Khan tells us is ubiquitous in media coverage of sexual threats to the child) is here unevenly confounded.[92] This immanent troubling begins to clear the ground to see something else, other modes of apprehending sexual harm—its sources, dimensions, and constraints. So what is the harm?

The sex harm in TCAP is not (entirely) about predatory men and the corruption of sexless girls and boys. Although TCAP's Hansen may think he is telling us a story about predators and prey, we are instead witnessing desiring but dependent sexual subjects—young people. This combination of sexual will and social vulnerability of the young person, rather than an inborn evilness of the adult, is partially what provokes such discontent around intergenerational sexual activity.[93] It is not simply that we want young people to be properly heterosexualized or forever asexualized or that discomfort around youth sexuality signifies fear of female erotic agency. Rather, young people desire, but on account of educational, experiential, and circumstantial phenomena, their desires are disproportionately subject to interference, constraint, and manipulation.

As we have also seen, TCAP treats all girls and boys as equivalently vulnerable and spoilable, and men searching for boys and men searching for girls as equivalently predatory and evil. What if queer boys go online, sometimes, for sexual partners and friends because their worlds are insufferably homophobic? What if girls go online, sometimes, for sexual partners and friends because of the cramped conditions of gendered enculturation and expectations?[94] Given how girls and boys are socialized to initiate and understand sex, must we assume that girls and boys experience sexual activity with older partners in the same fashion, as unequivocally traumatic?

Doesn't a social constructivist account of gender and sexuality require a presumption that sex across age is differently inflected by different sexual cultures, socialization, and gendered embodiment? In the remainder of the book, I more deeply contemplate and complicate the running stipulation that gender and sexuality matter in locating and remediating sexual harm across age difference.

2 Transcendent Homosexuals, Dangerous Sex Offenders

> [The framers and the drafters of the Fourteenth Amendment]
> knew times can blind us to certain truths and later generations can
> see that laws once thought necessary and proper in fact serve only
> to oppress.
>
> —*Lawrence v. Texas*, 539 U.S. 558, 579 (2003)

> The sexual fringe is a scary place.
>
> —Gayle Rubin

To Catch a Predator (*TCAP*) produces predators. By patterning pornography and reiterating tenets of law-and-order ideology, *TCAP* imagines sexual harm as resolvable by criminal law and presents criminal law as effectively compensatory. The show recursively generates the sexual harm it then eradicates, but only until the next episode. Sexual harm is about bad men (who do not always look so bad, upon closer inspection) violating asexual children (who look adolescent and sexual, upon closer inspection).

Now we want to ask, as we round the cultural circuit of life, law, and sexual harm, how does law incorporate cultural *doxa,* or becoming-*doxa,* to deliver its sex offender? And how, if at all, is the juridical construction of the sex offender related to law's characterizations of the child, the homosexual, and consent? To answer these questions, this chapter travels over to the Supreme Court and back to the spring/summer of 2003, a moment as celebratory for gays as it was devastating for convicted sex offenders.

For John Lawrence and Tyron Garner, metonymic figures for gays nationwide, June 2003 was nothing less than world transformative. The Supreme Court declared sodomy laws unconstitutional and granted previously withheld privacy and liberty protections to gays, lesbians, and their intimate (consensual, private, noncommercial) decisions. *Lawrence* is a landmark decision for the gay rights movement, as well as a landmark decision for the purchasing power of the Fourteenth Amendment. "When the history of our times is written, *Lawrence* may well be remembered as the *Brown v. Board* of gay and lesbian America."[1]

That is some pretty emancipatory stuff.[2]

Things did not bode so well in March of that same year for John Doe, John Doe, John Doe, and Jane Doe: three sex offenders and the wife of one, respectively and pseudonymously. The Supreme Court handed down twin decisions, *Smith v. Doe* and *Connecticut Department of Public Safety v. Doe*, rebuffing all of the Does' claims seeking constitutional protections from state sex offender registration and notification (SORN) requirements.[3] If the 2003 spring/summer court session ushered in the promise of juridical freedom for one historical sexual outcast, the homosexual, it recodified another sexual outcast, the sex offender, and declared open season on him.

Since the specter of the pedophile is and has been historically deployed to criminalize gays (e.g., J. Edgar Hoover), retract their rights (e.g., Anita Bryant and the "Save Our Children" campaign), or neutralize their political aspirations (e.g., Prop 8),[4] it may seem particularly cruel and politically naive—if not dangerous—to consider the setbacks faced by the John Does against the successes achieved by John Lawrence and Tyron Garner and to ask what rhetorical, discursive, political, juridical connections there are between these cases. Yet the formal similarities of the cases are evident and invite comparison: *Lawrence* and the sex offender cases involve regulating marginalized sexual personae, adjudicating the limit of law's reach in citizens' lives, delimiting the liberty afforded by due process protections, and discerning the proper figuration of harm and morality in lawmaking around sex. Moreover, if *Lawrence* and the sexual moral imaginary it animates and stokes *require* creating, disavowing, and then demonizing a sexual subclass, then theorizing the 2003 cases *in tandem* is neither cruel nor naive but necessary in diagnosing and interrogating how understandings of sexual freedom and sexual harm are currently, juridically inscribed. *Lawrence* argues that sex between consenting adults in private is constitutionally protected.[5] The fault line between the sexually acceptable and the sexually abject, between the terrain of progressive sexual politics and the terrain of sexual perversion, is brokered by the apparently transparent figure of the consenting adult. A riding presumption of *Lawrence* is that sexual harm is present only where the consenting adult is absent, or at least the kind of harm with which a liberal noninterfering state ought to interfere. But because the "consenting adult" cannot capture sexual ethics as cleanly or completely as the court or the nation would like—that is, on the one hand, because a whole lot of sex is still harmful that involves legally consenting adults,[6] and, on the other, because not all sex among minors or between minors and adults is necessarily harmful[7]—the figure of the sex offender, as reconstituted in *Smith* and *Connecticut,* contains the ambiguities of adult consent that threaten its coherence as a normative compass in the labyrinthine universe of sex and law. The sex offender, and what the court and the nation do with and to him, keeps alive, which is to say immunizes, adult consent as the story, the bright line, of sexual ethics, transmuting any fragility, ambiguity, loose ends, or displaced and disavowed erotic desire (for the child, or for riskiness) into violent reprisal.[8] The sexual pluralism in *Lawrence,* acerbically recognized by Justice Scalia, registers on both judicial and national fronts.[9] Americans, social-justice-loving people, and the legal system have entered (and created) an era—the age of consent, let's call it—where our traditional moral arguments and political capacity to identify and mitigate sexual harm are recalibrating. The legislative-turned-judicial understanding of, and punitive response to, the sex offender comfortingly and wrongly relocates the danger of sexual harm onto a discrete body (the stranger, the pathological recidivist, Jerry Sandusky, Jimmy Savile).[10] The figure reassuringly (re)partitions the moral universe on Manichean lines. The legislative-turned-judicial maneuver glosses over the complexities of sexual harm and danger and detracts from the primary sources of sexual abuse: fathers, family members, and family acquaintances.[11] Put slightly differently, while scholars, lawyers, and law students have argued that "sex offenders" ought to be treated with greater restraint, nuance, and fairness (especially juvenile offenders, as we have seen), my argument contends instead that the "sex offender" does not exist.[12] Or rather, that the figure of the sex offender has been legally created and codified, in part judicially, and that such creation and codification distinguishes sexual harm from sexual freedom, and sexual deviants from intimacy-valuing citizens, clearly and discretely, incorrectly and detrimentally.[13] The legislative attack on the "sex offender" (*To Catch a Predator*'s predator) and the judicial affirmation of this attack—both in its rhetorical and doctrinal dimensions—skew our understanding of sexual harm onto and into one person, thus simplifying the world and its multiply sourced dangers. The amplified legislative and judicial anxiety around sex offenders is contemporaneous with the judicial emancipation (or at least decriminalization)—and the changing social mores that underwrite that emancipation—of the homosexual. While the *Lawrence* opinion offers freedom and protection to the intimate, private homosexual, it neverthe-less retains a structural logic that imagines and then attributes sexual harm and dangerousness onto one body, a character type, a sex offender. Even though the characters changed, the script remained intact.

The first section of this chapter overviews the reemergence of sex offender laws and the variety of forms they take from the 1990s to the pres-ent and catalogs some common criticisms of them. This section analyzes notification and registration broadly as a national diffusion, rather than the specific statutes of the *Smith* and *Connecticut* jurisdictions (Alaska and Connecticut, respectively),[14] to situate these cases, their constitutional questions, and their cultural ramifications in a broader context. The second section explicates the twin sex offender cases, focusing on the constitu-tional claims of the respondents and the arguments invoked by the jus-tices against them. The third section reads the arguments of *Smith* and *Connecticut* against Justice Kennedy's opinion in *Lawrence*. The sort of juridical reasoning and rhetorical maneuvers of *Bowers v. Hardwick* that *Lawrence* so deftly reject are strikingly parallel to the reasoning and maneu-vers of the *Smith* and *Connecticut* cases. At the same historical moment— spring/summer 2003—when the Court (via Justice Kennedy) rejects cer-tain forms of argumentation in the sphere of sexuality, morality, and the law, it (via Justice Kennedy) then redeploys these strategies against sex offenders. The fourth section asks and begins to answer: Why? Why does the Court shift its *Bowers* strategies over to *Smith* and *Connecticut*? What can theorizing these cases together tell us about the juridical construction of sexual harm and sexual freedom and about the national-liberal fantasy of adult consent as simply and summarily morally determinative in the terrain of sexuality?

THE REEMERGENCE OF U.S. SEX OFFENDER LAWS

"Moral panic," as recalled in the first chapter, rapidly escalates around social and sexual deviancy in moments of political expediency and social dislocation.[15] At various times in American history, the supposed sexual threat embodied in and by Jewish men, black men, gay men, and "sex psy-chopaths" has been hyperbolized by media, political elites, mental health professionals, and social conservatives to regulate the sexuality of newly urbanized girls; to resanctify the heterosexual nuclear family and restitute gender norms in the postwar period; to crack down on gays, gay bars, and gay public spaces; to stifle or superimpose the sexuality of children; to win votes; to make a profit; and even to cut welfare.[16] It is beyond the scope of the chapter to historicize changing sex offender laws or the varied social interpretations and legal constructions of the sex offender since the turn of the twentieth century (as feeble-minded, as pathetic, as treatable, as evil, depending on the decade). I gesture at this history simply to note that the most recent panics around child sexual abuse and sex offenders inaugurated in the 1980s and continuing into the present, and the laws these panics sometimes motivate, have a genealogy. The important point is that there is a constructivist story to be told, and neither sex panics nor the laws that sometimes flow from them necessarily correlate to documented increases in sexual violence or sexual abuse against children.[17]

From the mid-1990s to the present, the United States has witnessed a tidal wave of state and federal sex offender laws. There are currently three main varieties of sex offender laws, all of which come into effect immediately prior to or upon the offender's release from prison: registration, community notification, and residency restrictions.[18]

Registration laws differ greatly by state, but generally offenders must register with local authorities and provide their address, bodily characteristics, place of employment, and social security number, along with their vehicle license number, make, and model. Offenders must periodically reregister—sometimes for life—or face federal criminal charges. States must meet minimum registration requirements under the Jacob Wetterling Crimes Against Children and Sexually Violent Offender Registration Act of 1994 or face federal budget cuts.[19]

Notification laws mandate that after an offender relocates from prison to civil life, either the offender himself or local authorities are required to notify members and/or institutions of the community. Like registration, the degree of community notification is often proportionate to the designated severity of the crime. Minimum state notification requirements were also first mandated federally under the 1996 "Megan's Law."[20] The federal Megan's Law and its state equivalents require sex offender information— often a picture of the offender, his address, the crime for which the offender was convicted, the age of the perpetrator and the victim at the time of the crime—to be made available for the public at large. States and the federal government post much of the information on online sex offender databases, which are, generally, freely accessible.

Residency restrictions are a newer iteration of sex offender laws, requiring that sex offenders live outside measured radii of places where children congregate, like schools or swimming pools. In some states, offenders cannot live within five hundred feet of schools; in other states the radius is two thousand feet.[21] These laws have some unintended consequences: offenders are effectively prohibited from living in entire municipalities, so they overflow into another; or, in Miami, sex offenders all lived together under a bridge, because it was the only locale legally far enough from protected institutions.[22]

The most recent federal minimum requirements for state sex offender laws are set in the Adam Walsh Act (AWA), and failure for state compliance results in federal funding cuts.[23] The AWA surpasses the baseline requirements of the Wetterling Act and Megan's Law, both in scope (whom it covers) and duration (how long offenders must register). The AWA creates a three-tiered system of sex offenses, potentially labels any crime vaguely sexual (public urination) a sex offense, requires certain juvenile offenders to register, compels registration for violent and nonviolent offenses alike, compels constant reregistration, and mandates that all offenders' personal information be posted online for fifteen years, twenty-five years, or life, depending on the tier of the crime. The AWA is offense based and does not allow for individualized, clinical risk assessment to determine whether an offender should or should not register and whether his personal information ought to be made publicly available.[24] The requirements of the AWA are stricter than those of most states, and some states have objected that compliance will be prohibitively costly.[25]

But cost is by no means the only objection to the array of sex offender laws. On a policy level, critics object: sex offender laws do not work (that is, they do not reduce sex offenses);[26] many laws make no or few assessments of risk, and so waste resources tracking the recidivist and the nonrecidivist, the violent offender and the nonviolent "Romeo";[27] and the stigmatizing and ostracizing effects of registration, notification, and residency restriction may encourage the violent behavior they are aimed to deter. The stress and depression resultant from social segregation, bullying, threats, verbal and physical attacks, and unemployment cultivate fertile psychological ground for recidivist, sexually aggressive behavior.[28]

On a humanitarian level, critics argue that these laws excessively burden offenders' lives and the lives of offenders' family members. Offenders often cannot reunite with their families because of residency restrictions.[29] As a result of online notification, offenders are sometimes harassed, publicly humiliated, and assaulted, and homes of offenders have been burned down or otherwise vandalized.[30] Facing such responses, some offenders have committed suicide.[31] The humanitarian criticism clusters around the wide net of registration and notification, which captures the "wrong place, wrong time" offender, or the "stupid teen," along with the playground abductor—a widely shared sentiment is that these laws are grossly overbroad (what I referred to as the "too far" argument in the Introduction). As mentioned, the AWA can require states to label anyone who commits any sexual crime a sex offender, including public urination, public indecency, statutory rape, and soliciting a prostitute.[32]

On a constitutional level, the laws have been challenged on wide-ranging grounds, only the most prevalent of which are mentioned here. One set of oppositions revolves around the laws as punishment: if notification, registration, and residency restrictions function to punish, their retroactive application violates the ex post facto clause of the Constitution.[33] Plaintiffs have also argued that the laws are uniquely harsh and disproportionate, violating the cruel and unusual punishment clause of the Eighth Amendment.[34] Another set of oppositions maintains that the laws are functional deprivations of liberty or equality, thus triggering Fourteenth Amendment protections. If the law singles out and subjects a class of people, that is, sex offenders, to unfair treatment without rational basis—without any reasonable relation to a legitimate state interest—the law contravenes equal protection guarantees.[35] If the law provides no administrative process to oppose registration and notification requirements, or no individualized risk-assessment, plaintiffs argue the laws violate procedural due process.[36] Finally, some claimants charge that the intrusions into their privacy, the restrictions on their travel and residency, and the consequent "stigma plus" the social consequences of that stigma amount to a violation of substantive due process, to infractions of fundamental rights that warrant strict scrutiny review.[37] On these Fourteenth Amendment challenges, the policy critique bleeds into the constitutional one: since there is evidence that these laws contravene their intended objectives, there may be no rational basis for them and, so the argument proceeds, for their enactment and enforcement.[38]

Why is all of this important? Because none of it matters.

Despite the laws' being bad policy, morally and physically devastating, and constitutionally questionable, legislatures continue to enact them, and courts (mostly) continue to reject objections on all counts. Some courts have placed temporary injunctions on the most egregious laws, and a few courts have ruled that blanket registration, notification, and residency requirements without attention to degrees of dangerousness and risk assessment, or without administrative processes of appeal, violate due process protections.[39] Nevertheless, the 2003 Supreme Court cases on sex offender laws soundly reject claims that registration and notification are either punitive or in conflict with procedural due process protections.

JOHN DOES AND THE SUPREME COURT

Two cases on sex offender laws made their way up to the Supreme Court in 2003. In *Smith v. Doe,* the respondents (two John Does and the wife of one) claimed that since they were convicted of sex offenses prior to the enactment of Alaska's registration and notification laws, retroactive application violated ex post facto. They argued that the continued requirement of registration and reregistration as sex offenders, and the continual community notification of their sex offender status via the Internet and other forms of public announcement, constituted a form of punishment.[40]

Delivering the majority opinion and reversing the ninth circuit decision, Justice Kennedy ruled that Alaska's notification and registration laws are regulatory, not punitive, and therefore trigger no ex post facto problem: one cannot be punished retroactively, but one can be regulated.[41] To determine if a statute is regulatory or punitive, the court first looks to legislative intent.[42] The manifest intent of the Alaskan legislature was evidently regulatory: it sought to protect the public health, not to punish offenders. Thus, the court turns to criteria enumerated under *Kennedy v. Mendoza-Martinez,* which may determine laws to be punitive despite their regulatory intent. The factors that may override legislative intent include whether the law (1) has historically been regarded as punitive, (2) imposes an affirmative disability or restraint, (3) has a rational connection to a nonpunitive objective, and (4) is excessive in respect to its purpose.[43] The court determined that sex offender laws reach none of these thresholds: the laws are dissimilar to colonial acts of shaming and humiliating; they are reasonably related to rates of recidivism; no physical restraint is imposed on offenders; and difficulty in finding employment or housing on account of notification is "conjecture."[44] Dissenting, Justice Ginsburg argued that the absence of an assessment of dangerousness or an assessment of individualized likelihood of recidivism marks the laws excessive, and Justice Stevens insisted that the majority's reliance on the presumptive recidivism of offenders in fact substantiates the ex post facto claim, as it singles out a subset of persons for legal restraint.[45] Both Ginsburg and Stevens also documented the threats, assaults, evictions, and arson faced by offenders, which Kennedy and the majority overlooked, that might constitute affirmative restraint.

In *Connecticut Department of Public Safety v. Doe,* Doe argued that Connecticut's registration and notification laws violated procedural due process protections guaranteed by the Fourteenth Amendment. Since the laws allegedly deprived him of protected liberty rights, the state, under prior case law, ought to be required to administer a "predeprivation hearing" to assess Doe's dangerousness and determine whether registration and notification are indeed applicable.[46]

The protected liberty interest in question is one of reputation. Although the court has consistently ruled that damage to reputation alone (from the dissemination of truthful information, for example) does not qualify as a protected liberty interest,[47] the "stigma plus" test outlined in *Paul v. Davis*[48] specifies that procedural protections are warranted when "the injury to reputation [is] accompanied by a change in the injured person's status or rights."[49] In Doe's case, the "plus" is his change in legal status to "sex offender."[50]

Delivering a brief, unanimous decision reversing the second circuit opinion, Chief Justice Rehnquist ruled that, first, there are no protected liberty interests of the sex offender violated by notification and registration laws and, second, even if there were, no predeprivation hearing would be necessary.[51] Such a hearing must be "material to the State's statutory scheme," must be related to the law in question.[52] John Doe, argued Rehnquist, mistakenly assumed that Connecticut's laws were enacted to supervise *dangerous* people and that his dangerousness ought to be assessed. But the laws target sex offenders as a *class* and make no reference to dangerousness, so dangerousness is irrelevant.[53] No hearing is necessary to establish his legal status as a sex offender, a status confirmed by conviction. In concurring opinions, Justices Ginsburg and Souter also rejected the procedural challenge but suggested that equal protection and substantive liberty claims might still be available to Doe and those similarly situated.

A REVISIONIST READING OF *SMITH* AND *CONNECTICUT,* OR HOW THE COURT DOES THINGS WITH SEX OFFENDERS

The analyses of the next two sections of this chapter closely track the arguments in *Smith* and *Connecticut* alongside the arguments advanced in *Bowers* that were subsequently rejected by *Lawrence.*[54] This comparison is made to substantiate the claim that, whether or not sex offender laws are ultimately constitutional, these laws, like the sociojuridical construction of the sex offender himself, inform an imaginary that fictively stabilizes sexual harm onto discrete bodies and character types. The court does so in, and because of, a national climate increasingly sexually pluralistic and socially progressive where the homosexual is no longer a sufficient repository for sexual amorality. Put perhaps too simply, where the homo/hetero distinction once divided the sexually moral from the amoral and consent/nonconsent divided the sexually harmful from the nonharmful, the consent/nonconsent divide, in the wake of *Lawrence,* does double duty, partitioning morality and harm.

The court's consent/nonconsent distinction, even if not comprehensive, is therefore overburdened and overdrawn, covering at once too little and too much. It is unable to diagnose or mitigate sexual injustice that is legally consensual (too little), and it smuggles in sexual practices considered amoral and designates them nonconsensual and harmful (too much). It is the fragility and volatility of this distinction that the figure of the sex offender stills and obscures. The following three subsections explicate how the court constructs the sociopolitical figure of the sex offender. The final section of the chapter suggests why.

Sodomizing and Recidivating

To overturn *Bowers,* the majority opinion of *Lawrence* deploys a battery of arguments, the first of which is an accusation of bad faith historicism.[55] For *Bowers,* part of the rational basis for sodomy laws was a presumably historic, uninterrupted, Judeo-Christian moral aversion to homosexuals and their sodomitical acts. *Bowers* maintained that long-standing proscriptions against sodomy testified to a universal moral code that disapproved of homosexuals and homosexuality.[56] In *Lawrence,* Justice Kennedy countermands this assertion. First, sodomy laws were originally enacted and enforced to protect people deemed incapable of consent—they were not aimed to target homosexuals; second, sodomy laws that did focus on same-sex sex were only recently drafted, in the 1970s; third, most states have repealed their sodomy statutes.[57] These three arguments taken together challenge both the claim that sodomy laws historically manifested disapproval of homosexuality and the claim that such disapproval is widely shared. Remarkably, Justice Kennedy observes that the homosexual is a historical invention of the nineteenth century and thus could not have been singled out by colonial sodomy laws because he did not—as a category—yet exist.[58]

Important here is the degree to which the *Lawrence* court felt compelled to do its history homework, citing scholars of colonial America and gay and lesbian studies.[59] Also important is that not far from the surface of *Lawrence* is the suspicion that homophobia directed and then marred *Bowers's* selective use of history and that homophobia does not a good constitutional decision make, blinding or mischaracterizing the facts of the case. "At the very least," writes Kennedy, *Bowers's* history was "overstated," and he scrutinizes Justice Burger's "sweeping references" to the moral reprobation of homosexuality.[60]

Just three months before Justice Kennedy's compelling performance as a revisionist historian, he and the majority for which he wrote categorically refused to ask similar constructivist questions about the ascriptive identities of sex offenders. The backbone of Kennedy's opinion in *Smith*, and Rehnquist's opinion in *Connecticut*, is the uncritical presumption of high recidivism, the great likelihood that sex offenders will reoffend.[61] Justice Kennedy approvingly cites Alaska's 1994 legislative finding that "sex offenders pose a high risk of reoffending" as evidencing a regulatory purpose, protecting public safety.[62] Reversing the ninth circuit's ruling that the Alaska requirements were "excessive in relation to its regulatory purpose" because the laws did not track dangerousness,[63] Kennedy writes:

> Alaska could conclude that a conviction for a sex offense provides evidence of a substantial risk of recidivism. The legislature's findings are consistent with grave concerns over the high rate of recidivism among convicted sex offenders and their dangerousness as a class. The risk of recidivism posed by sex offenders is "frightening and high."[64]

Kennedy also cites two Bureau of Justice Statistics (BJS) studies, conducted in 1983 and 1997, that allegedly claim that convicted sex offenders are more likely to commit sexual crimes than other criminals (more on the studies below). In other words, the classification "sex offender" indexes dangerousness, so no further assessment is necessary. Further, it is the presumption of dangerousness that hedges against a punitive reading of registration and notification requirements: although targeting "sex offenders" as a class may look like punishment, the "dangerousness as a class" makes the laws regulatory, protective, and constitutional.

Chief Justice Rehnquist introduces his opinion in *Connecticut* also citing *McKune v. Lile*, "Sex offenders are a serious threat to the nation," and reports as well that the victims of sex assaults are mostly juveniles and that recidivism runs disproportionately high among sex offenders.[65] It is the dangerousness inherent in the class of criminals, a dangerousness Connecticut has a legitimate interest in containing, that neutralizes any claim to an individualized risk-assessment under the due process clause. Sex offenders are threateningly recidivistic by legal designation. Respondents' "alleged nondangerousness simply does not matter," but only because that scheme depends on the presumption of "serious threat" or high recidivism (one may already sense the tautological force at work here).

Concurring, Justice Scalia asserts that since the notification scheme targets sex offenders as a class rather than dangerousness per se, an assessment of dangerousness is immaterial and void as a matter of due process protection.[66] He reasons by analogy: a sex offender who claims he has been deprived of liberty without due process because his dangerousness has not been individually determined is as nonsensical as a fifteen-year-old who claims that a law prohibiting him from driving on account of his young age is a due process violation unless his driving safety skills are tested.[67] He does not explain the analogy, but it seems to be about a shared obviousness and absurdity in both cases. It is obvious that most children are not capable of driving and absurd to suggest there is no rational state interest in barring children from driving. It is obvious that sex offenders sex offend and absurd to suggest there is no rational state interest in tracking and publicizing their location and activities.[68] Moreover, it is the sex offending that vitiates any claim to ethical or constitutional competency on the part of the offender—due process is inapplicable for those, like children and sexual sociopaths, legislatively scripted as incapable of self-assessment.[69] The law and its representatives are the competent constitutional surveyors.

The central problem with Kennedy's and Rehnquist's opinions, and Scalia's analogy, is that the social fact of recidivism is just social. Evidence of sex offender recidivism from the 1980s into the present is complicated and contested, but generally research studies suggest that, if anything, sex offenders have some of the *lowest* recidivism rates among criminals.[70] So too, recidivism varies hugely by the particular crime, so any generalized statistic is definitionally bogus.[71] There is much state discretion in determining who is a "sex offender," and that broadened category exceeds the typical subject populations of recidivist studies, namely violent offenders (the 1997 BJS study examines the behaviors of only those who were convicted of rape and sexual assault).[72] Given too that over 90 percent of sex offenses against children are committed either by family members or family acquaintances, the recidivist stranger seems like a doubly wrong concern for public or legislative attention.[73] The Justice Center, an organization critical of Alaska's statutes and the court's approval of them, notes that the "legislature did not attempt to distinguish among types of offenders or to evaluate which offenders were most likely to recidivate."[74] If an older teenager who has sex with a younger teenager is a "sex offender," what does it mean to say he is a high recidivist?

Perhaps most importantly, the BJS studies referenced by Kennedy and Rehnquist do not say what the justices want them to say. Sex offenders, according to these studies, do not recidivate at a higher rate than other criminals. If any fact could be comported to sustain the claim, it is the supposition that rapists are 10.5 percent more likely to commit rape than other convicts who have not raped, a number pared down to 4.2 percent in a 2003 BJS study.[75] But all this means is that rapists are more likely to rape than *other criminals who have not raped.* A rapist is more likely to commit rape in the future than is an armed robber. This simply cannot intend that sex offender recidivism is "frightening and high" or that "sex offenders are a serious threat to the nation." Indeed, what Kennedy omits to report is more illustrative than his selective citations. Violent sex offenders were *less* likely to be on "probation or parole prior to prison admission" than other violent offenders.[76] So too, rapists were less likely to be rearrested for violent felonies than "most categories of probationers with convictions of violence."[77] The studies offer no data on nonviolent offenders who would be labeled sex offenders by both the Connecticut and Alaska statutes and the AWA provisions.

Meanwhile, where the homosexual of *Lawrence* is a recent, historical, and conceptual figure of modernity, whose legal and cultural determinants have transformed dramatically over the last six decades,[78] the sex offender of *Smith* and *Connecticut* appears transhistoric, prediscursive, and perverted. Like hardcore pornography, the court knows a sex offender when it sees one.[79] That the "sex offender" is an explicitly legal construct seems to suggest to the court that the law applies a concept to a person, but that the concept ("sexually violent predator") is simply right in its ascription: these people are like this—threatening, recidivistic, pathologically violent. Recourse to false suppositions of recidivism, and to invocations of the impending threat of the sex offender, occludes the huge range of people classified as such and assumes their constitutive immunity to therapy and rehabilitation. The sex offender is imagined as a hypersexualized and unremorseful Voldemort who keeps coming back for Harry.[80]

The point is unequivocally not that sexual crimes are unserious or that they do not carry severe consequences for their victims. Rather, the severity and seriousness of these crimes are, by selective judicial interpretation and deployment of social scientific studies, legislators' rhetoric, and popular cultural accounts, transformed into a misleading characterization of these crimes' prevalence and persistence. In other words, it seems clear that both the judicial and national concern with sex offenses is not their comparative rate of occurrences but rather their heinousness. Yet the focus on rates and recidivism (and incidentally, almost no discussion about the physiological consequences to victims) constructs the problem in a particularly inaccurate but strangely comforting fashion. Perhaps the anxiety generated by the heinousness of sex crimes is offset by imagining a contained subpopulation—regulated, constricted, publicized—as the sole perpetrators (more substantive hypotheses follow below). In any event, Justice White in *Bowers* rehearsed a grand and inaccurate story about sodomy laws and transhistorical Judeo-Christian morality to characterize the homosexual as a criminological type undeserving of constitutional protections. Justice Kennedy refuted that story in *Lawrence* while recycling its rhetorical form in *Smith,* selectively using and misusing history and social science to project an image of a sex offender whose dangerousness and recidivism precludes constitutional questions about punishment and procedure. At the moment incapacitating history and debilitating myth are dislodged from the juridical image of the homosexual, analogous "truths" and behaviors are rebuilt into the figure of the sex offender on the premise of a seemingly solid social science.

Stuck (Again) between Acts and Identities

In *Lawrence,* the majority refused the narrowing interpretation *Bowers* gave to appellee Hardwick's liberty deprivation claim. Justice White's appraisal in *Bowers* of the liberty claim as "a fundamental right upon homosexuals to engage in sodomy," according to Justice Kennedy in *Lawrence,* "demea[ned] the claim the individual put forward."[81] Such misinterpretation, analogized Kennedy, is like suggesting married people's claims to privacy rights are tantamount to claims to copulate. More, much more for Kennedy, is packed into the liberties Michael Hardwick, John Lawrence, and Tyron Garner sought: rights of intimate association, spatial privacy, and finding meaning in human relations.[82]

Kennedy is drawing attention to the rhetorical shuttling between acts and identities that underwrites the *Bowers* decision throughout, a shuttling Janet Halley noted over two decades ago.[83] As Halley observes, in order to disfigure and then disparage Hardwick's rights claim, the court equated homosexual identity to the act of sodomy. Reframing the question as such, the court unsurprisingly found no fundamental constitutional liberty to engage in homosexual sodomy. You knew *Bowers* was over before it began when Justice White went looking into the Constitution for gay sex.[84] Conversely, when the *Bowers* court entertained whether or not a rational basis existed for Georgia's *gender-neutral* sodomy law, it found that basis in the supposedly long-standing moral condemnation of *homosexuality.*[85] Homosexual identity legitimates criminalizing sodomitical acts. Where one might conclude that maneuvering between acts and identities, between dismissing the claims lodged from one axis by invoking the other, might reveal the decision's self-contradiction, Halley instead maintains that there is a "homophobic power" in this kind of discursive incoherence. It is this incoherence that allows Justices White and Burger to bar the homosexual from constitutional shelter and to immunize heterosexual sodomy from state supervision.[86]

Is there a similar act/identity rhetorical strategy at play in *Smith* and *Connecticut*? (You might predict where I'm heading, given my rhetorical question about rhetorical questions.) In *Connecticut,* respondents argued that, because the state did not undertake individual risk-assessment of offenders or provide procedures for appealing the registration and notification requirements, the law violated procedural due process. The majority responded that since the law was not tracking dangerousness, but rather keeping the subpopulation of sex offenders in check, there was no procedural hang-up. There was no requirement for an administrative appeal process because the rational basis for monitoring sex offenders is that they are sex offenders, not that they are more or less dangerous. There is nothing in need of appeal. They are, after all, sex offenders, and that is who is being targeted by the state. However, in *Smith*, the Does argued that sex offender laws are punitive because they unfairly target a subpopulation, invasively interfere with their lives, have negative social consequences, and so on, triggering ex post facto protection. Here, the court responded that sex offender laws are not punitive because they have regulatory intent, because these laws are aimed to minimize dangerousness and protect public safety. When the offender argues he is punished, the court declares he is merely being regulated or prevented. When the offender argues he is being regulated or prevented (without procedural safeguards), the court countermands that he is being punished, or at least singled out by virtue of conviction.

The court maintains that singling out and regulating subpopulations based on prior conviction is not ipso facto punitive. This is true by precedent but deflects attention from—while relying upon—the antecedent directive of *Smith*: dangerousness. Dangerousness is the glue that holds the legal construction—and legal fiction—of the sex offender in place. The ruling in *Smith* relies upon its prior ruling in *Kansas v. Hendricks*, in which the court found that Kansas could civilly commit those sex offenders shown to have a "mental abnormality" indeterminately, because they pose continuous danger to the community.[87] *Hendricks* governs *Smith*: containing dangerousness is regulatory and outweighs the punitive potential. But *Hendricks* requires individual risk assessment, and *Smith* does not. Justice Kennedy argues that individualized risk assessment is not necessary because notification and registration are not as severe as the confinement of civil commitment and because sex offenders are definitionally high recidivists. We have now reached the apex of absurdity (or a rationalized irrationalism), and the more one reads *Smith* and *Connecticut* against each other, the more puzzlingly incoherent they both become. The court relies on *Hendricks* in *Smith* but dismisses what *Hendricks* held to be critical, the assessment of dangerousness, even though dangerousness is the regulatory target of Alaska. When the sex offender in *Connecticut* requests that his dangerousness be evaluated, his dangerousness is rendered immaterial to his legal status as a sex offender, even though future dangerousness is understood as what makes the sex offender a sex offender, by Justice Kennedy of *Smith* and Chief Justice Rehnquist and Justice Scalia of *Connecticut*. We can extend Halley's observation on the rhetorical management of the homosexual in the *Bowers* imaginary to the rhetorical management of the sex offender in the imaginaries of *Smith* and *Connecticut*. When the sex offender claims his identity (a convicted sex offender) is unfairly penalized, the court argues his (future dangerous) acts trump any incurred penalty. When the sex offender claims his acts (or lack of acting) deserve particularized treatment, the court rejoins that his (legal) identity renders his (lack of) acting moot. John Doe, like Michael Hardwick, juridically ricochets between acts and identities: acts are transmuted into identity, and identity comes to betray a set of presumed acts. Constitutional protections fall by the wayside.

The performative act, though, still matters for the making of the sex offender. We are not fully in the land of preemption, where a supposed propensity to act converts to criminalized identity, a dystopia featured, for example, in the 2002 film *Minority Report*. To be labeled a sex offender by the state or federal government, one must commit a "sex offense." But this begs the question, what constitutes a sex offense?[88] I mentioned earlier that the expansive net of AWA may reach public urination and some teenage sex. As we saw in chapter 1, "attempting lewd behavior on a minor"—or online solicitation—may qualify as a sex offense. So too, conduct that cannot be read as sexual in any way can and has been relabeled as a sex offense, such as kidnapping.[89] My contention here and below is not that this overcoding and recoding is unjust, which it might be, but that this overcoding and recoding reflect a national, paranoiac ambition to cohere, and then capture, sexual harm in an identity form.

Let me be clear, finally, about distinguishing acts not only from identities but also from one another: unlike Michael Hardwick and John Lawrence, who allegedly engaged in consensual oral and anal sex respectively,[90] the John Does sexually molested children. The actions of the Does are neither equated with those of Lawrence and Hardwick nor excused by analyzing the strategies utilized to frame the relevant constitutional and normative questions.

Straw Liberties

Justice White infamously contorted Hardwick's liberty claim of privacy into the patently spurious claim that the Constitution provides a "fundamental right upon homosexuals to engage in sodomy."[91] In contrast, for Kennedy, the liberty claim was rather about spatial privacy, consensual intimacy, discovering transcendental mysteries intersubjectively, and human flourishing. As far as I know, this is the most robust—which is not to say most consistent or justified—understanding of substantive due process to date.[92] (However, it should also be noted that this capaciously imagined liberty was not explicitly elevated to a "fundamental right.")

What happens when sex offenders claim their fundamental liberties have been infringed by the state?

Neither the John Does of *Smith* or of *Connecticut* make claims to substantive liberty, although Justice Souter's concurring opinion in *Connecticut* nods in that direction.[93] Aside from that, the protected liberty often claimed by sex offenders in lower court cases (and claimed as a liberty-warranting procedure in *Connecticut*) is the liberty of reputation, delimited by the "stigma plus" test. However, there are two significant drawbacks to claiming "stigma plus" as a violation of liberty interests. First, the stigmatizing information that triggers substantive due process protection by precedent affects the status or rights of the complainant.[94] There is nothing technically incorrect or status-changing in the legal fact that sex offenders are sex offenders, a classification determined by conviction, not SORN requirements. Second, the "plus"—loss of status or rights—must be a direct effect of government action.[95] All the state agencies do is register offenders and put their names online. Neither Alaska nor Connecticut burns down sex offenders' houses or terminates their employment—neighbors and employers do, so these are indirect consequences. Nonetheless, substantive cases materialized after *Smith* and *Connecticut,* and explicating the judicial reasoning and nonreasoning is illustrative.

Doe v. Tandeske rehears the case reversed by *Smith.*[96] This is the same court (ninth circuit) that originally held Alaska's registration and notification requirements in violation of ex post facto protections; now the court entertains the Does' procedural and substantive due process claims. *Connecticut* governs the procedural claim. As Alaska's registration and notification is also based on conviction status, not dangerousness, no hearing on dangerousness is necessary. On the question of fundamental liberty and substantive due process, the circuit judges mention neither *Lawrence* and its capacious if ill-defined understanding of protected liberties nor the suggestion in *Connecticut* that substantive due process may be a viable road for the Does. Instead, the court quickly cites the stricter liberty standards of *Washington v. Glucksberg* and writes that it is "bound by controlling Supreme Court law," notwithstanding that *Connecticut* avowedly did not entertain substantive claims. Here is the punch line: The Does argued that their "fundamental interests in life, liberty, and . . . property" are unconstitutionally infringed by Alaska's sex offender laws. The circuit court is "forced to conclude" that "persons who have been convicted of serious sex offenses do not have a fundamental right to be free from the registration and notification requirements set forth in the Alaska statute."[97] Michael Hardwick asked for privacy and was told he had no right to gay sodomy. John Doe asked for rights to life, property, and liberty and was told he had no right not to have his name on a sex offender list. So too, this court, like the *Connecticut* court, refuses to disambiguate the legal designation "sex offender" and the many nonviolent, nonrecidivist crimes that fall under its purview. *Doe v. Moore* and *United States of America v. Madera* pull the *Bowers* flip too.[98] In *Moore*, appellants argued that Florida's sex offender scheme violated their rights, inter alia, to "family association, to be free of threats to their persons and members of their immediate families . . . to find and/or keep any housing."[99] The district court finds that there is no fundamental right "of a person convicted of 'sexual offenses' to refuse subsequent registration of his or her personal information with Florida law enforcement and prevent publication of this information on Florida's Sexual Offender/Predator website."[100] Like *Tandeske*, the *Moore* court cites *Glucksberg* and Supreme Court rulings with similarly restrictive interpretations of due process. There is no mention here either of *Griswold v. Connecticut, Roe v. Wade, Eisenstadt v. Baird, Planned Parenthood v. Casey, Lawrence,* or the intimations of substantive due process in *Connecticut*. Finally, the opinion explicitly insists that it will dismiss the Does' broadened liberty claims in exchange for their own understanding of the Does' grievance, a fundamental liberty to be removed from a sex offender list.[101] The judges of *Madera* make the same maneuver, citing *Tandeske*.[102]

Obviously, appellants overstate substantive interests to make them sound fundamental. So too, because of reasons already mentioned—the indirect effects of the requirements, the "truth" of the stigmatizing facts (sex offenders are legally so, despite their individual crimes, recidivism rates, etc.)—substantive liberty claims are weak. Nonetheless, the juridical reductionist maneuver, collapsing a big liberty into a tiny risible one, allows the court neither to seriously engage appellants' arguments, nor to substantively canvass the physical, economic, and psychic harms incurred by these individuals, nor, ultimately, to perceive them as individuals at all.[103] It's all just about a name on a list. Or it's all just about gay sodomitical acts. The collapsing act sidesteps the long-standing debate among both jurists and legal theorists about the scope and application of substantive due process, thereby sidestepping too the constitutional interpretations that underwrite the debate.[104]

SEX OFFENDERS IN THE JUDICIAL IMAGINARY, OR WHY THE COURT DOES THINGS WITH SEX OFFENDERS

An insufficiently reductive distillation of the chapter might be this: the sex offender is the new homosexual.[105] He or it is the newly minoritized Other, a new outcast, a cultural mirage on whom to superordinate normative sexuality, to displace perversity outside ourselves, to localize, personalize, and smooth out deep structural injustices: sex abuse in the family, the pedophilia of capitalistic everyday life, the coerciveness of everyday heterosexuality.[106]

This does not capture the complete story, but it certainly captures a chunk of it. Yet it leaves unanswered still a host of questions. What makes, and makes efficacious, the rhetorical strategies employed by state legislatures[107] and courts to pin the sex offender where he is: the recidivist, the gravest threat, the primary and summary figure of the perverse, the dangerous, and the sexually harmful? If "recidivism" is overly prescribed at best and just wrong at worst, why do legislators and judges endlessly invoke its truth to enact or secure these laws? What motivates the court to conflate and thus officially equate dangerous acts with legal identities, taking the acts to be inevitable and the identities to be prediscursive? Why are substantive liberty claims miniaturized to a seemingly silly request to get one's name off a list? Objectors to sex offender laws have not answered these sorts of questions. Cultural criticism and liberal-leaning law journal articles uncritically assume it is either public anxiety that propels and maintains these laws and/or a fantasy of security that shields us from the main perpetrators of sexual abuse: family and family acquaintances.[108] But the laws are nonetheless rationalized as good, just, and constitutional, and fear is too blunt an emotion to do all that complicated justificatory work. The problem of liberal legal critique that calls for better actuarial models of registration and notification and demands more measured attention to dangerousness is that it accepts the juridical construction of the sex offender as such, as an organizing and disavowing figure for understandings of harm and sexual normalcy.[109] The sex offender *productively* blocks critical thinking about sex and harm. I am hypothesizing that what mechanizes these laws and their judicial defenses is an absence of measured theorizing on harm, sex, and power, an absence that has become a crisis as the homosexual is no longer fair game for subordination and projection, an absence that is then filled in by moralized and fictive certainties and reliably predictable tropes. These certainties and tropes provide not, or not only, a false sense of security, but a false sense of knowing, by locating harm and danger onto discrete bodies and stories.[110] The sex offender is not only a scapegoat but also a palliative, a way to literalize understandings of sexual harm and freedom that do not describe the world we live in but nevertheless make the world inhabitable for us. In this sense, the sex offender does more symbolic work than inhabit the position of the subjugated Other who upholds the regime of national sexual normativity—which might be looking more and more like adult consensuality and less like heterosexuality *simpliciter*. The figure of the sex offender also helps constellate an episteme of sexual harm, danger, and freedom. Under these lights, the rhetorical strategies of legislatures and courts might be perceived as efforts to manage harm and danger by a steadfast refusal to think more critically about them. Rather than consider the distribution of sexually harmful acts across populations, the law has fictively consolidated by categorizing that harm into a subpopulation. "Categorical thinking" is of course the business of the law,[111] but here law's categories are shaped into criminalized characters, identities understood to be, summarily, sources of sexual injury. On account of history, politics, and doctrinal developments, we can assuredly say that John Lawrence is a homosexual, that there are homosexuals.[112] But is John Doe a sex offender, or did we make him one? Does the law equate a particularly disturbing act with an even more disturbing identity to reorganize the world of good sex and bad sex, harmful sex and sexual freedom, when the homosexual is a now-untenable foil against the protected and potentially procreative heterosexuals of *Griswold, Eisenstadt, Casey,* and *Roe*?

Let us momentarily return to the rhetoric of *Lawrence* to clarify this argument and its stakes. Justice Kennedy continually presses that the *Lawrence* claimants are consenting adults, and that their consenting adultness portends any legal interferences as morally motivated, and not motivated to prevent harm:

> The present case does not involve minors . . . persons who might be injured or coerced or who are situated in relationships where consent might not be easily refused . . . or public conduct or prostitution. . . . The case does involve two adults who, with full and mutual consent from each other, engaged in sexual practices common to a homosexual lifestyle.[113]

A new boundary, or a new emphasis on an old boundary, gets its architecture in *Lawrence,* an architecture that reflects a changing national temperament. The hetero/homo divide in sexual morality is unworkable, archaic, and now defunct.[114] Kennedy's homosexuals, even if not (as of this writing) federally recognized as a suspect class, are loving people who make intimate, transcendent decisions; they are not sodomizers. What takes the place of the hetero/homo division is the division between consent and nonconsent.

This division is not as thorough or clean as I have led on. In her excellent work on the "becoming" and "unbecoming" of sexual citizens in the United States, Brenda Cossman warns against a premature assumption that consent is the new moral/legal metric of our neoliberal time.[115] She draws attention to legislation and court rulings that penalize obscenity, adultery, "welfare queens," "deadbeat dads," and the selling of sex toys.[116] She explicates as well cultural artifacts that value up sexual self-governance, nonreliance on the state, monogamy and commitment, consumer power, and sexiness (but not too much sexiness), while valuing down state dependency, graphic sexuality, and promiscuity. Her filmic, televisual, and legal case studies lead her to the following verdict on the normative, discursive, and juridical force of consent:

> Whose identities remain constituted in and through sexual practices that produce them as outsiders? . . . Rapists and child sexual abusers are outlaws par excellence. . . . *But, consensuality has not emerged as the new bright line between citizen and outlaw. . . . From sodomy to indecency, premarital sex to adultery, s/m sex to commercial sex workers, consent does not operate as an automatic citizenship sanction.*[117]

Cossman argues that the borders of sexual, cultural, and legal citizenship are barricaded not so much by consent as by neoliberal disciplinarity, the promise of freedom premised upon practices of responsible self-management. This seems right, and so I want to clarify the sort of power I am suggesting that consent is arrogating in U.S. law and cultural discourse.

First, my focus in this chapter and throughout is on the changing perception of sexual harm, not the making of sexual citizenship. To this extent, consent is, I believe, becoming dominant—which is not to say comprehensive—as an adjudicative determinant for actionable sexual injury: its presence an index of permissibility, its absence an index of impermissibility.

Second, and illustrative of this first claim, the legal regulation of consensual activity is now coming to be cast in the language of nonconsent, evidencing consent's normative currency.[118] Two of Cossman's own examples on the regulation of consensual sexual conduct are illustrative.

The Eleventh Circuit Court of Appeals, holding the criminalization of the commercial sale of sex toys constitutional, references child pornography in its ruling: should the court protect the use of sex toys in the bedroom as a privacy right, the constitutional doors would open to the similar use of child porn. Although the child porn analogy was neither necessary nor central to the holding, it gives to consensual activity the sheen of nonconsent.[119] Elsewhere in the decision, not cited by Cossman, the court comments, "There is nothing 'private' or 'consensual' about the advertising and sale of a dildo. And such advertising and sale is just as likely to be exhibited to children as to 'consenting adults.'"[120] The nonconsenting child circumambulates the appellate decision.

Likewise, in the obscenity case Cossman considers—again, as an example of the successful, post-*Lawrence* regulation of *consensual* sexual activity—the prosecuted company, Extreme Associates, is considered "the most extreme and violent within the genre [of pornography]."[121] Indeed, the company's depictions of assaults, rapes, and murders of women led even Larry Flynt to distance himself and *Hustler* from Extreme Associates, protesting, "I have always promoted consensual sex and portrayed consensual sex."[122] The federal government, in pursuing the obscenity charge, went after the most nonconsensual-looking representation of consensual activity.

We see too the appeal of nonconsent-talk in *Lawrence*. Justice Kennedy, carving out the kind of human activity that will not be constitutionally safeguarded by the ruling, writes, "This [a 'personal relationship that . . . is within the liberties of persons to choose'], as a general rule, should counsel against attempts by the State, or a court, to define the meaning of the relationship or to set its boundaries *absent injury to a person or abuse of an institution the law protects.*"[123] Later on, we know, Kennedy will specify that *Lawrence* does not protect prostitution or minor sexual activity from criminalization. By casting these practices as injurious to the person, in contradistinction to the consensual conduct of Lawrence and Garner, the "injury" here is synonymous with nonconsent.[124] And if the "institution" Kennedy is implying is marriage, then "abuse" is an odd, or revealing, word choice. "Abuse of an institution" reframes litigation for same-sex marriage, as if gays are taking marriage against her will, without consent. We think of children being abused, not institutions.

There is also evidence that the rhetoric of nonconsent has trafficked back into the justification of sodomy law, post-*Lawrence*. In 2013, former attorney general of Virginia Ken Cuccinelli appealed a Fourth Circuit Court of Appeals ruling holding the state's sodomy law unconstitutional.[125] The law criminalizes oral and anal sex outright, with no specifications regarding age or gender of the parties or monetary compensation for the conduct.[126] Nonetheless, as part of Cuccinelli's gubernatorial bid, he lobbied hard for retention of the law, arguing that repeal would give free range to "child sex predators" in Virginia. The Ken Cuccinelli for Governor campaign created an entire website in defense of the law that broadcasts "KEEP VIRGINIA KIDS SAFE!" and accuses his Democratic competitor, Terry McAuliffe, of "playing politics instead of protecting our children."[127] A law prohibiting consensual oral and anal sex between adults is refigured by Cuccinelli as a "child-protection" measure to ward off sexual predators.

I am pointing to two phenomena that clarify consent's magnetism in the juridical sphere. The first is the subsumption of consensual activity under nonconsent as a way to register that activity's harmfulness (discussed above). The second is the impoverished vocabulary of consent/nonconsent for diagnosing and redressing sexual harm (discussed in the following chapters). Are all activities portrayed in Extreme Associates pornography harm-free, if women contracted in to the performance? Is all violent sex harmless in consent's presence?[128]

Consent is certainly a phenomenally better metric of sexual harm than gender of object choice, but this has not been the point. Rather, the question of sexual morality is muted by and converted into the question of consent. Everyone classified as a sex offender has presumably violated consent—whether against the incapable child or the unwilling woman—and this is morally wrong. However, whether such acts are wrong, whether such acts are wrong solely because of the absence of consent, and whether rectifying those wrongs is best addressed by overreaching SORN requirements are separate issues, confused and collapsed by *Smith, Connecticut,* and *Lawrence*. In the language of *Smith* and *Connecticut*, SORN requirements are coded as harm prevention, not morality enforcement, and because they are coded as such they find constitutional shelter. Meanwhile, the set of proscribed acts where the application of consent seems relatively irrelevant—prostitution,[129] teenage sex, adult incest, public urination—

remain forms of behavior socially and juridically unacceptable, forms not as beautiful or mysterious as Kennedy's homosexual identity. However, these acts too are drafted as harmful and perpetually dangerous under Alaska's 1994 statute and now under the 2006 AWA and can be regulated accordingly, post—and yet regardless of, or maybe because of—the robust liberties discovered in *Lawrence.*

In *Lawrence,* for a case not about morality, morality is referred to all the time as the abstraction the court shall neither evaluate nor regulate. Kennedy presses the morality/harm distinction, insisting the law has no place in moral redress.[130] He cites the famous passage of *Casey:* our "obligation is to define the liberty of all, not to mandate our own moral code."[131] Like John Stuart Mill, Justice Kennedy insists on driving a wedge between morality and (other-regarding) harm, and bracketing morality from legal interference.[132] Like Mill, Kennedy's distinction must fail, as Justice Scalia bitingly reminds us. A law prohibiting harm reflects a moral investment. As Scalia notes, laws against bigamy, polygamy, and prostitution are morally motivated. Distinctions between self-regarding harm, other-regarding harm, and offense are always shifty. But unlike Mill, Kennedy has no cognizance of the division's inherent instability, its slipperiness; there is no humbled latitude that leaves open the harm/morality classification to future interpretation.[133] It is this absolute emphasis on a bright line where none exists that comes to be injuriously moralistic, that redivides sexual lives and acts between right and wrong, that overextends the law and overpenalizes its infractions, that designates some as "moral monsters" and then distances them from the normal citizen.[134] More, it is the very expansion of liberty Kennedy extends to homosexual identities, to consenting adults, that, in good binary form, in the hope of preserving a social order that is always already ruined, requires curtailing liberties elsewhere, in a newly republicized sexual minority, the sex offender.

Might it be the case that the "nameless," multidimensional character of the substantive liberty in *Lawrence*[135] is terrifyingly open-ended, that liberal agreement in principle is cushioned in practice by redrawing lines that are named and naturalized? Is the promise of robust substantive liberty also an abyss, patched over by the uncomfortable comfort of online sex offender registries—in which one finds, on one website, in one place, exhaustively, sex harm? Since offenders are perceived as uniformly harming, liberty curtailment here looks not like mandating a moral code, but like doing the right thing. Justice Kennedy is right that *Lawrence* is not

about minors, prostitution, or coerced adults, but rather than considering the ethical and legal questions presented by intergenerational sex, sex
for money, and differing forms of force in everyday sexual interaction,
Lawrence—combined with *Smith* and *Connecticut*—casts homosexuals on
the good side of sexuality and sexual morality and casts the others, unilaterally, as sex offenders.[136]

In "The Domesticated Liberty of *Lawrence v. Texas*" Katherine Franke
makes an argument orthogonal to mine, although at first blush it looks
antithetical. It is the limitedness, she argues, of the liberty protections
in *Lawrence*—afforded only to consensual adults in private spaces—that
depresses its utility for progressive sexual politics.[137] She notes that after
Lawrence, the Kansas Court of Appeals upheld a law mandating longer
prison sentences for homosexual sex with a minor than for heterosexual
sex with a minor.[138] The court held that *Lawrence* did not apply to differential sentencing based on sex, because the Kansas law restricted minors,
not adults. For Franke, this ruling evidences that *Lawrence* "offers little . . .
to those who seek to engage in non-normative heterosexual behavior."[139]
But it is not that *Lawrence* does not extend its reach to Matthew Limon
so much as *Lawrence* in some sense portends his imprisonment, that it
organizes and understands sexual harm such that the person who crosses
the boundary of legally defined consent, who crosses the boundary of
legally defined ages of majority and minority, is the anti–John Lawrence.
He makes no intimate decisions but recidivates impulsively; his liberty is
not to be contained in the domestic but constricted through public notification. There are no gradations between *Smith* and *Connecticut* on the one
hand and *Lawrence* on the other: either one is a consenting adult having
sex in private, whose sex is good and free, or one is a sex offender, whose
sex is harmful. Franke's concern is that the Kansas law punished gay teenagers for having sex more harshly than it did straight teenagers, and *Lawrence* has nothing to say about this. My concern is that this law punished
teenagers for having sex, and *Lawrence* has everything to say about this.[140]

Indeed, how else should we make sense of Kennedy's reference to *Smith*
and *Connecticut* in the *Lawrence* decision itself? He writes, "the stigma this
criminal statute imposes . . . is not trivial. . . . It remains a criminal offense
with all that imports for the dignity of the persons charged."[141] Justice
Kennedy, referencing the *Smith* decision of three months prior, admonishes that were sodomy statutes permitted, Lawrence would "come within
the registration laws of at least four States." Remarkably, he writes, "this

underscores the consequential nature of the punishment and the state-sponsored *condemnation attendant to the criminal prohibition.*"[142]

For homosexuals then, sex offender laws do amount to state condemnation, impose serious stigma, and undermine human dignity. The laws do all the sorts of things against homosexuals that they apparently do not do to other sex offenders, from prostitutes to sexually active teenagers to people who have committed violent sexual acts. This is because, for Kennedy, homosexuals are people. Sex offenders are not.[143] Less dramatically, homosexuals are subjects who fall under the apparently de-moralized (but not demoralized) ambit of consenting adults, with all the constitutional protection that (now) entails. The homosexual, though, is the limit case, and the sex offender takes up the vacated space, complicated of course, and also exacerbated, by the fact that subsets of those designated sex offenders do commit crimes that are indeed harmful.

Recourse to recidivism, the conflation of acts and identities, and the trivialization of liberty claims are three powerful strategies that triangulate to produce the sex offender. But why are the strategies powerful? Why is recidivism rhetoric appealing? What is so interesting about claims to recidivism is not that they are factually suspect, but that they propel legislation and judicial affirmation despite their factual faults. One recalls David Halperin's astute observation that homophobia is not countered merely by proving homophobic stereotypes false.[144] Homophobia is powerful precisely because it operates over facts, or makes up new ones. Recidivism, like escalating danger, like homophobia, is a trope, a discourse (and homophobia itself has been historically expressed through the language of addiction).[145] It allows us to manage harm, identify sexual deviance, and neatly trace harm to sexual deviance.[146] The very image of recidivism, of criminal conduct occurring and recurring, of ultimate and unrelenting sexually abhorrent behavior, of violence without a responsible agent behind the violence, is a marvel of a condensation point. The magnitude and uncontrollability of sexual dangerousness purportedly endemic to the recidivist reassures that the recidivist embodies sexual harm itself, is its exclusive, endlessly absorbing repository.

Responding to the concern that the Connecticut scheme does not adequately assess dangerousness, the state's then attorney general, Richard Blumenthal, countered, "In fact, we disclaim any assessment of individual dangerousness. . . . The reason *every* individual is on the registry is because he has been convicted of a sex offense, which unfortunately has an exceptionally high rate of recidivism."[147] Condensed in this quotation are both the irresolvable paradox at the root of the sex offender court cases (and legislation), as well as an explanation for the persistent power the paradox holds. Dangerousness in this context can mean nothing other than the likelihood of reoffense, and in one impressive move, the state attorney general posits that the state is both uninterested in convicted sex offenders' dangerousness and that their alleged dangerousness motivates the statutory scheme. In effect, Blumenthal, like the Rehnquist opinion and the Scalia concurrence, declares the convicts dangerous—they are dangerous because the law and the state says so, not because their dangerousness has been evaluated—so offenders' claims to the contrary are preemptively neutralized by sovereign authority. The maneuver works because there is already an operative preconception of what a sex offender is and does, his presumptive pathological recidivism, that makes him into a comprehensive yet always combustible container of sexual danger. The very language of recidivism, a language that trades in probabilities, social science, and actuarial models, a language that seems objective, neutral, and dispassionate, masks the kinds of cultural anxieties and juridical codification of those anxieties that create the monolithic figure of the sex offender as we know him.[148]

What is so appealing about the conflation of acts and identities? Janet Halley argues that the *Bowers* court shuttled between acts rhetoric and identity rhetoric to superordinate heterosexuality, to subordinate homosexuality, and ultimately to conceal the (sodomitical) sex of heterosexuality, to conceal heterosexuality as a social marker, because power resides in invisibility, in not being marked.[149] In *Smith* and *Connecticut,* the rhetorical relay between dangerous acts and punished identities isolates sex harm and remoralizes sex in a more gay-friendly nation and a more gay-friendly court. A 2004 *Harvard Law Review* Note, criticizing sex offender laws on this dangerousness/punishment disjuncture, argues that the government "cannot have its cake and eat it too."[150] However, the dangerousness/punishment contradiction, like its act/identity predecessor, is performative, it does something, and that something is exactly why the government can have and eat its sex offenders. By relaying between the two judicial postures, by inhabiting neither and both, the court imagines harm and danger on the same body, it requires that harm and dangerousness be ambiguated, and it warns that disambiguating them is to invite harm and danger rather than to engage critically and carefully. The sex offender in the judicial imaginary discourages thinking about sex harm because we already know it when we see it, and seeing otherwise, seeing shades of gray or ambiguity, is moral laxity. Seeing otherwise is nipped before it begins by traversing between the offender as uniformly perverse and punishable (identity) and the offender as uniformly dangerous (future, inevitable acts). It is all in one place and on one person.

In confirming the constitutionality and desirability of a public list of dangerous sex offenders whose dangerousness it is unnecessary to assess because sex offenders are declaratively dangerous, that public list is as much a normative imaginary for those who are not on it: us. "We," those not on the list, are not sex offenders; we do not sex offend; we are not the kinds of people who sex offend—as if dangerousness and harm could be partitioned by population.[151]

Invidiously, the response of dangerousness to the claim of punishment grants a liberally neutral or actuarial mask to a court that vilifies offenders when they request risk assessment. I am thinking here of the AWA tier system. Its division of sex offenders according to severity into three tiers seems ostensibly actuarial, neoliberal, and unobtrusively biopolitical, but the gratuitously wide cast of those tiers with few distinctions for violence, few distinctions for age, automatic valuing "up" of any sex involved with a minor, and the extended duration of registration and notification suggest that the punitive violence of AWA, as well as the Connecticut and Alaska statutes, are covered by a facade of probability talk.[152]

What is so appealing about the trivialization of sex offenders' liberty claims to privacy, familial association, employment, and safety? For Justice White, turning the homosexual into a sodomite purposefully devalued the homosexual. When the lower courts entertain substantive liberty claims, their rejections often start in some form of the question, *Does the sex offender have a right to remove his name from the sex offender list?* It is not the human John Doe the court considers, already a pseudonym to avoid the shame of public record, but the sex offender sex offending and sex reoffending, the presumption of recidivism tautologically built into the structural logic of the question. John Does are reduced to a personage, a personage automatically betraying a past and inevitable future of dangerous acts, a personage that is not a person but a pathology.[153]

We want there to be an Iago, a Voldemort, a Hannibal Lecter, particularly in a judicial era and a national climate marked by new acceptances of sexual life-forms and identities, in which consent does double duty as our major metric of morality and harm. No doubt, there are some pathologically abusive, harmful people who do very bad things. No doubt, consent is the necessary starting point for legal adjudication in the liberal state. But it is just the starting point. A more robust and attuned judicial and social vocabulary is required to address the array of sexually unjust and harmful practices that does not collapse into adjudicating, with wrongheaded certainty, between the normal everyday sexually ethical citizen and the unstoppably evil predator, between the transcendent and free homosexual and the dangerous sex offender. Evil is only anthropomorphized in the gothic, and the gothic is a genre, not a lived reality.[154] The gothic is an injurious but juridically consolidating and socially productive riposte. And where consent may be legally determinative, it masks a pre-*Lawrence* cultural morality, sublimated but salient, and a cultural longing for social and sexual simplicity, for fixed absolutes of right and wrong, for righteousness and vengeance, that cannot be disavowed through the juridical freedom promised to the post-*Lawrence* homosexual.

3 Numbers, Sex, Power

Age and Sexual Consent

In the last chapter, I described how sex offender registration and notification requirements and the judicial endorsement of those requirements produce a scene of sexual harm and freedom that is as spellbinding as it is invidious. Moralized symbolically—if not, as a matter of law, completely—on the fault line of the consenting adult, persons come to betray fairytale characters of evil (the sex offender), freedom (the homosexual), and violated innocence (the child).[1] This chapter shifts the gaze to another, related area of law and sex: age of consent statutes. In this realm of sexual regulation less saturated by pathos, fear, unwarranted certitude, and electoral pandering, there are possibilities to renarrate the story of sex, age, and harm: possibilities that point to objects of concern other than irredeemably predatory persons. If the analytic mode of the last chapter was diagnostic and expositive, this chapter's is reconstructive and rehabilitative. To that end, this chapter and the next take as a starting point that national anxieties over youth and sexual threat should not be disqualified but instead recalibrated.[2] Legislative, judicial, cultural, and popular "panic" around young people and sexuality should be understood not as a category mistake but as a miscalculation. If we care about the sexual autonomy of young people, and the disproportionate vulnerabilities and constraints they face, would we endorse a world of sexual demonization, of sex offender registry websites, of involuntary civil commitment? How else might we think and regulate sex and harm?

The comparatively greater latitude age of consent statutes allow us to think more inventively, less destructively, about sex and harm, yet popular discussion of age, sex, and law nonetheless usually devolves into a numbers game. We generally agree that it is unfair for a seventeen-year-old to go to prison for having sex with a fifteen-year-old.[3] We generally agree too that a high school teacher should be prohibited from having sex with his or her student. But what do we think about sex between a teenage girl and a man in his twenties when they are dating? Or about sex between a sixteen-year-old boy and a man in his thirties who meet online?

Numbers alone are not morally determinative. Blanket age of consent laws may be necessary to prevent harm and protect sexual autonomy, but they can obscure the moral concerns at stake in sexual relationships conditioned by imbalances of power. On the face of it, a legal age of consent, as one of the few and probably most widely known per se sexual proscriptions, imagines one set of people (children) as categorically incapable of sexual decision making and another set (women) as presumptively available for sex. More mildly, age of consent statutes may figuratively—if not quite functionally—figure sex below a certain age as guilty until proven innocent and sex over that age as innocent until proven guilty.[4] Such a calculation does not take into account the myriad other factors, besides age itself, that make young people more vulnerable to coercion and exploitation: inter alia, power, dependency, sexual and social experience, gender and gendered expectations. It seems reasonable that the age of consent in many U.S. states ought to be lowered, and sex between minors of the same age decriminalized, but only—and this is the central focus of this chapter—in conjunction with other correctives: a more robust standard of consent for adult–minor and minor–minor sexual relations and heightened regulation of sex among persons in relationships of dependency, trust, and/or radical differences in power.[5]

To contextualize and defend these claims, the chapter is divided into five sections. The first section briefly describes past and current age of consent laws in the United States. The second introduces the principle that I argue should inform age of consent statutes and that should underlie reforms to existing statutes: sexual autonomy.[6]

The third section advances four reforms to age of consent law that would encourage and be encouraged by sexual autonomy: lowering the age of consent and decriminalizing sex between teenagers; continuing the trend of codifying age-span provisions; regulating relations of trust and dependence; and establishing an affirmative consent standard for sex between minors and between minors and adults. By engaging objections liberal and feminist legal theorists might raise against my claims, I am better able to advance my argument and defend its theoretical underpinnings.

The concluding part of section three proposes that none of the theorists or theories discussed adequately addresses the intersection of age, sex, and sexual orientation, nor do they consider the possibility that queer relations may have different dynamics than heterosexual relations, either because gender and gendered inequality operate differently in these different domains and/or because queer cultures may have a distinguishable and (more) defendable place for intergenerational sex (a possibility to which gay rights organizations are absolutely allergic, and with good reason, given the historic pattern of equating gays with pedophiles to imprison the former or deny them civil rights).[7] In this chapter, a (slightly) stronger case is made that it is gendered inequality—and not queer exceptionality—that makes age difference different, depending on the genders of the participants. In any case, more nuanced thinking about gender and sexual orientation in this arena is necessary to protect the sexual autonomy of queer youth, to undermine gendered and heterosexist social imperatives, and finally to resist the conservative appropriation of child-protection discourse to propel homophobic and antisex policies. Nevertheless, the necessary limitations of color-blind—or in this case gender-blind, or gay-blind—liberal law initiate two wider concerns, cautionary reminders spelled out in the fourth and fifth sections. First, recourse to law, especially criminal law, to resolve social or sexual inequality always entails unintended and sometimes regressive consequences, for example, by solidifying the very norms agitators hope to dispel (boys as naturally desirous, girls as naturally wounded), or by authorizing the state's punitive power over already vulnerable subjects. Despite these serious objections to the juridicalization of social justice politics,[8] I argue adolescents—regardless of their gender or sexuality—should be considered a separate sex class under law (fourth section). Such classification is a better alternative to either maintaining existing laws governing sex and youth or to abolishing regulation altogether.

Finally, despite the seductive allure of adjudication as a vehicle for social change, and despite an equally seductive allure of moral theorizing in the adjudicative mode (yes/no, good sex/bad sex),[9] the law and its *thou shalt nots*[10] must be decentered from our moral concern if we aim to promote and protect young people's sexual autonomy (fifth section). The question no longer is (or never was) *how can the law solve the problem,* but rather *how can the law contribute to refiguring the problem, rather than codifying or reproducing it?* It is my hope that these proposals work synergistically, developing a more complicated and consequently more honest cartography of young people, the law, and sexuality.

U.S. AGE OF CONSENT STATUTES

This history of age of consent statutes in the United States is partial and illustrates some of the sociopolitical mores and objectives that mobilized age of consent reforms. It does not account for all changes to these laws over the past 120 years, nor does it contextualize in any sustained way age of consent reforms alongside other changes in U.S. law, sexual (sex trafficking proscriptions, sex offender registration and notification, and other protection measures for minors, for example) or otherwise (postwar Anglo-American liberalization, neoliberalization, 1990s broken windows, mandatory minimums, habitual offender, and truth-in-sentencing reforms, for example).[11] I document how age of consent law has changed, draw out the defining principles that influenced those changes, and point to the principles that continue to inform, or at least provide a palimpsest for, the present.

A History of U.S. Age of Consent Statutes

Reforms to age of consent laws pivot around three historical junctures: the 1890s–1910s, led by social reformers and religious groups; the 1970s–1980s, led by second-wave feminists; and the 1990s, led mostly by neoconservative and neoliberal politicians jointly advocating smaller government and a crackdown on crime.[12]

Prior to the 1890s, states adopted English common law regarding statutory rape. Statutory rape was a strict liability offense and covered only the sexual violation of young girls between the ages of ten and twelve. The object of protection was a girl's chastity, where laws aimed to secure the smooth transfer of property rights to a girl's chastity from her father to her husband.[13] Statutory rape laws were enforced only against violations of white girls, as black girls were sexualized as open territory.[14] If it were proven that a (white) girl had previously been "unchaste," the defendant was exonerated. That only white girls fell under the purview of protection, and that white girls who had been promiscuous ("promiscuity" could include being raped) forfeited protection, "shows that the purpose of statutory rape law was to protect virginity, rather than to punish men who coerce sex from young girls."[15]

In the late 1880s and 1890s, both in Britain and the United States, anti-vice organizations, feminist reform movements, and social purity campaigns advocated raising the age of consent. Industrialization, urbanization, and the attendant influx of working-class young women in public spaces fueled coalition campaigns. Fears around the sex trafficking of white girls and fears that young immigrant and minority women were offering their sexual services brought together a politically diverse coalition that was somewhat successful in changing state laws. Although many sought to raise the age of girls' legal consent to eighteen or twenty-one, most states compromised on ages between sixteen and eighteen.[16]

Both the marital exemption and the "promiscuity defense" were carried over from their common law adaptations into turn-of-the-century reforms. A man could not commit statutory rape (or rape proper, for that matter) against his underage wife. While the dominant historicism of the reform movement interprets the coalitional efforts of white middle-class feminists, social reformers, and religious groups as indicative of a deeply conservative and reactionary movement to sanctify white women's virginity, regulate immigrant women's bodies, and discourage sex outside marriage,[17] there is also some evidence that this is not the complete story. Feminists and purity reformers also insisted that legal intervention was necessary to check men's advances and their presumptive right of access to young women.[18] So too, female doctors, attorneys, and writers argued that a raised age of consent would allow young women to develop their decisional abilities and sexualities free(r) from coercion.[19] As others would argue a century later, extended statutory rape coverage also meant protecting girls from sex that, while coercive, did not meet the threshold of criminal rape liability. Like the early sodomy laws discussed in the last chapter, reformed age of consent statutes reached coerced sexual exchanges that were not technically "rape."[20]

A confluence of postwar legal liberalization, the drafting of the Model Penal Code, the emergence of second-wave feminism, and the sexual revolution of the 1960s set the terms for the next wave of age of consent reform.[21] Feminist legal activists targeted both the gender specificity of extant laws and the criminalization of young people's sexuality. By only penalizing sex against young girls, laws ignored sexual abuse against young boys and codified dominant assumption of young girls' sex and sexuality as passive and spoilable.[22] Between the 1970s and 2000s, all states gender-neutralized their age of consent statutes, and many implemented age-span reforms to replace blanket proscriptions. Feminists targeted age difference as a better proxy for coercive sexual relations than age per se. Legal attention shifted away from the preservation of gendered relations and toward abuses of power. Age of consent reforms were a fraction of the broader egalitarian changes in formal sex law.

There were at least two unintended consequences of the 1970s reforms, the legacies of which continue into the present. First, the formal gender neutrality of the law belies the nonneutrality of the problem. While boys are of course sexually coerced and manipulated by older partners, it is predominantly girls who report being victimized, being pressured into sex, and regretting their first sexual experiences.[23] Like in other areas of the law, there is a fear here that ostensibly neutral statutes disfigure the social problem: gender neutrality ignores the connection between age disparity and sex inequality, recasting the injustice as one of uniformly incapable and inexperienced boys and girls submitting to predatory older partners, rather than the paradigmatic case of a (somewhat) older man advancing on a younger girl.[24] Gender neutrality of age of consent statutes may present sexual coercion across age difference as a problem experienced between atomized nongendered individuals rather than as a problem strongly inflected by gender inequalities.[25]

The second problem revolves around queer sexualities and cuts two ways. First, age of consent statutes, now gender neutral, could be and were used alongside other statutory apparatuses to incarcerate gay men. As second-wave feminists brought attention to incest and family sexual abuse, police and prosecutors hunted down gay men and gay organizations under the pretense of child protection.[26]

Gay activists, some pedophile rights activists, and some queer youth in the 1970s argued for the abolition of age of consent statutes on the basis that such laws censored youth sexuality and particularly stymied queer youth, already marginalized by their families, schools, and other state institutions.[27] This is the second prong of the second problem: gender neutrality flattens out potential differences between queer sexuality and heterosexuality, obscuring the possibility that sexual relations across generations take on different meanings and are differently imbued with power, depending on the genders and sexualities of the participants. These concerns, as well as the liberationist argument for abolishing age of consent laws, are considered later on in this chapter.

Despite gender neutralization across states, however, in the only age of consent case heard by the Supreme Court, *Michael M. v. Superior Court of Sonoma County,* the plurality opinion held that California's law (since reformed) penalizing exclusively men for sexually violating exclusively underage women did not violate the equal protection guarantees of the Fourteenth Amendment.[28] Deterring teen pregnancy, the plurality opinion held, was a rational legislative objective to warrant gender specificity.[29] Despite testimony that the petitioner "slugged" the victim in the face until she acquiesced to sex, the consensuality of the sex went unquestioned.[30] In his concurrence, Justice Blackmun tangentially noted that the drinking and "foreplay" between the petitioner and the victim indicated that the victim was not an "unwilling participant."[31] He omits the part about her getting punched in the face. Meanwhile, the plurality insisted that pregnancy was punishment enough for girls—they need not also face jail time: "The risk of pregnancy itself constitutes a substantial deterrence to young females.... A criminal sanction imposed solely on males thus serves to roughly 'equalize' the deterrents on the sexes."[32] The dissent argued that jailing boys and girls would double the effectiveness of pregnancy deterrence.[33] The girl's body, her choice, and her resistance were incidental both to the prosecution and the court. Rather, the rational basis of gender specificity fell on the fetus and its (non)future.[34]

The latest wave of age of consent reforms occurred in the 1990s. These reforms mainly constituted changes in enforcement patterns, sentencing extensions, and funding redistributions, rather than in legislated changes to actual ages of consent or age-span provisions, although some states did raise their ages of sexual consent.[35] Reprioritized focus on statutory rape enforcement and boosted funding coincided with the Clinton-era overhaul of the federal criminal code in 1994, the rollback of welfare in 1996, and escalating sociopolitical anxiety throughout the 1980s and 1990s that childbearing, unwed, poor, teenage girls of color were the root cause of poverty, urban dysfunction, and wasteful government spending.[36] The federal Personal Responsibility and Work Opportunity Reconciliation Act of 1996 (PRWORA), restructuring welfare to workfare and replacing Aid to Families with Dependent Children with Temporary Assistance for Needy Families, declared unwed pregnancy a major cause of poverty.[37]

PRWORA encouraged states to bolster their enforcement of statutory rape laws to decrease rates of teen pregnancy. The underpinning, breathtaking logic: poverty is caused by unwed teenage girls having children; these children are mostly the result of sexual relations between younger girls and older men; more punitive sentences against older men for statutory rape and heightened enforcement (for example, requiring poor teenage girls to name the father of their child in order to receive social services) will act as a steady deterrent to age-differential sexual relations, reduce teen pregnancies, and ultimately reduce state and federal welfare spending.[38]

From the perspective of regulating underage sexual vulnerability, the most phenomenal aspect of these sentencing, funding, and enforcement changes was their comprehensive failure. In the 1990s, most unwed pregnant teens were between the ages of eighteen and twenty, putting these women over the age of consent in every state.[39] Furthermore, a good number of pregnant teens at the time were married, and marriage inoculates statutory rape liability. Data suggest that these policies did not accomplish their stated objectives of deterring teen pregnancy.[40] Criminal focus on teenage pregnant girls distracted attention from prepubescent and nonpregnant teenage girls in sexually coercive relations.[41] Finally, teenage pregnancy rates had been steadily declining since the 1950s (although the rate of teenage sex had been rising), putting into doubt whether teen pregnancy had explanatory power over poverty. Some critics argue that poverty is the better explanatory variable of unwed teen pregnancies, that the causal arrows point in the opposite directions legislators assume, and that targeting poverty to reduce teen pregnancy might have been more effective than targeting teen pregnancy to reduce poverty.

Increased prosecution of men for statutory rape, harsher sentences, and retargeted funding coincided with the gutting of other social welfare programs, childcare services, and parent and job training programs. The 1990s' refocalization of statutory rape prosecution and enforcement framed teenage pregnancy as (evidence of) a crime rather than as a public health concern or propellant of social inequality.[42] Federal and state legislators characterized poor teenage girls of color as saps on government spending and/or victims to predatory men of color. Many feminist scholars and legal theorists objected to these reforms as efforts to supervise and regulate the bodies of young black and brown women, to incarcerate black and brown men, and to drastically shrink social services under the guise of reducing poverty and protecting girls.[43]

Contemporary U.S. Age of Consent Statutes

Currently, laws vary by state and are complicated; generally, they retain the structure of the 1970s reforms and have been intensified through the 1990s reforms. Most states follow a two-tier system.[44] A person over a certain age, usually sixteen or eighteen, who engages in sexual activity with a younger person, usually under the age of twelve or thirteen, commits a "first-tier" crime of first degree rape or sexual assault; a "second-tier" crime of a lesser degree is committed when a person engages in sexual activity with someone under (most commonly) the age of sixteen.[45] Second-tier offenses are popularly understood as "statutory rape," and first-tier offenses as "child sexual abuse," although "statutory rape" is not typically the name of the charge in criminal codes. In a few states, a second-tier offense is committed when a person of any age has sex with someone under the age of consent.[46] In most states, the perpetrator must be a specific number of years older than the victim.

Age of consent statutes have a politically complicated and contentious history, sometimes securing the proprietary transfer of young girls from their fathers to their husbands, sometimes reflecting dominant mores of gender and sexuality, sometimes recognizing the structural vulnerability of young people, and sometimes leveraged as a club against unpopular minorities. Most often, the laws reflect all these political investments, and whatever normative propellant inspired the reform is attenuated or coopted by additional political interests.[47]

I have recounted the social and juridical history of age of consent statutes and their contemporary formulations in order to illustrate the conflicted arrangement of youth, sex, and coercion manifest in U.S. law and to map out the difficulties presented in the project of rethinking regulation. States have different age thresholds and varied age-span differentials; objectives of age of consent laws are progressive, protective, and/or paternalistic; and the imagined impressionability and innocence of youth make them symbolically exploitable for conservative political projects.

The reforms outlined in the following sections—as well as the principle mobilizing them—are therefore not intended as a cure-all to be uniformly superimposed over states' criminal or civil codes, as if these codes are all equally insufficient or oppressive. Instead, I advocate changes that retain elements of current law targeting power asymmetry, that reject regressive figurations of youth and sex, and that protect and promote young people's sexual choices in the face of structural vulnerability and dependence. I offer these changes not to supplement or supplant specific statutes, but to generate a more careful, capacious vision of the law and its relation to youth, power, and sexual autonomy.

TOWARD A SEXUAL AUTONOMY MODEL OF AGE AND SEXUAL CONSENT

In the section titled "Reforming and Rethinking Age of Consent Statutes" below, I propose reforms to extant age of consent statutes, and delineate justifications for these reforms, utilizing empirical research, statutes, case law, and legal theorists' contributions. Sexual autonomy is the principle that underlies the suggested reforms; here, I explain what Stephen Schulhofer understands sexual autonomy to entail, what I retain from that understanding, what tenets I disregard, and why I disregard them.

What Sexual Autonomy Entails

What holds greatest normative purchase in Schulhofer's account of sexual autonomy is its centralization of infringement-on-choice as paramount in determining sexual misconduct. The idea of sexual autonomy offers a way for law and legal theorizing to deemphasize sexual violations as violations of the body alone. *Sexual autonomy* helps us avoid two persistent juridical embroilments: sacralizing (and consequently pacifying) the (female) body, and overstressing "proper" levels of force and/or consent. The following explication of Schulhofer's model illustrates why sexual autonomy is a normatively superior framework for considering young people and their relation to sex, sexuality, and each other. However, and despite himself, Schulhofer at certain moments privileges the body and specializes sex, which I suggest is a fraught maneuver for theorizing questions of sex and power, particularly in relation to young people, for whom "innocence" and "incapacity" are reigning cultural metaphors.

In "Taking Sexual Autonomy Seriously" (1992) and *Unwanted Sex* (1998), Schulhofer develops an understanding of sexual autonomy as a set of entitlement rights that hold open and protect sexual choices. The need for a legal principle of sexual autonomy arises, he argues, on account of deficiencies in sexual abuse and assault laws, and in the face of limited success in prosecution arising from feminist reforms.[48] Since both sex law and feminist reforms to sex law have focused primarily on the issues of non-consent and force, too many coercive—but nominally consensual—sexual encounters fall through juridical cracks.[49] Rather than determining if there was "enough force" in the sexual encounter to make it criminal, or if there was "enough resistance" to determine nonconsent, the law—and the rest of us—ought to take a more comprehensive view of sexual encounters, asking if the context, the relation between the persons, and the facts of the case seem to undermine sexual choice or to promote freer decision making.[50] The notion of sexual autonomy allows the law to more carefully treat threats and offers made conditional on sex and to restrict sex in professional, familial, or other relationship forms where the validity of consent is indeterminable.[51] Schulhofer persuasively argues that incorporating sexual autonomy under the law is more practical and philosophically consistent than attempting to expand the legal definition of force to encompass more than violence against the body and threats of bodily injury and death. To concretize the distinction: one way of arguing that sex between a psychotherapist and her patient ought to be legally impermissible is to insist that the professional relation itself is a form of force that compels consent or that the patient is not "really" consenting on account of something like false consciousness. The problem with such arguments, Schulhofer insists, is that stretching "force" this far renders the term meaningless or collapses distinctions the law should not collapse, namely, between this situation and the stranger with a knife at a woman's throat.[52] So too—and this is more my point than his—the patient is (or at least might be) consenting, so making the sex legally *nonconsensual* disregards the desires (or at least, the preferences) of the patient.[53] Instead, arguing from a baseline commitment to sexual autonomy, the law can justify regulating sex by presuming that the sexual choices or choice structure of the patient cannot be adequately guaranteed on account of the structural vulnerability that defines the relationship: it is not consent that is at issue but rather the asymmetry that marks consent as an unacceptably ambiguous metric. We cannot know if the patient consents, which makes consent less useful. Similarly, the professional services offered in the relationship should not be contingent upon sex between the partners, a possibility that cannot be checked should the sex be unequivocally permissible.[54]

Schulhofer's advocacy for more robust standards of sexual consent also relies on his commitment to sexual autonomy. Schulhofer outlines a number of rape cases where defendants were cleared in which women were threatened but did not resist, or did resist but not enough to count legally, or resisted but then acquiesced, or were so financially dependent on the defendants that they could not reasonably resist.[55] None of these cases can be construed as respecting the sexual autonomy of the victim, and a legal schema that did respect the sexual autonomy of the victim—that considered her choices and desires protectable—would require a more exacting standard of consent that signals, at the least, some volitional attachment to the sex one is having.[56]

The valuing up of "autonomy" quickly triggers some hefty philosophical objections. The most significant and perhaps best-known criticism is that the notion of "autonomous subjects" presupposes an undifferentiated, unmoored person who is rational, reflective, and deliberative.[57] The concept, particularly in the realm of sexuality, may be complicit with the culturally compulsory figure of a unitary, consolidated psychic subject whose desire is unidirectional.[58] Autonomy belies our fundamental (but racially, economically, sexually, etc. differentiated) dependence on others; it belies the confluence of forces that influence our decisions, desires, and self-understanding.[59] Similarly, autonomy makes the individual the unit of analysis at the expense of group life, communal relations, or structural modes of exclusion or inequality that cannot be accounted for through a localized defense of the deliberating person.[60]

But sexual autonomy need not get lethally mired in problems connected to high liberal theories of the person:

> Legal protection of autonomous choice has a narrower objective [than the proposals of feminist legal theorists like Chamallas and Pineau, who argue for some form of mutuality standard], to permit individuals to act freely on their own unconstrained conception of what their bodies and their sexual capacities are for. This approach need not imply a naïve, laissez-faire liberalism blind to the inequalities of wealth and power. On the contrary, the objective is to protect individuals from real-world conditions that constrain freedom of choice, without dictating how that freedom can be used.[61]

This passage does not answer all objections, but sexual autonomy need not assume that we all come to the table—or bed—as unencumbered free agents. Instead, it can attempt to recognize differentiated relations of dependence, and to theorize acceptable and unacceptable forms of interference in the realm of sexual decision making, without prescribing what good sex should look like. The autonomy here is not an ontological truth of the human, but a guiding, revisable principle that recognizes available choices and checks certain constrictions on those choices. To that end, "sexual autonomy" is understood to be an aspiration, not an a priori.[62] It is not a synonym for freedom,[63] let alone justice, but a guiding principle for theorizing and regulating young sex and the young sexual subject. This, it should be noted, is a rather radical departure from autonomy as conceived by Kant, who saw young people as categorically heteronomous, and who saw sex (and masturbation)—with all its instrumentalizing, disordering, and impulsivity—as singularly threatening to self-restrained, autonomous decision making.[64] "Young sex" is, in this sense, a double whammy against Kantian autonomy. But in following Schulhofer's conception of sexual autonomy as pegged to the protection of choices rather than to the constitution of (an unduly influenced, morally developed, adult) character, I necessarily follow feminist reconstructions of autonomy as cultivated through social relations rather than apart from them. To that end, I am concerned foremost with (1) what sociolegal arrangements provide, in Marina Oshana's words, an "adequate range of options" to young persons and (2) how relations are structured and regulated to promote, in Jennifer Nedelsky's words, a "capacity for creative interaction."[65] There is an intended circularity to this "relational reconception"[66] of autonomy: What sort of social relations, and regulations of those relations, permit and encourage (young, sexual) subjects to participate most fully in the making of ongoing relations? When one understands autonomy as both generated by relations and as a normative aspiration of relations, one must also soften the "radical disjuncture between childhood development and the continuing development of human capacities."[67]

This autonomy right, so reconstructed, is therefore not set against relational rights and is not exclusively the prerogative of adults. And if we interpret sexual autonomy as an upshot of just structural arrangements rather than as a purely psychological state (achievable only at adulthood), then we need not eclipse, for example, how intimate partner violence, or how material and/or institutional power inequalities, influence (sexual) relations and decision making.[68] In fact, these sorts of phenomena become central to the sexual autonomy inquiry.

What Sexual Autonomy Need Not and Should Not Entail

As Schulhofer explicates sexual autonomy, the precept need not sanctify sex as a good that trumps all others, nor must it valorize the separateness and sanctity of the body as a treasured artifact. Unfortunately, Schulhofer sanctifies both sex and the body:

> Few of our other personal rights and liberties, perhaps only our right to life itself, are as important as our right to decide whether and when we will become sexually intimate with another person.[69]

> A second dimension of autonomy is also important. The core concept of personhood inherent in the common law . . . implies a physical boundary, the bodily integrity of the individual. Autonomy therefore, is not only the moral and intellectual, not only the capacity to choose. It is also physical, the distinctive separateness of the corporal person.[70]

For the purposes of both criminal law reform and normative legal theorizing, I suggest we reject these premiums placed on sex and body. Sexual intimacy and intimate decisions may or may not be monumentally important to the individual, but there is something uncompromising about nominating sex rights so special by fiat and in presuming that the special status of sex arises primordially, absent history and discourse.[71] By positioning sex rights as second only to life itself, we may amplify the harm resultant in the violation of that right. When sex is discursively constructed to be as special as life, and when the violation of sex rights is discursively constructed as a fate worse than death, this sociojuridical description animates and then redoubles the severity of the pain and harm it hopes to dispel.[72] The sacralization of sex and body undermines the normative utility of sexual autonomy. Schulhofer himself developed his version of sexual autonomy as a way to identify and then minimize the problems of sexual coercion *not* reducible to bodily violation. In fact, as Sharon Marcus and others have provocatively argued, when rape law or legal theory imagine the body as pristine, separate, and distinct, this figured body is complicit with rather than resistant to rape culture.[73] Such a body is without agency, a feminized and passive treasure, a temple whose only function is to await pollution, a body that is "already raped" or "already rapable."[74]

The problem is reinforced in the case of young people, whose bodies are culturally comprehended as either pure and therefore imminently contaminable, or as already sexualized and therefore not salvageable. When the problem of young people and their relations is sociolegally reduced to the problem of preserving bodies from sex rather than protecting choices within existing inequalities of power, the target becomes sex and its presumptive interference with innocence, rather than exploitation or manipulations of dependence.[75]

None of the remarks here is intended to suggest that rape is not harmful, that it does not harm the body, or that sexual violence against the body is not experienced traumatically or as singularly disturbing. But theorizing sexual harm as a constriction on choice, as an external imposition against or willful negligence toward desire, or as potentially manifest in structural relations of dependence allows one to take sex rights seriously without the pitfalls of specializing sex for everyone, a priori determining sexual harm to be the worst kind,[76] or discursively building up the body as a temple awaiting its defacement.

Let me clarify then two points of contrast between Schulhofer's perspective on sexual autonomy and my respectful appropriation. First, while it is necessary to enlarge our perspective on sexual harm in order to incorporate constraint on choice, a recursive valorizing of corporeality and sex risks replacing the legal figure of a desiring, volitional subject with the figure of an always endangered, passive one. Second, and consequently, Schulhofer's sexual autonomy ultimately overemphasizes sexual noninterference—the right to say no, to not be violated, to not have "unwanted sex." These rights are indispensable, but another promising feature of sexual autonomy as I see it is the right to desire, to have wanted sex—provided factors of coercion and constraint are accounted for. Articulating a right to make sexual decisions is more feasible when we resist attributing to sex and body positions of privileged passivity.

If sexual autonomy is a right to which we are entitled, and if the right, relationally reconstructed, entails the holding open, fostering, and respecting of choices, how might a commitment to sexual autonomy guide legal reforms in the realm of age and sex?

REFORMING AND RETHINKING
AGE OF CONSENT STATUTES

Lowering the Age of Consent, Decriminalizing Sex between Minors

A commitment to sexual autonomy advises lowering ages of sexual consent in jurisdictions where the age threshold is higher than the age at which the majority of adolescents are having sex. So too, sexual autonomy demands that jurisdictions that criminalize sex between minors of the same age repeal such statutes.

The median age of consent in the United States is sixteen.[77] In some states, however, the age of consent is seventeen or eighteen.[78] While most states now have age-span provisions, some do not, and others have narrow age-span provisions.[79] Functionally, this means that in several states minors commit a crime when they have sex with one another, as each has sex with someone under the age of consent. Criminalizing sexual activity among minors condemns sex not coercion, dampens the sexual autonomy of young people, and disrespects their choices. If many young people are first having sex while below the age of consent, our social and legal obligation is not to penalize the sex—making it more difficult for teenagers to report coercion—but to protect young people's choices, desires, and safety.[80] We fail this obligation if we criminalize teenagers for having sex. Meanwhile, where some jurisdictions treat minors who have consensual sex as incapable children, they concomitantly sentence them as culpable adults when they commit crimes.[81] The sociolegal impulse here is punitive rather than protective: adolescents are incapable children when they have sex, but deliberative, intentional adults when they commit crimes. Insofar as black male youth are disproportionately transferred to criminal court,[82] and insofar as age of consent statutes are and have been disproportionately enforced against black men and gay men, we ought to be alert to the tendency for criminal law to become conduit and codification of racism and homophobia in the arena of sexual regulation.

I am not particularly wedded to fixing the age of consent—which should probably be called something like the age of sexual majority or sexual citizenship[83]—once and for all. Indeed, as the rest of this chapter suggests, such fixation on fixity reinscribes volitional youth as ontologically incompetent, deflects attention from relations of power and dependency in young people's lives that constrain consent's transformative force, ignores the sociological and educational contexts that influence young people's sexual decisions and decision-making capacities, flattens out important differences between heterosexuality and queer sexualities, and perhaps flattens out differences between sexual acts.[84] Nonetheless, given the prevalence of teen sex, the number of young people who first have sex with older partners, the developing reasoning of many young people,[85] and the particular regulatory pressure the formally neutral law places on young queer people and racial minorities, the age of consent should probably be lowered from its most common current range of sixteen to eighteen, to something closer to fourteen, with age-span provisions for younger teenagers between twelve and sixteen.

Before addressing two objections to lowering the age of consent—the presumptive sexual incapacity of minors, and the presumptive sexual vulnerability of girls—I should pause to more carefully explain how this chapter is both deeply indebted to and departs from the arguments found in Heidi Kitrosser's "Meaningful Consent: Toward a New Generation of Statutory Rape Laws" (1996). Many of the suggestions put forth here are similar to those Kitrosser proffered two decades ago: specifically, defining an affirmative standard of consent for sex involving minors, and more stringently regulating sex in age-discrepant relations of dependence and trust.[86] She successfully evidences the conditions of vulnerability unique to minors (particularly girls) as a class that warrant her (and my) revisions.[87]

Despite our substantial areas of overlap, however, at least three lines of Kitrosser's argument remain troubling from the perspective of sexual autonomy. First, Kitrosser asks the law to treat all sex between minors as illegal but allows for an affirmative defense of consent to challenge a rebuttable presumption of nonconsent. For those jurisdictions in which sex between minors would be reclassified from strictly criminal without the possibility of rebuttal to presumptively criminal with the possibility of rebuttal, this is a welcome change. But this begs the question: Why is the sex criminalized from the start? Kitrosser herself suggests the law should punish coercion, not sex, so why make sex guilty until proven otherwise? If the consent standard is an affirmative one, the defendant charged with sexual assault must prove that the plaintiff willingly agreed to sexual activity. This should be adequate, without criminalizing minor sex wholesale. Moreover, if sex with and between minors is guilty until proven innocent, it will, by prosecutorial and police enforcement, be black and gay boys and men who are disproportionately convicted and white suburban teens who are let off the hook. The sexual/social relations forged against background hostility will be retargeted, while sex among white youth will be presumptively noncoercive.[88]

Second, Kitrosser insists that restrictions on sex in relations of dependence and the rebuttable presumption of nonconsent are both justified because in each situation the consent of the minor subject is not meaningful: either the subject does not know what she is doing or she is coerced

into doing what she does. In the absence of a principle like sexual autonomy, Kitrosser must either advance expanding definitions of force to capture asymmetrical relations or question the validity of minors' and/or
dependents' consent.[89] But relations of dependence need not be "criminally
coercive" for the sex in those relations to be regulated. By focusing on
infringements of choice and choice structure, relations may be regulated
without legally designating minors inherently incapable of consent and
without therefore marking minors as coerced or violated preemptively.

Third, at moments in her article, Kitrosser treats minors as a Trojan
horse to restructure rape laws more generally, for adults. Her proposals,
she suggests, would ideally be incorporated throughout all rape law, and
she surmises that statutory changes addressing the unique vulnerability of
minors could compel legislators to overhaul rape law for everyone.[90] Kitrosser too quickly assumes that children are simply vulnerable like women,
but doubly so, and that changes in law—and social responses to those
changes—will all operate evenly over different subpopulations. Ironically,
her maneuver potentially objectifies children and childhood to marshal
political and legal change for adults.[91]

Objection: Children Are Incapable of Consent

Scholars from many disciplines have documented how innocence and
(concomitantly) incompetence are pervasive tropes of childhood in modern and late modern Western societies, tropes to which Kitrosser intermittently takes recourse.[92] And while such tropes are always inflected through
other social divisions (for example, the skewed racial allocation of innocence, wherein white girls are endangered and black boys are endangering,
or the whitening of children of color in media forms to appear innocent),[93]
it is the presumptive innocence and incompetence of children and childhood that news pundits, activists, legislators, and judges extol (and lament
the loss of) when calling for greater protections for youth or harsher pun-
ishments for those desiring them.[94]

Lodged in the objection of constitutional incapacity ("she is just a kid!")
is dualistic thinking that is damaging to young people and sexual autonomy
and that precludes a more nuanced understanding of power and its legitimate and illegitimate injection into sexual relations. In response to this
objection, I suggest that we think of consent as a spectrum instead of a
switch. From childhood to adolescence to adulthood, the guiding metric of
sexual consent ought to gradually shift focus from capacity to voluntariness.

Currently, some age of consent laws suppose an uncomplicated division between incapable children and volitional adults (a switch).[95]

Before attempting to exposit a more nuanced understanding of consent (a sliding scale from capacity toward voluntariness as age increases) in relation to young sexual subjects, I want to cut off two potential challenges preemptively. First, this chapter (and this book) only considers young people in the United States, statistically sexually active or almost sexually active, confronting sexual decisions. I am not considering those subjects under "tier 1" law, usually children twelve and under, as we can reasonably assume that *capacity* is and ought to be the guiding legal metric, not only on cognitive or developmental grounds, but also on the presumption that sexual knowledge and information is limited.[96] Thus, consent should not be an affirmative defense for sexual relations with tier 1 children. This invites the second challenge: despite the pastiche attached to developmental psychology, neuroscience, or just science more generally, I place very little emphasis on discovering a neurological moment when young people fully understand sex, their sexual choices, and the ramifications of sex acts, because there is enough sociological evidence that such a moment is illusory: education, safer-sex education, resources, gender, regional location, family dynamics, and politics all mediate, dampen, empower, or in other ways give shape to a young person's sexual agency and her ability to consent.[97]

To think through more precisely the shift from capacity to volition, I focus on two legal theorists' analyses of age and sexual consent: David Archard's (1997) and Michelle Oberman's (1994; 2000; 2001).[98]

In *Sexual Consent*, Archard unpacks what he calls the "common view" that consent, and only consent, morally legitimizes sexual activity.[99] His book attempts to understand what consent means under different contexts and why and if it is morally transformative. I start with *Sexual Consent* because Archard's treatment of questions around sex and youth provide much of the architecture for the remainder of this chapter. Specifically, I develop three of the factors he takes to be pertinent in evaluating youth and sexual relations—age, age difference, and special relationships[100]—and then add another: an affirmative standard of consent for sex between youth and between youth and adults.

Archard is sensitive to cultural narratives that underwrite modern understandings of childhood and sexuality. He recognizes how the ubiquitous image of childhood innocence works at once to sexualize children and to deny them any sexual agency and decision-making capabilities. "A child's innocence is rather like the purity of the virginal woman which is the object of a certain male sexual desire—attractive for being that which is not yet but can be corrupted."[101] Accordingly, argues Archard, "a child is deemed incapable of offering real consent, and abuse is frequently defined in terms of an exploitation of that very fact."[102] Thus, child sexuality is often read as child sexual abuse, without nuance for age, age difference, sexual practices, the relationship of the persons involved, and any other factors relevant to the encounter or relationship. The project of pinpointing standards for sexual relations across age is complicated indeed if the law, media sensationalism, and eroticized myths of innocence re-sexualize the very children needing protection and demonize the adults who apparently desire them.[103] Against such a saturated backdrop, Archard teases out what he takes to be morally significant in defending and determining age of consent laws.

First, however, Archard proposes that the three central criteria implicit in the "standard account" of meaningful sexual consent—for all people, youth and adults—are voluntariness, knowledge, and capacity.[104] We should want to do what we are doing free of specific pressures and constraints (voluntariness), we should understand what it is that we are doing (knowledge—in the literal sense, as in knowing that a penis and not a medical instrument is the object of insertion),[105] and we ought to have the cognitive wherewithal—to be sober, not severely mentally disabled—to make sexual decisions (capacity). In Archard's first conceptual frame, childhood looks like mental disability: "A child is judged to lack the capacity of an adult but not to be permanently disabled in that she will acquire capacity with age. . . . Wherever the age of majority is fixed, we may presume normal sane adults to be capable of giving their consent."[106] Childhood is equivalent to a kind of immature insanity or mental underdevelopment, and so capacity is the criterion that counts. However, in a later chapter focused explicitly on youth, Archard complicates his assessment. The four evaluative criteria he introduces are "the nature of sexual activity, the age of the consenting party, the age differential between the parties, and the existence, if any, of a special relationship between the parties."[107] From these categories it is evident that capacity is just one of many considerations and is more or less salient depending on the specifics of the situation. It is important to contrast the earlier reflections of the book with the later ones, because it is the myth of eroticized childhood innocence that Archard himself observes that labels capacity, or incapacity, as the singularly relevant factor regarding minor sex and sexuality.

In discussing age differentials between partners, Archard focuses on situations in which the choices of the younger person are or reasonably seem to be constricted or unfairly manipulated by another person. Because young people, particularly girls, may seek validation, respect, or attention from an idealized older person, they may be willing to engage in sexual activity despite their not desiring to do so.[108] It is their voluntariness that is primarily at issue. The "special relationships" Archard describes are those of institutionalized power differentials: a father and daughter, an uncle and nephew, a coach and athlete—relationships that often characterize adult–minor sexual activity. In these relationships, Archard again emphasizes the constraints on a child's choice, rather than the child's capacities. As for age itself, Archard comments, "what matters is not just that one can have sex but that one has some understanding or appreciation of what is involved in having sex."[109] Puberty then is not adequate as a metric of capable consensuality; rather, one needs an awareness of what one is doing with one's sex and sexuality. This appears to be straightforwardly about capacity, but note that Archard is not simply interested in whether a young person is capable of literally saying yes or no to sex, but in whether a young person understands the physical and emotional ramifications of sexual activity. This understanding requires education, experience, and knowledge of sexual life. When the assumption of incapacity justifies the withholding of sexual education, then young people really are incapable of sex or giving sexual consent, but because of lack of information, not incapacity per se.[110]

Archard builds for us a solid foundation to better theorize age and sexual consent. Against a cultural imaginary that mostly envisions youth as sexually incompetent and/or duped sexualized commodities, Archard's distinctions between capacity and voluntariness recall that different young people, of different ages, are positioned differently in their relation to sex. Age-span provisions and "special relationships" are elaborated further in following subsections, with an emphasis on voluntariness and choice, rather than capacity. As I have been trying to make clear against the objections of innocence and incapacity, a moral or juridical insistence on capacity alone ensnares us in problems analogous to those we encounter in valorizing the body or sacralizing sex.

Although I follow Archard's schema, I depart from his reasoning somewhat. Archard explores the conditions under which age differences and special relations may invalidate consent. In contrast, I suggest that such divisions in positions of power sideline consent as the central moral or legal metric. And where Archard suggests that more robust standards of consent may be appropriate for sexual relations between people relatively unknown to each other, I will later apply such standards to youth as a legal class of persons.[111] The distinction is that Archard sees affirmative consent as a hedge against interpersonal forms of coercion; I see affirmative consent as a hedge against structural vulnerabilities and institutionalized dependencies particular to young people.

Objection: A Lowered Age of Consent and the Decriminalization of Sex between Minors Will Underprotect Girls

A compelling objection to lowering the age of consent and decriminalizing sex between minors comes from Michelle Oberman, who is concerned that such reforms would exacerbate the already subordinate condition of young girls.[112]

Oberman offers sociological and psychological research as well as case law to illustrate the sexual pressures young women face, the common regret they share after their first sexual experiences, and the recurring emotional and physical harms from sexual abuse and early-age sexual activity.[113] She observes:

> The vulnerability inherent in adolescence, including severely diminished self-esteem, ambivalence about one's changing body, and a marked reluctance to assert one's self, leads teenagers to consent to sexual contact that may not be fully, or even partially, desired.... [A] multiplicity of factors beyond sexual desire and love that lead teenagers to consent to sex ... [are] fear, confusion, coercion, peer pressure, and a desire for male attention.[114]

Outlining the coercive sexual experiences particular to girls and the legal failure to prevent these experiences, Oberman proposes her own reforms, among them "retaining a relatively high age of consent, while simultaneously enlisting victim cooperation in determining the course that a criminal action will take."[115] She recommends that the age of consent be no lower than sixteen and that victims be consulted to determine the appropriate punishment for perpetrators. For Oberman, law ought to be a social corrective to gender as it exists for young people, and laws that once commodified girls ought to be recuperated for their protection.

The problem with Oberman's proposals is that they criminalize all sex under age sixteen, regardless of the ages or desires of the parties. Although the "ideal" type of mutually pleasurable sex between teenagers of the same age is rarely prosecuted, and although Oberman encourages reduced sentencing and/or sexual education programs for first-time offenders of nonviolent, per se crimes, the message is unambiguous: sex is bad when you are young, there is always a perpetrator and always a victim, and the girl qua girl is always vulnerable, always in need of state protection from others and herself.[116]

Oberman maintains that a young girl's continued insistence that she wanted the sexual relations to occur may not exonerate the perpetrator, and this seems sometimes right. Oberman's statutory rape reform aims to shield young girls from a socialization process where they "want" to have sex in order to be respected, validated, and appreciated by men. But in all of her case examples, the girls were either silent or asked the perpetrator to stop.[117] The boys target the girls because they are younger and sequester them to places where they are alone and cannot reasonably resist. The boys often physically assault the girls or advance despite their resistance.[118] Oberman herself admits that, for several of her cases, it would be "absurd to consider these encounters consensual."[119] What is odd, then, is that Oberman's evidence against taking a girl's "yes" as "yes"—that her yes is coerced and thus ought to be discounted—exhibits precisely those times she has not said yes. The marshaling of coercive teen sex as evidence of a general unhealthiness of teen sex makes coercive sex seem less problematic (by defining it as a status crime) and mutually desired sex more suspect.

Oberman's age of consent law criminalizes sex in relations of dependence, sex across wide age spans, and sex in the "grey area"—when older teenage boys make unwelcome sexual advances against teenage girls. But she also wants to criminalize all mutually desired sex among minors. The line Oberman draws both overreaches and falls short. She casts too wide a proscriptive net over youth sexual activity and in doing so reiterates patriarchal assumptions about the universality of young female vulnerability.[120]

Like Archard, Oberman largely and mistakenly refuses to consider a more robust standard of consent for sex between young people and between young people and adults.[121] However, unlike Archard, Oberman importantly understands that questions and problems around age, sex, and consent are also always questions and problems about gender and power.

But such recognition of this interface need not collapse, legally, into the assumption that girls are either sexless or powerless.

Continuing the Trend in Age-Span Restrictions over Per Se Proscriptions

Feminist-led reforms in the 1970s both gender neutralized age of consent statutes and transformed blanket, one-age proscriptions into age-span provisions. In most states, a seventeen-year-old is no longer criminally liable for sex with a fifteen-year-old, but a nineteen- or twenty-year-old is.[122] Age-span reforms are doubly motivated. First, such reforms shift the punitive response away from sex per se. Age-span provisions can signal that there is nothing innately impermissible about sex at a young age. Second, and consequently, these reforms aim at eliminating coercion; age difference is considered an adequate proxy for coercive relations.[123] These provisions reflect the social and economic pressures young people, particularly girls, face to acquiesce to sex with older men; they reflect differences in sexual knowledge and experience between younger teenagers and older people;[124] they implicitly acknowledge young people as sexually volitional but vulnerable, rather than incompetent or incapable. Therefore, they are welcome substitutions to older laws. They should continue to replace one-age blanket proscriptions still on the books in some states.

Objection: Age Spans Are Not an Adequate Proxy for Sexual Coercion

There is, though, no necessary reason for sexual relations between younger people and older people to be any more coercive than sex between people of the same age.[125] Age-span provisions build in a presumption of coerciveness and power asymmetry, a presumption with empirical support,[126] but the age difference itself might not explain the coercive nature of the sex. In *Consent to Sexual Relations,* Alan Wertheimer suggests that age differences between partners may not accurately index sexually coercive encounters, and he therefore equivocally opts instead for blanket prohibitions effected through a single age of consent.[127] Oberman cautions that a focus on age spans may deflect attention from the coercive sexual experiences of young girls with partners of the same age and may naturalize the less-than-wanted sex between same-aged young people as an inevitable rite of passage into adulthood.[128] Below, I respond to Wertheimer and then Oberman.

Wertheimer begins his discussion on age and sex promisingly, asking, "positive law aside, when and why should we regard the consent of a young person as invalid?"[129] He continues with this counterconventional claim:

> It is not obvious that age, *per se,* should be a worry at all. Age may be a useful *proxy* for psychological capacities that are relevant to the validity of consent, but it is only a proxy. In principle, we could evaluate a person's competence by reference to the mental capacities that are relevant to that decision and there is no reason to think that the relevant mental capacities of many minors are lower than the mental capacities of many intoxicated or retarded adults whom we typically regard as capable of giving morally transformative consent.[130]

This challenge to the capacity model of age and sexual consent is clarified by the six hypothetical scenarios Wertheimer offers to illustrate the legal and moral difficulties around sex and age.[131] The most flagrant cases of illegitimate consent involve partners of different ages and positions of power: an eleven-year-old girl and an eighteen-year-old brother's friend, a thirty-four-year-old male babysitter and a fourteen-year-old girl, a seventeen-year-old gang member and a high school freshman, a thirty-three-year-old man and a fourteen-year-old girl who meet online.[132] What is bothersome here is not simply age, but age difference, relative positions of power, and the exploitation of that difference and power. Among Wertheimer's scenarios, he believes only consensual sex between two fifteen-year-olds is morally valid but is admittedly unsure about which relations should be legally valid.[133]

Yet despite Wertheimer's own examples, and his own evaluation, he insists that age spans are not necessarily problematic:

> it is possible that wide age spans are more *likely* to be coercive, that the proportion of peer relationships that are problematic on these grounds is lower than the proportion of wide-age-span relationships. This may or may not be so. But, absent evidence about the way in which age spans are, in fact, a good proxy for coercion, this argument provides little support for the age-span approach.[134]

But then why do we, or does Wertheimer, find sex between fifteen-year-olds unproblematic? In one of his more uncomfortable scenarios, two eleven-year-olds have sex. This is startling, but is it criminal? The situation of the eighteen-year-old, however, who advances on an eleven-year-old is suspect because he is more sexually knowledgeable, exploits her inexperience, and knows that she will willingly accede to appease her brother's friend.

Wertheimer summarizes his discussion by claiming that considerations of age spans and other differences in power are too complicated for any rigorous discussion or legal regulation and seems to suggest that blanket age of consent laws may be the best we can do, even though they may be no more (or less) defensible than other per se laws like age-span prohibitions.[135] Wertheimer asks a number of questions that are left unanswered, and ultimately little is developed on this front. Why? Because, despite his introductory remarks, Wertheimer collapses age into the problem of capacity. He does so because his theory on voluntariness—which is in fact his theory on sexual consent writ large—cannot canvass structural relations of power, nor the effects of power on choice and submission. In Wertheimer's analysis, choices are only compounded by individual and individualized threats, and so the status of the partners (employer-employee, different levels of intoxication, etc.) rarely matter unless one person has leveraged the authority to explicitly disadvantage another.[136] Because Wertheimer cannot address the kinds of pressures and constraints manifest in most relations between adults and minors, and because his theory cannot acknowledge socialization processes that condition girls to acquiesce or submit to sex with older partners, he is left with no other alternative but to make children incapable, to end where he began, with positive law.[137]

Oberman is also skeptical of age-span criteria. She reviews six cases in which underage girls did not want to have sex with their partners, but where the consent standard of criminal rape law would likely not have protected them, that is, would not have found the behavior of the men criminal.[138] The cases evidence the need, she says, for bolstered age of consent statutes. Although Oberman presents her examples to indicate why prosecutorial priority on age-span cases would be underprotective, Charles Phipps points out that "Oberman's case studies do more to demonstrate the legitimacy of age span provisions than to undermine them."[139] Indeed, all the cases involve girls at least several years younger than the boys. The facts of these cases[140] (like the facts of *Michael M.*) are incongruous with a plea to criminalize all teenage sex. Oberman is concerned that age-span provisions will skew social understandings of sexual violence as a problem of creepy old men and vulnerable young girls, thus detracting attention from peer-on-peer sexual coercion. But properly tailored and enforced provisions would strengthen the sexual autonomy of young people, particularly girls. Such provisions would not imply that the problem of sexual violence is and is only the problem of great age discrepancy, but rather that different ages reflect different degrees of experience and power, that older people intimidate younger people, and that younger people acquiesce to older people.

Regulating Relations of Dependence and Trust

If age-span provisions have been codified to approximate relations of coercion, why not regulate relations that are more proximately coercive? As discussed earlier, adult perpetrators of child sexual abuse are much more often fathers, stepfathers, or family acquaintances of the victim than they are strangers in the park. But when such stories are narrated (and legislated) as violations of innocent, asexual children rather than as manipulations of relational dependence, the fourteen-year-old victim (as portrayed—and not without immanent contradiction—in *To Catch a Predator*) is lumped into the same story as the four-year-old. Children and youth are written over as blank slates, unwanting and undesiring, whose corruption is inevitable.[141] The problem to be fixed becomes the pathological evildoer rather than the relation of trust or dependence leveraged for sexual satisfaction— morally exonerating and epistemically disprivileging everyday abuse and constraints on sexual choice.[142] All states criminalize some incestuous relations, and all states prohibit at least certain relations between young people and their custodians—teachers, principals, psychologists, etc. But these laws tend to target consanguinity rather than dependence and too narrowly delimit the set of proscribed relations. Normatively, from the perspective of sexual autonomy, and empirically, given patterns of reported sexual victimization, we should be more concerned with sexual relations between uncles and nieces, or minors and their mothers' boyfriends, *irrespective of bloodlines,* than with sex between siblings, half siblings, or cousins.[143] It is relations of trust, authority, and dependence, and not simply age, age difference, or consanguinity, that ought to be the centerpiece of regulating sex with minors.[144] By privileging relations of dependence over age, we are left with a rather different juridical imaginary, where differences of power and its abuses are targeted, and where young people are considered capable and volitional. In essence, the law would no longer assume that young people cannot say yes to sex, but that in certain relations of dependence they cannot reasonably say no. The law would no longer convey to young people, *you cannot know what you want, and you do not want sex,* but rather, *whatever you want, there are certain relations where the ambiguity is too great, where exit options are too few, and where harm and/or coercion is too likely to legally permit unregulated sex.*[145] An emphasis on relations of dependence signals that law takes young people's choices as paramount, and doubts the integrity of meaningful choice, and the holding open of options, when an uncle, stepfather, coach, or teacher makes sexual advances.

Objection: Dependency Is Ubiquitous and Too Variable to Be Regulable.

Sexual partners are rarely if ever equal; in fact, it is hard to make sense out of what equality might mean or along what dimensions it ought to be measured. In the absence of conceptual qualification, a stipulation to regulate sex in relations of dependence leads two ways: either all sex everywhere is impermissible since all power differentials functionally manufacture consent, or the stipulation is to be junked precisely because it holds all sex everywhere suspect, and this cannot be right, as sex is good or fun or mutually desired despite and sometimes because of power asymmetry.[146]

Let's return to Wertheimer, who helps tease out one compelling way to normatively distinguish relations of dependence that do and do not compromise sexual relations. At the point where Wertheimer's theoretical distinctions reach their limit, I concentrate on a debate between Schulhofer and Wertheimer to round out the specifications of regulating sex in relations of dependence between minors and adults.

Much of Wertheimer's *Consent to Sexual Relations* is concerned with distinguishing sexual threats from sexual offers and articulating principles of valid moral and/or legal consent under conditions of inequality or asymmetry. Wertheimer posits that tokened consent under conditions of inequality or asymmetry should be considered valid if the recipient of the proposition can reasonably expect to maintain or improve what Wertheimer labels her "moralized baseline."[147] In cases where her refusal to have sex results in a worsening of her condition below that baseline, consent is invalid and the sex illegitimate. For example, it is wrong for a woman's doctor to make performing her surgery conditional on her sexual reciprocation: the doctor has a conventionalized obligation to treat her, she has a reasonable expectation of treatment, and the withholding of treatment wrongly lowers her baseline standard of living.[148] However, if a wealthy man offers a poor woman one million dollars for sex, the consent is valid and the sex legitimate, if not morally ideal. She either remains poor or receives money, and neither the offer nor its fruition makes her worse off than she would otherwise be.[149]

There is much commendable in this approach—a kind of sexual realism, reminding us that sex often takes place in grids of asymmetry, that we do not always "want to want" to have sex, that choices are always constrained by circumstance but are choices nonetheless.[150] The moralized baseline approach is adaptable to the variety and inequality of everyday life and grounds a usable evaluative framework. On the other hand, it oversimplifies how power operates between sexual partners, ultimately limiting its utility for those situated unequally by institution or social convention, as is often the case with minors and adults.

The limited applicability of the moralized baseline approach for sex between minors and adults in relations of dependence is best illustrated in a disagreement between Wertheimer and Schulhofer over Wertheimer's *Higher Grade* hypothetical. In *Higher Grade,* a professor offers to raise the grade of his student should she have sex with him. If she refuses sex, she will receive the grade she deserves on merits. Wertheimer argues the professor is not as sexually coercive or as morally culpable as he is in *Lower Grade,* where a professor threatens to lower the student's grade below what she deserves unless she has sex: "One reason for thinking [the professor's] proposal in *Lower Grade* is wrong simply does not apply to *Higher Grade,* namely, that [the professor] is not proposing to violate [the student's] rights should she reject his proposal."[151] In *Lower Grade,* the student has a conventional right to a grade earned on merits confounded by the sexual threat, whereas in *Higher Grade* her baseline, supposedly, is unaffected. Schulhofer argues the professor is equally coercive and culpable in both scenarios. Because it is reasonable to assume that buried under the offer of a higher grade is retaliation "below the baseline" for refusal, the law and moral theory should treat these cases alike. The employee who refuses sex for a promotion often gets fired, the student who refuses sex for a higher grade often gets a lower one than she deserves—these offers are more often than not retrospectively threats, and therefore illegitimate.[152]

Wertheimer has responded to Schulhofer that if *Higher Grade* were "genuine"—that is, if in fact there were no punishment for refusal, but the student simply retained her earned grade—then the offer of *Higher Grade* and the threat of *Lower Grade* would (and should) be separate questions.[153]

Schulhofer does not have much of a reply. His claim is dependent upon the empirical evidence that this outcome, receiving the earned grade, is an outlier, but it need not be. Rather, the very fact that the student cannot know a priori whether this offer will ultimately violate her rights is itself tantamount to a suppression of her sexual autonomy. It is not the likelihood that the offer is a threat that is the problem, but the fact that the professor qua professor leverages that ambiguity, whether consciously or not, to his sexual advantage and the student's sexual disadvantage. Even if there is no retaliation, the professor secures sex by misusing a position of power and manipulating a relationship of dependence. The question ought not to be *did the student suffer as a result of the refusal,* but instead *can a student reasonably say no, given the power conditions of the relationship?*

Schulhofer offers a number of regulations and restrictions on sexual relations between teachers and students, (some) lawyers and clients, and psychiatrists and patients.[154] The impetus for regulation is that one party is highly dependent on the other and that this dependence undermines sexual autonomy. It is therefore unnecessary to argue that these relationships should be regulated based on some measured probability of retaliation. Given the dependency in certain unequal relations, it is the constraint on choice, the manipulation of one's will for sexual gratification, and the ambiguity of potential retaliation that require legal response. It is these forms of dependency that often characterize relations between adults and minors—stepfather and daughter, teacher and student, coach and athlete. It is impermissible for a father to have sex with his daughter not (necessarily) because the sex is incestuous or because it is automatically abusive or coercive, but because the sex is likely to be abusive or coercive with or without a threat. There is no way to tell, and that is the problem—an upshot of relational dependence, buffered by age differential and (most often) gender. In these circumstances, the giving of consent is indistinguishable from a necessary concession to maintain the baseline, to check violence, or to avoid deprivation.

It is not simply vulnerability and dependence that nullify consent, because sex frequently takes place in worlds and relations of inequality. Nor is sexual consent only nullified if one's moralized baseline is threatened through leveraging vulnerability and dependence. Rather, there are certain relations where the degree of vulnerability and dependence is so great that, to paraphrase but redirect MacKinnon, it is impossible to tell the difference between coerced submission and consent.[155]

In Alissa Nutting's 2013 novel *Tampa,* eighth-grade teacher Celeste Price—whose character combination of sexual addiction, ruthless manipulation, and unfeeling disregard for human suffering is so typically the reserve of fictional men—seduces her inexperienced, shy, and skinny fourteen-year-old student, Jack Patrick. Celeste tells us: "I could smell the mint chewing gum on his breath—he'd indeed prepared himself for a make-out session. Could consent have been any more transparent?"[156]

What I have argued in this last section is that Celeste might be right but the sex is still wrong. The wrongness of the sex need not be predicated upon nonconsent, an inquiry into the cognitive capacities of Jack, or traumatic sequelae (which in Jack's case are multiple and murderous). The sex is wrong because Jack cannot reasonably refuse, given—among other factors—the institutional parameters of the relationship.

Creating an Affirmative Standard of Sexual Consent for Minor–Minor and Adult–Minor Sexual Relations

Although Schulhofer and Archard promote a more robust standard of consent than the extant standards of most state laws, neither they, nor Oberman, nor Wertheimer, address the possibility of revising standards of sexual consent for young people as a class of persons. I argue for the construction of such a consent standard here, first situating this demand in the context of prior feminist reforms and then responding to potential objections. An affirmative standard of sexual consent unique to and for young people spurs concerns from all stripes—legal realists, critical theorists, protectionist feminists, prosex feminists, poststructuralists. Their concerns are not discountable, but the costs of stasis—for young people and for sex—are higher than the costs of the proposed alternative.

Beginning in the 1970s, states reformed their criminal rape laws under pressure from feminist legal activists and scholars. Marital exemptions to rape were mostly abolished (husbands can now be considered sexually coercive, as a matter of law), as was the requirement that a rape charge be corroborated (women are now believable, as a matter of law). Judges no longer peremptorily instruct juries that rape is often falsely accused, and many states have enacted "rape shield" laws that, to varying degrees, preclude testimony reporting the sexual history of the claimant.[157] Women are no longer required to display "utmost resistance" to satisfy the force requirement of rape and sexual assault statutes.[158] The force element has been relaxed, and a few states have switched from a force or resistance

requirement to a "nonconsent" requirement.[159] However, scholars and lawyers have noted that this change has not made much material difference
in successful prosecutions, as "nonconsent" and "forcible compulsion" are
interpreted by judges and juries to require a demonstrable act of resistance
by the alleged victim. The nonconsent standard has been rescripted as a
force element.[160]

While most states retain a force element in their rape or sexual assault
statutes, and while some states have transformed their force element into
a nonconsent standard, only a handful of states require an affirmative version of consent for the sex act to be noncriminal—some verbal or nonver-
bal freely made agreement that signals willingness beyond acquiescence
or compliance.[161] Although feminist legal theorists have argued for an affirmative standard of consent—to advocate a legal model of sexuality that
underscores mutuality and reciprocity and/or to militate against gendered
power imbalances[162]—the calls are mostly ignored juridically and challenged jurisprudentially.[163]

Whether or not feminist legal scholarship had, or has, the moral force
or empirical evidence to make the case for affirmative consent in adult
heterosexual relations, such a standard should be incorporated for regulating sex between minors and between minors and adults. A rationale for
that standard closely resembles rationales made by feminists over the past
twenty-five years but is more actionable and compelling in the context of
youth and sexuality.

An affirmative standard of consent promotes sexual autonomy—it
tracks, better than extant laws, young people's objectives. It checks sex
in the "gray area" among teens or between teens and adults in which sex
is secured through silence, nonresistance, or weak resistance. As far as I
know, only Heidi Kitrosser has explicitly argued for an affirmative standard of consent for sexual relations involving minors. Although I partially
agree with her rationales, I want to add another: a shift to affirmative consent in fact makes the standard no longer entirely about consent but about
sexual autonomy and young people's desires and choices. Affirmation displaces consent as the central metric in determining criminal sexual conduct, refocusing attention onto the choices and options of young people
instead. Sex and sexuality come to look less like a commodity reluctantly
ceded through contract—a thing one male person wants and one female
person relinquishes—and more like a collaboration of desiring subjects.[164]
Several feminist theorists make the case for more protective sex laws by

demonstrating the comparative robustness of laws guarding individual's proprietary rights to objects like cars and horses.[165] The body, they suggest, is surely as protection-worthy. The problem with this analogy is that it symbolically reproduces sex with women as a thing to be proprietarily protected and contractually traded, rendering female volition interchangeable with cars and horses.[166] If instead the law asks not *to what will young people accede,* but *what do young people want,* it acknowledges agency, hedging against the sexualizing of socially imagined childhood innocence or blankness the law had previously codified.[167] Insofar as consent presupposes incapable young people on one side of the line and reasoning-but-acquiescing people on the other, volition drops out of the equation, and eroticized innocence fills the vacuum.[168] To legally imagine a young person wanting sex is to legally imagine a young person wanting, puncturing fantasies of a child tabula rasa that fuels both conservative erotophobic politics and (some) pedophilic desires alike.[169]

I do not define explicitly what constitutes "affirmative consent." I am inclined though to agree with Schulhofer that "sexual intimacy must always be preceded by the affirmative, freely given permission of both parties."[170] The consent token need not be verbal. It can include body language, particular forms of conduct, and mutual initiation. A Washington statute defines consent as "actual words or conduct indicating freely given agreement to have sexual intercourse or sexual contact."[171] Indeed, a spoken requirement may be asking too much, since young people report being uncomfortable verbalizing their desires to each other.[172]

Objection: "Affirmative Consent" Can Be Coerced; "Affirmative Consent" Is Still Subject to Judicial Interpretation

There are considerable problems with an affirmative consent defense for minor sexual relations, two of which stand out readily: coercion and judicial interpretation. With regard to coercion, if perpetrators know the standard has shifted to an affirmative one, might they not coerce victims to "affirm" they want to have sex? Perhaps. As it stands, many young teenagers who are now having mutually desired sex are criminals. The many older teenagers who are having sex are underprotected by standards of consent and force that ultimately codify and normalize coercive sex. Girls are unlikely to say "no" to unwanted sex, and the law evaluates fearful silence as legitimate consent. At least with an affirmative consent standard, silence might no longer be transformative.[173] So too, one might hope that an affirmative standard would disqualify affirmations given on account of threats or force.[174]

With regard to judicial interpretation, the "welcomeness" standard developed under sexual harassment law since *Meritor Savings Bank v. Vinson*, and which has an obvious affinity with affirmative standards of consent, is riddled with the problem of dubious (one might say misogynist) interpretation.[175] Although presented as a more robust alternative to the consent standard of criminal rape law, "welcomeness" has sometimes hinged on the sexual character of the plaintiff, her choice of clothing, and her choices of speech and humor.[176] If judges have been capricious in interpreting "welcomeness," why would they do a better job interpreting "affirmative consent"? Will a teenager's sexual dress and sexual past be considered evidence of affirmation? Ultimately the issue here collapses into the issue of coercing a "yes," and my response is similarly, admittedly, unsatisfying: an affirmative standard beats the extant alternative, at least making it more likely that silenced submission or resistance without force will not qualify as consent. Similarly, narrowly tailored definitions of consent in sexual relations might address misogynistic, ad hoc judicial interpretation. It should not be exceedingly difficult to enact a consent standard that requires more than a short dress either to signal interest in sexual activity or to neutralize evidence of resistance.[177]

A similar feminist concern with the "welcomeness" standard of sexual harassment law is that it shifts evidentiary focus onto the behavior and desires of the plaintiff and away from the power hierarchy that constitutes the workplace relationship.[178] As for power hierarchies, regulations on relations of dependence and age-span provisions hedge against an overly individualized characterization of sexual coercion. As for transposing the burden of proof, theorists and activists have argued that rape law mistakenly queries the plaintiff, her character, and her behavior instead of querying the behavior of the defendant. Yet it strikes me that any reform more extensive than an affirmative standard of consent—for example, were nonconsent the rebuttable presumption in charges of sexual assault—veers into marking the defendant guilty until proven innocent. It potentially attributes guilt without fact finding, trial, or jury deliberation, and it portrays sex itself as an inherently unwelcome act equivalent to, say, theft or assault.[179] Susan Estrich analogizes that "consent" is not an affirmative defense to robbery, as we would not reasonably believe the plaintiff to have asked or consented to be robbed.[180] But we do not need to valuate sex like we valuate armed robbery to demand a more robust standard of consent in sexual relations between young people and between young people and adults. The law can require a form of affirmative consent that does not a priori assume that sex is, with occasional exceptions, experienced like armed robbery.

Objection: Why Not Adopt "Affirmative Consent" as a Standard for All Sex?

Liberal and feminist reformists alike have suggested that states augment their standards of consent for criminal rape law. Given that—as Catharine MacKinnon and Andrea Dworkin have famously remarked—a dead woman is legally capable of sexual consent in most jurisdictions, there is not all that much to rebut this demand.[181]

On the plane of gender, I have hesitations—but only hesitations—about fully incorporating affirmative consent reforms. Some critics point to problems with this move and the conceit that motivates it: it infantilizes women, it patronizes sexual partners, it imagines sex as conversational, it takes the sexy out of sex, it opens the door to endless legal retaliation and places unfair burdens on the defendant.[182] I sympathize with only some of these criticisms, but indeed there is a risk in the assumption, first, that adult women cannot say what they want and, second, that protectionist law is the best vehicle for women's empowerment.

These ambivalences aside, I have focused here on gender as it intersects with age. At this juncture, welcomeness carries fewer problems than it does when applied to rectifying women's inequality. As Oberman evidences, young people are disinclined to express their desires, and their silence is exploited. Young people are less experienced and less informed than adults. A standard of affirmative consent recognizes that sexual relations among minors and between minors and adults are more fraught, new, and vulnerable than sexual relations among adults, but that they occur frequently and ought to be safeguarded, not suppressed. Kitrosser argues that if the law cannot be reformed for everybody, perhaps at least the law can be adjusted for young people.[183] Rather than consider reforms for young people the best we can do, we might think of young people as a separate class of individuals for whom the law has a different function. Affirmative consent does not presuppose that young people are constitutionally helpless, powerless, or dependent, but recognizes instead forces, circumstances, and gendered socialization that disproportionately impact youth and that necessitate a more fortified legal shelter for sexual autonomy.

Objection: Who Says "Yes" to Sex?

A commonly invoked objection to an affirmative standard of consent is that sex is not a conversation, that people do not and do not want to speechify the sex they are having. They do not want to contractualize the encounter, deeroticize it, anesthetize what would have been seductive because subtle foreplay.[184] People who share a history of intimacy presumably share some level of familiarity with each other and need not explicitly agree to sex each and every time they have it.[185] This commonsensical skepticism is a powerful antidote to feminist agitation. In the 1990s, the infamous sexual consent policy of Antioch College was much maligned for requiring that students verbally consent to each "level" of sexual activity before proceeding to another.[186]

The first response to this objection is the reminder that affirmative consent need not be a "yes" or a clumsy nod of the head. It intends instead that lying still, submitting after resisting, or submitting after threats are leveled do not meet the threshold for exculpation. In the well-known rape cases discussed by Schulhofer, Estrich, Oberman, and so forth, the facts of the case are often not disputed—everyone agrees that the victim lay there, submitted after resisting, or submitted after threats were leveled.[187] It is rather the interpretation of the facts that are litigated. An affirmative consent standard excludes interpretation of such facts as constituting consent. Moaning, moving, kissing, saying "that feels good," removing some of one's own clothing, guiding a partner's hands, initiating a sexual act after one's partner initiated the first act: such behaviors might all be factors in determining consent. Lying scared, silent, and still, however, would not count.

In his survey of rape laws and attempted rape law reforms, David Bryden proffers a few critiques of an affirmative consent standard—all variants or derivatives of *but who says yes to sex?* While admitting that "symbolically and educationally, [affirmative consent] would be an excellent rule," Bryden objects that "in an ongoing sexual relationship the parties usually do not regard every sexual encounter as a momentous decision, fraught with dangers that need to be carefully evaluated."[188]

The claim presumes that affirmation or agreement to sex is only required if sexual decisions are momentous and if dangers run high. But what if affirmation is about respecting the wants and desires of the people having sex—respecting sexual autonomy—whether or not the act is momentous or the danger imminent? "With your lover," he writes, "a greater degree of spontaneity is acceptable," but can't one have the pleasures of spontaneity coterminous with the pleasures of wanted sex?[189] If I spontaneously jump my partner, and he lies there motionless, never signaling any verbal or bodily interest, is that the kind of spontaneity the law should recognize as permissible? Maybe, maybe not. But is it the kind of spontaneity young people, those newly entering into sexual relations, should learn is morally acceptable and legally allowable? No.

David Bryden criticizes the affirmative consent argument because it presupposes a "gross imbalance of power" that may not characterize relations between most men and women. Bryden suggests the argument for affirmative consent may stereotype and reify—rather than rectify—the power imbalance between men and women.[190] This hesitation is less applicable to sex among minors and between minors and adults. Between minors and adults, there are more often measurable or immeasurable imbalances of power, whether in different levels of knowledge and experience, in different forms of emotional investment and psychic need, or in different institutional locations. As for sex among minors, it seems plausible that the adoption of affirmative consent could be conceived of not as a reiteration of gender norms around aggression and passivity, but as a statutorily recognized commitment to sexual autonomy. While consent reform in the worlds of either adult sex or youth sex would be ostensibly gender-neutral, the reforms in the former (analytically, let's imagine they are discrete) would be more quickly and ubiquitously interpreted as protections for women, given that such reforms are spearheaded by women and that the history of rape reform is the history of figuring women's bodies and bodily availability to men. But the history of age of consent reform is not gendered as monolithically.[191] Reform to consent standards for teenage sex may be perceived as applying to youth as a class, rather than to young girls. In a perfectly sexually autonomous world, an affirmative standard of consent would be introduced alongside more egalitarian safer-sex programs that centralize both safety and desire and that articulate the import of respecting and defending sexual choice.[192] An affirmative standard of legal consent could be understood as both indicating and propelling a political appreciation of young people's sexual choices.

Finally, Bryden objects that an affirmative consent standard may conflate sexually amoral acts with sexually criminal acts, which would result in harsher sentencing:

while many of us might criticize a man who fails to ask, or at least to wait for an affirmative signal, in the absence of some sort of physical or at least verbal resistance by the woman few observers would say that the man's conduct was so unusual and immoral that it warrants the extreme sanction of imprisonment.[193]

While some disagree about whether "date rape" and "stranger rape" ought to be treated as different in degree or kind,[194] no one advocates uniform punishment for all sexually violent or coercive acts. Schulhofer specifies different degrees of proscribed sexual conduct that warrant different levels of punitive or civil response.[195] One can advance an affirmative standard of consent without presuming that all convicted defendants deserve the same punishment.

Objection: Why Not Abolish All Per Se Proscriptions and Status Distinctions in Place of Affirmative Consent?

If sexual choice matters, then what marks the difference between the law denying the sexual agency of a young person and a person constricting the choices of a young person? If an underthought problem of sexual coercion and violence is the fact of restricting another's choices and dismissing another's desires, then the law just as surely regulates desire when it forbids a young person to be sexual as does a person when he forces a young person to be sexual.[196]

The three replies here are cursory, since their substantive force has been implicit throughout this chapter. First, the analogy is not apt. In the case of law, sexual activity is being prohibited. In the case of forced sex, sexual activity is being compelled. Until the harms that result from abstaining from sex are shown to be equivalent to the harms of forced sex, the parallel between restriction by law and pressured sex by persons should not be overdrawn.

Second, the regulations on sex in relations of dependence are designed to encode autonomy, on the presumption that those relations pollute the possibility of willed agreement. A prohibitory law need not presuppose that a seventeen-year-old cannot want to have sex with her psychotherapist; rather, it presupposes that her autonomy is better protected through restriction, since the patient cannot reasonably say no in the relationship.

Third, desires are not prediscursive. In a 1978 France-Culture radio interview on intergenerational sex and the recriminalization of the "sex offender," Michel Foucault contends, "an age barrier laid down by law does not have much sense. Again, the child may be trusted to say whether or not he was subjected to violence." And Guy Hocquenghem seconds, "listen to what the child says and give it a certain credence. This notion of consent is a trap, in any case. What is sure is that the legal form of an intersexual consent is nonsense. No one signs a contract before making love."[197]

Philosopher Linda Alcoff effectively counters these arguments.[198] Although for Foucault power is diffuse, productive, micro- and multidirectional, its grounding coordinates for sex and sexuality—at least in the radio interview—are relatively fixed: the law, sexology, psychiatry, and their concomitant discourses. For Alcoff, gender and age too, as eroticized power differentials, constitute or at least mediate sexuality and the desire for object choices. Media, law, academia, and psychology condition the experiences of pleasure and desire; cultural judgments are internalized differentially across social strata:

> It is a mistake to think that putting forward such judgments [about sex between adults and minors] will necessarily result in an overall increase in repression: the repression of adult–child sex may effect a decrease in the constraints by which children's own sexual energies are policed, managed, and deflected.
>
> There is no necessary contradiction between a view that takes seriously the connection among discourse, power, and sexuality, and a politics of sexuality that repudiates various sexual pleasures.[199]

Foucault is not Foucauldian all the way down. The "truth" about our sex and sexuality in relation to external power, whether figured as the adult or the state, is a priori nothing, always already entrapped in discursive routes preformed in normative expectations; in this case, in a sexualized, authorial world of adults. The child verbalizes consent in the same discursive— not just juridical—regime that subordinates her. As Vikki Bell argues, "In this appeal to change the law and legal practice . . . Foucault seems to forget his well known scepticism of this notion of rights and this notion of 'no restraints' as freedom."[200] Listening to the child may be necessary to evaluate the facts of the relationship in question, but it is wholly insufficient as a matter of law. "Listening to what the child wants" can be critically appreciated without imagining that those wants are not inflected by psychic needs, socialization, and gender difference, and without supposing that law cannot work as an imperfect corrective to the manipulations of desire.

Is Gay Sex Exceptional?

But what if the consent of the child, as well as its sexual encounters, are neither uniformly manufactured nor necessarily damaging, respectively? What if the gender and sexuality of the child reorganizes scenes of consent, desire, sex, and harm? Alcoff's critique of Foucault's willing sexual child holds such traction in part because Foucault's child is genderless, and he does not address—either here or elsewhere[201]—how the child's consent, desire, self-understanding, and experience of the sexual encounter may be mediated through social meanings of gender and sexuality.

While Wertheimer, Archard, Schulhofer, Oberman, and MacKinnon, with varying degrees of success, incorporate gender and age as variables, or as systemic difficulties, in distilling down tokens of meaningful sexual consent, none of them treats same-sex sexuality sufficiently. Wertheimer's sociobiology naturalizes heterosexuality, male aggression, and female passivity and all but suggests that homosexual sex occurs only in the absence or frustration of available heterosexual options.[202] Oberman's argument rests on the presumption that girls' sexuality is categorically vulnerable and the law ought to function as a categorical corrective. She rarely mentions boys.[203] Boys are not, from the evidence Oberman retrieves, as susceptible to or suffer as much from sexual coercion as do girls. Archard (like Schulhofer), if we extrapolate from his case studies, assumes that the coercive dynamics of sex between men is equivalent to those between men and women. And MacKinnon has long maintained that force in same-sex relations simulates the eroticized dominance that is heterosexuality, that sadomasochistic, rough, or indeed abusive relations between same-sex partners mirror or reify sex inequality, in which the "bottom," "submissive," or "abused" is a placeholder for "woman."[204]

This is possibly true, but not always or necessarily: the social conditions of and constraints on same-sex sexuality versus the imperatives of "compulsory heterosexuality" distinguish intergenerational sex between a man and a younger woman and a man and a younger man as often markedly dissimilar situations. The dynamics of gay intergenerational sex brings into relief—as does Oberman—that our concern with age is more often than not a concern with gender and with the manipulation of young girls' anxieties and longings. Boys are no doubt sexually abused.[205] But a sexually curious and sexually frustrated teenage boy who searches for an older male partner may be a different scenario from Wertheimer's teenage girl who has sex with her babysitter.[206] Adolescent boys may seek out older men for companionship, for sexual experience, for an introduction to gay culture, and for a shelter from homophobic culture.[207] It is telling too that, according to Alcoff's research, "gay" pedophilic men are interested in teenage boys, "straight" pedophilic men are interested in prepubescent girls, and the average age of incest victims is seven.[208] In several European studies, boys did not suffer the sequential harms from early-age sex with older partners nearly as commonly as did girls.[209] Studies in the 1980s and 1990s in the Netherlands, Australia, and the United States also suggest that boys and adolescent men generally report their sexual experiences with older men as positive, reporting both as boys and later as adults.[210] Another study among gay and bisexual college men found that most responded positively to (noncoercive, reportedly consensual) sexual relations with adult men when they were younger; also, these boys (now adults) did not manifest the sequelae predicted in mainstream child sexual abuse literature.[211] In 1998, psychology researchers Andrea Nelson and Pamela Oliver found, in their large-sample study of college students, that men more often reported their cross-generational (and illegal) sexual encounters as "consensual and not harmful," whereas women reported them "as coerced and harmful." Their findings on same-sex sex among boys and men diverge though from the above-mentioned studies: "Boys generally said they had been coerced into contact with men, but that they had agreed to or wanted contact with women." However, only five men in their study reported that they had sexual experiences with older men when they were younger.[212]

It seems sex across age carries different meanings—social and subjective—depending in part on the genders and sexualities of the participants. I must caveat though that I am comparing the dynamics of sex between men and girls and men and boys, and I am not investigating sex between women and boys or women and girls. There is a dearth of research on younger girls' sexual experiences with women, although plenty of testimony to the formative, solidaristic power of lesbian intergenerational sexual encounters.[213] Regardless, I am not romanticizing gay culture as a world of gender parity free from sexual violence and coercion, nor making the naive claim that desire is freedom, that gender is discursively instantiated, and that sexual freedom from gender identity is the just sexual order of things.[214] However, the cultural dynamics and social inequalities that structure sexuality matter, a point made by feminist critics but not fully appreciated by the theorists discussed.

It is remarkable that in the debates around pedophilia between feminists and (very few) gay and queer theorists in the 1980s and 1990s, nobody, as far as I can tell, adequately observed that each camp had a different subject in mind. For the feminists, the person to be protected is the young female child at the mercy of parents or family friends.[215] For these gay and queer theorists, their reserved defenses of pedophilia imagined, interviewed, or sometimes recalled their own experiences as a teenage boy having sex with an older gay man.[216] It is surprising and disappointing that in the studies cited above, as well as other scholarly commentary on man–boy relations, there is such little attention to socialized gender difference. Indeed, a 2008 survey of several studies on man–boy relations, as well as the studies' authors themselves, use the data more to criticize dominant tropes of child sexual abuse literature (harm as foregone conclusion of intergenerational sex) than to interrogate why it might be "different for boys."[217] A similarly myopic interpretation can be found in Julian Marlowe's "It's Different for Boys" (1997). Marlowe posits that the phenomenon of male prostitution shores up arguments against female prostitution as patronizing and protectionist. He writes, "Concern for the mental health of female sex workers rests on a normative view of female sexuality as connected to love and relationship," and so feminist objections to prostitution are based on sexist assumptions about female chastity, victimhood, and passivity.[218] Since gay sex is just like straight sex and there is nothing normatively wrong with gay sex for pay, then there is nothing normatively wrong with straight sex for pay. Regardless of one's position on prostitution, one need not be a MacKinnonite all the way down to flip the argument on its head: precisely the fact that male–male sex for pay does not reflect the same systemic violence and exploitation as does female sex work makes gender difference and heterosexuality more suspect, not less. Marlowe undercuts his own argument when he writes that "many gay men have learned not only to accept but also take pride in sexual deviance," overlooking the possibility that pride in deviance may, at least in part, be a privilege of comparable social power or social capital between male partners.[219]

This brief discussion then intends two admonitions. First, legal theorists should not assume that age difference is gender indifferent, nor that gay sexuality is a copy of heterosexuality, replete with identical patterns of power, inequality, and socialization.[220] Second, the very fact that this area is a no-go zone for theory and discussion further incapacitates unpacking the intersection of gender and age inequalities. Because attempts to explore differences of straight and gay sexuality in terms of age are heard as defensive rationalizations or apologia for pedophiles, it is exceedingly difficult to assert that the discourse on sex predators—often (but not always) homophobic and usually hysterical—undermines critically interrogating family, home, heterosexuality, and other typical, unceremonious sites of abuse and coercion.

Rightfully, gay people hate talking about this. The North American Man–Boy Love Association (NAMBLA) is still the specter that haunts the gay rights movement. Political organizations against extending civil rights to queers continually deploy the rhetoric of child protection and child harm. This then is one reason law should not dictate different rules for gay sex and straight sex among minors and between minors and adults; one could only imagine the social response to statutes that make the latter more presumptively suspect than the former.

But a second and more subtle reason for resisting legal differentiation is that the comparative benignity of gay boys' sexual experiences with adults may have less to do with gayness and more to do with the social conditions of boyness and the ways in which boys, queer or not, learn that sex is enjoyable, inevitable, and something to which they are entitled, whereas girls, queer or not, learn that sex is invasive, dangerous, and something that they are expected to prevent, defer, and not desire.[221] If this is the case, then differentiated law codifies and reinforces just this sexual imaginary, in which boys get to get off and girls get to get hurt.

MINORS AS A SEPARATE SEX CLASS UNDER LAW

Although gender and sexuality then must register in considerations of sex and youth, they need not register in statute. Despite how the problem of youth and sex is (systemically, not comprehensively) differentiated by gender and sexuality, youth ought to be treated equally by law, since the benefits of uniform classification outweigh gendered juridical distinctions.

The converging point to which all the listed reforms (decriminalizing sex between minors, age-span provisions, relations-of-dependence provisions, affirmative consent) lead is the codification of minors—between the ages of twelve and seventeen, perhaps—as a separate sex class under law, distinguishable from "tier 1" children on the one hand and from adults on the other.[222] Defining this demographic as a particular class recognizes youth as vulnerable yet desiring agents—and it may be this combination of vulnerability and desire that is in part what makes youth sexuality altogether uncomfortable in the contemporary United States.[223] Historically, law and social policy have managed this discomfort by overdetermining vulnerability and deflecting desire.[224] The reforms I have delineated, as well as the principles that inform them, attend both to the sexual agency of young people and to the material, institutional, and psychic sources of their vulnerability. These proposed reforms are imperfect, but so is everything in the bluntness, formality, and ostensible neutrality of liberal law. They are, however, more normatively defensible than many extant statutes.

There is a body of feminist and queer-theoretic scholarship, influenced by Marxism, critical legal studies, and critical race studies, that is highly skeptical of sexual justice theories and politics that demand more, not less, legal intervention and disciplinary regulation.[225] Janet Halley scrutinizes what she calls a "governance feminism" that premiums the state as our salvation of sex inequality.[226] There are sound reasons to reject "governance feminism" and other such state-centered, state-sanctifying, juridical theories and politics: they depoliticize and disempower nonstate actors, they ossify rather than prevent injury, they are lodged in the language of liberal citizenship rights rather than the language of restructuring social power, and they further entrench the state in disciplining the practices and behaviors of its subjects.[227]

Yet I am inclined to think that when all is tallied, the reforms here would not add to legal intervention or further consolidate state power around sex and sexuality, but instead redirect the law and its priorities. Law already regulates young people's sex lives, and law is unlikely to retreat on this front soon. The challenge is how to regulate (and think about) sexuality better, rather than to imagine a stateless sexual politics.[228] These proposals are not a substitute for a more creative, multisite politics of sexual justice. Rather, they are envisioned as precursors to and part and parcel of such a politics.

LAW'S LIMIT

That power, desire, and sex interface variably with intergenerationality, sexuality, and gender provides but one piece of evidence that law is and ought to be a tiny component of building a more sexually just environment that minimizes harm and engenders autonomy. The bluntness and neutrality of liberal law—its strength and weakness—mean that the experiences and desires of queer kids will be more greatly disfigured in and by the juridical imaginary.

Here is another limitation of law's efficacy: the seductive appeal in transgressing sexual prohibition, the eroticizing of subjects marked out of bounds, because they are out of bounds.[229] Child pornography is a terrific example of a discourse eroticized by virtue of its legal condemnation.[230]

And another: moral theorizing in the adjudicative mode (*this is ethically acceptable sex, this is impermissible sex*) feels good, just, comforting, and simple, but grafting regulations and restrictions from on high neither implies social uptake nor ever attends to complex, noncodifiable histories and politics that produce inequality (or that generate desire).[231]

As a matter of policy, progressive, critical assessments of past and present statutory rape law (and of criminal rape law more generally) admonish that law and legal change are only a small part of the institutional, social, and economic overhaul required for a more comprehensive vision of sexual justice.[232] Law students, law professors, activists, and theorists all argue that guaranteeing the sexual autonomy of young people would require, beyond legal *thou shalt nots*, far more comprehensive health care, funded antipoverty programs, funded job-training programs, more sex-positive and egalitarian safer-sex educational programs, better resourced public schools, and more critical assessments of and creative alternatives to dominant cultural and media representations of young people's sexuality.[233]

However, there is a tendency in these hortatory appeals to split "law" off from "the social," so that changes in the former are understood as ancillary to or isolable from the latter. I am pressing for a more fluid picture, in which revised legal regulations are not just items on a checklist to implement before or after broader social restructuring. Instead, such reforms might contribute to identifying what those social problems are, and how they should be attenuated. By shifting legal focus from capacity to voluntariness, and from status prohibitions that reflect traditionally gendered mores to status prohibitions that reflect a commitment to sexual choices, the law produces a more nuanced figure of the young person. This young person is neither prima facie a sexually abused child nor, *primo coitu,* a sexually unfettered adult. Rather, she is a vulnerable and desiring subject before the law. Such a subject demands social and political changes that promote neither unqualified access to her body nor her strict and mythic abstinence, but her autonomy.

4 Growing Somewhere?

Journeys of Gendered Adolescence

"What do you do when you're not sure?"

—Father Flynn

In the last chapter, I proposed moderate reforms to existing age of consent statutes. I suggested that an emphasis away from age per se and toward relational rights and the protection of sexual autonomy would have several effects. Practically, reforms would entail the decriminalization of sex between minors and between some minors and adults. Discursively, reforms would help create an alternate juridical imagination, one capable of envisioning the young subject as at once desiring and vulnerable, at once volitional yet often dependent. This legal scene withstands gothic attribution, in which the child embodies incompetence and innocence, the sex offender personifies recidivistic evil, and the homosexual emerges as archetypal of the free, consenting adult. Considering instead relations of dependence, a more robust, affirmative standard of consent, and, consequently, adolescents as a separate sex class, the law still does its inevitable categorical, regulatory work. Yet it informs a terrain of sex harm and freedom that begins to more carefully canvass structures of vulnerability, allows for the existence of desire that is neither exclusively male nor exclusively predatory nor exclusively adult, and finds fault in constraints on and manipulations of sexual choice and choice structure, rather than locating fault in presumptively bad persons.

However, I also concluded that law may not be the normatively or practically appropriate venue to adjudicate the ways gender difference and sexuality inflect sex across age, or, rather, to adjudicate how the risks and propensities of harm in sex across age may be partially mediated by gender difference and sexuality. But that the law is a conflicted locale for addressing questions and problems of gender and sexuality as they intersect with age and age difference does not mean those questions and problems do not exist, or that we should not think critically about them.

I have so far made the case that consent, innocence, and predation are the nationally organizing terms for sexual harm and freedom. These terms are—when unreconstructed—damaging for young people, for sex offenders, and for sex. Whereas the prior chapter shifted focus from sexual consent to sexual autonomy and—by extension of this first move—from innocence to vulnerability, I now want to transition from predation to peremption. Peremption is a somewhat archaic, legalistic, and clunky term, not quite a neologism, but its clunkiness is part of its normative appeal—it holds at bay the anthropomorphizing of sexual harm that is narratively saturating, ethically insufficient, and mostly misleading.

This chapter stakes a claim for *peremption* as denotative of sexual harms irreducible to predation, that is, irreducible to the sex offenses committed by the legal fiction of the sex offender. I define peremption as *the uncontrolled disqualification of possibility*; for my purposes, I want to move our attention to the peremptory narrowing of *sexual* possibility. Peremption names a set of conditions that restrictively channel young people's desires, that disable young people not simply from achieving their interests but also from developing them.

Underneath and buoying the shifts I am proposing—from consent, innocence, and predation to autonomy, vulnerability, and peremption—is another, one that has gone heretofore relatively unremarked upon: a shift from the child, the sex offender, and the homosexual as our constellating characters of sexual harm and freedom to the gendered adolescent. What if adolescence—with its indexical if not universal mix of vulnerability and desire, its receding incompetencies—were exemplary of sexuality? What might it mean for our theorization and regulation of sexual harm if we take seriously adolescence as that weird space-time between the fictions of the adult rational actor (in contradistinction to the sex offender) and the unknowing child? I am thinking adolescence not as a separate sex class under law, as I did earlier, but as a kind of sexual orientation unto itself, defined less by gender of object choice (homo/hetero) than by an exploratory disposition. To consider adolescence as a sexual orientation is to consider sexuality not as always already organized by a predetermined gendered object, but rather sexuality as a becoming, as a figuring and refiguring of which objects matter and how, and as a series of formative screwups. The normative value of becomingness is sui generis, rather than as componential of any particular developmental theory of sexual identity formation.[1]

Perhaps this account of adolescence sounds romanticized or, worse, essentialist. But to place adolescence and its associated sexual becomingness at the center of normative inquiry need not disavow that adolescence is a historical construct, a consequence of and accommodation to the social and economic upheavals of the late nineteenth century and to the attendant fears of racial degeneration, emasculation, and national disunity.[2] Nor must we synonymize sexual becomingness with the tired rehearsal of hormonal overdrive and reckless impulsivity that so often demands ever-increasing parental and police surveillance.[3]

Rather, to conceive adolescence as exemplary of sexuality, and to render visible ways that sexual possibility is perempted, offers some alternative perspectives. We can canvass the young sexual subject as indeed a subject, rather than as a corporately commoditized identity or racialized threat.[4] We can perceive sexual harm as an ecological phenomenon that is identical neither with the wounding of girls' bodies nor with antigay bullying. In fact, under a peremption sensor, the social inscription of a putatively fixed sexual orientation—homo or hetero—may damage the young subject too, or at least overwrite her identifications and underdescribe her sexuality.[5] Nonetheless, peremption registers how pressures and constraints faced by the young sexual subject are asymmetrically gendered, as well as inflected by race and class inequalities.

Therefore, while this chapter explores the constrained conditions of gendered adolescents, "adolescence" also carries a symbolic function, a way to think sexuality, and therefore sexual harm, in a different frame—the frame of peremption, not predation.

The first section below defines *peremption* and provides some etymological and usage background. I then elaborate the meaning and normative implications of peremption against and alongside political theorist Philip Pettit's theory of freedom as nondomination. Pettit's articulation of domination, as the capacity for uncontrolled interference,[6] is the central conceptual referent for my delineation of peremption. I triangulate on Pettit's account of domination, feminist political theoretic critiques of Pettit, and my own assessment of this literature to shore up what kinds of injustice peremption makes noticeable and remediable (in this regard, my reworking of Pettit's domination to materialize peremption mirrors my critical appropriation of Stephen Schulhofer's sexual autonomy in the previous chapter). Foremost, and to foreground, peremption achieves two objectives domination cannot. First, whereas domination, for it to count as domination, requires an "avowed interest" that is or could be uncontrollably interfered with, peremption countenances what might count as harm when we do not yet know our interests, or when we are figuring them out. Second, and subsequently, whereas domination and freedom, for Pettit, bifurcate on the figure of the adult, capable of freedom, and the figure of the child, whose best interests are only knowable by others, peremption carves out a place for the adolescent as both an empirical referent and a symbolic placeholder of (sexual) becomingness.

The second section revisits cultural representation, where the discussion first began with *To Catch a Predator*. I explicate three U.S. films all produced in the first decade of the twenty-first century: *Doubt* (2008), *Thirteen* (2003), and *Superbad* (2007). In different ways, and hailing from several genres, these films tell us something ethically critical about youth, sex, and harm, in part by deprioritizing without disappearing young sex, sex across age, and queerness. The films keep these phenomena in their orbits while also elevating other circumstances the young subject confronts and navigates; and the films elevate these circumstances—racial difference, socioeconomic privilege and underprivilege, for example—in a more intimate, complex relation to the young subject than the empirical can admit.

I turn mainly to the filmic adolescent, and not to "identifiable, embodied youth,"[7] for three reasons. First, these films, like many mainstream films, are containers of contemporary cultural myths. They reflect to us what we see or want to see in ourselves and in others, solidifying stereotypes and mirroring normative cultural fantasies.[8]

Second, and by contrast, these films offer representations of the child and childhood that are not yet, to paraphrase Kathryn Bond Stockton, coded by history or codified by law.[9] The representations of children and childhood Stockton parses in her *Queer Child, or Growing Sideways in the Twentieth Century* (2009) both reflect social mores and are also uniquely positioned to expose and resist them. The filmic child is poised to inhabit and generate other worlds. "Mainstream teen comedies," J. Jack Halberstam concurs, "are replete with fantasies of otherness and difference, alternative embodiment, group affiliations, and eccentric desires."[10]

Third, film allows for a more capacious excavation of ethics, with its attention to "concrete characters," to the historical arc of the subject, and to subjective vulnerabilities ineluctably tied to sociality.[11] Political and legal theory, not to mention statutes and case law, do not and cannot capture this emotional and ethical complexity. Art humbles theory in its propositional mode, allows an encounter instead of inciting a pronouncement. At the same time, it points law and normative theory-gazing to a different kind of object to resolve or a different kind of injustice worth minimizing.

The films I explicate are not "real"—they do not provide "real" persons or problems, and in that sense the complexity they reveal is not referential to or representative of the empirical. The realness of film is precisely its ability to capture structuring forces and patterns of behavior by cartooning or broad-stroking the characters.[12] In this way, concepts are clarified by "amplification through simplification."[13] While films like *Doubt, Thirteen,* and *Superbad* are at moments cartoonish, or deliver caricatures, or deliver kinds of people metonymic of kinds of groups (unsure, protogay children of color; white or whitish girls in single-parent, working-class families; overwhelmed working-class white mothers; reckless white boys in suburbia), they are all the more worth interrogating, offering up raw material for thinking about and theorizing tropes. These films elucidate precisely by bringing an amplified, simplified realness to the ensemble of age, age difference, gender, and sex.

My hope is that both parts work in combination to dimensionalize *peremption* so that it is (1) theoretically parsimonious enough to identify a form of sexual harm otherwise obscured or only vaguely perceived, (2) politically capacious enough to capture how this harm is commonly endured and navigated, but (3) particularized enough to register how that harm articulates across ascriptive differences and social inequality.

FROM DOMINATION TO PEREMPTION, OR THE FUTURE IS ADULT STUFF

Peremption: Some Etymology and Usage

I define peremption as the *uncontrolled disqualification of possibility.*[14] This resembles the *Oxford English Dictionary* definition and registers similar normative concerns to those captured by Philip Pettit's neorepublican theory of domination.

Peremption derives from the classical Latin verb *perimere,* meaning "to kill or destroy."[15] In contemporary usage, *peremption,* or the more familiar adjectival form *peremptory,* is often found in and associated with legal

proceedings, namely the "peremptory challenge": "an objection to a potential juror made by counsel without obligation to give a reason."[16] *Peremption* and *peremptory* refer to "quashing" or "admitting no refusal"[17]—a
combination of obstinacy and unilateralism toward decisions and decision
making that, as a definitional rule, excludes discussion, debate, or input
from others, particularly from those others affected by whatever decision
is made. There is a fixity and finality to the peremptory challenge. The
juror is disqualified at once and at will—the absoluteness of that disqualification rests in part on the fact that the attorney need not offer reasons
for the dismissal—and whatever feelings or thoughts the juror herself or
the opposing counsel harbors make no difference whatsoever. Outside
the law, we see the same sort of disqualifying aspect of peremption. From
Dickens: "Tupman was somewhat indignant at the peremptory tone in
which he was desired to pass the wine." From the existentialist psychiatrist
R. D. Laing: "There was the peremptory bully who was always ordering
her about."[18] Note, again, that it makes no difference whether Tupman
wants to pass the wine, drink the wine, or do somersaults—peremption
does not contravene another's interest so much as it is indifferent to that
interest. Laing, it turns out, is reporting on a schizophrenic patient of his—
the "bully" and "her" are the same person.[19] Indeed, peremption presupposes no external, identifiable agent. Despite the fact that most examples
of peremptory challenges and peremptory conduct refer to attorneys, gen-
erals, kings, political leaders, or people otherwise in power, neither the
OED definition (of *peremptory,* not the archaic *peremption*) nor my account
require a doer behind the deed—*peremptory* may refer to a characteristic of the deed itself, a quality of action, a manner of speech, or indeed,
an internalized or internal directive (Laing's patient). *Peremptory* may also
characterize the force of a norm or the collateral of enculturation.

In repurposing peremption to name a harm, and to name here a kind
of sexual harm, it is important to notice how the original meaning of *perimere*—to kill or destroy—reverberates in contemporary usage. This is
best clarified by thinking peremption in contradistinction to its near hom-
onym, *preemption.* Both terms mark a time before, although only the latter
does so etymologically. Whereas *preemption* describes "the act or right of
claiming or purchasing before or in preference to others," *peremption* disqualifies certain future conduct.[20] In that sense, the "time" of both terms
antedates and anticipates the "time" of consent or nonconsent—the possibilities of the subject are quashed, disqualified, or killed before they are

entertained as possibilities, or perhaps even before they congeal as possibilities. But *preemptive,* whether regarding a purchase or a military strike, presupposes other parties' objectives or interests. The preemptive strike anticipates an attack. A preemptive right grants purchasing power over an object before that object is made available on the market. Preemption, *buying before,* recognizes another (opposing or hostile) subject and predicts the subject's objective; peremption, *killing or destroying,* cancels out that subject and is indifferent to the subject's objective. To preempt is to frustrate others' (perceived) potential pursuits. To perempt is "to do away with or quash," to obliterate rather than frustrate.[21] For Philip Pettit, domination disqualifies the adult as a political agent—it denies the freeness of the free person. For me, peremption disqualifies the adolescent as a sexual agent—it denies the (sexual, relational, becoming) autonomy of the young subject.

Peremption as Domination

In *On the People's Terms: A Republican Theory and Model of Democracy,* Philip Pettit updates his account of domination, thereby updating as well his normative prescriptions for democratic institutions, political processes, and public provisions.[22] For Pettit, republican democratic arrangements should be keyed to the promotion of freedom and the relief of domination. Domination, in the latest iteration of his theory, is the *capacity for uncontrolled interference.*[23] Unfreedom need not require actual interference; rather, Pettit is centrally concerned with relations—between citizens, citizens and state, employees and employers, spouses—where the more powerful party has the capacity to uncontrollably interfere with the less powerful party (my examples of "relations of dependence" in the previous chapter, if unchecked, fit the bill). Pettit argues that the democratic state has a responsibility to provide such goods, and to involve its citizenry in such a way, so that people are safeguarded from dominative relations. Central to Pettit's theory too is the notion of undominated choice; persons, in order to be free, are entitled to pursue a range of choices and should be equipped—educationally, financially, politically, socially—to realize those choices.[24]

In earlier work, Pettit defined domination as the capacity for *arbitrary* interference.[25] He now substitutes "uncontrolled" for "arbitrary."[26] Although he understands the meanings of these two words to be interchangeable, what he wants to specify is the injustice of someone interfering or potentially interfering with your choices, without regard for or input from you.

The problem of "uncontrolled interference" against you is that it is "uncontrolled" by *you*. This is particularly important as we rethink sexual harm. Abstinence only until marriage (AOUM) sexuality education and abstinence-plus programs may be nonarbitrary in the sense that they are "subject to established rules" and ostensibly "track the interests," or at least some interests, of young persons.[27] But AOUM might also count as domination insofar as it is designed and implemented without any input from teenagers—they have no say in the way the program is administered over their sexual lives.[28]

Pettit's domination, the capacity for uncontrolled interference, is an attractive model for articulating a theory of peremption, uncontrolled disqualification of possibility. Domination is less about malevolence and predatory bad actors—although bad actors are still in the script—than about safeguarding relations from abuses of power and securing persons with the means to exercise choices. Moreover, on Pettit's account, freedom is not possible absent human relations—this is not a vulgarized liberalism in which less interference equals greater freedom. Nondomination as a political goal, as opposed to some notions of noninterference, admits human sociality and relationality as the conditions of human freedom and asks how social relations should be structured to diminish domination and promote flourishing.[29]

To return to the realm of sexual harm, if the threat to consent is predation, then the threat to sexual autonomy is peremption, modeled on domination. Consent and predation discursively constitute a world where one says yes (figuratively, homosexuals) or no (figuratively, women) to sex, and where one is either sexually competent (the adult) or incompetent (the child, the sex offender). In this world, too, the avoidance of relations might constitute a form of freedom. Sexual autonomy and peremption emphasize restructuring and regulating the relations in which we already find ourselves. Consent and predation zero in on the frustration or non-existence of preference; sexual autonomy and peremption zero in on the figuring and formatting of preference, examining which relations and institutions allow or disallow the subject to imagine and pursue possibilities. The question in this discursive outlet is not, foremost, whether we say yes or no to sex, but rather (1) how are subjects made sexually literate, constituted as persons able to say yes or no to sex, and (2) what sort of sexual and relational opportunities are permitted or disqualified.

Four Insufficiencies of Domination

As useful as Pettit's theory of domination is for reimagining social, political, and now sexual injustice, there are several limitations to the account, four of which are germane as we redirect our attention to the scene of sex, gender, and the young person.[30] Peremption builds directly off of domination; but where the former departs from the latter is best clarified by working through these four insufficiencies.

Can Norms and "Internal Barriers" Be Dominating? Peremptory?

Political theorists Nancy Hirschmann, Sharon Krause, and Clarissa Hayward all favor Pettit's domination over liberal notions of unfreedom as (property) interference.[31] Nondomination calls for more robust state provisions than noninterference and requires a contestatory, not just consenting, citizenry to monitor political and civic relations.[32] Nonetheless, these thinkers each in overlapping but distinct ways question whether nondomination can reach the problem of the unjust norm. If women internalize a low or subservient sense of self-worth, or if women's imaginative horizons are artificially narrowed by social expectations of what women can do or who they can be, are these instances of unfreedom?[33] And if they are, might domination as the "uncontrolled capacity for arbitrary interference" overlook something crucial about unfreedom? If employers sub- or unconsciously disregard racial minority applicants on account of prevailing stereotypes, is this an equivalent injustice to workplace relations unchecked by safety regulations or labor protections? The latter is a textbook case of Pettit-style domination, but the former—the psychical and social pervasiveness of harmful stereotypes—seems at once not quite about (potential, intentional) interference and yet very much about the curtailment of freedom.[34]

In *Republicanism*, Pettit argues that the "dominating party" must always be an agent—it cannot be a "system or network or whatever."[35] This seems dispositive, and unfortunately so, for Pettit's critics. While domination may not require bad intentions on the part of the external agent, it does seem to require an external agent, and this conclusion worries Hirschmann, who asks us to depart from models of domination as "manipulation, coercion, oppression, brainwashing."[36] Instead, "if freedom is concerned with the capacity to choose, then social construction requires us to think about the broader conditions in which choices are made."[37] Hirschmann queries how "restraints" are distributed, internalized, and felt across social fields and axes of difference,[38] how "social construction," or I suppose what I am calling norms, delimits choices and legitimates inequality.

Pettit takes a second swing at the problem of the unjust norm and its socializing force in *On the People's Terms*. There, he distinguishes between hindrances that "vitiate" freedom and hindrances that are "invasive" of freedom. The former describes the "failures of resources" necessary for the subject to exercise her choices whereas the latter describes the deliberate (although not necessarily malicious) foiling of the subject's choice.[39] Vitiation is about withdrawals or deprivations that foreclose choice. This kind of barrier is on the whole less threatening to freedom, for Pettit, than invasion.[40] So, then, it does seem to be the case that "a system or network or whatever" can indeed be dominative, and perhaps Pettit believes he has adequately satisfied Hirschmann's concerns about "internal barriers" and Hayward's concerns about "systemic domination."[41]

But it is one matter to be deprived of choices and another to be steered toward choices and away from others by the force of normative order and social expectations. For Hayward, "systemic domination" names not only the way minoritized populations may be prohibited from participating in decisions that affect them, it also describes how "people can be unfree when they are subjected to social, yet impersonal forms of power, like the power of deeply entrenched constitutional arrangements, or unquestioned principles, or *norms that have been sacralized or otherwise universalized*."[42]

It is both out of fashion and patronizing to render what sounds a little bit too much like "false consciousness" as a threat to the realization of freedom, as if you are duped by the social and I am not. But as Hirschmann recognizes, when we examine the force of unjust or containing norms on the imaginative capacities of subjects, we are not presupposing that some subjects are entirely free of normative influence and others wholly puppets.[43] We are inquiring about degrees of normative influence, comparative imaginative containment. "Feminist freedom requires a double vision": to defend the subject's choices and to examine the discursive and material conditions that give shape to desires and aspirations.[44] From this perspective, the injustice of intimate partner violence, for example, is not only the imposition of physical injury but also the constraint on political liberty— women are dissuaded from envisioning exit options.[45]

What might this account—taking norms seriously as a threat to freedom—mean as we refigure adolescence, adolescents, and their gendered, sexual relations? When political theorist Sharon Krause's mother admonished her, as a young girl, to "take smaller steps," she was not exactly "dominated" by her mother, nor can we say that this advice was strictly contrary to Krause's interest.[46] Under a system of gendered value, there are many ways taking smaller steps might make Krause more "ladylike," attractive, approachable, and so forth. But to the extent that the advice expresses a norm of feminine docility, and to the extent that the norm disqualifies other ways of moving one's body through the world and delimits aspirational horizons, we should conceive of the norm as a harm, as a threat to relational freedom. "Yet from the earliest of ages—*and with special intensity from adolescence onward*—women are barraged with cultural messages that deny or debilitate their agency."[47]

In the ensuing encounter with our filmic adolescents, I shall be arguing that norms—especially norms around gender and sexuality—can be forms of peremption, can uncontrollably disqualify the relational possibilities of the young subject, and as such, can be just as threatening or damaging as more readily identifiable forms of violation. The harm I am pegging is not only the political interference of an interest, but also the normative-discursive crowding out of possibility.[48]

Subjective/Objective Interest; Subjective/Objective Possibility

Choice—meaning an adequate range of available options as well as the resourced, safeguarded ability to pursue those options—sits at the heart of Pettit's freedom. But are interests subjective or objective? If you believe it is in your interest to lie down in the middle of the freeway during rush hour or take brain-melting drugs, and I remove you from the freeway or take away your drugs, have I furthered your objective interests (life, health) or dominated you? According to Marilyn Friedman, Pettit is ambivalent on the question of whether interests are subjective or objective—whether your interests are best determined by you or by philosopher kings. Traveling through Pettit's oeuvre, she observes textual moments where it appears that domination is the overriding of a subject's interests as she perceives them, and other textual moments where it appears that domination is the overriding of a subject's interests as measured against an external standard of human welfare.[49] To resolve the ambiguity, Friedman argues that conduct should qualify as domination only in the former instance, when subjective interests are frustrated. It is patronizing and encroaching, she insists, to maintain that someone is dominated when, under her lights, no interests of hers are frustrated.[50] On the other hand, Friedman inserts a "well-being proviso" to the reconstructed theory of domination that hedges against perspectivism.[51] In scenarios where a subject's well-being—understood in objectivist if unspecified terms—is so imminently and seriously at risk, external parties may interfere on the subject's behalf, whether or not the subject agrees to the interference. And if the interference is "carried out with expressions of clear concern for the recipient's well-being," it will not qualify as domination.[52] Like Hirschmann, she returns to the figure of the acquiescent abused wife. To intervene on her behalf, suggests Friedman, is "paternalism (parentalism)" not "domination."[53] (The "parentalism" parenthetical, it turns out, will be helpful as we migrate to adolescence and preference formation.)

Pettit clears up whatever ambiguity Friedman found in his earlier texts. In *On the People's Terms,* Pettit states unequivocally that domination is the uncontrolled capacity to interfere against the choices of the subject and the interests of the subject as she determines them to be:

> when choices have the potential for harming the adult, able-minded agents who exercise them, the [republican approach] argues against criminalizing them or leaving them unprotected.... Take the choices associated with the use of recreational drugs or with certain forms of gambling. The [republican approach] suggests that such choices do not call for any active form of resourcing.... But it strongly supports the view that since any other approach would be paternalistic, failing to acknowledge the status of the agents ... the choices ought to be protected.[54]

It would seem then that contra Friedman, Pettit's republican account of domination would disallow intervention even in the case of threats to well-being, of intimate partner violence, if the assaulted partner rejects intervention. To do otherwise—unless we make the questionable assertion that the abused partner is not "able-minded"—disrespects her as a free agent.

Whoever is right about Pettit on interests—Friedman or Pettit—the conflict is illustrative as we shift focus from "interest" to "possibility" and from the (imagined) fully formed, "able-minded" adult to the developing, increasingly competent or decreasingly incompetent young person. Friedman's well-being proviso seems essential in the case of teenagers—relatively but not entirely inexperienced, categorically if neither universally nor equally dependent, and desiring. Self-injury, as we will see later, may be a young person's choice, but it is one that parents and guardians may justly, nondominatively, and nonperemptorily interfere with. Certain self-injury or certain drug use, to whatever degree they are chosen, may so fundamentally hinder or disqualify future possibilities that a caretaker may override a young person's preferences. But we need to be careful here, as the very point of carving out a theory of peremption is to hold off a form of overpowering that discounts and discredits young people's desires.[55]

On the other hand, precisely because young people's subjectivity is imitative, relational, and dialogic (which is to say not wholly distinguishable from subjectivity as such), withdrawal and absence can be, counterintuitively, their own forms of peremption. Withdrawal and absence, not just imperiousness, can function to uncontrollably disqualify possibilities too.

From Interference of Interest to Disqualification of Possibility

As I mentioned above, and what Pettit and feminist critics agree upon, is that domination, for it to qualify as domination, presupposes an identifiable interest of the subject. Harm is understood, following Joel Feinberg, as a (possible) setback to one's interest.[56] But what might qualify as harm if one does not yet know one's interests or is figuring them out? The adolescent is the figure for that question, which is altogether different from the violation of interest (for example, sex without consent) or "false interest" (for example, the acquiescent abused wife) or what we might consider a self-destructive interest (to be killed for sexual satisfaction).[57] It is a question, also, largely ignored by political theories of injustice. Therefore, with peremption, I shift from Pettit's "interference" of interest to "narrowing of possibility" to open up ways to think about harm that require the fiction of neither the rational actor whose interests are predetermined, nor the actor whose objective interests are warped by the social, nor the unaware child whose best interests are designated by others. If political theories of injustice largely target violations or foreclosures of preformed preferences, I shift emphasis to preference formation. If the formation of preferences is always relational, always in some sense requiring the "interference"[58] or influence of others, what influences are peremptory of young people's flourishing, and what forms are propulsive? In this sense, and unlike domination, peremption identifies "a *cramped* rather than an exploited existence."[59]

There is something, though, disingenuous about romantically reimagining adolescence as a figuring out of interests and peremption as the uncontrolled disqualification of that very "figuring out." Adolescents—the subjects of clinical research studies, their filmic counterparts, the ones we know in our lives—often have rather identifiable, quite concrete interests, whether mundane, fantastical, spiritual, sexual, boring, or bizarre. But my concern with the intersubjective, multiply mediated making of what Feinberg calls "ulterior interests" need not presuppose that young subjects are sans all interests, as if in some purgatory of the open-ended question.[60] And yet, when we are preoccupied with the already-cognized interest or expressed preference—whether the preference is conceived as objective, subjective, misguided, or, as it were, "juvenile"—we shelve equally important questions of (sexual) harm and freedom.

From Free Adults to Freeish Adolescents

For political theorist Patchen Markell, the "insufficiency" of Pettit's domination is its inability to capture the injustice of "usurpation." Usurpation refers to the ways actors and institutions may "narrow" the subject's "involvement" in, rather than control over, conduct concerning her and her political community.[61] Preemption therefore has a close normative affinity with usurpation, but unlike Markell, and unlike Pettit, I relax adulthood as the presupposition of human agency:

> But it is one thing to be treated like a piece of property, *and quite another to be treated, say, like a child*; and not just in having the protective hand of a parent interfere with your conduct for your own good, but also and more insidiously in having the world ordered in ways that narrow the field of situations in which any conduct on your part might be called for.[62]

For Markell, "being treated like a child" sharply identifies two relational phenomena domination cannot reach: first, intervention on behalf of, or pretextually on behalf of,[63] the subject without input from the subject herself, and second, worldly arrangements that disqualify people from participating in the direction of their lives. But reducing these two faces of involvement (paternalism and disqualification) to the analogy of being treated like a child begs crucial questions: Why should we treat children "like children"? Which children, of which ages and social ascriptions, do we treat like children?

The three insufficiencies of domination I have overviewed so far—undercounting the force of the norm, the primacy of subjective over objective interest, and the presumption of an already-identified, violable

interest—are the consequences of and ingredients for a more comprehensive insufficiency that underpins Pettit's neorepublican project: a total
conceptual separation of the adult as free and able-minded from the child
as unfree and incapable.[64] To that end, Pettit's neorepublicanism shares a
conceit with those liberal contract theories that it is designed to counteract: they all tend to "overlook" children while stabilizing assumptions of
adult rationality, reasonability, and freedom against a unitary and undifferentiated account of the child.[65] Adults, as discursively free agents, are
intellectually fortitudinous to withstand the force of a norm.[66] Their subjective interests or preferences may be ill advised, but because adults, in
this framework, are so thoroughly able-minded and deliberative, it is
unjust to override their preferences. The totalizing adult/child binary may
warrant too much intervention against children and too little intervention
in the lives of the adults. More to the point, the binary leaves no conceptual space for the adolescent subject, whom we may understand as the
person neither always able-minded nor categorically incompetent, neither
fully independent nor totally dependent, neither "adult" nor "child," neither free nor unfree, but freeish.[67]

It is not quite right to say Pettit overlooks the problem of children and
domination. But when Pettit references the needs and welfare of children,
these textual moments reiterate rather than rectify the cabining of freedom to adulthood and the political-theoretic erasure of the adolescent
subject:

> Children cannot be given the same opportunities as adults if they are to be
> enabled, when they become adults, to enjoy the sort of non-domination
> which a republic would confer: they must be subjected to the disciplines
> inherent, as any parents knows, in fostering education and development.
> But how then would children be treated under a regime for promoting free-
> dom as non-domination? Would they be reduced to living at the mercy of
> their guardians and teachers?
>
> Absolutely not.... [They should] seek to advance the relevant interests
> of the children.... Parents and teachers [should] be allowed to exercise
> considerable interference in the lives of children ... but the interference
> would track the children's interests according to standard ideas, and would
> not constitute a form of domination.[68]

To assert that this interference would "not constitute a form of domination" does not make it so. Although guardians cannot subject children to

any and all forms of capricious rule, this is only because children will someday "become adults." There is no affordance for, or theory of, injustices against the *becoming* of the becoming subject. Whose ideas are "standard," and how are they collectively or noncollectively determined?[69] Are children a monolithic social group, similarly situated across age, gender, race, sexuality, class, and geography? Who resides in the interstice between the child, governed through "standard ideas," and the adult, self-governed under the regime of nondomination?

Pettit argues that sometimes we ought to treat children as if they are free, in the sense of "fitness to be held responsible," in order to cultivate their freedom, but the priority is always ultimately placed on freedom synonymized with able-mindedness synonymized with adulthood.[70] His model of social justice is built to secure the political rights of "citizens," whom he defines as "all adult, able-minded, more or less permanent residents [of the state]."[71] The concern with freeing the free adult-to-be, therefore, displaces attention from the fact of becoming and from the ways becoming, or figuring out interests, or testing possibilities, are promoted or disqualified.

The problem is deeper than misapplication, as if freedom as nondomination could have been extended to check harms against young people but was not. In *A Theory of Freedom,* Pettit argues for a notion of freedom as "discursive control" as opposed to "rational" or "volitional" control. Where the latter conceptions of freedom may suffer from infinite regress (do you want what you want?) or the "bystander problem" (do you meaningfully endorse what you want?), respectively, discursive freedom, as "fitness to be held responsible," centralizes not acts and choices of the subject, but the development and constitution of the subject as such.[72] "[Agents] are fit to be held responsible . . . in virtue of being a reason-responsive type of agent, not in virtue of anything in a sequence of controlling events or states."[73] So Pettit solves the recursive riddle by pegging responsibility to a type of person rather than a self-endorsement of an act or belief. But this solution also makes freedom a children-free, adults-only zone;[74] when Pettit lists abusive parents as exemplars of dominating agents, it is unclear, on his own terms, if children could ever be dominated, because they are not the "types" of persons that are free. How can one's freedom be infringed if one is evacuated from the ambit of freedom's reach?

Other political theorists more attentive to children's and minority groups' welfare nevertheless replicate Pettit's equation of freedom with adulthood.

Martha Nussbaum's capabilities approach, as is well known, demands more robust political institutions and constitutional protections than does liberal contract theory (although Nussbaum's capabilities approach and Pettit's neorepublicanism seem to generate similar political arrangements).[75] Yet while Nussbaum goes to great lengths to insist that, in most cases, institutions ought to ensure capability development rather than compel functioning ("bodily health" should be achievable, but we should not be forced to visit the doctor), she shifts the standard for children: "Children, of course, are different; requiring certain sorts of functioning of them (as in compulsory education) is defensible as a necessary prelude to adult capability."[76]

Victoria Costa echoes Pettit and Nussbaum and states most explicitly what presumptions are shared across their approaches to the child:

> talk about "promoting the freedom" of children has a very strange ring to it, unless it is interpreted as shorthand for talk about the promotion of their future freedom as adults. For example, no one would say that young children are dominated by the state simply because they are disenfranchised, or because they are required to go to school. In order to extend Pettit's theory to apply to the situation of children, one would need to supplement it with an account of the objective interests of children . . . it would still be better to talk about protecting the interests of children rather than about promoting their freedom.[77]

It is Nussbaum's "of course" and Costa's "very strange ring" that I want to challenge—illocutionary performatives that naturalize children as objects of protection forced to do whatever it is adults think best for them, so they can someday be fully capable adults too.

Perhaps Costa is right about "very young children"—neither disenfranchisement nor compulsory education may be domination. But what about older children and younger adults? We may justifiably wonder whether compulsory education, disenfranchisement, and impoverished or inaccurate sexuality education are forms of domination against them, especially if young subjects are not consulted about, let alone participatory in producing, the policies that affect them. Costa shuts out any normative aspiration between "protecting objective interests" and "promoting freedom." These are the two and only two political objectives, and they track exactly and without remainder the concerns of children and adults respectively.

If these are the only existing normative metrics, the "young" of Costa's "young children" is unnecessary. Either you are a child, whose interests are protected, or an adult, whose freedom is promoted—there is no process, no becoming, no adolescence. It is this space that I am trying to wedge open with "possibility," where the controlled (or nonarbitrary) enabling of possibility is a political good, and the uncontrolled disqualification of possibility is an injustice, peremption.

Pettit, Nussbaum, Costa, and others encountering the political problem of the child are, to varying degrees, beset by the presumptive power of the biological determinant. What is more easily revealed as prejudice in the case of other social axes of difference, namely biological inferiority or underdevelopment on the basis of gender or race, tenaciously clings to our account of age.[78] Some critics negotiate the dominant developmental narrative with alternative strategies: assuming its (qualified) truth but criticizing its current influence on law and policy;[79] insisting that the child's differences require modified or entirely transformed political and institutional arrangements; drawing attention to the ways vulnerability is shared across, rather than distinguishable by and definitive of, age populations; and/or discarding the development narrative (almost entirely) as a social construct that maintains hierarchy and the fiction of liberal personhood.[80] But whatever strategy is employed, many of these critical efforts to inject the child into political theoretic models of social justice ultimately focus on ensuring the development of the happy, choice-capable, and choice-rich adult. Emphases on dignity and futurity revolve around the hope of a freer tomorrow of mature, sound decision making, an important but inadequate objective.

To refigure adolescence as a space and symbol of receding incompetency, as both imitative and exploratory, also means valuing up the mistake, the risk, and momentary failures. This perspective "requires that we see risk not as a zero sum game but as a condition of development, part of the work of growing up."[81] Failure, or what Jen Gilbert calls "risk" in this context, is not by itself an antidote to (hetero)normative order.[82] The receding incompetence that risky behavior registers activates no necessary politically progressive project. Yet, insofar as receding incompetency and trial by fuck-up are constitutive components of growing somewhere, it is politically, ethically necessary to inquire about the material and discursive structures that cushion or convert the consequences of "the mistake" for some young people and not others. When is an obstacle the condition of possibility for growing somewhere, and when does it get you stuck? How and why are some young people peremptorily disqualified from social and sexual possibilities, while others are permitted to risk failure and suffer fewer—or even formative—consequences? Finally, how are young people differentially equipped to figure out their interests, to explore possibilities, to mess up and move on? The films I explicate in the next part, through the concept of peremption and the attendant, refurbished fiction of the "freeish" adolescent, begin to answer these questions.

PEREMPTED JOURNEYS OF GENDERED ADOLESCENCE

Above I enumerated three insufficiencies (and one meta-insufficiency) of domination as a theory of social injustice and suggested that peremption might better detect otherwise un- or undercounted harms against the (young, sexual) subject. Below I explicate three films that capture some of the ways young sexual subjects are perempted by and/or navigate through ideological, material, and discursive impediments. Despite the apparent symmetry (three insufficiencies, three films), it is not the case that each of the films reflects, exactly, each of the harms peremption captures. While some filmic scenes do perfectly correspond to the enumerated harms of peremption (for example, the subordination of "objective" interests to self-injuring "subjective" interests), most do not. These films, their characters, and their relational dynamics proffer a dynamic complexity to peremption. This chapter is neither as clean nor as prescriptively concrete as the previous three; rather, it is a first shot at a cartography of peremption. I pay attention both to the way young subjects are crowded out or crowded in—disqualified from possibilities—as well as to the ways some of those same subjects attempt to navigate themselves and their relations into social and sexual intelligibility.

Doubt: Perempted by Narrative

What do you do when you're not sure? . . . "No one knows I'm sick. . . . No one knows I've done something wrong." Imagine the isolation. You see the world as through a window. On the one side of the glass: happy, untroubled people. On the other side you.[83]

Father Flynn's sermon, which opens both the play and film versions of John Patrick Shanley's *Doubt,* is intended for several audiences, but not Donald Miller (Joseph Foster), the twelve-year-old black boy in the all-white

Bronx Catholic school whom Flynn (Philip Seymour Hoffman) will soon be accused of sexually molesting.[84] The sermon might be a closeted confession, as the inquisitor Sister Aloysius (Meryl Streep) believes, of Flynn's own pedophilic past; it might be prolepsis, warning of Aloysius's compensatory brutality in the face of uncertainty; it might be a public service announcement to the church audience's audience, us, asking that we forestall reaching a verdict as our method for comprehending sexual injury and confirming our good personhood.[85] *What do you do when you're not sure* could be directed to any number of listeners, but the question is not poised to Donald, who will nonetheless thank the priest for speaking to and for him (see "Ballerina Toys and Magnetic Subjectivity," below).

Doubt cannot be the story it flirtingly and fleetingly gestures toward: the story of a queer, intergenerational sexual encounter that might be the launchpad to a less hostile elsewhere, a way to relieve the affective residual of racism, family abuse, and bullying.[86] This relief might be pleasurable, not (just) desperate or forced. But this is all speculative, which is the point. Donald Miller never appears in the play, shows up for less than five minutes of the film, and is rarely called upon to speak.[87] We have little idea what this boy wants, what his interests might be, or how he might go about discovering them.[88]

Instead, *Doubt* is the story of reconciling the liberal reforms of the Second Vatican Council with the impunity historically enjoyed by male clergy; of pre-Stonewall homosexuality and the prickly refuge of priesthood;[89] of church power as patriarchal, hegemonic, and mostly unyielding; of (depoliticized) racial desegregation and well-meaning white people. St. Nicholas School, its administrators, and the possibility of interracial, intergenerational sexual abuse on its grounds all function as metonymy for these macro conflicts, conflicts that predate and *perempt* Donald. The boy is the eye of a storm (and wind is *Doubt*'s ceaseless metaphor) that has nothing to do with him.

Father Flynn is an affable mentor to the junior high boys, an irreverent rule-bender who countervails the draconian (or "dragon," as Flynn calls her) stickler, Principal Sister Aloysius. Flynn's quirks—his long fingernails, his sweet tooth, his preoccupation with the boys' self-presentation—may or may not betray a closeted homosexuality or a camouflaged pedophilia.

Father Flynn, powerful, perhaps pedophilic, perhaps gay, and perhaps predatory, takes special care of Donald, an altar boy who is reserved, bullied, and black. Donald might be gay too. In Donald's first full line (and one of few), he asks his friend, "You think I'm fat?"[90] At the outset, white liberal sympathies over integration are transmuted into detections of effeminacy. Whether or not Donald's "feminine" concern is deployed to defang what might otherwise be a hypermasculinized blackness, the maneuver allays one anxiety only to introduce another.[91] Meanwhile, the usual fear of desegregation, miscegenation, is replaced by the fear of homosexual predation, and the black boy who might otherwise be read as a threat in proximity to white girlhood is momentarily made innocent in proximity to white manhood.[92]

Sister Aloysius's dislike and distrust of Flynn crystallizes when Sister James (Amy Adams), a doe-eyed eighth-grade teacher, reports that Flynn is Donald's self-appointed "protector." Flynn calls Donald out of James's class to the rectory, either to help him out of trouble or to have sex with him, to cover up Donald's drinking the altar wine (a "screw-up," here not formative) or to ply him with booze. These are the ambiguities that drive Aloysius's crusade against Flynn. Where at first the film offloads the would-be villainy of the progressive Flynn onto the regressive, prudish school-marm Aloysius, gender soon gets more troubling. The viewer is therefore not awarded the resolution *To Catch a Predator* stages on repeat—the cultural castration of a predator it first had to produce.[93] Unceremoniously, Flynn sits in Aloysius's chair when he arrives in her office, arrogating command. When Aloysius challenges Flynn more stringently, he castigates her for defying the gendered chain of command: "You have taken vows!" he spits, "obedience being one." "Obedience" is the rebuttal Flynn knows, and it is the easiest, and the procedural is where you turn when the substantive leaves you vulnerable, but that does not make power any less fraternal or Flynn any more likeable. Sister Aloysius's hortatory appeal to Sister James, "Men run everything. We are going to have to stop him ourselves," may be heavy-handed but resonates as we see the church machinery operate to shield men from being held accountable. The offscreen monsignor dismisses Aloysius's account, and Flynn is relocated to and promoted in a nearby school, a now painfully familiar response to sexual abuse in the Catholic Church.[94] The film disturbs us not because, ultimately, Flynn abused Donald and goes unpunished (we never know; we know only to doubt our certitude); rather, the film is disturbing because church officials are indifferent—they would rather not know.

But while the "'did he or didn't he' binary plot"[95] enthralls us to macro conflicts of race, sex, and church power, we are ultimately twice removed from the protogay child and his desire for anything: sex, love, support, whatever. Donald is perempted by narrative, by the discursive structure and compulsory affect of a sex scandal. He and his sexual possibilities are disqualified because he is a pretextual prop, and the pretext of his abuse effaces any deeper inquiry into the conditions and constraints of his sexuality.[96] "The truth makes for a bad sermon," Father Flynn explains to Sister James in the play. "It tends to be confusing and have no clear conclusion."[97] But there is a difference between indeterminacy (what happened) and polysemy (multiple meanings), and this is nowhere more apparent than in the devastating exchange between Sister Aloysius and Donald's mother, Mrs. Miller (Viola Davis), in which Aloysius alerts Miller to Flynn's alleged advances against her son (Figure 7).[98] This scene should be transformative but has nowhere to go, narratively or normatively:

SISTER ALOYSIUS: I am concerned about Donald's welfare.
. . .
MRS. MILLER: Sister you ain't going against no man in a robe and win. He's got the position.
SISTER ALOYSIUS: And he's got your son.
MRS. MILLER: Let him have him then.
. . .

Figure 7. "Well maybe some of them boys want to get caught," challenges Mrs. Miller, on behalf of the absent Donald. *Doubt* (2008).

SISTER ALOYSIUS: Do you know what you're saying? . . . What kind of
mother are you? . . . He is after the boys.

MRS. MILLER: Well, maybe some of them boys want to get caught!
. . . That's why his father beat him. . . .

SISTER ALOYSIUS: W-What are you telling me?

MRS. MILLER: I'm talking about the boy's nature now. . . . You can't hold
a child responsible for what God gave him to be.

SISTER ALOYSIUS: I'm only interested in actions, Mrs. Miller.

MRS. MILLER: But then there's the boy's nature.

SISTER ALOYSIUS: Leave that out of it.

MRS. MILLER: Forget it, then! . . . My boy came to your school 'cause they
were gonna kill him in the public school. His father don't like him. . . .
One man is good to him—this priest. . . . Do I ask the man why he's good
to my son? No. I don't care why. My son . . . needs some man to care about
him . . . and to see him through the way he wants to go. And thank God
this educated man with some kind of kindness wants to do just that.

SISTER ALOYSIUS: This will not do.[99]

Recall that in chapter 1, Chris Hansen reprimanded his predator du jour
and his television audience, "This isn't about gay or straight. Nobody cares
what adults do."[100] Mrs. Miller wonders otherwise: Is it possible that
there is a sexual relation between her son and the priest, and that, rather
than serving as yet another injury to the litany Donald endures, this is
sexual activity that might be wanted and comforting? Is this sexual activity
an insufficient antidote? For the most part, the film canvasses two possibilities, neither of which is confirmed: either Father Flynn sexually abused
Donald (morally wrong) or Father Flynn sheltered a black gay boy from
the unfairness of the world (morally right). But the really hard doubt,
the doubt that *Doubt* can only but broach, is that sex happened and it
was, if not morally right, benign or beneficial.[101] This is the subtext of
Father Flynn's final "confession": "I can't say everything, you understand . . .
remember, there are things beyond your knowledge. . . . I've done nothing
wrong. . . . I care about that boy."[102] And this possibility—that Donald
advanced on Flynn first, and that sex across age, even across vast power
differentials, might not ipso facto damage—is what circulates nearly im-
perceptibly when Sister Aloysius, in the play, lectures Sister James that
"[she] cannot afford an excessively innocent instructor in my eighth grade
class . . . innocence is a form of laziness," and when Aloysius complains,

referring to a white classmate of Donald's, that "puberty has got a hold of him."[103] Both the indictment of innocence and the acknowledgment of adolescent sexuality (here coded as "puberty") are transferred onto characters that can bear their consequences—Sister James and a white schoolboy, respectively. Innocence is questioned as the organizing episteme, which allows Aloysius to later charge that Flynn is exploiting Donald's isolation as "our First Negro student"—if the sex is improper, its impropriety is about the manipulation of dependence and vulnerability, not innocence.

For Mrs. Miller, Donald's "nature" (presumably his gayness, but for all we know, his desire for older men of the cloth),[104] does not exonerate Father Flynn's actions, if they occurred, nor should it. But what Mrs. Miller clarifies is that the greatest threats to Donald's flourishing, sexual or otherwise, may not be Flynn, but the deadly gender normativity of junior high school, the intergenerational transmission of racism, an abusive father, and political power struggles for which Donald is a pawn but not a player.

The "this" that "will not do" for Aloysius may be, to cite Hocquenghem's provocation, that "it's worse when children are consenting."[105] "This" cannot be assimilated into any of *Doubt's* manifest parables, not simply because consensual sex across age and power is normatively icky, but because consensual sex across age and power leaves us with no predator pruned of complexity. "What kind of mother are you?" is Aloysius's futile attempt to stitch back the gothic as it is unraveling. Maternal and "mucousy," Mrs. Miller emphatically and empathetically complicates sexual harm in a way no positivism can.[106]

Several times throughout the film, characters propose that Donald should be consulted to determine "what happened in the rectory." "Ask the boy then," demands Father Flynn, a request Sister Aloysius brusquely dismisses: "Oh, he'd protect you . . . because you have seduced him."[107] If the perspective of the pedophile is nearly nonexistent in visual representation, the perspective of the "victim" is even less likely, save when it reaffirms trauma.[108] We need not hear from Donald because we already have interpretive mastery over anything he will say: self-reported scarring is true, self-reported enjoyment is deluded.[109] As I argued in the last chapter, I agree with Alcoff that "listen[ing] to what the child says" can never be fully determinative, precisely because power is productive and disciplinary, not just juridical.[110] But giving "credence" to the child's testimony need not be equivalent to granting it moral let alone legal authority.[111] Donald is almost always spoken for, his feelings and behaviors reported by adults. Donald is peremptorily disbarred from the scene of his own subjectivity—never called upon to codetermine his present or future. The removal of Flynn is "carried out with expressions of clear concern for [Donald's] well-being," but Donald is nowhere involved, his noninvolvement not simply rationalized but mandated by the figure of the innocent child unduly influenced.[112] The "quashing" of Donald is hastened rather than alleviated on one of the rare occasions he is obliged to speak.[113] Punitively, Sister James makes Donald stand up in class and recite "Patrick Henry's famous remark," which he does not know.[114] Illiberally demanded to "give me liberty or give me death," the performative contradiction entitles Donald to neither. The pedagogic echo of Rousseau's paradox notwithstanding—noncompliant men must be forced to be free—this adolescent subject is in no sense (morally, politically, sexually) free or freeish.[115]

Ballerina Toys and Magnetic Subjectivity

Let's hold open our doubts by way of return to Father Flynn's opening sermon, the one in which Donald interjects himself as audience. Flynn ends the sermon and retires to a changing room in the back area of the church, where Donald finds him to express his own admirations and aspirations: "Hey Father, that was some sermon. . . . I wanna do that." Shanley's film locates this tiny space (air time, lines offered, the cramped quarters of the changing room) for Donald to make himself receptive, a supplicant.

"You'd be a good [priest], I'm sure," replies Flynn, and sits Donald down to offer him a small toy ballerina (Figure 8).[116] The ballerina, Flynn demonstrates, is controlled by a mirrored magnet. Donald imitates Flynn, learning to manipulate the miniature. Cullingford proposes that Donald's "effeminacy is suggested by Father Flynn's present of a toy ballerina."[117] The boy's effeminacy is the visual evidence of a protogayness that inaugurates the hardly developed challenge against the verdict on queer intergenerational intimacy, which crescendos and dissipates with Mrs. Miller's later testimony.

This is probably right—the toy is a good gay cue. Yet it also presents a more troubling but latent element to this story than the desiring gay child. Subjectivity, sexual or otherwise, adolescent or otherwise, is not just relational; it is imitative and requires superintendence.[118] Donald needs and wants *controlled* disqualification, an older person to give him love but also direction, somewhere to spin. Donald learns to control the toy the way he

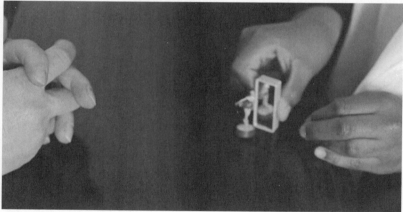

Figure 8. Young, gendered, queer subjectivity: mirrored, magnetic, imitative. *Doubt*.

wants to be "controlled" by Flynn. The problem is that the magnet that is this Other, the object that motivates movement, looks a whole lot like Pettit's "arbitrary rule," or being "under the thumb" of another.[119] It is nearly impossible to distinguish, in this instance, between malicious manipulation and the manipulation that is the necessary but insufficient condition for growing somewhere. What sort of superintendence fosters the figuring out of interests, and what sort of superintendence denies the very autonomy it purports to develop? And on top of this ambiguity is layered another: post-2002, we cannot see a priest giving a toy to a boy in a backroom without alarm. What sort of superintendence, we now also must ask, is sex abuse? Amy Adler provocatively argues that our presumption of child sex abuse "perversely" incites a "pedophilic gaze": our never-ending search for abused or about-to-be-abused children in scenes like this one eroticizes the child.[120] Conjectured prurience libidinizes the intergenerational relation. On the other hand, this sort of critique can unintentionally obscure that it is not the child's innocence that is spoiled, but his becoming autonomy that is perempted.

A white boy (the one Sister Aloysius worries is pubescent) shoves Donald, and the toy falls and breaks. Flynn picks up the pieces and caresses Donald (Figure 9), worrying Sister James—and us, again—about his intentions: care, lust, or both, commingled? Foreshadowed by the broken toy is the broken Flynn, Donald's magnet, forced out by Aloysius. That Donald is "heartbroken" by Flynn's departure seems to bother nobody, or bothers only as controvertible proof that maybe Father Flynn didn't do it after all.[121]

Despite momentary ruptures, *Doubt* cannot canvass Donald's imitative, becoming, sexual subjectivity to the exact degree it presupposes his abuse/nonabuse as the motor of every parable in the film's repertoire. Shanley has said that his text is a cautionary tale of *preemption,* the play written and staged shortly after the 2003 U.S.-led invasion of Iraq.[122] Sister Aloysius preemptively strikes against Father Flynn, perhaps mistakenly assuming he is a weapon of mass destruction. But preemption is still about Flynn. Peremption is about Donald. The emphasis on Flynn's identifiable "interest"

Figure 9. Pedagogic, pederastic, or both? *Doubt.*

(Donald), and then Aloysius's neutralization of Flynn, saturates *Doubt's* (sexual) ethics. Unavailable therefore is any lasting diegetic or theoretic space for Donald, the adolescent boy, to figure out his interests, to forge alternative possibilities. On the other hand, it is the toy that is shattered, not Donald. He will graduate, we are to believe, despite his mother's worries. The effects of Father Flynn's buoying outlast the effects of his exiting. It should "get better" for Donald. He will grow somewhere, even if that growth is forever deferred offscreen.[123]

But if Donald is presented a future, however fragmented by the narrative of sex scandal, what of *Doubt's* girls; where do they get to grow? Father Flynn recommends to Sister Aloysius that they should take "the boys" out for ice cream and on camping trips in order to modernize the Catholic school. Cullingford observes that Flynn's proposal injects the specter of the pedophile—ice cream and camping trips are readily interpretable as grooming tactics.[124] But the more fundamental question, as obvious as it is unasked, is why, in this coed school, are ice cream and camping "boy" privileges? Who is mentoring the girls, mirroring/modeling subjectivity for them? Earlier in the film, Sister Aloysius charges Sister James to keep one of her more flirtatious female students "intact" until graduation. The girl's sexuality is rendered a threat to her future, and adults are tasked to guard her against her own desire. Throughout the film, we see boys and men move—get out of line, act up, play basketball, break things, eat rare, red meat. Girls mostly sit still and look pretty or dignified, occasionally expressing an unremarkable desire.[125] All of this might cavalierly be dispensed with as postwar, prelib gender roles from which we late moderns have ethically graduated, but as *Thirteen* and *Superbad* help evidence, peremption—its contemporary manifestations, felt ramifications, and elicited resistances—is gender asymmetric. Uncontrolled disqualifications of possibility take varied but nonetheless gender-patterned forms.

Thirteen: Perempted by Absence

Tracy Freeland (Evan Rachel Wood), *Thirteen's* thirteen-year-old white protagonist, enters seventh grade as a seemingly socially adjusted and appropriately attractive teenager, but placed low on a hierarchy of coolness and beauty she has only just encountered. Tracy befriends queen bee Evie Zamora (Nikki Reed) by sharing stolen money to shop for low-cut jeans, midriff-baring tops, makeup, and shoes. This friendship apparently initiates Tracy's free fall into drugs, sexual precocity and promiscuity, anorexia, and unbridled anger—a fall that occurs with terrifying, terrorizing speed. But background information reveals the bitterness, sadness, and confusion that Tracy harbored before Evie. Tracy's resentment travels fast but discriminately and oedipally: to her mother Mel (Holly Hunter), a recovering alcoholic hairdresser who has little time to hear Tracy's poetry; to her mother's boyfriend Brady (Jeremy Sisto), who shares a history of substance abuse; to her father (D. W. Moffett), whose unspecified corporate job (it has something to do with NASA, but "he might as well be on the fucking moon," as far as Tracy is concerned) absents him from the family.

Thirteen is about crowding, and not in any solidaristic way, like a youth subculture or a worker's collective or even Facebook.[126] Rooms and homes are cluttered with things and people; kids and dogs are sleeping in the same bed; self-eroding commodities and sexist advertisements swamp the screen; the mother's boyfriend occupies the shared bathroom, his clothes occupy the dryer; camera shots zoom in too close. We are as trapped as Tracy feels. Her downward spiral from "straight A" tween to drugged delinquent entails as well a crowding in of Tracy's readily penetrable body: she snorts, imbibes, performs oral sex, gets "poked" and pierced. Excruciatingly, Tracy cuts herself—first with a scissors, then a straight-edge razor. Cutting reveals (for her mother) by epidermalizing that Tracy is in pain. If Donald Miller is crowded out by narrative, Tracy Freeland is crowded in— by commodities, neighbors, unsorted clutter, and corporeal incursions of all kinds.

Given all this crowdedness from all these directions, it might seem peculiar to insist that what *Thirteen* demonstrates is peremption by *absence*— withdrawal, unavailability, cultural, psychical, and material impoverishment. But what all these disturbances ultimately dramatize are the disturbances of which Tracy is deprived: a lifeworld that is materially and psychically buoying rather than attritional; nontoxic affiliation; caretakers not chained so unforgivingly to labor.

Unlike *Doubt,* though, young sex is not a big problem in *Thirteen,* despite the film's surface of moral panic around white girlhood under the metastasizing precariousness of neoliberalism. I first describe the "sex" scenes in *Thirteen,* because these scenes, and critics' misreading of them, clarify that it is not sex but social structures in proximity to sex that perempt Tracy. But if sex is not the perempting problem, what is? Tracy's father is unsure, which further reveals the ways (sexual) harm against the young subject is not always actionable, not always translatable into the juridical.[127] The best way to perceive the contours of this gendered peremption is to catalog the ways Tracy resists it: through racial appropriation and cutting. These strategies, though, grow Tracy nowhere, and Tracy's mother ultimately must override her daughter's "subjective interest," cutting, to secure her objective ones.

Young Sex Is Not a Big Problem

In "Irreconcilable Feminisms and the Construction of a Cultural Memory of Virginity's Loss: À ma soeur! and Thirteen," Carol Siegel offers a broadside of Thirteen for the retrograde messages it delivers about girls, women, and mothers, as well as for its missing analysis of structural inequalities in the twenty-first-century United States. Siegel and other film critics suggest that Thirteen informs its audience that young girls are undone by sex and that sex initiates girls into patterns of reckless undoing.[128]

It strikes me that Thirteen is indifferent to the consequences of young sex, emphasizing other forms of gendered coercion and disadvantage irreducible to blow jobs or same-sex sexual experimentation, and therefore irreducible to the question did she consent, yes or no? Rather than demonizing individual girls and women, as Siegel believes, the film textures inequality through the performance of pained bodies and undirected emotion.[129] The film wedges open a site for young female sexual curiosity, but critics of the film by and large claim the film performs the contrary.

There are three "sex scenes" that involve Tracy: Tracy makes out with Evie to practice for her hook-up with their popular classmate, Javi (Charles Duckworth), although this "practice" edges toward the noninstrumental; Tracy hooks up with Javi; and Tracy and Evie attempt a threesome with the neighbor, Luke (Kip Pardue), a white, toned lifeguard in his twenties.

For Tracy and Evie, sex is not a terribly entangling predicament, although gender is—in part because its norms are so commoditized and the girls have such little money. Sex and pleasure are problems for the adults of the film, who, unlike the girls, must care for dependents, making pleasure a problem of priority. There is only a little room spatially and temporally for Mel, the mother, to wrest her pleasure, and that pleasure is interrupted by Tracy's demands. Figuring out sex and pleasure amid single motherhood is a practice of ongoing negotiations. By contrast, kissing one's same-sex best friend, performing oral sex on one's new boyfriend, and trying to score with a man in his twenties are not prima facie discombobulating or even terribly momentous for these girls (Figure 10).

Figure 10. Young sex is not a big problem. *Thirteen* (2003).

One evidentiary slice of nontrauma is the direction of action in the sex scenes. Tracy spends many of the nonsex scenes of the film being poked, prodded, punctured, and penetrated—by piercings, scissors, blades, her mother, and bullies. In the sex scenes, where we would anticipate violations and penetrations, Tracy commands the action, or learns to. Tracy confidently kisses Evie as they roll on the floor together; she puts a beer bottle to Javi's lips and undoes his belt buckle, as she first imitates Evie's movements (Evie is with a boyfriend, too), but then takes her own initiative; finally, and again imitatively (but here sartorially), Tracy makes out with Luke as both girls caress his leg.

Siegel and others see different dynamics in these scenes. Of Tracy's fellatio, Siegel comments, "oral sex is presented as something to be avoided, not because it brings risk of sexually transmitted diseases, but because it is dangerous in some mysterious, unarticulated, and thus naturalized way"— except there is no filmic evidence to suggest the sex is mysteriously dangerous.[130] Kathleen Karlyn suggests that Tracy performs oral sex on Javi at his persistence.[131] Her proof, it would appear, is that Tracy reports to Evie that "it tasted kinda nasty." But to read Tracy's dissatisfaction with the taste of semen as nonconsent is to disallow the prospect of nonharmful young heterosexual female desire at exactly the moment that it presents itself, or narrates itself, since young sex cannot legally be screened.[132] Javi does not coerce Tracy, and there is no suggestion he would. Predatory male desire is not in the film:[133] a close-up of Javi's unsure eyes brings us to an innocence that is rarely accorded to the black teen boy. In *Doubt*, Donald Miller's effeminacy marks him both noninnocent (queer) and also nonpredatory; in *Thirteen*, Javi's innocence is the invitation to the scene of sex, the vehicle for young black male heterosexuality to arrive as an unthreatening prospect for Tracy.

Postfellatio, aglow from a candle,[134] Tracy dreams aloud that prejudice would dissolve if everyone married interracially. Of course, no marriages, just blowjobs, have occurred, but her appeal is not simply naive. Rather, in encountering her own pleasure, she can, for the first and only time in the film, imagine a future, if heteronormative.[135]

What I take to be the film's deliberate nonchalance on interracial sex, Siegel and Karlyn interpret as reactionary. Here is Karlyn:

> The film suggests that for girls like Evie and Tracy, having sex with non-
> white men has less to do with rebelling against racism than with making a

"fashion statement" and appropriating the "coolness" of hip hop and other forms of black culture now reigning in youth-oriented fashion and music.[136]

And Siegel:

> The young men who pursue the girls are almost all not only African-American but gotten up in threatening gang-style attire. Once the girls attempt to seduce a white boy, who almost gives in to their seductive posturing but then catches himself and rejects them because of his fear of being charged with statutory rape, or perhaps even out of a moral desire to obey the law. Dark-skinned boys in the film lack such impulses, freely taking advantage of whatever girls offer them.[137]

Why is it so hard for us to look at these scenes and see: Tracy is enjoying sex, or at least learning how she might?[138] The black boys are objects of desire neither to credential the girls' antiracism nor for the girls to appropriate coolness. These boys are playful and *not* threatening. Nor are the boys wearing "gang-style attire," unless we assume that any black, underprivileged male sartorial style is always already equivalent to gang-wear. The "white boy" Siegel mentions is twenty-something, and the black boys are Tracy and Evie's schoolmates. So it is age difference, not racial difference, which here differentiates impulse control. The sentence structure of Siegel's "the young men who pursue the girls" is "man fucks woman; subject verb object."[139] But Tracy and Evie arrange the date, initiate the sex, and want to experiment with sex and pleasure (if not without betrayal).

But not all sex is benign in *Thirteen*. The harnessing of sex abuse's perlocutionary power delimits the film's otherwise indifference to or even weak encouragement of sexual discovery. Tracy and Evie's strategic deployment of sex abuse talk seems to confirm James Kincaid's thesis that sex abuse is lodged irrevocably in the gothic form: when "predators" are no longer viable, uncomplicated repositories of evil, the sex abuse story turns on itself, and we accuse the accusers.[140] Evie stingingly calls Luke a "fucking pervert" after he rejects the girls' advances; Tracy calls her mom a "child abuser" when she asks Tracy to wait for the bathroom; finally, Evie and Tracy report to Tracy's mother that Evie was sexually abused by her uncle, in the hopes that this information will convince Mel to let Evie move in. Evie and Tracy, villainous, no longer victims, exploit the powerful effects the sex abuse narrative compels. However, this last exchange among Tracy,

Evie, and Mel begins to disrupt the gothic form, challenging Kincaid's thesis while taking up his call to "change" or complicate "the stories."[141]

Anticipating Mel's hesitation to Evie's move-in, Tracy sensationally announces that Evie was abused by her uncle. Evie corroborates: her uncle put things inside her and threw her into a fire, she says pleadingly. "You could maybe even save me," begs Evie. An earlier scene reveals Evie's bruising, and a newspaper clipping Mel has discovered later confirms the avuncular abuse. Critics of the film miss this evidence, doubting Evie.[142] The truth of the abuse does not exonerate the manipulative force of its deployment, but the truth textures, rather than flattens, Evie's character: we understand why Evie grows so attached, daughter-like, to Mel, and we see more clearly why Evie's self-validation is organized around sexual and social appreciation from others, appreciation that is too often distracted, fleeting, or nonexistent.

Evie's testimony to abuse is heartfelt, earnest, manipulative, self-serving, and true. *Thirteen* complicates the weight of sex abuse origins, but the film is also cognizant of this rhetorical force for mothers and families when the little girl is its object. Evie is not fabricating, but neither is she confessing an interiorized wound that is now her self after the fact of male predation. *Thirteen* asks us neither to discount the formative consequences of child sex abuse nor to grant it epistemological or political primacy. Like Evie, the film is unsure how psychically damaging the abuse was or is. There are myriad other obstacles affecting Tracy and Evie. They are barraged with billboard messages and advertisements telling them to be skinnier and prettier ("Beauty is truth," teaches a recurring bus stop advertisement), to wear less clothing, or to wear clothing with tags like "I wanna bone" (Figure 11).[143] What they learn from the world, like too many of the girls for whom they are metonymic (and, admittedly, hyperbolic), is how to be available rather than agentive.[144] The adult women of *Thirteen* (Mel, Mel's hairdressing clients, Evie's caretaker) bleach and burn themselves and knife away aging skin. The more they absent themselves the more they are worth, both as service economy laborers and as objects of men's desire.[145] These injuries, unlike Tracy's cutting or Evie's abuse, are not plotted as spectacle but as routine and uneventful. So although Evie and Tracy manage to direct their curiosities and desires in the scenes of sex (and return from sex unharmed), they are open territory to commoditized sexualizing. Sexual objectification, as prerequisite for social intelligibility (and economic survival, middle-school popularity, etc.), preempts sexual subjectivity.[146]

Figure 11. Learning how to be available rather than agentive. *Thirteen.*

The recitation of child sexual abuse and male predation potentially overwhelms attention—Mel's, the viewer's—to a broader, deeper constellation of agency, desire, and constrained relations. *Thirteen* moves from—without abandoning—the static problem of predation to the dynamic problems of relation. It queries how material and affective scarcity imbricates with heteronormativity to pressure, pervert, and perempt Tracy's and Evie's relations with each other, with boys, and with their caretakers. It leaves open whether Evie's uncle or mass-mediated messages to girls, whether sex abuse by predators or gendered effacement by the social, are more responsible for the deterioration of these girls' lives.[147]

Although *Thirteen* diegetically displaces sex as "the problem" of gendered adolescence, sex reappears as "the problem" in the production of the film. A child welfare officer was on the set of *Thirteen* for the duration of production, as were the parents of the teenage girls. Hiding behind the couch in the almost-sex scene with the lifeguard, the child welfare officer instructed the girls not to touch the area too close to the lifeguard's nipples. The girls were permitted to slide their hands up his shorts but not unbutton them.[148] So too, *Thirteen* was rated "R" by the Motion Picture Association of America, so that teenagers themselves had restricted access to a film reflecting on and critiquing their own social/sexual circumstances.[149] Teen sex is for adult audiences. The obsessive, pornographic focus on what the child can see or touch eclipses the very processes of gendered socialization *Thirteen* foregrounds. The legal supervision of the film redounds by fiat: sex harms the child.

"What's the Problem?"

Midway through *Thirteen*, Tracy's father arrives to stave off what is by now the evident anticlimax, Tracy's emotional, physical implosion. As an absent parental figure whose central function is the provision of child support, and as the masculine authorial voice of dispassionate but firm reason, the father is the film's closest symbol of legal intervention.[150]

The fatherly, legalistic intervention fails blisteringly. Things sour immediately: the father tells Mel that Tracy cannot live with him; the father informs an unsurprised Tracy that he has to renege on his upcoming plans with her, but then confirms plans with his son to go surfing together, betraying his investment in overseeing his son's but not his daughter's maturation;[151] he speaks of Tracy as a "client" on an interrupting cell phone call, signaling his marketization of familial care; he exits quickly and uncomfortably, effecting no character or narrative redirection.

His mantra, "What's the problem?" is the most revealing component of the scene and tells us about the inadequacy of either juridical epistemology or juridical intervention in relation to the vulnerable, constrained, sexualized girl. He asks Tracy's mother, "What's the problem?" and repeats to Tracy, "What's the problem? What's going on?" He is unanswered. Angered, he asks his son Mason to explain the problem "in a nutshell." Mason sighs disappointingly, flaps his hands in the air, and walks away.

One part of the problem, as we saw, was sexual objectification as a substitute for sexual subjectivity. Here are other related dimensions: Tracy wants outlets for sexual and social exploration with no educative role models other than Evie; she wants to be sexy in Los Angeles environs that make sexiness synonymous with accessorized starvations; she wants maternal care from her mother who is too taxed providing material care (and trying herself to squeeze in moments of intimacy and pleasure); and Tracy wants space but also sociality, neither of which are on offer in Tracy's small, rundown house or in her harshly hierarchized school. Tracy is not "acting out," but acting to find something or feel something for which there is no good aspirational image or buoying lifeworld.

There is no one problem, or no problem concisely articulable, and that is the problem. One might want to say the problem is the problem of addiction, or the problem of adolescence under conditions of material scarcity, or the problem of gender under conditions of unrelenting hetero-sexuality, or the problem of a friend's bad influence. But the problem is all of these and none of them, a whirlwind of converging forces for which there is no origin the father, like law, can uproot and solve by fiat. "It's happening so fast," taglines the film, and it is both the rapidity and multi-causality of Tracy's deterioration that make her a bad subject for the law. The combination of crowdedness and absence, untraceable to a singular source, preempts the possibility for the nontoxic articulation of a girl's uncongealed longings for undetermined objects—what in the idiom of the last chapter was called sexual autonomy.

Navigating Peremption, Growing Nowhere: Racial Appropriation and Cutting

Racial appropriation and cutting are the conduits *Thirteen* offers for Tracy to navigate her way out of crowded conditions and absented relations (the phenomena that never fully congeal into a singular "problem"). Both, in different ways, are phenomenological ammunition for Tracy to propel herself out of childhood (racial appropriation) and to counteract the affec-tive residual of withdrawal or betrayal (cutting). Both strategies—although not executed consciously enough to be called strategies—fail. They grow Tracy nowhere, engendering an invitation to subjection, not subjectivity.[152]

At first blush, *Thirteen* appears banally racist: racial otherness throws into relief and into crisis Tracy's white innocence. The story begins with thirteen-year-old Tracy accompanied by model minority, Asian American prepubescent girlfriends who are study buddies; the story ends with Tracy threatened by menacing, butch black teenagers, their speech affected "black" and "poor" ("you's nasty"). In the time between, she has been seduced away from innocence by the Edenic "Evie," a Latina whose booty-shaking and skin-revealing attire bespeak a mythically brown, primal, seducing sexuality that neutralizes ascriptions of childhood innocence.[153]

If we bracket the racial tropes, though, we can read something else: racial difference models nothing. Racial difference fails to deliver what Tracy wants from it, a way to look or be otherwise. The racial diversity of the film may alternate between the benign and stereotypical, but in neither case is it an appropriable provision for growing up, sideways, or somewhere. An hour into the film, Tracy dons tight, high hair braids, not quite cornrows, but this cosmetic change only amps up the leers and catcalls from the men on Melrose Avenue; racialized props for Tracy are not propulsive. She looks sexy as she saunters down the street in her new hairdo, low-cut jeans, and skimpy crop top, but then rapidly finds herself spiraling in a garishly green-lit, drug-induced stupor, frantically searching for the absconded Evie, until she once again bitterly returns to the confining conditions of her mother's overcrowded home.

In fact, when racial difference gets closest to offering a future it offers instead "reproductive futurism," a political, hygienic fantasy of a better future governed by collective attachment to the presumptively best interests of children, the modus operandi of contemporary politics as such, according to Lee Edelman.[154] Tracy's sexual encounter with Javi provides the raw material for possibly imagining a future of herself as a growing sexual subject, but that possibility is squandered for a depersonalized vision of a racially indecipherable child: "You know, if everybody married someone from a different race ... then in one generation there would be no prejudice."[155] Tracy unwittingly substitutes a desexualized, vapid vision of future racial sameness, a future that is uninhabitable but also uninteresting, for an affirmation of a present, personal, sexual pleasure (Figure 12). Replying to Tracy's ethereal reflection, Evie caresses her, asking, "So, you had a good time?" It is as if Evie must remind Tracy to remain in the present, to allow her pleasure to be felt as pleasure and not deferred into a desexualized heteronormative fantasy whose alibi is racial equality.

The fantasy of the racially indecipherable subject produced through heterosexual reproduction also appeared over two decades ago on the cover of the 1993 *Time* magazine issue, "The New Face of America," its promise of racial fusion dispelled by Lauren Berlant and Michael Warner.[156] Berlant and Warner call attention to the unnoticed but operative

Figure 12. Tracy imagines a future of racial sameness. *Thirteen.*

role "national heterosexuality" plays in a sanitized vision of a multicultural America that obliterates its unjust racial and immigrant histories while wedding citizenship to the metaphor of family rather than public contestation.[157] What Tracy Freeland magnifies for us is the internalization of that projection by the young girl subject as a nonaspiring aspiration for a future that is not hers, but the nation's. Unwilling but more likely unable[158] to articulate the nascent pleasure she discovers in heterosexual sexuality, she defers to a more digestible, defensible fantasy of nonprejudice guaranteed through heterosexual reproduction.

If racial appropriation grows Tracy nowhere, self-injury diminishes the very subjectivity and autonomy she wants to cultivate.

Tracy cuts herself when Brady, Mel's boyfriend, returns to the Freeland house. After his arrival, Tracy flashes back to Brady's home-wrecking overdose. She later cuts herself when she feels abandoned by her mother and Evie. Tracy directs a scissors to her arm and blots the blood with cloth as the camera zooms out above her, capturing her sated detachment from disappointment. Finally, Tracy cuts herself when her brother tells her he "can't wait" until Tracy is kicked out of the house to go live with their father. Tracy believes her mother does not want her, and now it seems nobody does. Evie has ditched her, as have her former friends. She is inundated by unlove and opts for a razor blade. She cuts too deep; there is too much blood. She falls to the floor, moaning, as the scene fades. We see her the next morning running limply behind her gym class, almost translucently pale, massaging her scarred arm.

There is plenty of research on cutting, its etiology and objectives. Presciently, there is one historical observation and one contemporary point of contention to relay. The observation: cutting used to be understood by mental health experts as a "cry for help" that typically indexed a suicidal tendency in the patient.[159] This is not necessarily so. Cutters, mostly girls and women, conceal their cuts and their cutting behavior, often wearing long shirts, like Tracy.[160] The point of contention: there is debate as to whether cutting is a pathological, compulsive behavior particular to emotionally unbalanced persons, or a prevalent phenomenon that might be better classified as a voluntaristic, deviant strategy of realizing relief or "reconfirm[ing] the presence of one's body."[161]

Why might Tracy cut herself? Not as a cry for help. Tracy's "cries"—for her father to stay, for her mother's boyfriend to leave—are enunciated clearly. But her cutting is neither impulsive nor fully voluntaristic either. It is a secreted embarrassment, neither a badge of honor nor solidarity with other angry young girls.

Tracy cuts not because circumstances are out of control but because she is too controlled, she is crowded in, materially—for example, by the family friend's child and dog who sleep in her bed—and psychically, as when her mother and her friend leave her. Withdrawal is peremptory, leaving Tracy without interlocutors to articulate either her frustrations or her desires.[162] She cuts when she feels abandoned, when she senses a loss of relations and a desire to recapture them.

Tracy and Evie are fastened to and terrified by the logic of heterosexual and affective scarcity, in which lust and love are depleting resources that if spent on one girl will be lost on the other.[163] We see this in the wanting gazes that travel across the screen: Evie stares at Javi when he pursues Tracy; Tracy stares at Evie when she kisses Luke. It is in the absence of, and desire for, any reliable, intimate, friend or familial relations to make life more navigable that Tracy cuts. She cuts when she is remanded by neglect or by will to a cramped position.

Tracy's last name, "Freeland," points out Karlyn, may refer not only to Tracy's frustrated hopes to be unencumbered, but also to the current U.S. neoliberal economic landscape that has made working-class folks like Mel and her daughter ever more susceptible to the fluctuations of capital (subprime homes are bellying up in their neighborhood).[164] Distinctly, we might interpret "free land" as *terra nova,* the colonial myth of an uninhabited new land awaiting both conquest and cultivation. The borders of Tracy's body and bedroom are continually breached. Sometimes she likes the prodding and sometimes she loathes it, and it is hard to tell the difference between liking and loathing because conquest and cultivation come in the same form (like a priest with a magnetic ballerina). But the risks of feeling something new are disproportionately borne and internalized by Tracy as a girl subject, rather than displaced outward toward alternative intimacies, which, as we will see, the boys of *Superbad* are entitled to imagine but not fully realize.[165]

"I'll die for you, but I won't leave you alone right now": Peremption and Preference

Tracy's body, bedroom, and home are all punctured by disruptions, whether in the form of family friends who sleep over, blows to the head from Evie as they huff ("hit me!" she cries, but then gets hit too hard, her temple bleeding, repaired not by medical aid but by makeup, replacing one flesh wound with another),[166] or self-cutting. These disruptions and perturbances range from unannounced and unexpected to insisted upon and self-inflicted, but *consent* does not cleanly demarcate the harmful from the benign or the harmful from the beneficial.

In one of the last breachings of Tracy, Evie's caretaker Brooke (Deborah Kara Unger), botched from elective plastic surgery, peels Tracy's sleeve back to show Mel Tracy's scars. "None of your business you fucking Frankenstein!" cries Tracy. This is requisite moral relativizing—is Tracy's arm cutting any worse than Brooke's facial cutting, or any worse than Mel's hairdressing products that burn her clients? But there is a more powerful implication. Tracy has no one and no thing to aspire toward that is not already marred; no figures to guide her somewhere that is productively, not destructively, disorganizing; no horizons that do not disfigure her.[167] Tracy is oppressed, depressed, and angry, none of which reflects gender-neutral teen ennui but rather symptomize enervating sociopolitical arrangements.[168]

Mel finally intervenes on Tracy's self-destruction, spurred by the revelation of her cutting. No longer concerned either with appeasing her daughter's capriciousness or acquiescing to her rage, Mel hugs Tracy, draws back her sleeve, and kisses her scars. Tracy cries, falling to the kitchen floor (Figure 13):

TRACY: Get off of me. I hate you. Stop!

MEL: . . . I'll die for you, but I won't leave you alone right now. . . . I want you here with me. You're my heart. I'll make it right.

TRACY: It can never be right. Get off of me. . . . Don't hold me! Don't! Stop![169]

But for a merciless blue, all color is drained from the characters and the kitchen. Tracy's voice falls to a whisper; she barely protests her mother's hug between her sobs. The final scene brings us to Tracy's bedroom, where she and her mother sleep, embracing. A dreamscape shows Tracy circling on a playground merry-go-round, and a varied palette refills the screen. Tracy appears flesh-colored and ebullient, but the metaphor remains ambiguous.[170] Has Mel returned Tracy to a less damaging but still risky (and therefore fun) girlhood, or has the centrifugal force of self-injury hurled her into an unredeemed future, which is to say a paralyzing present?

Mel holds Tracy; she does not send her to rehab or outline any other twelve-step plan of action. We have no idea what happens next. But the hug, unconsented, signals that Mel is superintending her daughter, refusing to let Tracy, who is otherwise untethered, self-injuring, and foundering, go. In this moment, it is ethically necessary for Mel to override the desires of her daughter ("Get off of me!"). Such a supposition might come as little surprise to any parent or guardian, but what I am trying to show is

Figure 13. "I won't leave you alone right now." *Thirteen.*

that Mel's intervention is ethically necessary not because Tracy is a "child," that is, incapable of consent or self-governance. Rather, what *Thirteen* so carefully catalogs is that Mel's unwanted presence, at this moment, prevents more than it performs peremption. Tracy can and does consent, desire, and deliberate (if often only to conform better, the telltale sign of mainstream, filmic, feminine adolescence).[171] And it is precisely to secure Tracy's becoming—her sexual and social adventures, her figuring out relations and relationality—that Mel does not let her daughter continue onward, downward. It is because self-injury, to the degree inflicted here, disqualifies or "quashes" so many social and relational possibilities that Mel overrides Tracy's wishes. From this perspective, what authorizes intervention is not solely Tracy's age. *Thirteen* is not about the natural impulsiveness of teenagers, but about the ways the zero sum logic of heterosexual value, violent beauty norms, and material inequalities are asymmetrically absorbed and therefore mismanaged by young subjects. When that mismanagement (e.g., cutting) so evidently undermines the subject's flourishing and her capacity for figuring new and varied relational possibilities, it is perhaps not only warranted but also required that others act in and for her interest.

I am not hashing out here a full-blown theory of paternalism/parentalism.[172] Instead, I am suggesting that peremption offers a different way to think about restricting and cultivating (young, sexual) subjects, where neither consent nor age warrants—by themselves and/or as equivalences for one another—ethical primacy. Throughout the film, Mel encourages Tracy to eat more and questions the pornographic messages on Tracy's newly revealing clothing. But Mel neither forces her daughter to eat nor dresses her more conservatively, conduct that might arguably "track the [child's] interests according to standard ideas," but that would nonetheless be impermissible, not simply because Tracy is capable of decision making but because such conduct would hinder Tracy from figuring out possibilities, what Mill called "experiments of living," however misguided they might be.[173] When Mel refuses to release Tracy in this penultimate scene, the refusal is justified not because "mothers know best," but because some experiments in living, like relentless drug intake or deeper and deeper cutting, evidently and intensively disqualify future possibilities—relational, social, and sexual.[174]

To care about Tracy and her thriving, sexual or otherwise, entails caring about more than age, age difference, and consent. It entails caring about microscopic and macroscopic conditions that perempt her and her ambitions, that make most but not all of her aspirations attritional. Despite its continual spectacles of gendered downfall, *Thirteen* refuses to reproduce girlhood in crisis terms and temporalities. The sheer volume of crises—snorting, cutting, stealing, familial fighting—compound to negate what they appear to prove. Girlhood is not a series of hazards, each to be discretely quelled. Rather, for Tracy, metonymic, girlhood is the angered mismanagement of realizing and confronting diminished horizons. Things might get better, but they might not. Tracy might grow somewhere, she might discover avenues of self-exploration and self-expansion that are not self-injurious, at least not as much. Tracy's mother is ultimately there for her, but so much else is not: friends who are not also racked by the fear of love and lust as zero sum; worlds to be sexual that do not demand self-mutilation; a future for her beyond an antiracist futurism sealed by heterosexual reproduction.

Superbad: Propelled (and Perempted) by Incompetent Masculinities

In the previous chapter I cited studies finding that boys are less often harmed by sex at a young age and/or across wide age differences than are girls.[175] These studies' authors argue that what may explain some of this gender difference is gendered socialization. Part (but only part) of what sex feels like has to do with what we are told, implicitly, explicitly, and gender-differentially, sex should feel like. It is neither gay exceptionalism nor embodied sexual difference that best explains differences in young people's self-reported sexual experiences, but a sense (or lack) of sexual subjectivity, forged in the interstice between activity and context.[176]

In this regard, *Superbad* is more about *propulsion* than it is about *peremption*. Adolescent boys overcome impediments rather than succumb to them. The film follows three dorky white boys as they are "guided," not "blocked," through a series of obstacles that begin at the close of the school day (and high school, synecdochally) and end at a house party. Best friends Evan (Michael Cera) and Seth (Jonah Hill) aspire to impress and have sex with Becca (Martha MacIsaac) and Jules (Emma Stone), respectively. Evan is skinny, shy, and uncomfortably earnest. Seth is overweight, crude, and mannerless. Fogell (Christopher Mintz-Plasse), tiny, voice-cracking, rounds out the trio as the most unrelenting loser. Charged with the responsibility of purchasing booze for the party, Fogell acquires a fake driver's license, according to which he is Hawaiian, twenty-five, and named McLovin. The liquor store patronized by the unconvincingly adultified McLovin is robbed. From here begin two parallel journeys. In one, McLovin rides in the backseat of the cop car driven by officers Michaels (Seth Rogen) and Slater (Bill Hader), learning shortcuts to and compromises with manhood. In the other, Evan and Seth ride off with a strange man to a different party in the hopes of stealing alcohol. The adults at this party are reckless, violent, and oversexed, threats the boys dodge or neutralize. Escaping the party, they reunite with McLovin, and the two journeys braid as they arrive at the proper (read: age-appropriate) house party. Seth is too drunk to have sex with Jules, Becca is too drunk to have sex with Evan, and McLovin is interrupted midcoitus by the return of the bumbling officers. The following day, Evan and Seth reconvene at the mall where they run into Jules and Becca. Girls in tow, Seth and Evan walk off in opposite directions with their opposite-sex interests. Both are hesitant to separate from one another, but recover confidence as the camera pans out to the mall and its consumer traffic, a wide shot sanctioning their paths from boyhood homosociality to young adult heterosexuality.

My reading of *Superbad,* juxtaposed against *Thirteen,* tracks subtle, indirect ways (white, middle-class) boys may be emboldened—gender socialized—to feel agentive in proximity to sex and intimate sociality. Like in *Thirteen,* young sex is not a big problem. Here, though, predatory adults reemerge, but as foils to vindicate rather than vitiate boys' (hetero)sexual discovery. Unlike in *Thirteen,* law (and its authorial figures) is lubricating, its knowing absence and selective withdrawals propelling, not inapposite. And where racial appropriation transports *Thirteen*'s Tracy nowhere but to an emptied futurism, racial appropriation is the main discursive vehicle for the *Superbad* boys to grow somewhere. I draw attention to the ways law's lubrication and racial imitation are propulsive not to offer them as unproblematic solutions to peremption, as if all would be well if only white girls could successfully "act black" too. I instead want to prod thinking about when and under what conditions discursive repertoires cultivate or frustrate relational possibilities.

Still, the boys of *Superbad,* despite the social affirmation of their (white, middle-class) boyness, are perempted. What perempts them is neither the violence of masculinist competition nor homophobia (although a healthy portion of each grounds much of the narrative), but the impossibility of male–male intimacy that is neither homosexual nor homosocial nor homophobic. *Doubt*'s Donald was overwritten, too scripted by scandal. Seth and Evan are too unscripted (which does not mean they are rudderless). But despite being perempted by social scriptlessness, a trace of their intimacy, the unsure beginnings of its articulation, is found in the series of fantasies shared among the unlikely male heroes.

Predation as Vindication

Superbad normalizes rather than neutralizes young male heterosexual desire by juxtaposing it against a cast of predatory, pathetic adults.[177] But while *Superbad* ingratiates the boys' sexuality by locating predation elsewhere, it also confers upon the boys enough social dexterity and comedic capital to maneuver themselves out of any danger.

The hapless stranger-predator, "Francis the driver" (Joe Lo Truglio), offers to take Evan and Seth to a house party, at which he promises there will be booze for them to bring to their crushes. Seth and Evan agree, unknowingly committing themselves to a party of burned-out adults in which fights break out, cocaine is snorted, Evan is forced by drug addicts to sing for them, and the girlfriend of the surly host menstruates on Seth's pants.

As they enter Francis's car, Evan hesitates: "This guy's fucking creepy, man. Look at him." Seth is unconvinced: "What? He looks like a guy. That's what guys look like." Francis is the problem of the predator in the public imagination. He is both fucking creepy and looks just like any other guy, so danger is distributed across all male strangers and yet also identified in its particularity: it turns out he is a creep, one that motors the narrative. While all strange adult men may be closet offenders, because all guys who look like guys look like offenders, Francis the driver vacuums up this potentially metastasizing danger. Light under the steering wheel (campily) haunts Francis's face, as Evan and Seth rebuff his offers to "sit up front" (Figure 14). Attempting to develop a rapport, he asks, "You guys on MySpace, or ..." the question convicting him as a certifiable creep. MySpace is a social network site initially marketed to teens, whose adult members were considered sexually suspect.

Seth and Evan's ambitions to score alcohol and score girls are pacified as harmless kids' stuff against this predatory but pathetic character. Seth's earlier appeal to Evan, "You know when you hear girls saying, like, 'Oh, I was so shitfaced last night. I shouldn't have fucked that guy.' We could be that mistake!" looks less like an incitement to date rape and more like the ordinary adventures of boyhood. (It might be more apt to say that what the predatory adult helps make possible is the funniness of this proposition rather than the ordinariness of its eventuation.)

Figure 14. Evan and Seth rebuff Francis, the driver. *Superbad* (2007).

Francis, on account of past transgressions, is beaten up by the host of the party. The scene echoes the police brutalization of the men on *To Catch a Predator*, although here violence is more comical because more self-commenting—the host kicks Francis "right in the nads"—and more didactic: direct your desires to proper objects (college, same-age girls) or imperil your testicles.

The teens' house party, their drunkenness, and their beleaguered attempts to lose their virginity are digestible, read as proper, against the potentially predatory Francis and the social space he introduces to the boys. The Latina-looking woman who menstruates on Seth's pant leg cannot self-govern, nor can the party's Italian-ish host, who pummels whatever men are in the vicinity. The lot of ethnically tinted characters demonstrates the threat of adulthood as well as the kinds of adults that the boys should not become. These adults are perpetual adolescents—not in the normatively desirable way I've been theorizing, but as stereotype: unbalanced, impulsive. Their becomingness is unbecoming, and they are a threat to themselves and anyone nearby, especially teen boys.

However, the danger is not all that dangerous, because the boys are self-assured and socially dexterous. Evan atonally but precociously performs The Guess Who's "These Eyes" to a circle of druggies, subduing any potential conflict.[178] And Seth, horrified by the blood on his pant leg, shouts, "You used my leg as a tampon!" Seth and Evan, it appears, are unharmed.

Regardless, the comparative scariness of a grown woman's menstrual blood, a grown man's fists, and cocaine subdues anything that might look like a problem later. The sex, or failed sex, that Evan, Seth, and McLovin pursue is acceptable, even encouraged, by its now established benignity. The point here, of course, is not that all the sex or almost-sex that ensues after the adult party, at the teen party, should be read as harmful, dangerous, bad, or bad for girls. Rather, the film parallels these two parties and their attendees in such a way that nothing sexually or gender-problematic *could* happen at the high school party. Young sex is not a big problem, but in this frame it never could be. The possibility is precluded by symbolically locating danger and threat elsewhere, and this maneuver representationally reifies the stratification of sexual harm and freedom that I have been objecting to as normatively misguided for youth, law, and sexual autonomy. As cultural prognosis, *boys will be boys* is not the inversion of *sex harms the child,* but a refortification of the adult/child binary, albeit with a different alibi.[179]

The near-traumas of the first three quarters of *Superbad* set up the ensuing young near-sex as harmless, certainly, but also as awkward, slapstick, and unsynchronized. Evan is disarmed by Becca's avowed desire. "I'm so wet right now," she drunkenly whispers, to which Evan uncomfortably musters, "Yeah, they said that would happen in health." (Interestingly, Becca is the most sexually confident character in *Superbad,* but her unselfconscious assertiveness is mostly written off as drunken and castrating, and therefore as testing ground for Evan to display that other virtue of manliness, forbearance.) McLovin is so overstimulated he must speechify the sex he is having in real time: "I got a boner! . . . It's in, oh my god it's in!" And Seth admits to Jules he wanted to get her drunk to have sex with her, only before passing out and falling into her face.

These boys fumble, say stupid things, overcompensate, and underperform. Yet these mistakes barely register as mistakes, and unlike Tracy's failed experiments in feeling new sensations, these mess-ups are far from disqualifying. They are misadventures of maturation, goofed explorations of possibility requisite for growing anywhere new. For Tracy and Evie, sex is, ironically, one of the few social loci where the feeling of aliveness is *unlinked* to the girls' attrition.[180] In a way, the sexual is a haven from the social (and "sexualization"). For Seth, Evan, and McLovin, the social is a series of alley-oops to their graceless (almost) sex. The sexual is buoyed by the social. Here, the phenomena that propel boys, as opposed to girls, are not the usual culprits: media representation, sexuality education, differential parental treatment, etc. More subtly, *Superbad* demonstrates how law's lubrication and racial appropriation ready the boys to grow somewhere.

Law as Lubricant

The first few lessons the skinny, pasty, whiny McLovin receives from the police officers include the following: the in-credibility of a black woman's testimony, the soul-sucking power of wives, and the femininity of Asian men. That is to say, he observes the privileges not only of law but also of white manhood and learns the rhetorics of ridicule and forms of exclusion on which that privilege produces itself. The cashier in the liquor store, Mindy (Erica Vittina Phillips), is the only black character in the film, and the officers mishear what she is saying, record the opposite of what she says, and then, insinuating that the robber sexually molested her, grope across the counter toward her breasts. After Mindy hurriedly exits, the officers turn their attention to McLovin. While they approve his one-word name ("that's bad ass"), they opine on a Vietnamese "man-lady" they arrested "who was legally named 'Fuck.'" Pretending to approve McLovin's ludicrous identification, they observe he is an organ donor. The officer too, we learn, is an organ donor, at his wife's insistence. "Women," even after you're dead, they warn McLovin, want to "tear your heart out."

The twist though—what makes the scene funny—is that the joke is on the officers, or the joke is the officers. Their blunderings, their witless delays, make obvious the blindness of a white dude worldview that pretends its universality.[181] While McLovin witnesses a black woman disbelieved and humiliated, we witness a deflation of police arrogance, of prejudicial idiocy that wields itself as fact-finding. And although this scene might be both satirical and, well, patriarchal, it confers upon McLovin, upon the young and nervous boy, different forms of status: pedagogic subject, proper addressee of the law, and the object of a didactic homosocial couple, the officers. McLovin is about to grow, not so much under the supervision of law as through its strategic incompetency and its selective nonenforcement.

En route to drop off McLovin at the house party, Officers Michaels and Slater are radioed in to restrain a disruptive homeless man at a bar. The "bum" acts up, and the officers are spectacularly unable to reel him in. "Stop him, McLovin!" yells Michaels as the bum crashes into McLovin, who, in high caricature feminine, shrieks and shields himself. McLovin does nothing impressive, but circumstances, kitchen obstacles, and slippery floors collaborate to make him a hero, as if he is responsible for felling the bum.

McLovin tumbles into a position of masculine achievement—he is primed by law's pullback. And his frail body, high voice, and gangly affect lengthen his distance from adulthood, but only to make his surmounting the gap more of an accomplishment. McLovin's innocence is propped up not as a blank slate to be hyperbolized or eroticized, but as the starting point to measure his growth. In this instance, the distance traveled—from socially awkward boy to still socially awkward but confident "bad-ass" nonvirgin—signals success, not violation.

A sexually ennobled McLovin arrives at the high school house party and swiftly wins over Nikola (Aviva), but at the moment of penetration, the officers enter the bedroom to kick out any partying teenagers. Remorseful for crimping this would-be rite of passage, Officer Michaels laments, "we should be guiding his cock, not blocking it." As the two cops and McLovin sit uncomfortably close together on the bed (see Figure 15; unacceptably close, were they Donald and Father Flynn), we learn the cops knew "the whole time" that McLovin was lying about his age, but they granted him a free ride anyway. "I guess we saw a bit of ourselves [in you]," says Slater, and then apologizes, "I'm really sorry that I blocked your cock."[182]

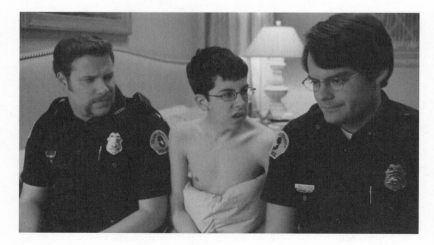

Figure 15. Guiding McLovin. *Superbad.*

Law's intentional withdrawal generates the possibility of sexual passage. This implicit admission that not all transgressions transgress equally encourages McLovin to venture outward.[183] The officers' identification with McLovin prefigures their relationship to him: role models, but as legal authorities who eschew law. The combination of identification, aspiration, and sanctioned outlawness catapults McLovin, but smoothly and safely, guiding his cock.[184]

As we have seen, sex law is all too often peremptory rather than promotional of young people's sexual autonomy. Kathryn Bond Stockton, in her reading of the sexual agency of *Lolita's* Lolita, proposes that the more apt analogue to the pedophilic yet often cruelly indifferent Humbert Humbert is the law itself, rather than Clare Quilty, Lolita's "preferred pedophile."[185] U.S. law in the 1950s did not recognize the personhood of the child let alone her or his sexual capacities or ambitions. Law is thus blind to Lolita and a threat to her flourishing.[186] *Thirteen* and *Superbad*, both produced half a century after *Lolita*, present addenda to Stockton's observation, gesturing toward qualifications of sexual and certainly racialized difference.[187] To Tracy, law is belated (in the form of the father), beside the point, juridical, prohibitory, but ineffectual (witness shoplifting, sex with the lifeguard). In the face of law, Tracy's objective is to not get caught. For McLovin, law is engendering, lubricating in its non- or selective-enforcement, pedagogic in its entreaty to homosociality.

Navigating Peremption, Growing Somewhere: Racial Appropriation (redux)

In *Giovanni's Room,* argues Mae Henderson, James Baldwin dons "racial drag" under the whiteness of its tragic protagonist, David.[188] It is only from a position of white manhood that Baldwin could launch his literary assault on the constraining, heteronormative[189] predicaments of postwar American masculinity. White American assumptions surrounding black men would have otherwise neutralized the critique of masculinity (and marital) norms.

An inverse racial costuming propels the white boys of *Superbad,* which exploits the stereotyped black hypermasculinity Baldwin might have been eschewing. Blackness, or the appropriation of historically (sometimes stereotypically) black music, humor, and style, drive the boys into adulthood.[190] Blackness indexes a manhood that is neither threatening nor overwhelming, but appreciable and approachable (on white boys). Blackness is everywhere in *Superbad* but for the almost total whiteness of the cast—the title, the 1970s funk soundtrack, the boys' stylized speech acts and body comportments.

The title of the film is taken from James Brown's classic "Super Bad" (1970), a funk ode to sensual manliness.[191] So confident is Brown's sexiness that he finds his own sexiness sexy; the song's nod to self-arousal runs alongside *Superbad*'s homoeroticism. Unlike James Brown, the clumsy, unsmooth trio that are *Superbad*'s white boys are anything but super bad. Titling the film *Superbad* wedges an interval between their dorkiness and adult, "black" coolness but makes it a surmountable interval to close or at least to narrow by film's end.

The soundtrack raises up (without calling it) racial difference as a proxy for surmountable age difference and figures acts of racial imitation as manliness. The boys ride the bus to the Four Tops' "Are You Man Enough?" (1973): "Are you man enough / Big and bad enough / Are you gonna let them shoot you down?"[192] The lyric fades on a shot of McLovin picking his nose (Figure 16). More than four decades prior, "Are You Man Enough" introduced Shaft in *Shaft in Africa* (1973). McLovin is not Shaft. The song's incongruity to the scene is its humor.

Yet these boys' journeys continue beyond the bus stop; they do not get "shot down." McLovin is ultimately heralded as more than "man enough," when later the cops allow him to stage resisting arrest in front of his classmates. The Motown lyric is a challenge but an eventual affirmation. If the

Figure 16. "Are you man enough?" *Superbad.*

black soundtrack works to buoy the boys into manhood, it also shortens the interval from the other direction, from adulthood to boyhood. Having kicked out all the teenagers at the house party, Officer Slater dances by himself—hip hop lite (or white)—on the living room floor (Figure 17), to The Coup's "Pork and Beef" (2001): "Don't trust the police / No justice no peace / They got me face down in the middle of the street." Again, the incongruence makes for the humor, but in this case more insidious since the humor neuters The Coup's political critique.[193] Slater has literally taken up the position of the vacated adolescents, closing the distance McLovin travels to meet him or be him.

When Jules asks Seth if he can secure a fake ID, he replies, "fo sho, fo sho . . . I'm gettin' that fo sho," but he overdoes it, embarrassing himself. Nonetheless, his "street talk" is an exercise by which he tries to assume and impress responsibility. For the first quarter of the film, Seth sports a T-shirt with an enlarged, goofy print of Richard Pryor's face. Seth's "mature" skill at puncturing "small talk" with startling vulgarity might find its progenitor in Pryor.

At the film's near close, we witness another act of racialized imitation, this one more successful. McLovin and the officers douse the police car in gasoline and light it on fire, and McLovin shoots a gun at it (Figure 18). His first shot overexcites him—he draws back, squeals. Now familiarized

Figure 17. Officer Slater closes the distance to manhood. *Superbad.*

Figure 18. McLovin unloads. *Superbad.*

with the kickback, he reestablishes authority: "Break yo' self fool!" he warns the anthropomorphized vehicle and, tilting the gun sideways, opens fire until drawing blanks.

We see a young white boy in an oversized, adult white dress shirt joyfully shooting at a blazing police vehicle while two officers stand by approvingly. This scene—the overcoming of an authorial object one stands beside—is paradigmatic of "dude" movie finales that enlist their young male subjects into "the phallic order," and the twinning of criminality with legal sanctification marks McLovin as both outlaw and ascending man.[194] As in other moments shared with McLovin and the officers, the knowing absence of law, its selective withdrawal, its congealing homosociality, open out trajectories of sexual growth and masculinizing enculturation. Unlike Seth's "fo sho," this adoption of "gangsta" talk hits the mark—his boyness is emphasized while paradoxically erasing itself through racial imitation. Imagine if McLovin were black—it would not be humorous *at all.* Watching a black boy shoot a gun at a cop car on fire triggers other audience responses, namely fear (of the boy) or disappointment (at social failure). For this boy, "black" talk and behavior is a launchpad. If for Baldwin, racial drag permits a critique of American masculinity and its hetero imperatives, racial drag for McLovin facilitates assimilation into masculinity and dictates of self-control: over himself, his erection with Nikola, and his gun.

Homosomething Intimacies

Despite the ways law's lubrication and racial imitation boost *Superbad*'s boys man-ward, they too are perempted, uncontrollably disqualified from generating or figuring out alternative relations. This disqualification comes not from discrete perpetrators, like parents or bullies (parents are absented in *Superbad*, and there is one "bully," who gets his comeuppance), but rather from the few and inflexible social scripts available for the enactment of early twenty-first-century young American masculinity. Despite (or because of) increasing gay friendliness and decreasing gender differentiation, boys and young men are perempted from developing deeper, intimate relations with one another—relations that might refigure the very dictates of masculinity that exclude them.[195]

The boys, though, (get to) try. *Superbad* orbits entirely around male affective attachments, cross- and same-generational, always unsure whether those attachments are sutured homosocially (and depending on a mediating woman or womankind), homophobically ("fag," "pussy," and their synonyms permeate the script), or homoerotically (some form of boys' and men's sexual or sexually inflected longing for one another).[196] From this perspective, the film is one extended but ultimately failed attempt to forge homosomething relations, where male-male intimacy is coded neither as protogayness nor as childish stopover on the way to the heterosexual or at least heteronormative couple form. That experiment begins with penises—sketched and fantasized—swells into a sleepover, and fizzles out at a shopping mall.

Penises parade through *Superbad*. Early in the film and over the closing credits rolls a montage of penis images: penises in costumes, as persons, as mythic or historic heroes and villains. These illustrations are the product of Seth's confessed ("super gay") addiction to drawing penises ("mandicks") when he was a younger boy. Seth's youthful impulse to sketch penises has morphed into the (male) ensemble's predilection to discourse relentlessly on them and their discharges. "Cum," "jizz," "dicks," "cocks," and "erections" are the most frequent utterances in the film. There is an ambivalence in all this incitement to cock talk, as it does not simply point to the discovery or wielding of male sex right. The cock talk is homoerotic, especially in its disavowals, but more importantly and complexly, the speech acts are both a defensive response to and also a projection of an unspecified male–male intimacy—the intimacy and sociality the boys of *Superbad* are perempted from experiencing and enjoying. Young Seth's repetitive-compulsive penis-drawing is not primarily about stuckness, mastery, or loss,[197] but points instead toward relations that can be visualized but not yet verbalized.

Superbad's fantasies of the future are inconsistent experiments in boys' not doing violence to women in the forging of homosomething bonds. These experiments constitute articulations of unnameable and undecidable male intimacies that historically tend to stabilize themselves in the devaluation or one-dimensionalization of the female or feminine.[198] We are presented with three fantasies of a different future, one of which belongs to Evan and his erections, another to Officer Michaels and criminal semen, and the last of which is verbalized by Seth near the film's end, and then shared with Evan, who together see themselves on rooftops, declaring their love for one another.

First, as Evan and Seth admire a naked, big-breasted woman on the cover of a porn magazine, Evan bemoans, "It's not fair they get to flaunt that stuff... and I have to hide every erection I get." He envisions, "just imagine if girls weren't weirded out by our boners and stuff... and just, like, wanted to see them." He looks past Seth into this future: "I mean, that's the world I one day want to live in."

Second, McLovin inquires if the officers will successfully apprehend the man who robbed the liquor store. Certainly not, agree the officers. Officer Michaels clarifies, "if the man had ejaculated and then punched you in the face, we'd have a real good shot at catching him." Like Evan, he imagines an alternative universe: "I often go to sleep and dream of waking up in a world where everything is covered in semen."

Finally, in the penultimate scene of the film, Evan and Seth fall asleep together on Evan's basement floor, after the failed sex acts with their future girlfriends. Lying close to one other, they exchange apologies for conflicts in their friendship. Reconciled, Evan thanks Seth for helping him out of the house party:

> EVAN: You carried me. I love you. I love you, man.
> SETH: I love you. I love you. I'm not even embarrassed to say it. I just, I lo- I love you.
> EVAN: I'm not embarrassed.
> SETH: I love you.
> EVAN: I love you. Why don't we say that everyday? Why can't we say it more often?

SETH: I just love you. I just want to go to the rooftops and scream, "I love my best friend Evan."

EVAN: We should go up on my roof.[199]

They do not go to the roof, but hold each other on the floor until, it seems, both do not know what to do with the newfound intimacy between them. Seth pats Evan on the back too many times until the scene fades out (Figure 19). The morning finds them hung over and separated from

Figure 19. "I love you. I'm not even embarrassed to say it." *Superbad.*

one another. Transparently, Seth yells to Evan that his mom has "great tits," reinstalling heterosexuality's momentary leave of absence.

These three different dreams share much but they are not the same. All travel among the homosocial, the homoerotic, and something in between or above but unable to announce itself. Evan dreams not about his boners but "our boners," and what he wants is a collectivity not of homosexuals but of men whose arousal will be nonthreatening to the same sex and possibly inviting to the other. The dream is framed around women and their reception, though, so here homosociality invokes its third term, a woman or image of a community of women to mediate or heterosexualize male–male attachment. In the second dream, women are absented, but a world of crime scenes covered in semen manifestly invokes sexual violence against them. Under these lights, this homosociality is of the garden variety: the degradation of women binds men to one another and Teflons homosexuality.[200] And yet, the cops are jointly dreaming of semen and wishing McLovin had semen on him, too. That the dialogue is at times jarringly funny is not because it is antigay, but because it is dangerously close, yet nonidentical, to gayness in its vulgar honesty. The cops' recurring discussion of jizz and cocks—their offer to "guide" McLovin's cock—are fledgling exercises in nonmisogynist homosociality, forms of connection that might not triangulate around a third term. The vocabulary is genitalized because this envisioned intimacy—homosocial but maybe not homosexual or misogynistic, erotically pedagogic but maybe not pederastic—has no other language for its narration.

Except for the untenable language of "love." Evan and Seth ratchet up the homosocial imaginary beyond free-floating erections or free-flowing semen. In this third dream there are no cathected genitals. They want to love each other and declare it publicly. Their refusals to be "embarrassed" underline that they know they should be; that boys' intimate attachments to each other can only be publicly registered in their lifeworld as homosexual, girlish, or childish.[201] Earlier, when Seth accuses Evan of "bailing" on him in ways small and large, Evan yells back, "I've wasted the last three years of my life sitting around talking bullshit with you, man. Instead of chasing girls and making friends, I've just sat around wasting all my time with you." The repetition of "waste" and "with you" bespeaks the "embarrassing" anxiety that this attachment is the very opposite of waste, both nourishing and necessary. Or rather, this "queer temporality"—delay, lingering, "bullshitting"—is made "time wasted" (and made to feel like time wasted) by the normative mandates of adult manhood, in which "growing" should never be directionless, sideways, or to be determined, but only and always "up" into the presumably monogamous, preferably heterosexual, intimacy-exhausting couple form.[202]

Evan and Seth are not gay. But they do feel something, and that something includes love and commitment and desire to grow with each other. When the cops break up the teens' house party, Seth carries a passed-out Evan to safety. "I'm gonna save you, Evan!" he cries, as the slow-motion that satirizes the feat as faux-heroic also exposes by poorly camouflaging care. What is Seth saving Evan from? He is not rescuing homosexuality from criminalization (the police officers) or a socially structuring homophobia (the high school party). What Seth and Evan momentarily evade is the pedagogic priming of law, its assimilative rather than its exclusionary power. Seth saves Evan, for one last night, from the "law" of socially sanctioned, scripted masculinity, where development into young American manhood is indexed not only by heterosexual object choice, but also, as Niobe Way so convincingly demonstrates, by the demotion of serious friends into superficial "buddies" and the conversion of intimacy into resigned indifference.[203] For "it is not the externalized women they fear, but the instability of their own fractured identities" rendered by the intensities of their attachment.[204]

Evan and Seth end their boyhoods at the mall, not on the rooftop. Consumerism, far from lethal, becomes a first step out of childhood and into the responsibilities of a foreclosing adulthood. The boys get some running room, some space and airtime to have a desire and imagine their sociality otherwise, but that sociality refuses materialization. The boys experiment in nonnormative desire but must find women, head to the mall, and then to college. (*Thirteen*'s Tracy experiments in nonnormative desire too, but she feels the repercussions—she's held back in seventh grade: "If a girl experiments it's a failure to do something; if a boy does it's called courage and vision—*all too often*.")[205] Evan and Seth match up with their newly acquired girlfriends and leave each other, which is as much about the film selling out to its genre-expected conclusion as it is a cognizance that it cannot conclude anywhere else, despite Seth's final, mournful gaze at the retreating, reheterosexualized Evan (Figure 20).

Robert Bulman and Nicole McCants argue that the boys of *Superbad* emblematize the possibility of "enlightened masculinity": boys willing to care for one another without the fear of expressing their "vulnerability and tenderness."[206]

Figure 20. The end of boyhood. *Superbad.*

> A film like *Superbad* challenges us to ask how adolescent boys can learn
> to be men without ridiculing and dominating women, and without fear-
> ing that close friendships with other men undermine their masculinity or
> heterosexuality.[207]

This question—how to be men without screwing women or screwing
over other men—"marks a cultural turning point in teen sex comedies."[208]
It might, but Evan and Seth's friendship does undermine (their) heterosexuality, and that is why it cannot sustain itself, or why that friendship has
to grow up, bifurcate on women, and detach from its own intensity. By
ridiculing their ridiculing of women, the film asks us to think about productions of young masculinity that might arrange themselves otherwise.
In assuming the boys are ontologically heterosexual and that their rear-
rangements of masculinity implicate no alternatives, Bulman and McCants
miss an important if unintentional lesson of the film: adult heterosexuality
is a learned achievement, one that comes with a defining loss, a foreclosure
of polymorphous possibility.[209]

Peremption captures the problem of homophobia, but in a different
way than we have come to expect (as bullying and brutality). We should
not trivialize the traumas that gay, protogay, and effeminate boys endure,
but the notion of peremption allows us to ask, what kinds of relations and
intimacies—same-sex, cross-generational, or otherwise—are disqualified

by our stunted, instantly applied vocabulary of sexual identity, and by the coding of adolescent boys' intimacy, deep friendships, or sexual relations with one another as either "gay" or meaningless prologue?[210] The severing and self-sabotaging of such intimacies, suggests Niobe Way, lead to American boys' increasing sense of disconnection, isolation, and depression.[211]

If the cock talk and fantasies of male–male intimate sociality aim to generate or sustain what might be called queer relations between Evan and Seth as well as McLovin and the officers, it is the confidences and assurances brokered in the very relations between boys and men that, recursively, empower dreaming anew. The friendship and quasi-pederastic pedagogic relationship are the resources, the material and psychical stuff that cocoon while cultivating the characters' capacities and desires to grow. As with Tracy, to care about Evan and Seth, sexual or otherwise, entails caring about more than age, age difference, and consent. To care about them and their flourishing means thinking about what remains inarticulable in the relations between them: forms of intimacy and relationality for which there is sparse vocabulary and a receding social landscape.[212] It means thinking as well about how the very possibility of experimenting with intimacies and relations, of being permitted or expected to adventure, is often a gendered prerogative. This leads to a paradox. The friendship between *Thirteen*'s Tracy and Evie is deep, even nontaxonomically intimate, but the girls' confiding in each other is overpowered by competing with each other in the attritional, winner-take-not-much economy of heteronormativity. Seth, Evan, and McLovin are given—by policemen or gender enculturation or both—a nonattritional shot to play and mess up, to draw cocks and guns, talk about them, and talk about sex, but all this talk orbits and gestures toward without ever realizing its alternative, always deferring the queerness (but not homosexuality) that is its stimulant. They are "lost but alive and unvanquished in their displacement" until they rediscover normativity, girls, and the couple form.[213] It is because McLovin is in some sense queer—odd, effeminate, nerdy—that he requires and benefits from the priming of the older officers. It is because Evan and Seth are in some sense queer—awkward around girls, too much in love with one another for masculinist propriety—that they need each other to dream of unembarrassed erections and declarations of love. It is their very boyness, though, or cultural constructions of and conferrals to boyness, that codes their pedagogic priming and homoerotic dreaming as moving modi of opportunity and not static loci of trauma.

CONCLUSION

The argument of this chapter is not that boys should have sex with their priests, that girls are uniformly consigned to a pleasureless, attritional social station, that white kids should more craftily appropriate racial minority (stereotyped) styles, or that the greatest sexual threat to adolescent boys is rigidified, denigrated scripts for their intimacies. What this analysis of *Doubt, Thirteen,* and *Superbad* proposes, inflected by a nascent political theory of peremption, is that we see other kinds of sexual harm when we substitute the gendered adolescent for the child, the homosexual, and the sex offender, and when we substitute the figuring out of interests for interests that are predetermined.

Donald is perempted by the narrative requirements of scandal, and his sexual possibilities are uncontrollably disqualified by macro social conflicts for which he is always only a metaphor or a trump card. Tracy is perempted by discursive, material, and familial absences, by norms that are attritional and glorify girls' attrition. Evan and Seth are perempted by a cultural landscape inhospitable to boys' homosomething intimacies and by the severely limited options for those intimacies to articulate themselves. These sorts of harms are less spectacular, intentional, and locatable than predation, molestation, or bullying, and therefore less fixable by law. These harms are barely perceptible as injuries when *consent* is ethically saturating and discursively diacritical.

Indeed, these sorts of harms have the unsatisfying tendency to be sourced back to "narratives," "norms," "culture," and "scripts," both in the arguments of this chapter and in the psychological research that has buttressed them.[214] What I have hoped to show, though, is how these narratives, norms, scripts, and cultural processes not only damage gendered subjectivity but also differentially perempt sexual and relational autonomy. By traveling (or staying still) with *Doubt's* Donald, *Thirteen's* girls, and *Superbad's* boys, we have seen some of the ways those norms, narratives, scripts, and socialization processes are varyingly installed, gendered, and navigated.

Conclusion

Other Sex Scandals

Over a decade ago, James Kincaid half-seriously proposed that we generate other scandals to dislodge the damaging, eroticizing, and so completely captivating narratives of sex predators and (formerly) innocent children.[1] The following sections of this Conclusion do not really point to other scandals so much as other sexual conflict zones—in life, law, and theory.

The four sections serve as postscripts to the four preceding chapters. They are by no means dispositive over their objects of inquiry. Rather, they wed more recent developments in U.S. popular discourse, law, legal theory, and queer studies to this book's explications of moral panic, the sociolegal construction of the sex offender (and homosexual-cum-consenting adult), sexual autonomy, and (gendered, perempted) adolescence. As other forms of sexual violence scandalize, as gays and sex offenders are reiteratively, respectively sanctified and demonized, as sexual autonomy is profoundly problematized by legal thinkers, and as the child is revivified in queer studies, how might we rearrange (and how are some already rearranging) the constellation of sex, harm, consent, and age?

FOOTBALL PLAYERS AND FRAT BROTHERS: A NEW MORAL PANIC?

As of this writing—although the tides may shift yet again as of your reading[2]—popular discussion and media attention surrounding sexual violence in the United States seems to be in transition. The folk devils with whom we have become accustomed (Sandusky, Savile, child pornographers, Internet predators) are fading into the background as new characters emerge front and center: football players and frat brothers. Although these characters are by no means the only loci of national anxiety concerning sexual violence, various media outlets are awash with reports of unchecked or underchecked campus rape and sexual assault.[3] Sexual violence in colleges and universities has long been a target of feminist activism, but the issue reemerged full scale in the national spotlight in the spring of 2011. In April of that year, the Department of Education's Office for Civil Rights sent out a "Dear Colleague" letter to educational institutions, stating in no uncertain terms that such institutions have an affirmative obligation to transparently and thoroughly redress reported sexual violence.[4] Otherwise, reminded the letter, schools may be found in violation of Title IX of the Education Amendments of 1972, which "prohibit[s] discrimination on the basis of sex in education programs or activities operated by recipients of Federal financial assistance."[5] Sexual violence and harassment can be forms of sex discrimination, as can be institutional indifference.[6] Schools found in violation of Title IX may lose federal funding or be subject to further litigation, or they may be fined if held in violation of other federal law, like the Clery Act, which requires schools to report on and disclose crimes committed on campus.[7] Meanwhile, less than a month before the publication of the "Dear Colleague" letter, students and alumni of Yale filed a federal complaint against the university claiming just such a IX violation. The school, alleged the complainants, inadequately and incompetently dealt with sexual misconduct and sexism on its campus, thus "fail[ing] to eliminate a hostile sexual environment."[8] Since the letter from the Department of Education and the complaint against Yale, federal agencies have stepped up their coordination efforts to hold universities and colleges accountable, and students and/or their advocates at many other schools have collaborated to file federal complaints or civil suits against their colleges.[9] Students object to universities' underreporting of sexual assault, inadequate disciplinary procedures, and failure to offer meaningful support to victims. Survivors and their allies are particularly incensed that perpetrators—even those definitively determined to have violated their schools' sexual misconduct policies—are rarely, let alone seriously, punished.[10]

This begs the question: Are we in the midst of a new moral panic? Have we turned our pitchforks to new bad guys, young men with otherwise "promising futures," because we have exhausted, for now, the sociopolitical assurances we can squeeze out of child predators?[11] If, as I have argued, we manufactured sex offenders in order to simplify sexual violence, sanctify the consenting adult, and desexualize young people, what might account for renewed attention to sexual violence on our campuses, if such attention is not entirely explainable by, say, the rising incidence of said violence?

The question is leading, as I do not at all believe we are in the throes of a new moral panic. One could only make such an equivalence based on formal, superficial similarities between contemporary accounts of campus sexual violence and yesteryear accounts of child predation. Indeed, some contemporary news stories rehearse the gothic structure, pornographically positioning a solitary, young, female victim against a group of pathological football players and an equally pathological university that provides the players safe harbor.[12] A few outspoken activists and politicos insist that seriousness is best measured only and always by punitiveness and demand expulsion for any disciplinary finding of sexual misconduct.[13] Some protest that universities should get out of the sexual assault adjudication business altogether and leave such cases in the hands of law enforcement officials.[14] And the list of schools the Department of Education publicly released as under Title IX investigation, like the names of alleged sexual assault assailants scribbled on bathroom doors by anonymous activists at Columbia University, calls to mind sex offender websites and other public notification mechanisms that do so much to make us feel good and so little to minimize sexual violence.[15] Meanwhile, as others once leveraged children's supposed sexual endangerment to reheterosexualize and renormativize the public sphere, some have capitalized on campus sexual assault to complain about the casualization of sex, "hook-up culture," and the end of (domesticated, gendered, mannered) romance.[16] Policing sexual violence has long been pretext for policing sex.[17]

But the resonances between the child sex crimes of the mid-1990s and the sex offender registration and notification (SORN) laws and media attention they catalyzed and the college sexual assaults of the 2010s and the activism and media attention they have catalyzed mostly stop at the surface. Digging a little deeper, it is quickly apparent that current activism and federal involvement around college sexual assault is more sophisticated, careful, and efficacious than a cursory overview suggests.

A name on a bathroom wall is local, removable, and written by justifiably enraged nonstate actors. A sex offender listing on a state notification site (which includes a home address and many other details) is global, nearly permanent, and posted by unjustifiably vindictive state actors. And there are far more important distinctions to be noted between these spheres of anti–sexual violence politics.

First, there are the numbers, which are always fuzzy and manipulable, but still tell us something. Studies on the incidence and prevalence of child sexual abuse in the United States report wildly divergent findings, but studies tend to document decreasing rates (and victimization by strangers has always been exceedingly uncommon).[18] Meanwhile, "substantiated cases of sexual abuse dropped from 23 per 10,000 children under 18 to 8.6 per 10,000, a 62 percent decrease, with a 3 percent drop from 2009 to 2010."[19] While the numbers on incidence and prevalence of sexual violence against women in college also vary, and while studies carry attendant definitional problems (Is all sex with children child sexual abuse? Is all sexual misconduct sexual assault?), the studies are not *that* varied or uncertain. They tend to cluster around the same finding: one in four or one in five women are victims of sexual assault, attempted or completed, during their undergraduate careers.[20] Meanwhile, Corey Yung recently assembled data showing that the rate of sexual violence against women may in fact be rising.[21] So in the case of child sex crimes, we have a statistical oddity, possibly downward sloping, remedied through SORN regulations that are inefficient and counterproductive. In the case of campus sexual assault, we have a statistical commonplace, possibly upward sloping, remedied through, at its best, creative activism, collaboration across stakeholders, and data-driven best practices keyed to prevention and gender equality (see below).

Indeed, student activists are not in fact making folk devils out of football players and frat brothers. Their primary targets are their host colleges, and their objectives are neither to humiliate nor to demonize university administrators, but to install or revise disciplinary procedures and reporting systems. The guiding impulse is not retributive but reformist. In addition to calling for and instituting more systematized and fair disciplinary and adjudicative procedures, IX activists, and some university IX coordinators, are spearheading a multipronged approach to combat sexual violence. This approach entails workshops on bystander intervention, campus-wide discussions of sexual communication (beyond what counts or does not count as consent), sexual climate surveys (which will likely be federally mandated in the near future), and more honest assessments of the ways drugs and alcohol can impede decision making.[22] This approach is neither univocal nor persecutory and does not wholly depend upon anthropo-morphizing evil for its political credibility. Many activists recognize that not all forms of sexual assault and misconduct are identical, that expulsion of an offender is not always or necessarily the best resolution (yet we do well to remember that expulsion is not incarceration), and that the uni-versity has an obligation above and beyond criminal law enforcement to ensure an environment where everyone can equally participate (this is but one reason why universities cannot and must not delegate their responsi-bilities to local authorities).[23]

The movement is organic and not driven by a desire for votes, profit, or ratings. The latest wave of anti–sexual violence activism has been spurred by student survivors, working with their friends and peers across the nation and the world. For example, several students from different univer-sities collaborated in 2013 to create Know Your IX, an organization that provides resources to other survivors, undertakes education initiatives, and has successfully put pressure on federal agencies to more strenuously oversee university compliance with Title IX. As its name suggests, Know Your IX encourages people to learn for themselves—about civil rights legislation, about available online and offline resources for survivors of sexual assault, and about ways individuals can work independently and collectively to make their environments safer.[24]

There is (if not always) a productive humility in this emerging arena of anti–sexual violence organizing, a collective awareness that governmental agencies, universities, and student organizations need to work in coalition and learn from one another, need to experiment with innovative preventa-tive and educational programs and test their success. Such expressed open-ness and curiosity is rarely the case among those promoting and enacting SORN and other sex offender regulations, whose certitude barrels over any inconvenient facts. The difference between 1990s and early 2000s SORN activism and legislation and 2010s campus sexual assault activism is nowhere better demonstrated than in the exemplary "First Report of the White House Task Force to Protect Students from Sexual Assault." In drafting the report, the task force sought input from a variety of "stake-holders": survivors, parents, alumni, administrators, and so on.[25] The sug-gestions of the report—get men involved in sexual violence prevention, administer campus sexual climate surveys, properly train advocates, encour-age bystander intervention, partner with local rape crisis centers—are informed directly by said stakeholders and Know Your IX activists.[26] The report makes men comrades in the campaign, rather than protectors or predators.[27] The unambiguous declaration that Title IX protects students from gender identity and sexual orientation discrimination dissipates any unitary construction of the victim.[28] And the constant refrains that we should follow "best practices" to prevent sexual violence, that we should conduct new research and gather more data, and that there is so much more to learn about effective intervention are worlds removed from dominant official and unofficial discourse on SORN requirements.[29] Compare the tempered, nuanced language of the report to congressional debates on Megan's Law ("when I think of an innocent child, one who cannot defend herself or himself... who is now with someone who preys upon them... then my voice raises for that innocent child against that violent sex offender, against that child abuser, against that murderer"), or to President George W. Bush's speech as he signed the Adam Walsh Act ("When a child's life or innocence is taken it is a terrible loss—it's an act of unforgivable cruelty.... We're sending a clear message across the country: those who prey on our children will be caught, prosecuted, and punished to the fullest extent of the law").[30]

What is perhaps most promising about this new wave of activism is its deprioritization of refurbished consent as a primary political objective and its displacement of woundedness and trauma as sources of normative authority. Certainly, colleges have been successfully called upon to redefine consent in their sexual misconduct policies, and student groups politick on consent's behalf.[31] Likewise, documented sequelae of sexual assault add ethical urgency to calls for action, particularly calls for improved reporting procedures and support training.[32] But this is a movement about gender equality: equal access to education, equal participation in the social and academic life of the university, equal opportunities to codetermine sexual and social relationships. Unlike other student sexual safety campaigns, IX activists do not inadvertently constrict their ambitions by the language of consent. Consent Is Sexy, a Know Your IX predecessor, ends up overemphasizing the sexual event and underemphasizing campus sexual culture. And it is forced by its own agenda, sexifying consent, to repackage its normative values (mutuality, sobriety, respect, etc.) as consent proper, stretching *consent* past any credible meaning of the term.[33] Know Your IX can call a spade a spade—this is not just about consent, but about prevention, intervention, communication, due process, accountability, and affecting campus sexual climate. This activism avoids, if not always,[34] unhelpful embroilments about consent technicalities—determining the exact line between agreement and acquiescence, for example, or determining the exact line between incapacitated inebriation and fun drunkenness. When these sorts of inquiries preoccupy discussions of sexual violence, one has the queasy sense that what is being calculated is not *what can I do to promote a flourishing sexual culture* but *what can I get away with*.[35] So too, by focusing its mandate on changing university disciplinary and adjudicative systems, this newer activism is not beset by recrimination and ressentiment.[36] Unlike the earlier years of Take Back the Night marches, the focus here is less on "breaking the silence" and speaking wounds to power and more on ridding campus life of sexual violence outright—by changing communication, behavior (bystanders' and partners'), and institutional responses.[37] Moreover, the language and concept of "sexual climate" invites a needed integration of sex positivity organizing with anti–sexual violence organizing—indeed, "climatory" is a far more versatile idiom than "predatory." In the wake of the IX complaint filed against Yale, some students, university administrators, and an external oversight committee sought to shut down Yale's 2012 "Sex Week," a biennial, week-plus-long series of events, lectures, performances, and sometimes over-the-top celebrations of sex, intimacy, and sexualities of all stripes.[38] Explicit sex exploits seemed to be the concern. But as the organizers of Sex Week eloquently argued, as did keynote speaker Ann Olivarius, public sexual culture is not the catalyst to sexual violence but an antidote.[39] To speak sex—not as deep truth, confessional, or interiorized wound, but as unshamed, pleasuring, risky inquiry—is elemental in the formation of sexual subjectivities that are not foregone conclusions. This sort of sex talk, like comprehensive sex education, facilitates the capacity to codetermine sexual relations that may otherwise be rote, deadening, or worse.[40]

I may sound like a cheerleader in my effort to distance this incipient organizing from SORN and its attendant politics of the child. But if I've overstated the differences, it is to firmly ask and answer: A new moral panic? No. We may be witnessing a reversal, but nongothic, and with a nonpanicky twist. For too long, argues Claire Potter, Sandusky stories, those that orbit the innocent child, have captured our attention, while stories of sexual violence against women are trivialized and rationalized ("Since most people don't believe that ten year olds want to be anally penetrated by grown men . . . people tend not to spin alternative scenarios about little boys like: 'look what he was wearing'").[41] But whereas Sandusky stories centralize predation and innocence and anthropomorphize sexual harm, IX stories centralize prevention, vulnerability, and sexual autonomy, canvassing sexual harm as multiply mediated and multiply remedied. This sexual harm is eradicable not through chemical castration but through (campus) cultural transformation.

FEDERALIZED LESBIANS, RECIDIVATING RECIDIVISTS, AND THE MYTH OF CONSENT

Speaking of cultural transformation: since 2003, gays have morphed from sodomites to spouses in the juridical imaginary, while sex offenders have, unsurprisingly, symbolically stagnated. In the Supreme Court's summer 2013 term, on the tenth anniversary of *Lawrence v. Texas, Smith v. Doe,* and *Connecticut Department of Public Safety v. Doe,* we witnessed anew the mystifying, discursive, and doubled-down power of consent. As in 2003, the 2013 court ruled on sex offender law and laws regulating the intimate lives of gays and lesbians.

United States v. Windsor is more lauded and well known than *United States v. Kebodeaux.*[42] *Windsor* holds section 3 of the federal Defense of Marriage Act (DOMA) unconstitutional, as a violation of the Fifth Amendment's due process clause.[43] Section 3, for federal purposes, defined marriage as a legal union between one man and one woman. *Kebodeaux* holds the federal registration requirements of the Sex Offender Registration and Notification Act (SORNA, Title I of the Adam Walsh Act) constitutional as applied to Anthony Kebodeaux, a veteran of the U.S. Air Force who was convicted of and served his sentence for a federal sex offense prior to SORNA's enactment.[44]

From the perspective of this book—querying the consent paradigm and its correlating characters—what is remarkable about these cases is not so much the holdings as their rhetorical maneuvers. These maneuvers tell us, ten years after *Lawrence, Smith,* and *Connecticut,* that the legal fiction of consent and the legal fiction of the sex offender have lasting, reigning, and interlocking normative appeal. And the appeal of the sex offender, like the appeal of the consenting adult, reverberates beyond the Supreme Court. As lower courts continue to strike down state same-sex marriage bans, states forge ahead enacting new sex offender regulation requirements, as severe as they are inefficacious.[45]

Penning the opinion for *Kebodeaux,* Justice Breyer irrelevantly enumerates the alleged benefits of the federal SORN system. The social value of

SORNA, in this instance, is immaterial to the constitutional question, which hinges on the scope of federal power under the necessary and proper clause.[46] And while *Kebodeaux*, unlike *Smith* and *Connecticut*, concedes conflicting studies on sex offender recidivism, the holding nonetheless maintains that the registration requirements are sound constitutional policy for the promotion of public safety: "Congress' decision to impose such a civil requirement that would apply upon the release of *an offender like Kebodeaux* is eminently reasonable."[47]

Who is "an offender like Kebodeaux"? Positioning Kebodeaux in textual and conceptual proximity to the 2003 Bureau of Justice Statistics (BJS) study—which the court reports as finding comparatively high rates of sex offender recidivism—suggests he is a rapist or child molester.[48] We learn from Justice Breyer's opinion that Kebodeaux was convicted of "carnal knowledge," and from Justice Roberts's concurrence that "Kebodeaux violated the Uniform Code of Military Justice by having sexual relations with a minor."[49] If we—as I believe we are expected to do—deductively triangulate from the cited BJS study, the conviction of "carnal knowledge" with a minor, and the repeated reference to "an offender like Kebodeaux," then we arrive at the dominant fiction of the sex offender: one sex offender is like all the others, all sex offenders are recidivistic, most violate women or children, and all violate consent.

But only upon reading Justice Thomas's dissent do we come to learn that, in fact, Kebodeaux was convicted for having "consensual sex with a 15-year-old girl when he was a 20-year-old Airman in the U.S. Air Force."[50] He received a three-month prison sentence. The sexual encounter is read as "consensual" by Justice Thomas, but U.S. military records do not, of course, tell us whether the sex was wanted, acquiesced to, pressured, awesome, mediocre. Regardless, these details of the conviction undermine the figure of the sex offender as uniformly manufactured by the court, legislatures, and popular culture. It is through the mystification of Kebodeaux's crime, and through the court's subsequent reconstitution of Kebodeaux as a sexually violent recidivist—as consent's violator—that the SORN provisions and federal prerogatives of the Adam Walsh Act are discursively reaffirmed. The discursive reaffirmation brooks, or at least lubricates, the doctrinal reaffirmation. As I make clear in the Introduction, my point here is not that Romeos and Juliets should be granted special political sympathy while everyone else rots on the registry. Rather, I am suggesting that the court must make Romeo into Voldemort to confirm the goodness of federal SORN requirements. But Romeos perpetuate sexual violence too, while Voldemorts remain palliative yet terrorizing fictions.

If sexual harm is refigured as the violation of consent, which the sex offender is then produced to personify, how is sexual freedom refigured as consent's presence?

In Justice Alito's dissent in *Windsor,* he outlines "two competing views" of marriage that he takes to be in contest before the court: "traditional" or "conjugal" marriage and "*consent*-based marriage."[51] The former denotes a view of marriage as inhabited by "opposite-sex" partners and as purposed for, almost exclusively, procreation.[52] The latter denotes a view of marriage as "the solemnization of mutual commitment"—the statutory privileging of two individuals' reciprocal choices.[53] Expectedly, Alito argues that Edith Windsor is asking the court to "implicitly endorse" one view and that such an endorsement is judicial overreach.[54]

As dissent, important here is not the doctrinal force (nil), but the way "consent-based marriage" captures the most powerful and persuasive way of thinking about gay marriage. The notion of mutual choice underscores Kennedy's celebration of Lawrence and Garner in *Lawrence* and infuses his defense of Windsor in *Windsor.*[55] "Consent-based marriage," were it catchier, could very well be the campaign slogan for marriage-equality organizations—it is a normative if usually unstated prerequisite to slogans like "freedom to marry" or "love is love."[56] (As I have argued elsewhere, the apotheosis of the consenting adult may impede mainstream LGBT rights groups from generating a more coalitional, less identitarian contestation of state-sponsored sexual injustice.)[57]

But as Kennedy's opinion also recognizes, "consent" does not immunize all marriages from federal interference, such as those entered into by immigrants fraudulently seeking citizenship status.[58] And, of course, states prohibit polygamy and incestuous marriages.[59] Consent is perhaps a necessary normative concept for a defense of gay (or late modern) marriage, but it is not sufficient, at least not if we want to withhold other consensual relations from statutory privilege.

Justice Alito's dissent in *Windsor* and Justice Breyer's opinion in *Kebodeaux* illustrate the extent to which, when it comes to sexual harm and freedom, we think we are thinking about consent. But consent is only a heuristic, and a treacherous one. Because consent magnetizes liberal discourse around sex, because it makes the world of sex intelligible and justiciable, the debate over same-sex marriage appears to be a standoff between gendered tradition (injurious to gays and lesbians and probably heterosexuals too) and individual consent (freedom for gays and lesbians and probably heterosexuals too), and the problem of sex offenders appears to be—or is made to be—the problem of nonconsent.

Might sex between twenty-year-old Kebodeaux and a fifteen-year-old girl be impermissible (or permissible) whether or not Kebodeaux is pathologically predatory? Might the impermissibility (or permissibility) of this sex have nothing to do, or not everything to do, with consent? What social or sexual value, and legal justification, might be accorded to same-sex marriages that have nothing to do, or not everything to do, with consent? How might we defend the official sanction of same-sex marriage over other forms of nonhetero, nondyadic, or nonexogamous intimate relations, if consent cannot get the normative job done? What other concepts invite a more just, more feminist, less vilifying, and less myopic perspective on sex and harm—concepts that might allow us to identify and militate against sexual harm when that harm does not appear in the form of adult male predation and the violation of innocence?

To answer this last question, I have proposed that autonomy, peremption, and adolescence might productively disenchant our allegiance to consent, predation, and the child. The penultimate question—on the privileging or depriviledging of same-sex marriage against other relational forms—is for another book.

AUTONOMY ≠ CONSENT

Two stinging critiques of sexual autonomy were published in law journals after I wrote the substantive material for the third chapter: Marc Spindelman's "Sexuality's Law" (2013) and Jed Rubenfeld's "The Riddle of Rape-by-Deception and the Myth of Sexual Autonomy" (2013). Rubenfeld's and Spindelman's controversial articles provide an opportunity to further clarify the contours of my feminist-inflected, relationally reconstructed sexual autonomy, as well as its implications for law and legal theory.

Rubenfeld and Spindelman arrive at wildly opposing assessments of sexual autonomy's normative consequences for criminal law, constitutional law, and our cultural episteme. For both authors, autonomy is probably incompatible with sexuality.[60] If it is compatible, it is nevertheless a catastrophic principle for sex law. Despite their conflicting conclusions, they seem to agree about what sexual autonomy is: a right to individual sexual decision making and "self-determination" demonstrable through and activated by consent.[61] But by reading sexual autonomy off of the first person, present, active, consenting or nonconsenting subject, both Rubenfeld and Spindelman miss opportunities to reconstruct autonomy in more broad-based, ecological, and relational terms. Their respective, identical constructions of sexual autonomy rig their normative conclusions, but their constructions of sexual autonomy could be otherwise, and thus so could their conclusions.

Rubenfeld's riddle of "The Riddle of Rape-by-Deception" is this: sexual autonomy is ascending as the "single, unifying principle" in "sex law," demarcating permissible from impermissible sexual conduct, or sex from rape (a questionable assumption from the outset).[62] This, if true, would present a serious problem for criminal law, because sexual autonomy is tethered to respecting people's choices, and "from autonomy's viewpoint, fraud is as great an evil as force."[63] Thus, any form of deception that induces sex—not disclosing your HIV status, saying you went to Yale when you went to Wesleyan, "make-up and hair dye", etc.[64]—corrupts consent. The deceiver, on a sexual autonomy model, should be convicted of rape. Because such convictions would be plainly (to Rubenfeld) ridiculous, we ought to discard sexual autonomy and reinsert a force requirement back into rape law. What rape violates is not sexual autonomy but a right to bodily self-possession, and that right is only abrogated by force (overpowering, pinning down, imprisonment, etc.) or threats of force.[65]

I am less concerned than others are with solving (or dissolving)[66] the riddle, and more concerned with his containing configuration of sexual autonomy. However, because I think the riddle presents a significant challenge to sexual autonomy as a governing principle of sex offense, I will say a word about it here, mostly channeling the thoughtful insights of others.[67] As Deborah Tuerkheimer points out, under conditions of heteronormativity, material scarcity, and late night drinking, our consent is hardly if ever fully informed.[68] The space between (or among) sexual partners is often filled with fantasy, partial concealments, selective disclosures, embellishments, and indeed, sometimes lies.[69]

Tuerkheimer opts for "sexual agency" rather than "autonomy" as her preferred governing principle for sexual regulation, since, for her, the former better connotes choice under subordinated conditions, whereas the latter connotes self-governance unpolluted by the world.[70] I argued in the third and fourth chapters that "autonomy" reaches the constrained decision making Tuerkheimer catalogs as "agency." Regardless, and conceding conceptual overlap,[71] Tuerkheimer posits that, in most cases, we better respect sexual agency when we endorse rather than vitiate consent in information-insufficient, power-differential scenes of sexual exchange, since information insufficiency and power difference are ineradicable. Some deceptions and lies are worse than others, however, so certain lies and deceptions might be eligible as legal harms.[72] For me though, as for others, the "materiality" of the deception matters more, juridically speaking, than the supposed sequelae or allegedly objective "reprehensibility" of the deception.[73] As metrics, sequelae and reprehensibility too easily buttress bigotry and too easily lend themselves to moralization.[74] "Materiality," or something like explicit conditionality, protects autonomous choice while leaving room for the fantasies and embellishments sometimes surrounding sex. Here is what I mean: I do not believe, for reasons I will elaborate in my discussion of Spindelman's article, that nondisclosure of HIV-positive status should be criminalized, nor do I think we should criminalize HIV-positive people who engage in unprotected sex. Regarding HIV and other STIs, there are better ways to engender sexual autonomy than through legal penalty. To the extent that there is any role here for criminal or civil law, it arises, I think, in the highly specific scenario where one partner conditions sex on a preferred serostatus and the other partner, knowing his serostatus, lies in order to have sex. Notice that the status itself—positive or negative—is irrelevant. What matters is the flat-out lie to the conditional requirement of the other party. If Jane says to Jill she will have sex with Jill if and only if Jill went to Yale, and Jill lies about her alma mater, it is not inconceivable to make the deception actionable as some form of sexual misconduct.[75] Perhaps this sounds like governance feminism gone wild, but consider for a moment how infrequently such a case would arise—when, if ever, is an alma mater actually made exclusively, explicitly conditional to sex? Nil. Rubenfeld argues we cannot integrate consent from other arenas of criminal law into sex law because absurd results follow. But when the state convicts a person of trespassing because he enters someone's house posing as a "meter reader," it is not deception sui generis that is penalized.[76] Posing as a meter reader is positively elemental to entry. If, on a date, Jill tells Jane she is a meter reader when in fact she is an attorney, or tells Jane she went to Yale when she did not, and several hours later they go to Jane's home and have sex, Jill could not possibly be convicted for either trespassing or sexual misconduct. This may all seem silly—doctrinal theory in search of a problem—but insofar as Rubenfeld highlights a real tension regarding consent's growing jurisdiction in rape law, then "we must bite this bullet: when the deception is material to someone's sexual consent, then sex-by-deception is a serious wrong."[77]

A last note: not all conditionals are answerable as truth claims. What sexual misconduct cases involving gender-nonconforming or trans-identified people (often cases where one party thought they were having sex with another party sex-assigned male, but said party was sex-assigned female)[78] seem to reveal is a staple of third-wave feminism: gender is not the kind of thing that we can transparently subject to a truth claim—gender is not anatomy, it is not always binary or stationary. For many of us, *what gender are you* turns out to be a qualitatively different question than *(where) did you go to college*. When courts subject gender to a truth claim, phobic results usually follow.[79]

Materiality mostly aside, more prescient from my perspective is Rubenfeld's conflation of sexual autonomy with consent, and with the reduction of sexual autonomy to individual (present tense) choice rather than relational (present and futural) possibilities.[80]

The consequences of this conflation are most apparent through Rubenfeld's repeated invocation of a fictional seventeen-year-old girl, whom he employs to substantiate three interrelated arguments: the absurdity of rape-by-deception, the necessity for injecting a force requirement back into rape law, and the legitimacy of morality as a basis for the state criminalization of certain sexual practices. I briefly consider each of Rubenfeld's teenagers to emphasize two points: first, that sexual autonomy is a necessary "myth" (or more forgivingly, concept) for sex law; and second, that securing sexual autonomy, relationally reconceived, requires more than the performance of first person, present, active (imperfectly informed) consent—it requires the restructuring of legal (and many other) relations.[81]

Seventeen-year-old girl 1. If sexual autonomy governed sex law, warns Rubenfeld, seventeen-year-old girls could be charged with rape if they told their suitors they were eighteen (lying about your age, at any age, would violate sexual autonomy as Rubenfeld characterizes the myth—demanding absolutely informed consent where "materiality" stretches to any and every embellishment, falsity, and lie).[82] In a reply to his critics, Rubenfeld recounts this lying teenager no less than three times, twice in the first three pages: Are we really prepared to charge the teen with rape, just like we charge her suitor with statutory rape (or however the age infraction is terminologically codified)?[83] The example "speaks for itself," writes Rubenfeld (although if it really spoke for itself it might not need to be repeated).[84] Ergo, we should not criminalize inducements to sex as sexual misconduct. Moreover, and here I agree with him, the basis for thinking such criminalization absurd is not the lack of harmful results that follow the sex. The older partner, as we well know, will face prison time and will likely be subjected to SORN requirements.[85]

Never does it occur to Rubenfeld that if the teenager is lying because of the law—an unstated implication of the hypothetical—maybe it is the law, not the teenager, that is in the wrong. And it seems to me that the easiest, most honest way to advocate scaling back remaining higher-age of consent statutes is to ground our argument in a principle of sexual autonomy. The law itself violates the teenager's autonomy, disqualifying her ability to codetermine her relations. Such a solution does not merely reduplicate by aging down the problem. If a fourteen-year-old says she is fifteen to convince a nineteen-year-old to have sex with her, we can more comfortably declare, on account of experiential and educational difference, developmental processes, and gendered patterns of acquiescence, that the younger teen is incapable of consenting and likewise un- or less accountable for lying. The fiction of the incapable fourteen-year-old may still be a fiction, but less damaging than the legal fiction of the incompetent, incapable seventeen-year-old. When the autonomy inquiry focuses summarily on the capacities and behaviors of the individuals, and not also on those background conditions cultivating capacities or influencing behaviors, the inquiry necessarily falls short.

Seventeen-year-old girl 2. A high school principal who tells a seventeen-year-old student he will expel her unless she has sex with him should not be convicted of sexual assault, argues Rubenfeld.[86] As he sees it, the scenario involves coercion, and since coercion, in the final instance, is about the vitiation of consent, it cannot qualify as rape, if rape is, as Rubenfeld would like it to be, a "violation of self-possession."[87] Opening the rape law door to coercion opens the door to deception, which is what his theory of rape as sexual slavery seeks to avoid in the first place.[88] Rubenfeld supports the conviction of a foster parent who threatens to send his fourteen-year-old female ward back to juvenile detention unless she has sex with him, because Rubenfeld sees "force" in this scenario ("threat of imprisonment"). But he sees no colorable force claim regarding the principal and the teenager.[89]

There are at least two counterarguments for criminalizing or otherwise penalizing the principal's behavior as sexual, not just professional, misconduct.[90] Both arguments are principled on sexual autonomy.

First, as with the materiality of deception, so with the materiality of coercion. The principal enforces sex on the student by explicitly, purposefully leveraging his institutional power. The threat positively dispossesses her—by contravening her moralized baseline, Wertheimer might say[91]—of a right to codetermine sexual relations. This dispossession is the very purpose of the threat. The principal makes himself the sole governor of the relational terms.

Second, a more robust account of sexual autonomy, removed a few steps back from the immediacy of the sexual (mis)conduct, portends prohibiting sexual relations between a high school principal and a high school student. Full stop. Here, again, is where sexual autonomy and consent part ways. The teen cannot reasonably say no to the principal; she cannot easily extract herself from the dependent relation; her ability to constitute and reconstitute (other) sexual relations is unacceptably curtailed by the institutional power differential. Whether or not the teenager consents, her sexual autonomy may be better secured through regulating sex in relations of direct authority and substantial dependence.[92] In this second counterargument, the case against the sex is not a case against coercion, and thus not a case against nonconsent. It is a case for sexual autonomy as a check on uncontrollable disqualification of relational possibilities (peremption).[93]

Seventeen-year-old girl 3.[94] Near the end of his article, Rubenfeld asks whether rape as a violation of bodily self-possession will reach sex with underage persons. The answer: no.[95] Since statutory rape law is largely premised on the presumption that young people are incapable of consent, his rape law would not reach this sex, since his rape law relegates consent to a transformative metric only for violent, rough, or sadomasochistic sex.[96] But, he then assures, consent is not actually the premise of statutory rape law anyhow, since everyone knows teens can consent to sex: otherwise, we would not charge adults who sexually assault teens with both "real" and "statutory" rape.[97] What undergirds statutory rape law is the state-endorsed belief that "such sex is deemed immoral and harmful even though consensual."[98] Because statutory rape is a "different and independent crime" from "real rape," his proposed reforms would have no bearing on regulations and proscriptions against underage sex.[99]

Rubenfeld is right, which is all the more reason we should constitution-alize or otherwise codify sexual autonomy as a governing principle for the regulation of sexual relations. In the absence of an enshrined sexual auton-omy principle, "traditional morality" might still be a good basis for the criminalization of nonnormative sexual conduct. And in the absence of any countervailing jurisprudence—say, suspect classification, equal protec-tion, or privacy—this grants the state remarkable regulatory and punitive powers. Suppose the state criminalizes sexual intercourse with overweight, unintelligent, less attractive, or mean people, or criminalizes group sex, kinky but nonviolent sex, commercial sex (which it mostly does), or, indeed, gay sex, because the state deems such activities "immoral and harmful even though consensual"? Remember: according to Rubenfeld, the regu-lation of youthful sex is not based on youthfulness, since seventeen-year-olds are consenting adults; the regulation is based on morality.

Rubenfeld argues that the central holding of *Lawrence,* if it is a sexual autonomy holding, is rightly called into question by his logic.[100] This seems like a stretch: one may believe that Jill can tell a sex-inducing lie to Jane without incurring penalty and also believe, without contradiction, that the state should not criminalize the ensuing sex between Jill and Jane. We might think it permissible for Jill to impinge Jane's sexual autonomy, but impermissible for the state to do so.[101] Yet his limited discussion of statutory rape law suggests Rubenfeld wants to excise sexual autonomy from both criminal and constitutional law (despite the fact that there is not much to excise in either locale). This is flatly unacceptable, reverting law to shield from state invasion only that sex that is proximate to marital bed-rooms, babymaking, and abortions. A constitutionalized, "thin"[102] sexual autonomy right checks state proscriptions against a wider set of relational, sexual possibilities. The challenge, as I described in the second chapter, is how to respect and promote sexual autonomy without synonymizing autonomy to consent, and without valorizing the consenting adult and demonizing or dismissing everyone else (sex offenders, young people).[103]

Whereas Rubenfeld worries that sexual autonomy authorizes too much state power and expands criminal law too widely, Marc Spindelman wor-ries that sexual autonomy impermissibly curbs state power and contracts criminal law too narrowly.

I am engaging with just a small aspect of Spindelman's mostly unpersua-sive yet strangely stunning, and stunningly smart, tirade, "Sexuality's Law." Spindelman's preoccupation is with the "ideology of sexual freedom," and far less with "sexual autonomy."[104] As Spindelman tells it, the ideology of sexual freedom is a pervasive but heretofore imperceptible force governing the lives and relations of late modern Euro-American gay men. Its intellectual founders are authors like de Sade, Genet, Sartre, Bataille, and Foucault; its social and political refractors are hegemonic masculinity, HIV/AIDS, and homophobia; its contemporary flag bearers—not always consciously, not without contradictions, and never totally—are activists and theorists like Douglas Crimp, David Chambers, Richard Mohr, Leo Bersani, and Tim Dean.[105] In this ideology, sex "is the value of all values":[106] it is world-generating, world-excluding, subject-creating, subject-shattering, relation-forging, and antirelational. Sex leads to new vistas of the possible and, when done right, ground clears extant social order.[107] Where all these conflicting but superlative values of sex inexorably devolve is toward an "erotics of death," the sacralization of violence that, at its limitless limit, "entails a right to die for sex and also a right to kill in its name."[108]

Needless to say, none of this is good for Spindelman. The ideology of sexual freedom does bad things for gay male sexuality and sexual subjectivity: gay men internalize homophobia, equate sexual violence with sexual freedom, underreport sexual abuse, censor and self-censor dissenting viewpoints, prize sex over life itself.[109]

"Sexual autonomy" enters this grim picture of gay sexuality conflictingly, through Spindelman's interlocution of Richard Mohr's *Gays/Justice*, and it is here that I want to focus my attention for the remainder of this section.[110] It seems at first that sexual autonomy is a counterpunch to sexual freedom: as a moral, rights-based abstraction side-constrained by consent, sexual autonomy provides the legally recognizable limit to the ideology of sexual freedom.[111] Spindelman is unconvinced. First, given that, under Mohr's lights, sex is phenomenologically fabulous, and given that what sex is for, under the ideology of sexual freedom, is the breaking of each and every boundary,[112] sexual autonomy does not hold a candle. But second, even if autonomy withstands the tidal force of sexual freedom, sexual autonomy is nevertheless hospitable to an erotics of death: "If autonomy means anything, it is that one must be able to sacrifice oneself and one's life for one's deepest belief."[113] Consent, argues Spindelman, grants "an immunity . . . to deal a sexual death blow. [One's] partner's underlying consent vitiates any notion that his death, sexually achieved as a result, is a harm. There can be no victims in this sex."[114]

Like Rubenfeld, Spindelman rehearses sexual autonomy as an abstraction exhaustively readable off first person, present, active, consent. Conceptualized as such, Spindelman concludes that sexual autonomy, despite itself, allows the ideology of sexual freedom reentry into law. Syllogistically, Spindelman's argument could be put the following way:

1. The state has an affirmative obligation to prevent and punish individual harmful conduct.[115]
2. HIV = serious injury and/as death.[116]
3. Sexual autonomy licenses each and every act of consensual sex, including sex between and among serodiscordant partners.[117]
4. Sexual autonomy = death.[118]
5. Therefore, sexual autonomy should be excised from sex law (and from our gay cultural lexicon).[119]

Let me tackle first the biggest and most dangerous misstep here, step two, HIV = death, which is the sine qua non of Spindelman's broadside. For Spindelman's critique to hold traction, for there to be an ideology of sexual freedom that is "laying waste" to gay men, Spindelman must figure HIV/ AIDS, and HIV nondisclosure and transmission, in a particularly invidious, phobic, regressive way.[120] At his rhetorical peak, HIV appears as a weapon brandished by sex-crazed, death-crazed homosexuals hell-bent on spreading, with impunity, their virus.[121] It is as if Spindelman imagines, or wishes, there really are patient zeroes, predators primarily responsible for the stubborn incidence and prevalence of HIV among U.S. gay men.[122] HIV-positive men are both Spindelman's sex victims and sex offenders. And in this way, HIV/AIDS literalizes the "erotics of death" that sits at the heart of gay men's alleged fidelity to sexual freedom.[123]

Spindelman would likely say that my critique performs a disavowal, in a long line of disavowals, of gay male responsibility for the perpetuation of sexual injury and "sexual death" in the form of HIV/AIDS.[124] But such a rebuttal misapprehends opposition to HIV criminalization laws, assuming in advance that resistance to law is resistance to responsibility. HIV nondisclosure and transmission laws were mostly codified midepidemic and midpanic.[125] They overestimate risks of certain sexual activities, assume risk where none exists, add stigma to an already stigmatized identity category, take little or no account of risk-reducing behavior (like taking antiretrovirals), and may very well deter HIV-testing by incentiv-izing ignorance.[126] Enforcement of potential HIV exposure laws is often vindictive, likely racially disparate in impact, and disproportionately tar-geted against men, and for heterosexual conduct.[127] There is no evidence that criminalization lowers either risks or rates of HIV transmission.[128] Meanwhile, safer-sex campaigns, antiretroviral therapies, serosorting, harm-reduction practices, and now, perhaps game-changing, preexposure pro-phylaxis, did not materialize solely so that men who have sex with men could fuck without consequence.[129] These are efforts to redress the harms of HIV without anthropomorphizing harm, to change the medical and cultural import of HIV so it is not a death sentence but a manageable health condition. Some of these efforts, across some demographics, have worked. If we care about minimizing and remediating HIV, if we care (like Spindelman does) about generating less toxic sexual relations, we should advocate for lowering the cost of treatment, making screening and treat-ment more accessible, and better funding for comprehensive sexuality and prevention education.[130]

So Spindelman is wrong about the medical and cultural meaning of HIV, and therefore wrong in supporting the criminalization of HIV transmission, especially if he is invested in lowering population rates of HIV.

On the other hand, step three of the syllogism—sexual autonomy licenses any consensual sexual activity—should give us some normative pause, and Spindelman states more eloquently than most the unbearable costs of sexual autonomy so conceived. Hiding in the shadows of "Sex-uality's Law," and in the footnotes, are accounts of other kinds of injuries and harms that, however consensual, may be intolerable from the liberal, democratic state's point of view. He references the "German Cannibal" case, in which one partner castrated, killed, further dismembered, and then consumed the other partner, acts partially videotaped and demonstrably consensual.[131] He references BDSM sex more generally, questioning its advocates' kneejerk recourse to consent as summarily determinative.[132] He worries that *Lawrence* authorizes, if not doctrinally counterbalanced, same-sex sexual violence under the sign of "freedom."[133] And he laments, rightfully, that gay men underreport sexual harassment, abuse, and rape, and that when gay men do report sexual injury, their accounts are too often dismissed or trivialized.[134]

I agree that the state might have a role to play in regulating, even proscribing, some harms of consensual sexual conduct—but I disagree that HIV nondisclosure is one of those harms.

The solution to addressing these other injuries is not to abandon sexual autonomy but to reconstruct its meaning, to reconceive it relationally. Jennifer Nedelsky understands "the capacity for creative interaction" as a core element of autonomy, and Gowri Ramachandran defends a right "connected to cultural and political expression and identity development," a right that protects "cultural velocity."[135] In Ramachandran's response to Rubenfeld, she supposes sexual autonomy may be "useful as a proxy," the normative ground on which we might declare that "neither the state nor anyone else should have a monopoly on one's sexuality . . . individual rights to define sexual identity facilitate cultural contest and change."[136] Again, whether we call this relational right sexual agency or sexual autonomy, whether we think of a right to "cultural velocity" as independent from or part and parcel of sexual autonomy, Schulhofer, Nedelsky, Ramachandran, Tuerkheimer, and many others converge on a qualified right to figuring out and codetermining our sexual and social relations. What this means, practically speaking, is that some (sexual) conduct, even if consensual, too broadly disqualifies the possibility for future relations, disqualifies the capacity to codetermine those relations and to participate in "cultural contest and change." That conduct might include sex that involves homicide or suicide.[137] It might also include sex that involves permanent, severe injury, like the removal of limbs or organs or some forms of psychological torture.

We need to be extremely careful here, as we were with *Thirteen*'s Tracy and her self-cutting. "Harm," even in its physical dimensions, is readily susceptible to moralization, as the infamous "Spanner Case" attests.[138] There, "harm," consensual and impermanent, served as pretext for a breathtakingly homophobic, AIDS-phobic ruling (whereas, just a few years after the Spanner Case, similar but marital, heterosexual SM conduct was held immune from England's law prohibiting "assault occasioning actual bodily harm").[139] And a focus on the removal of limbs and organs, likewise, must be qualified by competing, nuanced normative concerns regarding transgender identification, gender-confirming surgery, amputee devoteeism, apotemnophilia, and so forth.[140] These problems shelved (for someone else to pick up; one might, in this instance, utilize a competing harms analysis, or a competing state interest analysis), it seems to me more promising to redefine sexual autonomy as relational and futural, thereby targeting threats to future relations, rather than receding sexual autonomy to individual choice, thereby licensing, as Spindelman fears, sexual carte blanche.

TOWARD AN ADOLESCENT QUEERNESS

Queer studies scholars might take a cue from Rubenfeld and think more about teenagers, but think about them better. My parting thought, though, is not to "queer" adolescence. Adolescence is inescapably queer, in its contradictory constructions as liminal; "dangerous but endangered";[141] allegedly physiologically universal (that is, not a "construct" but a discovery) yet so evidently racially, culturally, and nationally inflected; a figural site of gender and sexuality possibilities but also the figural site of gender and sexuality disqualifications, attritions, winnowing. Instead, I want to ask how adolescence—as a category of analysis, cultural signifier, and, indeed, empirical referent—might inform, perhaps even queer, queer studies. There is, as this book has cited throughout, a plethora of work in gender and sexuality studies on the child and its tropic, organizing force.[142] Since the inception of what has come to be called queer theory, scholars have engaged with the child and its meaning-making capacity—as regressive, subversive, constitutive, terroristic, eroticizing, deeroticizing, normalizing, denaturalizing, etc.—in literature, law, social movements, and political climates. I want to spend a final moment on more recent queer-theoretic discussions of children and the child, reinaugurated by Lee Edelman and complicated by, among others, José Esteban Muñoz and J. Jack Halberstam, to make the case that thinking adolescence might open onto other possibilities for queer-theoretic interventions.

In his brilliant polemic, *No Future: Queer Theory and the Death Drive* (2004), Lee Edelman rails against—while admitting that we are always held hostage to—"reproductive futurism" as the organizing episteme for politics and for social identification. Edelman argues that, to stave off the "the hole in the Symbolic"—the disorganizing, self-shattering *jouissance* that limns our attachments (to our identities, to others) and fidelities (to liberalism, to reason, to narrative meaning)—we suture ourselves to the promise of the future, a future redeemed and embodied by the innocence, sameness, and simplicity of the child.[143] The child is "futurity's condensation," a bipartisan fetish and symbolic fulcrum, in the absence of which there would be no recognizable politics as such: "we are no more able to conceive of a politics without a fantasy of the future than we are able to conceive of a future without the figure of the Child."[144] The structure of reproductive futurism, psychical and political, redounds to the "absolute privilege of heteronormativity," delimits our political rights and imaginative capacities, and secures social consensus through the child, despite the fact that we are "collectively terrorized" by the child as the "beneficiary of every political intervention."[145] This is one way the death drive is recircuited. The other way is through queerness, which, for Edelman, names the negativity that undercuts the future, the child, politics, and narrative. Queerness is a *"structural position,"* not an immutable identity.[146] Gay or gayish adult men, like Scrooge or Voldemort, historically and contemporarily occupy that position, dangerously proximate to the little boy (Tiny Tim, Harry Potter) in whom the future is invested.[147] In Edelman's account, we are captured and captivated by the figure of the child, who installs and reinstalls straight(jacketed) sociopolitical and sexual order.

In contiguous ways, queer theorists José Esteban Muñoz and J. Jack Halberstam put pressure on Edelman's child. In *Cruising Utopia: The Then and There of Queer Futurity* (2009), Muñoz's rebuttal to *No Future*, Muñoz argues that queerness is best understood not as poised against the future, but as itself "futurity and hope," where queerness is a utopic promise always "in the horizon," pointing toward social, sexual, intergenerational collectives and world-making that liberal gay and lesbian politics have forsaken for pragmatism and assimilation.[148] While Muñoz endorses Edelman's "disdain for the culture of the child," he will later question this undifferentiated, ahistoricized child in whose name the social propagates itself: "all children are not the privileged white babies to whom contemporary society caters."[149] Marshaling hate crimes against young people of color as evidence, Muñoz drives the point home:

> The future is only the stuff of some kids. Racialized kids, queer kids, are not the sovereign princes of futurity. Although Edelman does indicate that the future of the child as futurity is different from the future of actual children, his framing nonetheless accepts and reproduces this monolithic figure of the child that is indeed always already white.[150]

For Muñoz, imagining a world "where queer youths of color actually get to grow up" is not symptomatic of reproductive futurism, but a restoration of what queer should be—an aspiration for a more democratic, pluralistic, supportive world.[151]

If futurity is or should be queer for Muñoz, the child is or should be queer for J. Jack Halberstam. He too critiques Edelman explicitly, but more interesting for our purposes is the way he refigures children and childhood.[152] In *The Queer Art of Failure* (2011), Halberstam too alleges an embrace of negativity, unproductivity, forgetting, and failure (as modes of political address rather than as a refusal of politics), but he looks to "alternative productions of the child," youth, and youth subcultures as engines rather than enemies of resistance to normative order.[153] Surveying computer-animated films like *Finding Nemo, A Bug's Life,* and *Toy Story* and teen comedies like *Dude, Where's My Car?,* Halberstam argues that such representations offer a "utopian alternative" in the childlike—that "tell[s] of the real change that children may still believe is possible and desirable."[154] "The beauty of these films," writes Halberstam, "is that they do not fear failure, they do not favor success, and they picture children not as pre-adults figuring the future but as anarchic beings who partake in strange and inconsistent temporal logics."[155] Halberstam observes how, in his archive, friendships, cross-generational partnerships, and collectivities are valued over individual achievement, the couple form, and the nuclear family. Capitalistic and corporate powers are directly or indirectly challenged by youthful irreverence, wilding, and refusal to be productive.[156] Halberstam picks up this thread of the productively disassembling, revolutionary child in his more recent *Gaga Feminism: Sex, Gender, and the End of Normal* (2012). There, the brief for children is made even more strongly: as "anarchic, ungendered blobs," children are the vanguard of "gaga feminism," a feminism keyed to gender dedifferentiation, nonidentitarian sexual and intimacy formations, street protest, and aesthetic experimentation.[157] "Change . . . is the air children breathe," and despite Halberstam's acknowledgment that the "child" has so often served reactionary politics, he argues that it is the younger generation that embodies and engenders new (dis) order.[158] In this utopia, "queers counsel the straight, [and] the children teach their parents."[159] Halberstam's child could not be further from Edelman's, but this child is also not Muñoz's suffering queer youth of color. Halberstam's kids are making a future and unmaking the gendered and sexual constrictions of the present.

I recount Muñoz's and Halberstam's critiques of Edelman because I think they are both misguided and yet have something important to offer, and that this something might be better delivered through a more careful canvassing of adolescence, rather than through rescue missions to recover the child (rescue missions that necessarily retain the very binary between childhood and adulthood Halberstam elsewhere hopes to dispel).[160] Muñoz's reference to victimized children of color (or adults of color he makes into children) *confirms* the very logic of reproductive futurism, which organizes politics around a fantasy figure—a childlike fetus, for example—while unceremoniously discounting the daily and structural injustices endured by children and adults alike.[161] And as other scholars have documented, children of color have been enlisted as figures of innocence to mobilize political action, both reactionary and progressive, although certainly innocence has historically and pervasively been the providence of white children.[162] The *symbol* of the child—white or of color—has no necessary correspondence to political projects that promote the welfare of children. Meanwhile, Halberstam's reimagining of children veers toward abstractly rather than concretely utopic.[163] The vision of children floating free from history, politics, and inequalities, as potentialities of the anarchy we like, is secured through his sample selection: those films that confirm (or, as foil, oppose) a transvaluation of "immaturity and a refusal of adulthood . . . a queer form of antidevelopment."[164] If we turn not only to CGI films like *Finding Nemo* and *A Bug's Life,* but also to films like *Thirteen* or, say, *Mysterious Skin, Precious,* or *Pariah,* we see young people who are, like Halberstam's favored characters, navigating possibilities, figuring out interests, and striving for nontoxic, nonnuclear, cross-generational relations, but doing so against backdrops of suffocating norms, material deprivations, and familial absence (it is less prescriptively appealing to "forget family" when you never had one that worked).[165]

If Muñoz's invocation of the child is too real, understating the force of fantasy, Halberstam's invocation of the child is too fantastical, divorced from unanimated realities, constraints, and inequalities. And yet, Muñoz and Halberstam are right, I think, to ask if the child must always be undifferentiated and ahistorical, must always figure as an object to be protected rather than a becoming subject to be propelled. What if the child, figuratively, were not a child, but a teenager?

Let me return to Edelman's child then, to propose one way the interjection of adolescence into the story and stronghold of reproductive futurism might amend Edelman's queer theory. Edelman tells us that "those of us inhabiting the place of the queer may be able to cast off that queerness and enter the properly political sphere, but only by shifting the figural burden of queerness to someone else."[166] As I've demonstrated, that "someone else" may now be the sex offender, and gay normalcy may be purchased through the demonization of the "future-negating" sex offender,[167] whose violation of consent violates social order. But whereas queerness, for Edelman, is a container fillable by whatever identity formation, the child references only and always children, despite Edelman's insistence that the child must not "be confused with the lived experiences of any historical discourse."[168] But if the tenants of queerness come and go, can different children occupy the sociopolitical figure of the child? Must it be the innocent, unknowing child, or could that position be held by the vulnerable yet desiring adolescent? We cannot, on Edelman's *own* terms, "fuck the poor, innocent kid on the Net" in refusal of reproductive futurism, because the symbolic appeal of the child is "impossible to refuse," because there is "no ground we could stand on outside that logic [of the Symbolic]," because "the signifying order will always necessitate the production of some figural repository for excess that precludes its ultimate realization of the One."[169] In other words, in the structure of politics, as in the structure of the self, there will always be a figural child and there will always be figural queerness. And if that's the case, if this is an inescapable structure, what, then, if we resignify the child in addition to avowing our queerness? Maybe it's not up to us. But Edelman knows, I think, that we cannot actually "choose . . . not to choose the Child," so maybe it is not so farfetched that we choose *other* children, that we generate other fictions of the child, adolescent fictions, less brutalizing in their social and sexual consequences.[170] On this reading, the child is neither the prop of extant social order (Edelman) nor an unadulterated revolutionary heralding a gender-fluid, anarchic future (Halberstam). As vulnerable rather than innocent, as indexically perempted (by norms, material inequalities, discursive repertoires) but not always or necessarily violated or bullied (by persons), the adolescent may expand the political horizon. We might still invest in, identify with, and want to protect this child, but this child is becoming sexually and socially autonomous, figuring out her interests, although under sociopolitical constraints that uncontrollably disqualify certain possibilities. For Edelman, the child that we are politically beholden to "condenses a fantasy of vulnerability to the queerness of queer sexualities," but another fantasy of the child, the teenager, might allow us to consider those material obstacles that preempt and perempt, or asymmetrically penalize, the child's queerness.[171] Queerness, that is, as exploration, experimentation, and formative mistake-making.

If the adolescent is our figure for the child, a figure intrinsically marked by a combination of protection and propulsion, qualified autonomy and peremption, we might more richly attend to axes of social difference and inequality, as Muñoz would like us to do. This rendition of the child bypasses the somewhat overstated conclusions that white kids have futures where kids of color do not, or that innocence is only the preserve of white childhood. The conflicted, relatively recent fabrication of adolescence—as liminal, social but also biological, imitative but also inventive, vulnerable but agentive—itself invites reading difference (race, gender, class, ability, sexuality) back into rather than washed out of the theoretical framework. More avowedly than the child, the adolescent is a pluralized, resolutely historicized, and eroticized construct. While the adolescent is no less ideologically saturated than the child, the former's avowed differences—*within the very category itself*—engender an engagement with social inequalities more promising than *add x and stir.*

This is but one location for queer-theoretic engagement with the adolescent. Surely there are others.[172]

Notes

INTRODUCTION

The Introduction title is adapted from a roundtable at Brown University, "The End(s) of Consent," sponsored by the Pembroke Center for Teaching and Research on Women in April 2012.

1. Convicted sex offenders are indexically and almost always male, a fact that probably has more to do with reporting patterns, prosecutorial enforcement, and cultural norms than empirics. See the subsection "The (Elusive) Female Sex Offender" in this chapter.

2. Assumptions 1 and 2 are dispelled by research presented in the second chapter. Assumption 4, indirectly challenged in all four chapters ("indirectly," for there are no measurements on the effectiveness of the signs), mislocates the principal site of sexual abuse as *other* people's homes, rather than our own, our workplaces, and our schools. On the ineffectiveness, possible countereffectiveness, and more general foolishness of sex offender residency restrictions (a policy correlate to assumption 3), see chapter 2, notes 21–22; see also Duwe, Donnay, and Tewksbury 2008, 500. On the ineffectiveness of sex offender residency restrictions in Jacksonville, Florida, a city northeast of Bradford County, see Nobles, Levenson, and Youstin 2012.

3. Under Florida law, a "sexual predator" has not necessarily been convicted of a crime against a minor. A person may be classified as a sexual predator, for example, if he has been convicted of more than one sex offense, or if the offense involved "physical violence." Fla. Stat. § 775.21(3)(a) (2012). Nonetheless, promoters and defenders of the public sign campaign have invoked its necessity for the protection of children. See, for example, Dunn and Dobilas 2013 ("[Bradford County's] sheriff is taking a bold move to warn families about child molesters in his community"); "The Florida County" 2013; Bechara 2013 (commented one Bradford County resident, "They go after our kids, we need to know where they're at").

4. On the cultural and legal characterization of homosexuals as violent, child-recruiting, death-driven, and addicted to their own desire, see, for example, Dalton 2001; Howe 2001; McCreery 2008; Stychin 1995, 117–39; Watney 1996, 22–37.

5. Mich. Comp. Law § 28.733–28.734 (2005).

6. See, for example, Adler 2012; Garfinkle 2003, 184–205; Human Rights Watch 2007, 65–77; Janus and Polacheck 2009, 159–62; Michels 2012; Pittman 2013. Asks Adler (2012, 134), "How did the law come to picture the predator and the victim as one and the same person?"

7. On the overall inadequacy and ineffectiveness of the most prevalent forms of U.S. sex offender laws, see, generally, chapter 2; Agan 2011; Prescott and Rockoff 2011; Wright 2009b. Prescott and Rockoff demonstrate that registration is deterrent in some instances and that notification may reduce *overall* crime rates; however, notification sometimes correlates with an *increase* in recidivism among registered sex offenders.

8. Pesta 2012.

9. For an account of the pressured and/or unwanted sex teenage girls experience as a result of teenage boys' (normalized, condoned) advances, see, for example, Oberman 2000. For an account of high school boys' ongoing and largely unchecked sexual harassment of girls, see, for example, Rahimi and Liston 2012, 170: "Underlying ALL of sexual harassment and bullying are sexist assumptions. Chief among these is 'boys will be boys.' Violence against women and against 'effeminate' males is not only tolerated but is often condoned and encouraged." For an account of how "too far" affordances are racially and heternormatively distributed, see Meiners 2015.

10. Both boys were convicted (judged "delinquent," as juveniles) of rape as defined by the Ohio Revised Code. One boy was also convicted of "illegal use of minor in nudity-oriented material or performance," for photographing the girl naked. See Oppel 2013.

11. Goddard 2012, emphasis added.

12. See Estes 2013. As of this writing, one of the two boys has been ordered to register as a "tier 2" sex offender in Ohio (on the federal tier system, see chapter 2), although his name will not be posted on state or federal sex offender registry websites. See Welsh-Huggins 2013.

13. See, for example, Ortberg 2013; Shapiro 2013.

14. It should be noted that a few voices in the blogosphere parlayed the Steubenville case into a broader discussion about the diffusion and prevalence of sexual violence and about our discursive overreliance on prosecution and predation as terms of comprehension. See, for example, McBride 2013; McKenzie 2013. On the other hand, some critics, while nodding to "rape culture" and the ordinariness of gendered violence, nonetheless reverted to the frame of the predatory perpetrator (or newscaster). For them, the problem of CNN's tone-deaf coverage was not that it symptomized wider inattention to enculturation that aggrandizes male aggression and converts female nonconsent into consent, but that the two Steubenville teenage boys really are

absolutely horrible human beings. See, for example, Beck 2013; Marcotte 2013 ("The phrase *'rape culture'* that feminists kick around describes, above all else, the way that sexual predators move about freely because other men don't stand up to them"); Murtha 2013.

15. E. Bernstein 2010.

16. See, for example, Carmon 2013.

17. See note 10.

18. Ohio Rev. Code Ann. § 2907.01 (M) (2008); § 2907.323 (2011).

19. See Fischel 2013b for a critical summary of left scholarship on child pornography law. See also Place 2010, 238 ("The real object of today's crime is not the victim, not the state, but the idea of safety and inviolability, of pure heart and best intentions").

20. According to a report by the Human Rights Watch (2007, 12), "national polls indicate that Americans fear sex offenders more than terrorists" (citing a Gallup poll reporting that "66 percent of people surveyed were 'very concerned' about sex offenders").

21. See also Corrigan 2006; Meiners 2009.

22. On the (waning?) nationalized supremacy of heterosexuality in the United States, see, for example, Berlant 1997, 16–19. On the resurgence of heterosexual supremacy within certain postcolonial nations alongside the concurrent normativizing of homosexuality in certain "Western" nations, see, for example, Stychin 1998, 11. Stychin presages contemporary debates on "pinkwashing."

23. Berlant 2007, 763.

24. A disciplinary analogue to this project would be something like, *what sort of sexual political landscape is foregrounded by Rousseau's Émile or the nonconsenting children of modern liberalism?* See Brewer 2005.

25. See Rubin 1993.

26. See, for example, Adler 2001; Fischel 2013a; Kleinhans 2004.

27. The social-historical episode presented here should not eclipse the more creative, capacious political ambition of the LGBT movement prior to the 1990s, which has almost collapsed under the heavy press of litigating for military and marriage inclusion (see D'Emilio 2007). Nonetheless, both LGBT visibility and the enactment of LGBT antidiscrimination laws from the 1990s and into the present are unparalleled.

28. But see Cossman 2007, 197. A fuller discussion on the limits of my argument—that adult consensuality has replaced heterosexuality as the national sexuality—can be found in chapter 2. As Cossman rightly points out, when it comes to sex acts, consent is not a constitutional get-out-of-jail-free card.

29. What young people in the United States do know about sex and sexuality is primarily learned from mainstream media that—so often but not always—portrays the very narrowest and therefore damaging version of normative sexuality (in terms of age, race, body, gendered conduct, and so on). See, for example, Lamb and Peterson 2012, 710; Levesque 2007, 118–26. On the insufficiencies, misinformation, erotophobia,

and sexism of mainstream sexuality education in the United States, see chapter 3, note 233; see also Fine and McClelland 2006; Rahimi and Liston 2012, 26, 39, 60–61, 178–79.

30. See Adler 2012, 133–34, 157; Szymialis 2010, 314–22, 339.

31. Age and nonconsent are not, though, the universal gravamen for sexual assault offenses, either across all states or within individual states' criminal codes. Many statutes retain a "force" element, for example, irrespective of nonconsent. Incest is often a strict liability offense. Regulations on public sex, prostitution, obscenity, and the sale of sex toys are not explicitly predicated upon nonconsent. See Cossman 2007, 35–37, 55–59, 197.

32. For a critique of the operative force of consent in modern and contemporary political theory, see, for example, Brewer 2005; Pateman 1980; Pateman 2007, 205.

33. On the interjection (and not) of consent into U.S. sex law, see chapter 3, notes 157–63. On the privileged role of consent in some feminist activism around sexual violence, see, for example, the "Consent Is Sexy" campaign (http://www.consentissexy .net/).

34. It seems somewhat absurd to provide specific citations for Marx, Gramsci, and Althusser, given how much these thinkers aimed to puncture, in different degrees of directedness, the fiction of consent as a presupposition, consequence, or index of freedom. Nonetheless, particularly prescient texts would include Althusser 2001 ("Ideology and Ideological State Apparatuses"); Gramsci 1971; Marx and Engels 1998 (in *The German Ideology,* the critique of social consent as an achievement of ideology is incipient, and developed by Gramsci and Althusser); Nussbaum 2001, 111–66.

35. De Beauvoir 1989; MacKinnon 1983; MacKinnon 1989; MacKinnon 2001; MacKinnon 2007a; Mill 1998 ("The Subjection of Women"); Pateman 1980; Pateman 1988. Of course, de Beauvoir is more sanguine about the transformative (potential) power of female sexual desire and pleasure than these other thinkers. While de Beauvoir also documents the many ways women dispute or disdain paradigmatic male heterosex practices, resistance usually cashes out at submission, however resigned.

36. Caringella 2009; Chamallas 1987–88; Gavey 2005; Oberman 1994; Oberman 2000; Oberman 2001; Schulhofer 1992; Schulhofer 1998. See also chapter 3.

37. Butler 2011; Eskridge 1995; Rubin 1993.

38. See W. Brown 2001, 18–44.

39. Ibid., 22–25.

40. Schulhofer 1992; Schulhofer 1998. On autonomy as relational, see, for example, Nedelsky 2011; Oshana 1998; but see also M. Friedman 2003. Friedman (87) cautions against feminist caricatures of autonomy theory, arguing that much "mainstream philosophical theorizing about autonomy" admits the importance (both conditioning and constraining) of social contexts and relations.

41. I understand vulnerability as human susceptibility to injury that is both universal and ineliminable, but exacerbated or minimized by political arrangements and power inequalities. Most helpful for my thinking here has been Fineman 2008, but

also, and sometimes inharmoniously, Butler 2006; Ezard 2001; Herring 2012; Nussbaum 2006b; Satz 2008; Turner 2006.

42. Elsewhere (Fischel 2013b), I wonder if innocence itself might be politically polysemic, even for sex. Whereas Fineman (2008) articulates the political arrangements that might result from replacing the autonomous subject of liberalism with the vulnerable subject, I am querying what sort of political and legal consequences follow if we understand vulnerability and autonomy as complementary (if competing) normative priors, rather than as mutually exclusive. On the distinction between vulnerability and innocence as idioms for children's social condition, see Dixon and Nussbaum 2012, 572.

43. See, for example, Dewan 2007; Keller 2012; Searcey 2009.

44. See chapter 1, note 3.

45. Lancaster 2011, 2, emphasis added.

46. Ibid., 255–56, emphasis added.

47. See also Berlant 1997; Edelman 2004.

48. See Kincaid 1998, 12–13.

49. See Kincaid 2004, 15.

50. Lancaster 2011, 17.

51. See Chauncey 1993.

52. Shane Phelan (2001) argues that lesbians and gays occupy the position of paradigmatic stranger in U.S. politics and political discourse; neither liberal, neighborly friend nor mutually constituting enemy, the liminal sexual stranger is faced with powerful if contradictory reproaches, as she is both enmeshed in and apart from the imagined citizen body. Phelan further contends that assimilationist approaches to political inclusion have reified bisexuals and gender-deviant queers as the new strangers demarcating political respectability (115–38). Oddly, Phelan says next to nothing (133) about "stranger danger" or the sexual stranger as embodied in the convicted sex offender. The sex offender, whose name is publicly broadcast in the interest of safer neighborhoods, and whose body blends in with the community's, surely functions as a structuring stranger to the norms of both political solidarity and sexual decency.

53. My thinking on the "queering" of sex offenders has been influenced by Cathy Cohen (1997, 1999, 2009), who powerfully argues that state regulatory policies and the exonerative dissociations of respectability politics render minority populations sexually suspect (and thus "queer").

54. See Janus 2006, 101–9.

55. I borrow the oft-cited phrase "the embarrassed etc." from Judith Butler (1990, 143). Of course, she was up to something quite different, but germane. For her, the "etc." that accompanies feminist laundry lists of women qualified by differences (race, class, sexuality, etc.) illustrates the impossibility of securing epistemological certainty of women's identity in advance of political engagement. The "etc." marks a failure, but one that should impel feminists to turn political attention toward signifying practices that naturalize identity, and away from prefiguring identities prior to making claims.

56. Of course this list could be endless. There are a multitude of identities, relations, sexualized phenomena, and sexual regulations that this project does not canvass or only canvasses cursorily. I am particularly concerned about my omission of transgender subjects and transgender desire (and therefore the project's tacit collusion in a gender binary). The omission is in part a function of diagnosing and then challenging dominant representations and regulations of sex harm and danger: although the child-at-risk in the contemporary national imaginary may be more or less gender-neutral, it is still dimorphically gendered. The transgender child is not understood to be either a subject or object of desire but a problem to be medicalized or psychologized. As a social problem and representational entity, the operating narrative of the transgender child is its and its parents' confrontation with gender deviation; desire (for another, not for one's identitarian truth) drops out, in part because socially intelligible desire is desire for one of two genders (see Valentine 2006, although he is concerned more broadly with the scholarly and social language of identity to gauge complexities of desire). Insofar as transgender adults are perceived to embody threat, it is the threat of gender dissolution and its ensuing social, familial, and identity confusions (Bornstein 2006; Gamson 1995; Gamson 1998), not the threat of predation on the child, that propel narratives of either incrementally enlightened acceptance or allergic aversion. Nonetheless, future work certainly should pursue questions of gender orderliness, gender-determined ordinariness, and trans subjectivity/subjection in the production and mediation of sex offense and sex harm in contemporary U.S. law and popular culture.

57. See Center for Sex Offender Management 2007; Denov 2003; Vandiver and Kercher 2004, 126.

58. See Denov 2003, 309–10. The laws target men—the anatomy specifications are decidedly not recognitions of gender fluidity.

59. See Kaplan and Green 1995, 299.

60. See Center for Sex Offender Management 2007, 3; Denov 2003, 311–12.

61. See Denov 2003, 311; Kaplan and Green 1995, 288.

62. There are few medium- or large-scale studies of female sex offenders, most of which are interested in generating taxonomies, not assessing recidivism. See, for example, Vandiver and Kercher 2004.

63. See Cocca 2004, 63–92.

64. But see Nutting 2013 for a (rather flat) countercharacterization of the female sex offender as ruthlessly predatory.

65. *48 Hours* 2011.

66. *Today* 2011.

67. See Jenkins 2001, 34–37.

68. See, for example, Gagnon 2003, 45; Jenkins 2001, 76–83; Lancaster 2011, 73–75; Loseke 2003, 9–10.

69. See Gamson 2001, 188–91.

70. See Loseke 2003, 7.

71. See Gorrell 2006.

72. See also Loseke 2003.

73. Jenkins 2001, 79.

74. But see Gorrell 2006.

1. "ESPECIALLY HEINOUS"

The phrase "especially heinous" is taken from the voiceover introduction of NBC's television series, *Law & Order: Special Victims Unit* (*SVU*): "In the criminal justice system, sexually based offenses are considered especially heinous." Because, in the series, the "criminal justice system" is synonymous with "law," which is usually synonymous with "order," "sexually based offenses" just are "especially heinous." *To Catch a Predator* (*TCAP*) too comprehends sexual offense as always already especially heinous. *SVU* is a fictionalized series that heavily borrows from "real life" events whereas *TCAP* is a "reality" show whose plotline and denouement are so routinized and contrived as to be fictitious. I am ambivalent about the ontological heinousness of sexual offense (as opposed to other offenses), but I will be suggesting that, for shows like *SVU* and *TCAP*, the heinousness of sex crimes is an upshot of violated innocence and that such a framework forecloses more helpful accounts of impositions to sexual autonomy. So sexual violation may be heinous, but not (only or always) for the reasons inferred from or explicitly announced in the scripts of *SVU* or *TCAP*.

1. See, for example, Best 1990; Hacking 1991. On the similar symbolic functions of the terrorist and the sex offender see Douard 2008–9.

2. See, for example, Angelides 2004; Califia 2000; Levine 2002. These authors are not so doctrinaire in their analyses, but their polemics against reigning conservative political achievements are not always precise.

3. Kincaid 1998.

4. See, for example, Wright 2009a and Corrigan 2006, respectively.

5. Foucault 1990, 17.

6. See Hacking 1991.

7. On the Anglo-American making and remaking of the homosexual subject through law, see, for example, Stychin 1995; Stychin 2003, 25–47. For a more cosmopolitan account of the legal construction of gay subjectivity, see Stychin 1998; Stychin 2003. Stychin's oeuvre tracks how the legal constitution of homosexuality develops over time. The history is not one of linear progress, although Stychin evidences the many ways the "homosexual" has traveled, in law, from subjugated, abnormal Other (against whom a stable, superior heterosexuality could be produced and maintained) to rights-bearing subject to harbinger of cosmopolitanism to the epitome of the neoliberal, responsible subject. As this and subsequent chapters will argue, the contemporary legal construction of and rhetoric surrounding the sex offender is largely inflexible and unforgiving.

8. Wright 2009a.

9. Adler 2012, 138, 142–43.

10. See Grigoriadis 2007; McCollam 2007, 31–32.

11. "Expensive Home Rich with Potential Predators" 2007 (my transcription).

12. See, for example, Grigoriadis 2007; Kohm 2009; McCollam 2007.

13. "Potential Predators Go South in Kentucky" 2007. I have corrected the punctuation and stylized the transcript.

14. See Adler 2001; Adler 2012; Casper and Moore 2009, 47–53; Khan 2009a. As Place (2010, 206) brilliantly summarizes, "This is where *Dateline: To Catch a Predator* is genius: it too comes into your home [like the predator] with the same titillating temptation, as it offers an immediate absolution from sin. We'll get off on this, then we'll get him."

15. See Adler 2012, 149; Place 2010, 196.

16. In her media discourse analysis of a child pornography/child sexual abuse investigation, Ummni Khan (2009a, 407) observes, "There is a kind of voyeurism of voyeurism that is engaged when the media expounds on how sickening the images are that the perverts consume."

17. See Lynch 2004.

18. See Kitzinger 2004. However, Hacking observes that as incest increasingly fell under the category "child abuse" in the 1970s and 1980s, it was more available for public redress: "thus the medicalization and 'societization' of incest as child abuse makes it possible to deal with a 'problem'" (1991, 280).

19. See Khan 2009a.

20. Berlant 1997, 96. See also Wood and Skeggs 2004.

21. Gamson (1998) similarly describes how talk shows immanently trouble their own normatively gendered and heterosexualized scripts, when trans and queer "freaks talk back," resisting the pathological characters they are expected to portray.

22. S. Cohen 2002, xxx–xxxi.

23. Ibid, 1.

24. See, for example, Atmore 1999; Burgett 2009; Kitzinger 2006.

25. This now obvious point about the interpenetration of "society" and "media," or rather, the collapsing of the distinction altogether, was forecasted a generation ago by Angela McRobbie and Sarah L. Thornton (1995, 570): "the media is no longer something separable from society. Social reality is experienced through language, communication, and imagery. Social meanings and social differences are inextricably tied up with representation." For an account that countenances this sort of interactivity between media covering sexual violence against children and public opinion, see Kitzinger 2006.

26. The observation is excavated from Rose (1999), but it is not hers; rather, she draws attention to the ways intensified moral discourse strengthens hegemonic interpretations of meaning and solidifies community identity. She argues that analysts of moral panic emphasize the social-structural conditions that generate panic at the expense of exploring the recurrent meanings and relations of power and order sustained or arranged through panicked discourse.

27. See Cavender 1998, 88–92; A. Doyle 1998, 99–102.

28. See Kohm 2009.

29. See Valier 2004.

30. See Adler 2012, 141–45.

31. S. Cohen 2002, 1.

32. Ibid., 90, emphasis added.

33. Ibid., 90, 146–47. Cohen critiques his and others' accounting of law in relation to moral panic, but the critiques do not capture more thoroughly the constructive force of law in continuing and contorting social and sexual anxiogenic phenomena. On sex law itself as historically reconstituted through social movement activists and "ordinary citizens," see Robertson 2005, 235.

34. Adler 2012.

35. Ibid., 152–57.

36. See Burgett 2009.

37. See, for example, Janus and Polacheck 2010, 166–68.

38. See Sarat 2009, 183. The argument presented here and elaborated in chapter 2 is indebted to Robert Cover's (1986, 1610) exposition of the "unseverable connection between legal interpretation and violence." I focus on the illocutionary, subject-constituting violence of legal categories rather than the perlocutionary, socially co-ordinated violence of judicial sentencing.

39. Pratt (2000) tracks how and why episodes of symbolic, brutal punishment are executed legally and extralegally within the otherwise increasingly bureaucratized penal practices of Western nations. He proposes that more emotive modes of punishment assuage communal feelings of distrust and dislocation in an era of detached communication and economic tension.

40. In the December 28, 2007, episode of *TCAP* (from which Figures 2–4 are extracted), the "predator" begins to express doubts to the decoy and mutters "it's not right, you know, and it's really bothering me." It is exactly at this moment of equivocation, when the "predator" appears less than predatory, when in fact he might get up and leave, that Hansen switches places with the decoy and course corrects: "you seemed pretty confident on the Internet." See "To Catch a Predator—Bowling Green, Kentucky" 2015.

41. See Cavender 1998; Kohm 2009.

42. See L. Williams 1999.

43. See Casper and Moore 2009, 52. It is not arbitrary that most of the clips of the show available from MSNBC.com are of the "money shots": Hansen choreographing the predator and law enforcement coming on (top of) him. Adler (2012, 137, 152) also refers to these scenes as "money shots."

44. See also Irvine 2006.

45. Rubin 1993, 4.

46. Burgett (2009) contends that Rubin and cultural and literary historians of "sex panics" may isolate "sex" and naturalize the "nation" in their inquiries, while also

conflating mass-mediated affect with public opinion. Inheriting "sex" and "nation" as predetermined terms of analysis and accepting media reports as proxies for popular attitudes may foreclose broader assessments of citizen intimacies, social phenomena, and transnational or subnational relays of power.

47. Rubin 1993, 6–7, 12; emphasis added.

48. See, for example, Janus 2006; Lancaster 2011; Meiners 2009, 32–35, 41–45, 51–54.

49. See, for example, Family Research Council 2014. The Family Research Council is too careful to equate homosexuals with pedophiles or child recruiters to substantiate their campaign against gay marriage. Nevertheless, two of their "Ten Arguments from Social Science against Same-Sex Marriage" are the increased rates of girls' sexual promiscuity and the increased rates of sexual and gender disorders (homoerotic attractions, detouring from gendered behavioral norms) among both boys and girls that will likely result from the legalization of gay marriage.

50. See, for example, Dowd 2010.

51. See, for example, Human Rights Campaign 2010.

52. See Corrigan 2006.

53. Hansen admits early in his book that children are most often sexually abused by relatives or people they know (2007, 6) and devotes a later chapter to parsing different psychological and social factors that predispose persons toward sexually violent behavior (189–208). These moments are throwaways. He banks on good parenting and online monitoring to rescue children and determines in a boldly unscientific calculation that a third of the men are "sick, evil, or wired to want to have sex with young teens," another third are "opportunists" having trouble getting lucky with age-concordant partners, and another third are sexually reprogrammed by the appeal of the Internet (7). See also Place 2010, 205.

54. Hansen et al. 2007.

55. See Phelan 2001, 40–45.

56. See Stanley 2006. Place (2010, 205) asks, "Are the people *Predator* catches really predators? Legally, they are. Morally, they may or may not be, because online is virtual reality, and virtual reality is partial fantasy."

57. See Adler 2012, 136.

58. In their meta-analysis, Wolak et al. (2008) found that every component of this scenario is atypical regarding youth and sexual violence. The great majority of sex crimes committed against youth do not involve online solicitation. Of the sex crimes that do involve online solicitation of a minor, almost none involve deception or force (these crimes are instead equivalent to what we commonly call "statutory rape," or the crime is the online sexual solicitation itself). "Most victims who meet offenders face to face go to such meetings expecting to engage in sexual activity" (113). They advise that "predator" is therefore a misnomer for online offenders (125). According to Potter and Potter (2001), U.S. and Australia media attention to children threatened by online sexual predators is disproportionate, given both the higher prevalence of other

online (and offline) threats young people face, as well as the comparatively low rate of interaction with strangers seeking sex, as reported by young people. Adler (2012, 144–45) references studies reporting that adult online solicitation of minors occurs infrequently, and at a decreasing rate from 2000 to 2006.

59. Rubin 1993, 18–19.

60. Ibid., 30–31.

61. Ibid., 20.

62. Ibid., 30.

63. See, for example, MacKinnon 2007a, 240–48; Schulhofer 1998, 1–16.

64. See Caringella 2009, 17.

65. See Cocca 2004, 38; Oliveri 2000, 467.

66. Atmore (1999) takes to task what she calls "contextualist" academics—Rubin, for example—utilizing moral panic models to explain media and public attention to child sexual abuse. She claims that contextualists lump together feminist and religious right protests against child sexual abuse as hysterical and reactionary. However, she dismisses all moral panic diagnosticians as quickly as she claims they dismiss feminism, implicitly reduces the problem of child sexual abuse exclusively to gender (Rubin's admonition), and canvasses neither the role of law, the place of sexuality, nor a concept of harm in her critique.

67. Rubin 1993, 15.

68. Ibid., 6, 7, 20.

69. Ibid., 15, 21, 23, 31.

70. See Alcoff 1996, 113–15. Alcoff's critique of "Thinking Sex" strongly influenced my own.

71. In another addition to moral panic literature, Gilbert Herdt reproduces a similarly unsatisfying normative framework in which the subject and subjection of the latest "folk devil" is what alone warrants political sympathy and redress: "moral panics overwhelm individual rights and require a new attention to the role that sexual panics play in perpetuating structural violence and reproducing forms of inferior citizenship" (2009b, 17). The structuralist account of sexual hierarchy leads Herdt to contest the lost rights of the demonized, without consideration that it may also be the precariousness of others' rights and relations that incites social fear. For Herdt, there are harms and threats that are "real," but only those leveraged against sexually minoritized subjects (19). However, he also points out that in a late modern era supposedly marked by the expansion of formal rights to different social groups, the affect of moral panic overpowers a more generous distribution of those rights (17).

72. Rubin 2011a, 36.

73. Ibid., 37–38.

74. Ibid., 29.

75. See also Rubin 2011b, 134.

76. See Alcoff 1996, 120–22.

77. The concurrence of vulnerability and desire intensifies, or at least appears to intensify, or is made more transparent, with the advent of technological forms of communication and social networking less familiar to older generations. See Potter and Potter 2001.

78. See, for example, Critcher 2002; de Young 2006; Herdt 2009a; Jackson and Scott 1999; Jenkins 1998; Kitzinger 2006; Lancaster 2011.

79. Hawkes and Egan 2008, 199.

80. See, for example, Angelides 2004.

81. Hawkes and Egan 2008, 196; see also Halberstam 2005 for an analogous discussion of "reproductive temporality" (4) and "reproductive maturity" (162) as heteronormative mandates. For a broader consideration of Halberstam, adolescence and/as sexuality, and the "stretched-out adolescences of queer culture makers" (153), see chapter 4 and the Conclusion.

82. Kelleher 2004, 159.

83. See Harcourt 2007; Janus 2006.

84. See Davis 2007, emphasis added.

85. See Jackson and Scott 1999, 87. Herdt (2009b, 26–32) extends the argument, positing that sex panics, not just child sex panics, are framed and enflamed by conservatives capitalizing on contemporary risks against family and imagined familial simplicity.

86. Hawkes and Egan 2008, 200–201. If age blunts inquiries of gender, innocence blunts inquiries of power, and each misreading reinforces the other. As Jackson and Scott (1999, 104) observe, "When children are sexually abused, this is frequently constructed as a despoliation of innocence rather than an abuse of power."

87. Hawkes and Egan 2008, 196–97; see also Rose 1999.

88. "Expensive Home Rich with Potential Predators" 2007 (my transcription).

89. See also Jackson and Scott 1999, 100.

90. "To Catch a Predator—Bowling Green, Kentucky" 2015.

91. See Connell and Messershmidt 2005.

92. Khan 2009a.

93. See also Wolak et al. 2008, 116: "In summary, what creates risk for teens online is not innocence about sex. The factors that make youths vulnerable to seduction by online molesters are complex and related to immaturity, inexperience, and the impulsiveness with which some youths respond to and explore normal sexual urges."

94. See ibid., 118.

2. TRANSCENDENT HOMOSEXUALS, DANGEROUS SEX OFFENDERS

1. Tribe 2004, 1895.

2. Of course, not everyone agrees that the promised freedoms and constitutional guarantees of *Lawrence* are purely emancipatory. Katherine Franke (2004, 1418) contends that *Lawrence* "domesticates" the concept of liberty, affording liberty only as a privatized right to those who mimic heterosexual, bourgeois sexual practices and

lifestyles, and only at the expense of a resanitized, reregulated public sphere that no longer defends a more capacious understanding of sexual pluralism and sexual freedom. Similarly, Mary Anne Case (2003, 80, 96–97) suggests the liberty in *Lawrence* distills down to a right of gays and lesbians not to face criminal sanctions for their homebound sex, scaling back any potential the ruling offered to promote sexual equality. Jasbir Puar (2007, 84, 120) argues that the protected intimacy of the private gay couple found in *Lawrence* is made intelligible and valuable through the "reracialization of sodomy elsewhere." The cultural and media-inflected sexualizing of Arabs and Muslims after September 11, 2001 (from Abu Ghraib to news cartoons), as well as the legal withdrawal of intimacy and privacy rights to indefinite detainees authorized the "national queer liberal subject before the law" as white and worthy of judicial safeguards. Bernard Harcourt (2004, 512) warns that decriminalization of sodomy might serve to deradicalize queer activism, which hinges in part on the power of transgression. The corollary to these objections might be that while *Lawrence* is not purely emancipatory, emancipation is never pure—the best one can hope for is minimizing the costs rather than eliminating them. The legal proposals offered in chapter 3 for the reregulation of sex across age differences take as a starting point that the effects of juridical intervention always entail collateral.

3. *Connecticut Department of Public Safety v. Doe*, 538 U.S. 1 (2003); *Smith v. Doe*, 538 U.S. 84 (2003).

4. See, e.g., Chauncey 1993; McCreery 2001; McCreery 2008. Supporters of Proposition 8, the 2008 anti–gay marriage referendum in California, successfully made the protection of children the main topic of debate in a referendum on the statutory recognition of and distribution of benefits to adult citizens. See, for example, two television advertisements produced by ProtectMarriage.com, a major supporter of Proposition 8 in California: "Yes on 8 TV Ad: It's Already Happened" 2008; "Yes on 8 TV Ad: Everything to Do with Schools" 2008.

5. *Lawrence v. Texas*, 539 U.S. 558, 578 (2003).

6. On forms of coercive sex that escape the ambit of criminal rape law, see, for example, MacKinnon 1989, 171–83; MacKinnon 2007b, 240–48; Peterson 2008; Schulhofer 1998, 1–16. See also Lynne Huffer's (2013, 91–117) "intertextual" interpretation of *Powell v. State*, 270 Ga. 327, 510 S. E. 2d 18 (1998) against *Lawrence*. In *Powell*, itself cited in *Lawrence* (at 576), the Supreme Court of Georgia held its sodomy statute unconstitutional (the statute upheld twelve years earlier in *Bowers v. Hardwick*, 478 U.S. 186 [1986]). The case involved a man, Anthony Powell, having sex with and performing cunnilingus on his wife's teenage niece. Initially, Powell was charged with rape and aggravated sodomy, but the trial court jury found no evidence of nonconsent—despite the niece's alternating between crying and silence (Huffer 2013, 109–11). Thus, Powell was found guilty only of sodomy. For Huffer, that "Powell became a figure . . . for the sexual autonomy of consenting adults in a larger emancipatory narrative about freedom" (92) erases "a story about sexual violation" (113) and betrays the law's inability to adequately redress sexual harm (114–15). For me, though,

Powell is less about consensual sexual harm (like, arguably, some extreme forms of sadomasochistic sex) than about the state's failure to adequately protect young people through (1) an affirmative standard of consent and (2) tighter regulations on relations of dependence. I thus disagree that, in this instance, "the event . . . resists articulation in the idiom of the law" (114). No articulation of injury in law perfectly corresponds to injury in life, but some articulations are better than others. See the subsections, "Creating an Affirmative Standard of Sexual Consent for Minor–Minor and Adult–Minor Sexual Relations" and "Regulating Relations of Dependence and Trust" in chapter 3.

7. On sex between minors and adults for which harm is not the default presupposition or the foregone conclusion, see, for example, Levine 2002; Rind 2001; Rind and Tromovitch 1997; Stanley, Bartholomew, and Oram 2004; Tsang 1981; Waites 2005.

8. On the collective anxieties and latent desires that animate the violent police, legal, and social response to sex offenders, see, for example, chapter 1; Adler 2012; Bruhm and Hurley 2004, xxi–xxx; Kincaid 1998, 74–109; Kipnis 1999, 3–63; Levine 2002, 20–44.

9. See *Lawrence*, at 590, Scalia, J., dissenting. Now infamously, Justice Scalia warned, "state laws against bigamy, same-sex marriage, adult incest, prostitution, masturbation, adultery, fornication, bestiality, and obscenity are likewise sustainable only in light of *Bowers'* validation of laws based on moral choices. Every single one of these laws is called into question by today's decision." Scalia, this chapter argues, is right. Scalia is right not because laws against prostitution and adultery will necessarily be nullified, but because such laws may now require legislative and judicial rationales that trade not in the idiom of "public morality" but in the idioms of "harm" and/or "non-consent." See Eskridge 2008, 340–41. The *Lawrence* opinion maintains that sexual regulatory laws are permissible only to the extent that they stop harm rather than enforce morality, without any cognizance that what counts as harm is animated by moral understanding and deliberation. By running roughshod over the array of ethical questions raised by sexual practices that are *not* reducible to the presence or absence of consent, which the *Lawrence* opinion takes to be as the prominent metric of sexual harm—questions about gender hierarchy, dependency, and family sexual abuse, for example—it, as well as the *Smith* and *Connecticut* rulings, smuggles the law's and the court's sexual moralism as an apparently nonmoral concern with harm prevention. By pinning the "sex offender" as the purveyor of sexual harm, the court both disavows its own sexual morality and shields its moral investments and distinctions as decidedly not moral, but rather neutral and Millian. To hedge against the tidal wave of legally sanctioned sexual pluralism prophesied by Scalia, the *Lawrence*, *Smith*, and *Connecticut* opinions collapse questions of morality into questions of harm (detected foremost by the absence of consent) as a way to narrow the more capacious sexual field it has helped inaugurate. The third and fourth sections of this chapter extend and elaborate upon this argument. See also Harcourt 1999. Mary Anne Case (2003, 79) argues that, despite Scalia's apocalyptic fears (and progressives' hopes), *Lawrence* spatially and

conceptually contains protected sexual freedom far more than it extends it. I am not sure my assertion conflicts with hers: as a matter of law, the reach of *Lawrence* may be short and yet to be fully determined. Symbolically, however, the juridical promise to safeguard adult consensual sex and the juridical dignification of the homosexual are politically and morally vast, and it is to this symbolic transformation that I believe Scalia's dissent, the majority opinion, and the *Smith* and *Connecticut* decisions respond. On both the capaciousness and constraints of substantive privacy protections enunciated in *Lawrence,* see Herald 2004 and Eskridge 2008, 339–59.

10. For comprehensive accounts on the historical emergence of "sexual pathology" as a conceptual category, the medicalization of sexual deviance, the influence of psychiatry on the legislative response to sex crimes and sex criminals, and the three waves of "sexual psychopath" and sex offender laws enacted in the United States (the late 1930s, the postwar era, and the 1990s–present), see Denno 1998; Jenkins 1998.

11. See American Psychological Association 2015; Human Rights Watch 2007; Snyder 2000. Rose Corrigan (2006) argues that sex offender laws frame sexual violence as a pathological problem that inheres in predatory persons, undermining feminist attention to sexual violence as a common, persistent, and often-sanctioned feature of everyday life and sexual relations. Similarly, Janus (2006, 88) writes, "by focusing intensely on rare but horrific crimes, the predator laws convey a clear message that the feminists—and the solid empirical science—are wrong. . . . Rather, these laws tell us that the real sex criminals are those who lurk in the bushes and parking lots."

12. See, for example, Agudo 2008; Boland 1995; Kunz 1997; "Making Outcasts Out of Outlaws" 2004; "Prevention Versus Punishment" 1996. On the medical and juridical construction of sexual subjects—and the consolidation of discrete sexual acts into congealed identities—see Foucault 1990. Foucault's most popularized contribution is that the "homosexual" is a modern production of multiple discourses rather than a stable figure throughout history. As Foucault himself observed, the argument extends to all sexual subjects, from the heterosexual to the sex offender. Judith Butler, like Carl Stychin (1995), picks up the argument and extends it to the juridical: "Juridical notions of power appear to regulate political life in purely negative terms— that is, through the limitation, prohibition, regulation . . . of individuals. . . . But the subjects regulated by such structures are, by virtue of being subjected to them, formed, defined, and reproduced in accordance with the requirements of those structures" (1990, 2).

13. For the historical analogue, the juridical characterization of homosexuality and the consequent privileging and cohering of heterosexuality, see Stychin 1995.

14. *Smith,* at 90–91; *Connecticut,* at 4–5.

15. See, for example, S. Cohen 2002; Hall et al. 1978; Jenkins 1998; Watney 1996. Denno—in a critique contiguous with Burgett's (2009)—challenges whether "panic" is the best descriptive category to explain enactment of "sexual psychopath" and sex offender laws (1998, 1355–68). She argues that "moral panic" literature does not

empirically ground the assertion that sensationalist media accounts and public fear are the primary explanatory variables for sex crime legislation.

16. See Angelides 2004; Califia 2000; Chauncey 1993; Cocca 2002; Cocca 2004, 12–14; Denno 1998, 1368–73; Freedman 1987, 83, 96–98, 103–4; Kincaid 1998.

17. See Best 1990, 22–31. According to Denno (1998, 1363), "the number of statutes passed each year appears to be largely unrelated to the rates of rape or sex offenses." The Human Rights Watch (2007, 23) puts it frankly: "Sexual violence in the US is, fortunately, decreasing."

18. Some states also civilly commit certain offenders past their prison release date, a practice held constitutional in *Kansas v. Hendricks,* 521 U.S. 346 (1997). On the reemergence of sex predator commitment laws and the ways they distort national perceptions of sexual violence, see Janus 2006. GPS tracking and chemical or surgical castration have also become statutory methods of sex offender supervision and regulation over the past twenty years. For summaries of sex offender laws, their costs, empirical validity, deterrent effects, and unintended or unknown consequences, see, for example, the collection of essays in Wright 2009b.

19. Jacob Wetterling Crimes Against Children and Sexually Violent Offender Registration Act, 42 U.S.C. § 14071 (1994). For a discussion of the act and its mandates, see Kunz 1997; Logan 1999, 1172–73.

20. Megan's Law, Pub. L. No. 104-145, 110 Stat. 1345 (1996).

21. See Loudon-Brown 2007, 798–800.

22. See Cave 2009; Davey 2006; Singer 2008.

23. Adam Walsh Child Protection and Safety Act, 42 U.S.C. § 16901 (2006).

24. See Farley 2008; Human Rights Watch 2007.

25. See Goodnough and Davey 2009.

26. See, for example, Agudo 2008, 309; Boyd 2007, 230; Kunz 1997, 476; Levenson and Cotter 2005, 52; Orben 2005, 806.

27. See, for example, Agudo 2008, 332–33; C. Carpenter 2006, 318.

28. See, for example, Agudo 2008, 309; Human Rights Watch 2007, 9–10; Kunz 1997, 477; Levenson and Cotter 2005, 61–62.

29. See, for example, Loudon-Brown 2007, 797–98; Saxer 2009.

30. See, for example, Farley 2008, 494; Kunz 1997, 476; Orben 2005, 808.

31. See, for example, Farley 2008, 472; Purdum 1998.

32. Although these are "tier 1" offenders, the least serious in the three-tiered system, they may nonetheless be listed online as sex offenders for fifteen years, reducible to ten at judicial discretion. See Adam Walsh Child Protection and Safety Act, 42 U.S.C. § 16915(a)(1)–(3), 16915(b)(2)(A) (2006).

33. See *Doe v. Poritz,* 662 A.2d 367, 404 (N.J. 1995), holding that registration and notification laws are not punitive; Boland (1995, 202) reports, "registration is frequently applied retrospectively, but it has been upheld against ex post facto challenges in nearly every instance because most courts view registration as a regulation, not a punishment. Notification has faced limited challenges and the results have varied."

34. See *Rainer v. Georgia*, 286 Ga. 675, *4 (Ga. 2010): "Because the registration requirements themselves do not constitute punishment, it is of no consequence whether or not one has committed an offense that is 'sexual' in nature before being required to register.... The nature of the offense requiring the registration would not somehow change the registration requirements themselves into a form of 'punishment' for purposes of an Eighth Amendment cruel and unusual punishment analysis."

35. See *Poritz*, at 413: "Classification of plaintiff based on his conviction of one of the enumerated sex offenses and his characterization as a repetitive compulsive offender is rationally related to the government's interest in protection of the public. The need for public safety outweighs the restrictions placed upon plaintiff as a result of his inclusion in this class. We conclude therefore that the registration and notification requirements do not violate plaintiff's right to equal protection under either the Federal or State Constitution."

36. Procedural due process claims are discussed in the third section of this chapter.

37. See *Doe v. Moore*, 410 F.3d 1337 (11th Cir. 2005); *Doe v. Tandeske*, 361 F.3d 594 (9th Cir. 2004). Hobson (2006, 972) documents the failed efforts of sex offenders on these grounds: "Convicted sex offenders have brought unsuccessful substantive due process challenges against various types of post-release restrictions.... Circuit courts have ruled that the statutes in question do not infringe the asserted fundamental right." Regarding a liberty interest in reputation, see *Paul v. Davis*, 424 U.S. 693 (1976); regarding *Tandeske* and similar dismissals of substantive due process claims, see the third section of this chapter.

38. See, for example, Boland 1995; Loudon-Brown 2007; Singer 2008.

39. See, for example, Chen 2009; Einhorn 2008; and *State v. Bani*, 36 P.3d 1255, 1257 (Haw. 2001), holding that conviction-based requirements, "without notice, an opportunity to be heard, or any preliminary determination of whether and to what extent [defendant] actually represent[ed] a danger to society," violated due process protections.

40. *Smith*, at 91. John Doe I was convicted of sexually abusing his daughter for two years, when she was nine to eleven years old. John Doe II was convicted of sexually abusing a fourteen-year-old. Both pleaded nolo contendere. They were released from prison in 1990 and completed rehabilitation programs. The Alaska Sex Offender Registration Act was passed on May 12, 1994.

41. *Doe I v. Otte*, 259 F.3d 979, 982 (9th Cir. 2001), holding that the Alaska Sex Offender Registration Act violated the ex post facto clause. Janus (2006, 20) observes that states enacted sex offender registration, notification, and commitment laws under civil codes precisely to bypass the constitutional checks that restrain criminal law.

42. *Smith*, at 94.

43. *Kennedy v. Mendoza-Martinez*, 72 U.S. 144, 168–69 (1963).

44. *Smith*, at 97–106.

45. *Smith*, at 116–17, Ginsburg, J., dissenting; *Smith*, at 113, Stevens, J., dissenting.

46. *Connecticut,* at 4. *Mathews v. Eldridge,* 424 U.S. 319, 335 (1976), requires inquiry into additional procedural safeguards; *Fullmer v. Mich. Dep't of State Police,* 207 F. Supp. 2d 650, 654–55 (E.D. Mich. 2002), holds that the plaintiff, a sex offender, has a right to be free from government defamation, entitling him to certain procedural protections.

47. See, for example, *Codd v. Velger,* 429 U.S. 624, 628 (1977).

48. *Davis,* at 705.

49. *Beitzell v. Jeffrey,* 643 F.2d 870, 878 (1st Cir. 1981).

50. *Doe v. Dep't of Pub. Safety ex rel. Lee,* 271 F.3d 38, 45–46 (2d Cir. 2001), holds that a change in legal status to sex offender constituted a "plus," a finding reversed by *Connecticut.*

51. *Connecticut,* at 7–8.

52. Ibid., at 4.

53. However, the Connecticut statute grants judicial discretion in exempting some offenders from registration and notification requirements, a detail that Justice Rehnquist omits and that may compromise (and authorize) his ruling that dangerousness is immaterial. See Conn. Gen. Stat. Ann. § 54-251(b), (c) (West 2009). Particular offenders may be exempted if determined not to threaten public safety. I owe this well-made point to Gabriel Baldwin (2004, 393–94).

54. I borrow the phrase "how the court does things with sex offenders" from J. L. Austin's *How to Do Things with Words* (1975). Although Austin initially sought to distinguish "constantive" speech acts that correspond to objective reality ("the cloud is in the sky") from "performative" speech acts that produce reality ("I do," at a wedding ceremony), he eventually confounds his own categorizations, proposing instead that all speech acts produce certain effects or perform functions that exceed or subtend the simply referential component. While the court understands itself as describing, referencing, and reporting on sex offenders and sex offender law, it simultaneously, through that very same "speech," produces the sex offender and the ancillary concepts of sexual harm (*Smith* and *Connecticut*) and sexual freedom (*Lawrence*). On the adoption of Austin's theory of performative speech to the cultural construction of gender, see Butler 1990; see also Kelleher 2004.

55. *Lawrence,* at 568.

56. *Bowers,* at 191–94.

57. *Lawrence,* at 568–70.

58. *Lawrence,* at 568, citing Katz 1995 and D'Emilio and Freedman 1997. See also Foucault 1990.

59. *Lawrence,* at 568. Justice Kennedy had help. *Bowers's* bad history was dispelled by the historians' amicus brief in support of the petitioners. See Chauncey 2004.

60. *Lawrence,* at 571–72.

61. *Smith,* at 103; *Connecticut,* at 4.

62. *Smith,* at 103.

63. *Otte,* at 992–94.

64. *Smith,* at 103, citing *McKune v. Lile,* 536 U.S. 24, 34 (2002).

65. *Connecticut,* at 3.

66. *Connecticut,* at 8–9, Scalia, J., concurring.

67. Ibid., at 8–9. Justice Scalia quips, "A convicted sex offender has no more right to additional 'process' enabling him to establish that he is not dangerous . . . than a 15-year-old has a right to 'process' enabling him to establish that he is a safe driver."

68. Baldwin (2004, 395–96) proposes that the analogy may overlook the judicial exemptions to the Connecticut notification requirements premised on an individualized assessment of dangerousness. However, both the infantilization of the sex offender and the naturalization of his alleged dangerousness advance a judicial "subject creation" of the sex offender as a childlike container for lawlessness and sexual perversity. On jurisprudence, policing, and the creation of criminal subjects, see Harcourt 2001, 160–84.

69. See Douard 2008–9, 48–49. Despite Scalia's analogy, however, children are entitled to qualified due process constitutional protections. *In re Gault,* 387 U.S. 1 (1967). See also Allender 2009.

70. Center for Sex Offender Management 2000. See also multiple studies cited in Boyd 2007, 230; Hobson 2006, 965; Human Rights Watch 2007, 25–35; Kincaid 1998, 95; Kunz 1997, 471–73; Terry and Ackerman 2009; F. Williams 2009. Kim English (2009), like many others, convincingly suggests that low recidivism rates may result in part from low reporting rates by victims, yet this is precisely the policy problem with registration and notification laws. They target convicted offenders who have been reported, leaving unaddressed unreported sexual violence usually committed by family members and acquaintances.

71. The Center for Sex Offender Management (2000) unsurprisingly finds (but no less ignorable for being unsurprising), "reoffense rates vary among different types of sex offenders and are related to specific characteristics of the offender and the offense."

72. Greenfeld 1997.

73. See Human Rights Watch 2007, 24–25; Wright 2009a.

74. Periman 2008, 2.

75. Langan, Schmitt, and Durose 2003, cited in Human Rights Watch 2007, 28.

76. Greenfeld 1997, 25.

77. Ibid., 25–26.

78. See, for example, Canaday 2012; Cossman 2007; Stychin 1995; Stychin 1998; Stychin 2003.

79. *Jacobellis v. Ohio,* 378 U.S. 184, 197 (1964), Stewart, J., concurring. Of course, the question before the Warren court was whether or not a film was obscene (Stewart concluded it was not). Before the Rehnquist court, John Doe is already a sex offender, settling the question prior to its being asked. Thus, the question *Are sex offender registries and notification systems rational and regulatory?* comes to be synonymous with the tautological and self-evident *Do sex offenders sex offend?* This is the logic underpinning Justice Scalia's concurrence-by-analogy in *Connecticut.*

80. See Edelman 2004, 1–31.

81. *Lawrence,* at 566–67, citing *Bowers,* at 190.

82. See Tribe 2004.

83. Halley 1993.

84. Ibid., 1750.

85. Ibid., 1768–70.

86. Ibid., 1756–57.

87. *Hendricks,* at 357.

88. According to the Sex Offender Registration and Notification Act (SORNA), Title I of AWA, a sex offender is an "individual who was convicted of a sex offense." See SMART 2010.

89. See Fischel 2013a, 82.

90. Tyron Garner and John Lawrence were most likely not having sex when police entered Lawrence's apartment. See D. Carpenter 2012, 73–74.

91. *Bowers,* at 191.

92. But see note 2, particularly Franke (2004, 1403–4), who argues that the liberty in *Lawrence* is actually a winnowing departure from more relational, less territorialized understandings of protected liberty as developed in *Griswold v. Connecticut, Eisenstadt v. Baird,* and *Roe v. Wade.*

93. *Connecticut,* at 9–10, Souter, J., concurring.

94. *Davis,* at 708–9.

95. *Siegert v. Gilley,* 500 U.S. 226, 233–34 (1991).

96. *Doe v. Tandeske,* 361 F.3d. 594 (9th Cir. 2004).

97. *Tandeske,* at 596–97, citing *Washington v. Glucksberg,* 521 U.S. 702 (1997).

98. *Doe v. Moore,* 410 F.3d 1337 (11th Cir. 2005); *United States of America v. Madera,* 474 F. Supp.2d 1257 (M.D. Fla. 2007).

99. *Moore,* at 1343.

100. Ibid., at 1344.

101. Ibid., at 1343–44, holds: "Despite Appellants' broad framing of their rights in this case, however, we must endeavor to create a more careful description of the asserted right in order to analyze its importance. . . . The right at issue here is the right of a person, convicted of 'sexual offenses,' to refuse subsequent registration of his or her personal information with Florida law enforcement and prevent publication of this information on Florida's Sexual Offender/Predator website."

102. *Madera,* at 1264–65. Unlike the *Tandeske* and *Moore* courts, the district court did not canvass the defendant's particular substantive liberty claims to reconfigure them, but omitted them from the opinion altogether. The district court ruling was subsequently reversed in *United States v. Madera,* 528 F.3d 852 (11th Cir. 2008), finding that the retroactive application of the AWA had not been clearly specified at the time of Madera's conviction.

103. As Marybeth Herald observes: "Whether an activity 'wins' fundamental right status often seems to depend on how broadly or narrowly the courts frame the question

before them. . . . Framing the question in a particular way provides an easy way to influence the outcome. Asking the question at a very specific level is not only a way to constrict the doctrine [of substantive due process], but to shut it down if that outcome is preferred" (2004, 9–11). Herald notices this judicial practice ("straw liberties," as I have called it) in her research on substantive due process challenges to state laws banning sex aids. She (2004, 10) cites *Yorko v. State*, 690 S.W.2d 260, 262 (Tex. Crim. App. 1985): "Does the due process clause of the Fourteenth Amendment guarantee a citizen the right to stimulate his, her or another's genitals with an object designed or marketed primarily for that purpose?"

104. Laurence Tribe (1980, 1070–71) identifies an ideological split over the nature and purview of substantive due process in the course of court history since the *Lochner* era. He argues the split is conceptually nonsensical while also favoring a more expansive reading of liberty protections: "If process is constitutionally valued, therefore, it must be valued not only as a means to some independent end, but for its intrinsic characteristics: being heard is part of what it means to be a person. Process itself, therefore, becomes substantive." On the traditionalist side of the bench, substantive protections are strictly limited to state infringements against liberties that are "deeply rooted in the Nation's history and tradition" (*Washington*, at 721). Substantive due process, on this reading, covers a finite set of liberties, like freedom of expression or choices regarding family upbringing, and no more. See also *Palko v. Connecticut*, 302 U.S. 319, 324–25 (1937). On the more progressive side of the bench, substantive protections do not cover concretized liberties, specific individual acts and phenomena, but rather shield expressive and intimate forms of association—and autonomy in determining and partaking in those associations—from government infringement. The case history supporting this reading runs from *Griswold v. Connecticut*, 381 U.S. 479 (1965) (holding that a state statute prohibiting contraceptive use among married couples infringed the right to privacy), *Eisenstadt v. Baird*, 405 U.S. 438 (1972) (extending *Griswold*'s protections to individuals), *Roe v. Wade*, 410 U.S. 113, 153 (1973) (holding that a right to privacy encompasses a woman's decision to terminate her pregnancy), arguably *Moore v. City of East Cleveland*, 431 U.S. 494 (1977) (protecting family arrangements outside marriage from government housing discrimination), *Planned Parenthood v. Casey*, 505 U.S. 833, 851 (1992) (confirming but constricting *Roe*; however—and crucial to *Lawrence* and the due process debate—"at the heart of liberty is the right to define one's own concept of existence, of meaning, of the universe, and of the mystery of human life"), and finally to *Lawrence*. Among legal scholars, the debate has centered on whether the judicial branch—as opposed to the legislative or executive—should ensure any protections to individuals besides proceduralist ones, and if so, on what moral and/or constitutional grounds. See R. Dworkin 2006; Ely 1980; Sunstein 2008; Tribe 1980; Tribe 2004, 1922–31. I recount these ideological, interpretive disputes as a counterpoint to my suggestion that the Does' claims to substantive liberty protections are weak; they are, but one could interpret both the Does' claims (as claims for privacy or rights to self-determination, say, instead

of claims to be taken off a sex offender website) and also due process case law (as more capacious, covering relational and intimate association, rather than as restricted to foundational, predetermined sets of practices) in such a way that grants more credibility to the petitioners. As the Does' liberty claims are restructured in *Tandeske, Madera,* and *Moore,* such claims cannot enter these debates, let alone win them.

105. See Stychin 1995; see also "Are Sex Offenders the New Queers?" in the Introduction.

106. Richard Mohr (2004) makes an evident but overlooked point that current social hysteria around pedophilia is matched by an endless eroticization of, and voyeuristic fascination with, children and teenagers in advertisements, film, and news media.

107. Mona Lynch (2002) examines congressional records of four 1990s sex offender legislative bills and documents the language of pollution, contagion, and purity-violation that infuses the discussions. Lynch argues that the visceral emotionality of these debates overrides constitutional caution and empirical investigation and silences opposition to sex offender notification and registration laws. Daniel Filler (2001) also investigates the rhetoric of legislative debate on Megan's Law in the U.S. Congress and the New York state legislature, evidencing the use of graphic anecdotes of child victimization, (often misinformed or misrepresented) statistical claims, and demonic characterizations of offenders.

108. See, for example, Human Rights Watch 2007.

109. But see Janus (2006, 103–4), who writes, "as constructed by the predator laws, risk tells us something essential—rather than accidental—about the person. This characteristic—sometimes called 'dangerousness'—is portrayed as a stable ingredient of the person, a part of him even if it is now not visible." Rose Corrigan (2006) objects to liberal assessments of sex offender laws for similar but separate reasons. Although many have drawn attention to the laws' punitive excess and their potential violations of civil liberties, critics have not carefully considered how the sex offender laws, through their selective enforcement, categorical exceptions, and symbolic configuration, regress to an individualistic and antifeminist portrayal of sexual violence.

110. On the "will to know" the criminal and to partition criminal and normal behavior, see Harcourt 2007, 173–92.

111. Stychin 1995, 141–42.

112. See note 78.

113. *Lawrence,* at 578.

114. See Burgess 2006.

115. Cossman 2007.

116. Ibid., 1–158.

117. Ibid., 197, emphasis added.

118. On the analogous currency of "harm" in political and juridical discourse, see Harcourt 1999.

119. Cossman 2007, 36–37, citing *Williams v. Attorney General of Alabama,* 378 F.3d 1232, 1241 (11th Cir. 2004).

120. *Williams,* at 1238.

121. Cossman 2007, 56; *United States v. Extreme Associates,* 431 F.3d 150 (3rd Cir. 2005).

122. Cossman 2007, 62, citing T. Brown 2004.

123. *Lawrence,* at 567, emphasis added.

124. Ibid., at 564.

125. Johnson 2013; *MacDonald v. Moose,* 710 F.3d 154 (4th Cir. 2012).

126. Crime Against Nature, Va. Code § 18.2–361(A) (2005).

127. "KEEP VIRGINIA KIDS SAFE!" 2013.

128. See Spindelman 2013, 172–88; West 2008; see also the section, "Autonomy ≠ Consent" in the Conclusion.

129. I am not ignoring the considerable feminist literature challenging the validity of consent under the structural and economic constraints of prostitution. Rather, I am suggesting that by positioning the consenting adult as the bearer of constitutional privilege and protection against those cases involving minors, prostitution, and other sex offenses, *Lawrence* comes close to assuming the nonconsensuality and harmful effects of these latter cases by assertion instead of argument.

130. *Lawrence,* at 571.

131. *Casey,* at 850.

132. Mill 1998.

133. Perhaps Mill is not completely cognizant of the slipperiness of his categories, but over the course of *On Liberty* what counts as harmful action requiring legal intervention comes to look less like an objective and ontological matter and more like a societal determination. See Harcourt 1999, 121; Munro 2007, 3.

134. Simon 2000, 1130; see also Douard 2008–9.

135. Tribe 2004.

136. Rather than conceive *Bowers* in terms of judicial restraint as a "romantic stabilization" narrative of the foregone past, or *Lawrence* in terms of judicial activism as a "comedic liberation" narrative of a promising future, Susan Burgess (2006) ironizes the judicial trajectory from 1986 to 2003. She suggests that *Lawrence* is a kind of queer makeover of *Bowers,* in which the justices grew savvier, more cosmopolitan, indeed more queer in their appreciation of gay relations. I find her reading persuasive, and yet I think *Smith* and *Connecticut* are stuck in the genre of gothic, of Manichean morality and justice that subtends the justices' moments of queer irony. The risk of fluid cosmopolitan sensibilities is acquiesced by the rigid installment of a gothic—which is to say fictional—villain. See also Kincaid 1998, 30.

137. Franke 2004, 1412–13.

138. *State v. Limon,* 32 Kan. App.2d 369, 383–84 (2004). Eighteen-year-old Matthew Limon received a seventeen-year sentence for having oral sex with a fourteen-year-old. However, the appeals court ruling was reversed by the Kansas Supreme

Court in *State v. Limon,* 280 Kan. 275 (Kan. 2005), which held that the law violated equal protection guarantees, not due process. State supreme courts in North Carolina (*In re R.L.C.,* 643 S.E.2d 920 [N.C. 2007]) and Virginia (*McDonald v. Commonwealth,* 645 S.E.2d 918 [Va. 2007]) have ruled that *Lawrence* does not constitutionally protect "nontraditional" (sodomical) sex between minors from criminalization. See Allender 2009.

139. Franke 2004, 1413. Allender (2009, 1842) argues that *Lawrence,* read through prior case law establishing young people's qualified right to sexual privacy, should reach "nontraditional sexual activity" among minors, but only "in a context in which traditional sexual activity is legal." Allender reaffirms the "extremely significant state interest" in criminalizing minor or intergenerational sex by distinguishing it against the state's interest in criminalizing queer minor sex, which can now only be rationalized as "promoting morality" (1847, 1850). Again, *Lawrence* becomes a license to criminalize young sex, so long as the state criminalizes uniformly across age (protection from harm) and not differentially across acts (morality promotion).

140. See Lancaster 2011, 67. Unfortunately, William Eskridge (2008, 339–42), moralizing consent, endorses Kansas's penalization of teenage sex in *Limon* to defend *Lawrence* from slippery slope detractors. Claiming that "consent is essential for regulating sexual activities," he uncritically accepts the impossibility of a fourteen-year-old's ability to consent and writes that "there is enormous evidence of the possible harm such encounters pose for youth," without citing any such evidence, let alone evidence germane to the conduct in question: oral sex between two teenage boys with mental disabilities.

141. *Lawrence,* at 575.

142. *Lawrence,* at 576, emphasis added. According to Mary Anne Case (2003, 131), "a substantial driving force for the result in *Lawrence* may be that the majority and concurring Justices see people like Lawrence and Garner . . . as precisely not the sort of people who should be spending the night in jail, or registering as sex offenders." But who are these "sort of people"? Does one become a sex offender, a persona, in the act of registering as one? At the very moment a particular form of sexual privacy is secured and codified there is a concomitant codification of intensified publicizing of sexual deviance and crime. It is as if, now that we can neither know nor regulate what gay people do in their homes, we must know what happens outside, and knowing feels like doing something, or preventing something, even if the "who" we know (the sex offenders in our neighborhood) has no correlation to the "what" (the practices and variations of, as well as the regulatory effects of the laws on, sex offense and offenders).

143. Between earlier gay rights cases and *Lawrence,* notes Case (2003, 106), "it appears Kennedy has . . . come to understand that the law is implicated in creating stigma, rather than stigma being just a social fact unrelated to the law." I would qualify that Kennedy's revelation of law's constitutive functions stops dead at the homosexual and plays no parallel role for sex offenders. In his appraisal of *Lawrence* and its relation

to stigma and sex offenders, Eric Janus comments: "After the Supreme Court's *Lawrence* decision declared that homosexuality may not be used as a degraded status, we might have been tempted to pronounce American outsider jurisprudence all but dead. . . . But there is evidence that the existence of the degraded other has not been a horrible historical diversion but is rather a central—though tragic—addiction of our liberal democracy" (2006, 105–6). By "outsider jurisprudence," Janus refers to the legal discrimination of subject populations deemed threatening to the social order. My argument is that *Lawrence,* rather than being a leaky stopgap to outsider jurisprudence, continues its logic.

144. Halperin 1995, 37–38; see also Sedgwick 2008, 5–7.

145. See Stychin 1995, 128–29, citing Sedgwick 1992.

146. Foucault 1995, 100.

147. J. Gordon 2003, emphasis added.

148. In fact, in both popular and scholarly discourse, the figure of the sex offender is not monolithic, and there has been increasingly vocal concern about young and nonviolent persons designated sex offenders by the state (see Introduction). Nevertheless, *Smith, Connecticut,* and the AWA suppress the disagreement where it matters most—the law—as far as the offender is concerned.

149. Halley 1993, 1770.

150. "Making Outcasts Out of Outlaws" 2004, 2732.

151. Thanks to Kendall Thomas for thinking this point through with me. See also Place 2010, 10 ("But the sinful pride lies in our putting sex offenders in a category of evil that allows us to define ourselves in opposition to them. . . . There will always be people guilty of great evil. But evil is an act, not a cultural metaphor, not a social backdrop, and not entertainment").

152. The argument is influenced by Foucault 2003 and Harcourt 2007. A tiered system of sex offender notification and registration purports to gauge the probability of reoffense (actuarial) and to relieve government agencies of invasive regulatory and rehabilitative techniques in favor of a seemingly more hands-off monitoring and deterrent approach (neoliberal); it also aims in its manifest purpose at preserving public health and safety rather than corporally or capitally punishing individuals (biopolitical). These advantages may work to obscure the singling out of sex offenders for this kind of regulation, the breadth of the regulation, and its psychic and physical consequences for offenders. For a broader critique of actuarial models of crime prediction and punishment, see Harcourt 2007. Janus (2006, 93–109) also suggests that the legal focus on sex offender commitment reflects and authorizes the state's turn to preventing crimes yet to have happened over punishing crimes that have already occurred. The emphasis on prevention enables broader police and surveillance powers.

Jonathan Simon (2000, 1135–42) contends that sex offender registration and notification symptomize what he calls "governing through crime," wherein the state's raison d'être is crime prevention and prosecution. He underscores the discursive, extralegal, collateral effects of registration and notification eclipsed by what appears as noninvasive and actuarial. Among these effects are the centralization of the "victim" as the ideal citizen type, the manufacturing of children as always imperiled, and the management of risk as a responsibility of the individual parent rather than as a dilemma for collective political deliberation.

153. See Foucault 1990; Foucault 1995; but see also Small (2015), who finds that Michigan prosecutors and defenders identify and thus construct sexual perpetrators not as monsters but as "lower class" men. In this way, economically privileged men are granted greater impunity whereas disadvantaged men are rendered suspect.

154. See Kincaid 1998, 30.

3. NUMBERS, SEX, POWER

1. See Khan 2009a, 396–401.

2. Lancaster 2011, 255–56.

3. In 2005, Genarlow Wilson received a ten-year prison sentence for aggravated child molestation for having had oral sex with a fifteen-year-old girl when he was seventeen. Amid much public outcry and charges of prosecutorial racial bias (Wilson is black), the Georgia General Assembly recategorized the statutory crime of teenage sex, formerly a felony, as a misdemeanor. Wilson was released in 2007 following a Georgia Supreme Court ruling holding the punishment cruel and unusual. *Humphrey v. Wilson*, 282 Ga. 520 (Ga. 2007). See also M. Cohen 2008; Goodman 2007. The details of the Wilson case, however, imply that the sexual activity may have been unwanted, or at least not wanted: a group of teenagers were drunk in a motel room; a seventeen-year-old girl accused Wilson and another boy of rape; a video tape "[shows] Wilson having sexual intercourse with an apparently semiconscious L.M. [the seventeen-year-old] and T.C. [the fifteen-year-old] performing oral sex on Wilson." *Wilson v. State*, 631 S.E.2d 391 (Ga. Ct. App. 2006). These are the kinds of details more culturally perceptible and more justiciable when the frame of sexual harm is more forgiving and less dichotomous than *predator or prey*.

4. Catharine MacKinnon writes, "If the rape law worked, there would be no need for statutory rape laws. Abuse of power, access, trust, and exploitation of vulnerabilities to pressure people into sex that is not wanted for its own sake would be illegal. . . . Young age or age differential below a certain age is . . . ossified into an absolute rule. This segregates out some of the most sympathetic cases for relative structural powerlessness in sexual interactions and leaves the rest of the victims . . . unprotected, their inequalities uncounted. By cushioning its excesses, this helps keep male dominance as a social system in place" (2007a, 245–46). MacKinnon overlooks state criminal laws that do account for other differences in power besides age, but such nuance would rob the argument of its rhetorical force, which stages gender difference as the primary and paramount inequality (notice the slippage from "abuse of power, trust, and exploitation of vulnerabilities" to "male dominance").

5. As explained below, the chapter is agnostic about gender—not as to whether gender manifests social hierarchy, but whether as a system of power inequality gender

requires the same legal or moral qualifiers as does intergenerational sex. Much feminist legal theory is incorporated into my argument but is applied to minors, not women. Although it is possibly true that the cultural obsession with age appropriateness might stall an appreciation of gender hierarchy, MacKinnon's structural account tacks too far, reducing problems of age and sex to gender subordination. We might do better thinking about children as if they were MacKinnon women rather than thinking about women as if they were children, as MacKinnon sometimes does. See, for example, MacKinnon 2007b, 1341; MacKinnon 1989, 110. For similar critiques of MacKinnon, see Berlant 1999, 49, 73, n. 44; Roiphe 1993, 148.

6. I call sexual autonomy a "principle" as it is both a propellant and an objective of the reforms and theoretic revisions delineated below. Despite the important admonition against feminist political projects miring themselves in determining epistemological certainties at the expense of open-ended democratic engagement (see Zerilli 2005), I cannot figure another way to intervene in law and legal theorizing, discourses of principles, foundations, and rules all the way down.

7. See chapter 2, note 4.

8. See Butler 1997a, 50.

9. In a rather different but contiguous consideration of gay men and bareback sex, Tim Dean (2009, 26) comments: "I'm claiming that thinking about bareback subculture happens most productively when judgments concerning whether it is good or bad are deferred. I'm arguing that intellectual and political work involves more than adjudication among positive and negative images of others or of ourselves. . . . I contend that sexual ethics begins not with making judgments about (or trying to regulate) others' sex lives but with establishing others' freedom from interference, even as we recognize our mutual sexual interdependence." Although I agree that good politics and good thinking are foreclosed by unreflexive recourse to adjudication, I am not certain that "judgments" and noninterference can be juxtaposed so definitely, nor that noninterference is an uncomplicated ethical commitment (precisely because of our "mutual sexual interdependence").

10. Foucault 1990, 155.

11. See, for example, Denno 1998; Eskridge 2008, 53–55; Harcourt 2001; Harcourt 2007; Posner and Silbaugh 1996; Wacquant 2009.

12. This periodization is adopted from Cocca (2004, 9–28) and complemented with other researchers' insights and observations as well as my own. For a richly textured history documenting the uneven protection of children and adolescents from sexual violence in New York City from the late nineteenth to mid-twentieth century, see Robertson 2005. Robertson documents how competing, interclass understandings of children, gender, and sexuality both informed and were informed by sex crime codification, prosecution, and enforcement.

13. See Oberman 2001, 802; on rapists' marriage to their girl victims as property compensation, see Robertson 2005, 95–115.

14. See Cocca 2004, 11; but see also Freedman 2013, 142–46, 155.

15. Oberman 1994, 27.

16. See Cocca 2004, 14–15; Freedman 2013, 125–36.

17. See Odem 1995.

18. See, for example, Ehrlich 2009, 244–45; Freedman 2013, 136; Oberman 2001, 803, citing Larson 1997.

19. Ehrlich 2009, 237–38.

20. See Caringella 2009, 41–42; Oberman 2000, 714–17. As Eskridge (2008, 53–67) points out, sodomy and age of consent reforms were not separate movements; sodomy laws were expanded in part to better protect children, and mostly enforced against men who had sex with minors. Age of consent reforms criminalized a broader range of sexual activity to reach nonpenetrative sex with youth. However, Robertson (2005, 98–99, 117–35) reveals that early age of consent reforms on the books in practice often led to less protection for adolescents.

21. See Olsen 1984, 404–7.

22. See W. Williams 1997, 76–77. Estelle Freedman (2013, 168–90) documents earlier, Progressive Era efforts to protect boys from sexual predation. Given the gender-specificity of age of consent statutes, "sodomy law served as a kind of unofficial age-of-consent mechanism for male–male sexual relations" (172). Freedman also describes how 1930s sexual predator laws, predecessors to contemporary sex offender statutes, were enacted to protect boys from both assault and homosexuality (189–90).

23. See Oberman 1994, 63–70; Oberman 2001, 707–10; Phillips 1999, 95. But see also "The Embarrassed Etc.: Adult Women and Predatory Priests," in the Introduction.

24. Elizabeth Hollenberg (1999) finds that older male partners are most often within five-year age spans of older teenage girls. However, younger sexually active girls between eleven and fifteen years of age are more likely than older sexually active girls to describe their sexual experiences as unwanted, and more likely to have had those experiences with significantly older men (271). This younger, more often coerced subset has been neglected by 1990s statutory rape enforcement targeting pregnancy prevention.

25. Notes MacKinnon (1991, 1305), "Underage girls form a credible disadvantaged group for equal protection purposes when the social facts of sexual assault are faced, facts which prominently feature one-sided sexual aggression by older males."

26. See Califia 2000, 56–57; Cocca 2004, 76–77; V. Doyle 2008; Jenkins 1998, 156–57.

27. See Tsang 1981; Wardenski 2005.

28. *Michael M. v. Superior Court of Sonoma County,* 450 U.S. 464 (1981).

29. Ibid., at 471–73.

30. Ibid., at 467, 475.

31. Ibid., at 483–85, Blackmun, J., concurring.

32. Ibid., at 473.

33. Ibid., at 494, Brennan, J., dissenting. Acerbically, MacKinnon comments, "the plurality opinion grasped the sex-differential reality at the cost of attributing it to

biology. The dissent understood the reality of sexual assault of girls to be socially created rather than biological, at the cost of failing to understand it as nonetheless gender-based. The plurality saw a hierarchy but thought it was biologically fixed. The dissent saw the possibilities for change, but missed the hierarchy" (2001, 1305).

34. On the organization of U.S. politics around the always vulnerable fetus, on the political infantilizing of U.S. citizenry that contains capitalist inequalities and privatizes racial and sexual pluralism outside and beneath civic contestation, and on the political possibilities eclipsed or assaulted by the sanctification of "reproductive futurism," see Berlant 1997, 25–82; Edelman 2004, 1–32.

35. See Hollenberg 1999, 273; K. Sutherland 2003, 323.

36. See Cocca 2004, 24–26; Fineman 2004, 238; Smith 2001, 303.

37. Personal Responsibility and Work Opportunity Reconciliation Act of 1996, Pub. L. No. 104–193, § 101(9)(A), 110 Stat. 2349–50 (1996).

38. See Duggan 2004.

39. See Hollenberg 1999, 270.

40. See Oliveri 2000, 505.

41. See Hollenberg 1999, 271.

42. Ibid., 268.

43. See, for example, Cocca 2004, 93–128; C. Cohen 1997, 455–56; Delgado 1996; Duggan 2004; D. Roberts 1997, 244–45; Smith 2001.

44. See Oberman 2000, 761.

45. See Phipps 1997, 56–62.

46. In twelve states, sexual activity between minors is a crime, and in several of those states it is a felony (see Phipps, 2003, 444, listing then current age of consent statutes).

47. On the more generalized marshaling of children's assumed innocence to invigorate conservative political projects, see, for example, Duggan 1994; L. Gordon 1988; McCreery 2001; McCreery 2008; Rubin 1993.

48. Schulhofer 1998, 38.

49. Ibid., 267–73.

50. Ibid., 103.

51. Ibid., 168–252.

52. Schulhofer 1992, 55–58.

53. See Schaffner 2005.

54. Schulhofer 1992, 84–87.

55. Schulhofer 1998, 33–38, 75, 77–78.

56. See also Chamallas 1987–88, 836.

57. See, for example, Benhabib 1992, 161–68, 170; Fineman 2004; Hirschmann 2002, 35–39; Sandel 1982.

58. See, for example, Bersani 1987, 220–22; Butler 1997b, 132–50.

59. See, for example, Cowan 2007; Young 1990.

60. See, for example, Sanders 1997; Young 1990.

61. Schulhofer 1992, 70.

62. In Tronto's words (2013, 125), "Human autonomy is an *achievement*, not a starting premise, and it is an achievement that requires many years."

63. Nancy Hirschmann (2002, 35–39) argues that "freedom" is more workable than "autonomy" for retheorizing social justice, as the latter points too myopically to rationality, reflection, and "internal" barriers on the subject. As an aspiration, autonomy presupposes a cool-headed, always-calculating, and unconstructed person—a person undiscoverable in social reality. I have chosen to employ "sexual autonomy" and not "sexual freedom" for two reasons. First, because I think the capacity-to-self-direct embedded in "autonomy" invites forms of governance that may be, at first blush, anathema to the presumptive entitlements of "freedom." Secondly, and intertwining, because "sexual freedom" carries with it unsavory associations of defensive gay muscularity, an unapologetic will to fuck that, while perhaps dignity- and life-saving for some gay men in the early, hyperphobic years of the AIDS crisis, is insufficient for the task of adjudicating sex between minors and sex across generations. On the normative allure and political downsides of "sexual freedom," see Spindelman 2013.

64. On Kant's views of children's moral and physical development (and on masturbation as retarding that development), see Rasmussen 2011, 27, 31–33. On Kant's views of sex as particularly dangerous to self-governance, see Halwani 2010, 200–210.

65. Oshana 1998, 97; Nedelsky 2011, 46, 158–94.

66. Nedelsky 2011, 42. As Iris Young (1990, 25) proposes, "Rights are not fruitfully conceived as possessions. Rights are relationships, not things; they are institutionally defined rules specifying what people can do in relation to one another. Rights refer to doing more than having, to social relationships that enable or constrain action." Martha Minow (1986) defends a conception of children's rights as "relational" as well. For Minow, rights mediate between reforms aimed at promoting children's autonomy and paternalistic protections. Unlike pure contract, relational rights entail presupposed duties by parents, young people, and the state (see also Minow and Shanley 1996). Framed as such, autonomy rights seem to be juxtaposed against relational rights. But, as mentioned above, I wonder if the young sexual subject, in particular, offers a way to legally think autonomy as a thoroughly relational good. Minow's analysis gestures in this direction (1986, 23): "In this sense, rights would represent not only a social commitment to preserve individual freedom from the injuries and intrusions of others [what Minow considers 'autonomy rights'], but also individual freedom to form relationships with others."

67. Nedelsky 2011, 55.

68. On intimate partner violence as conditioning and constraining autonomy, see, for example, M. Friedman 2003, 140–59; Nedelsky 2011, 307–34; Oshana 1998, 89–91.

69. Schulhofer 1998, 100.

70. Schulhofer 1992, 71.

71. See Foucault 1980, 56–57; Foucault 1990.

72. Concerned with a parallel centralization of sexed injury in some feminist critique, Janet Halley (2006, 346) remarks, "so much feminist rape discourse insists on women's objectlike status in the rape situation: man fucks woman—subject verb object. Could feminism be contributing to, rather than resisting, the alienation of women from their own agency in narratives and events of sexual violence? . . . Oddly, representing women as end points of pain, imagining them as lacking the agency to cause harm to others and particularly to harm men, feminists refuse also to see women—even injured ones—as powerful actors."

73. Marcus 1992, 400. Hirschmann (2002, 135–37) theorizes intimate partner violence as a constraint on a (indexically) woman's ability to make choices. The injury she identifies is thus not brutalization alone, but the injury to women's freedom resultant from brutalization. Mohr (1988) argues that control over one's body is and ought to be elemental both to constitutional law regulating sexual conduct as well as to any normatively defensible concept of sexual autonomy. While he tethers autonomy to corporeal self-direction, he carefully defends an individual right "to do *to* one's body as one pleases," rather than a right "to do *with* his body as he pleases" (117).

74. Marcus 1992, 386; see also Butler 1993a, 29. Like Schulhofer, Nedelsky (2011, 189–93) centralizes human embodiment in her reconstruction of autonomy, but she is concerned with how bodily deprivations undermine autonomous decision making. She pointedly differentiates her account of embodiment from those accounts that dramatize pain and suffering, in which "bodily violation comes to define the subject" (191).

75. Surveying the uneven development of British child pornography and sexual grooming laws, Ost (2009) argues that innocence and communal standards of decency have too often been the foci of protective attention, rather than the minimization of coercion and exploitation of children.

76. See Ost 2009, 140.

77. See Oberman 2001, 809.

78. In California, for example, sexual contact with someone under eighteen is a crime, unless the partners are married. Cal. Penal Code § 261.5 (a) (2010).

79. In Utah and Ohio, for example, an eighteen-year-old can be criminally liable for sexual contact with a fifteen-year-old. Utah Code Ann. § 76–5–406 (11) (2010); Ohio Rev. Code Ann. § 2907.04 (A) (2010).

80. Based on a 1994 Allan Guttmacher Institute study, Oberman (2001, 809) reports that most U.S. teenagers have had sex, so there are "potentially millions of statutory rapes every year." Opposing Oberman, Phipps (2003, 393) suggests that a more nuanced study of criminal sex laws would reveal that most sexually active teens are above statutory age thresholds. According to a more recent Guttmacher Institute study, "nearly half (46%) of all 15–19-year-olds in the United States have had sex at least once." However, the study also finds that most younger teens, under age seventeen, have not had sex. See Guttmacher Institute 2014.

81. See Schaffner 2005.

82. See Bishop 2000; Schaffner 2005.

83. See Waites 2005, 37–38. Age of consent laws clearly cannot and do not locate the transformative moment, sixteen years after the day of one's birth, where a person may meaningfully consent to sexual activity.

84. See Waites 2005, 29, 211–12. States generally distinguish crimes of sexual penetration with a minor from sexual contact with a minor, penalizing the former more heavily (see Phipps 1997, 43–47). Popular discussion ("what's the age of consent in Illinois?") obscures these nuances. Although such criminal gradations may be somewhat commendable under the rubric of sexual autonomy—recognizing the diversity of sexual experiences and contacts, intimating differentiated degrees of violation—the statutes portray a manifestly phallocentric and heteronormative account of sex. See also Higdon 2008.

85. On these two points, see Guttmacher Institute 2014: "The majority (59%) of sexually experienced teen females had a first sexual partner who was 1–3 years their senior"; M. Cohen 2008, 730.

86. Kitrosser 1996, 329–30, 333–34.

87. Ibid., 323–26.

88. See Cocca 2004, 136–38.

89. Kitrosser 1996, 321.

90. Ibid., 309, 329–30.

91. On the portrayal of wounded children to affect public opinion, see Holland 2004, 143–71; Wark 1995.

92. See, for example, Archard 1997, 118; Archard 2004, 19–50; Kincaid 1998, 14–17, 53–56; Kitzinger 1988.

93. For varying accounts of the ways childhood innocence is and has been racialized in the United States, see R. Bernstein 2011; Fields 2005; Fischel 2013b; Kincaid 1998, 20; D. Roberts 1997, 21; Stockton 2009, 31–33, 207–14.

94. See, for example, Kitzinger 2004; Ost 2009, 180–91; Schultz 2008.

95. On the political and political-theoretic origins of this division, see Brewer 2005.

96. See Waites 2005, 233.

97. See Lamb and Peterson 2012, 706.

98. I depart from Schulhofer here because, surprisingly, he does not investigate age, age difference, and constraints on choice, while Archard and Oberman do. Despite an otherwise prescient comment that age of consent statutes often neglect power relations by collapsing power inequality into a line-drawing game (1998, 196), Schulhofer repeatedly writes off the sexual consent of a hypothetical fifteen-year-old as meaningless, on the ungrounded rationale of presumed incapacity, therefore perpetuating the deficiency of the statutes he questions (102): "Intercourse with an apparently willing fifteen-year-old or with a mentally incompetent woman," asserts Schulhofer, "is not prohibited because the man is a potential killer; it is prohibited because the preconditions for meaningful choice are absent." Although Schulhofer stages the teen and the

"incompetent" to advance his argument for an expanded legal understanding of sexual violation, he unfortunately throws them under the bus to do so—both are declared unilaterally and equivalently incapable of decision making, their desires irrelevant to law.

99. Archard 1997, 1.

100. Ibid., 120.

101. Ibid., 119.

102. Ibid., 117.

103. See also Kincaid 1998; Kipnis 1999; Levine 2002.

104. Archard 1997, 44.

105. Ibid., 46.

106. Ibid., 44–45. However, while Archard writes that mentally disabled and drunk people are incapable, he uses the passive voice in considering children, intimating that such incapacity may be a determination of law and not biological fact: "The lack of such a capacity may be permanent, as would be the case with someone who is seriously mentally ill or disabled . . . a child *is judged* to lack the capacity of an adult. . . . Clearly a comatose person *is not able to consent to* . . . sexual activity" (44–45, emphasis added). Further along: "Sexual activity by someone below the age of majority *is characterized as* non-consensual" (119, emphasis added).

107. Ibid., 120. When Archard considers the "nature of sexual activity," he is primarily commenting on the then different age of consent laws in Britain for homosexual and heterosexual sexual activity, and he suggests the legal difference should be abolished (it has), since it has nothing to do with capacity, knowledge, or voluntariness, but rather homophobia. See also Waites 2005, 166–82.

108. Archard 1997, 126–27. See also Oberman 1994, 63–70; Oberman 2000, 725–26; Oberman 2001, 820–21.

109. Archard 1997, 124.

110. Ibid., 125. See also Levine 2002, 90–116.

111. Archard 1997, 37–38.

112. Oberman 1994; Oberman 2000; Oberman 2001.

113. Oberman 2000, 714.

114. Ibid., 709.

115. Ibid., 778.

116. See Phipps 2003, 386, 424.

117. Oberman 2000, 718–28.

118. Charles Phipps (2003, 434), reviewing Oberman's cases, observes, "the members of the Spur Posse committed rape, not statutory rape; the older adolescents in the Chicago case abused eleven- and twelve-year-old children; and Joshua Hemme raped two girls."

119. Oberman 2000, 721, quoted in Phipps 2003, 380.

120. See Phipps 2003, 424–45.

121. Phipps (2003, 425, 439–40) cursorily suggests that progressive proposals to revise statutory standards of sexual consent might be promisingly applied to young

people. Oberman is less hopeful: "One can easily imagine the consequences of this [consent reform] approach, were it to be permitted in cases involving young victims. Owing to factors with which we are well acquainted, girls are less likely to take an active role in rejecting a sexual advance. And if their silence may be taken as consent ... this 'reform' would enslave them to male sexual predilections" (2000, 767). Oberman's criticism does not account for the possibility of criminal statutes explicitly rejecting silence as a token of consent.

122. In Hawaii, for example, a twenty-year-old commits sexual assault in the first degree (felony) for penetrative sex with a fifteen-year-old, unless the partners are married. Haw. Rev. Stat. Ann. § 707–730 (1)(c)(i–ii) (2010). In Maryland, a seventeen-year-old commits a second degree sex offense (felony) for sexual contact with a thirteen-year-old. Md. Code Ann., Crim. Law § 3–306(a)(3) (2010).

123. See Cocca 2004, 19.

124. See Elstein and Davis 1997; Phillips 1999; Waites 2005, 238–41. However, in the United States the gap in sexual knowledge between teenagers and adults may not be so wide, as younger adults often have little or incorrect information about sex, contraception, and reproduction. See Landau 2009.

125. See Oberman 2000, 752.

126. See, for example, Elstein and Davis 1997; Lamb 2002.

127. Wertheimer 2003, 221–22. Wertheimer argues that Oberman opposes per se proscriptions, which is incorrect. Oberman advances per se proscriptions, but with qualifications regarding prosecuting and sentencing.

128. Oberman 2000, 751–52.

129. Wertheimer 2003, 216.

130. Ibid., 217.

131. Ibid., 216–22.

132. Wertheimer 2003, 217. Although Wertheimer's scenarios are hypotheticals (person A does x, person B does y), many of them are taken from court cases. The gang members and high school freshman scenario refers to the "Spur Posse" scandal, discussed in Oberman 2000, 718.

133. Wertheimer 2003, 217.

134. Ibid., 218.

135. Ibid., 218, 222. Wertheimer suggests that wide age-spans may be inherently exploitive (not coercive), but nevertheless endorses per se proscriptions.

136. Ibid., 180–82.

137. Ibid., 222.

138. Oberman 2000, 713.

139. Phipps 2003, 408.

140. See Oberman 2000, 718–28.

141. See Kincaid 1998.

142. See Kipnis 1999. See also chapter 2.

143. For discussion regarding the limitations of state laws regulating sex in relations of dependence, see Bienen 1998, 1564–76; Buchhandler-Raphael 2011, 221–28; Decker and Baroni 2011, 1127–31; Falk 1998, 79–81. Most states make "biological relation" the touchstone of their incest provisions. See, for example, D.C. Code Ann. § 22–1901 (2013) ("If any person in the District related to another person within and not including the fourth degree of consanguinity . . . shall marry or cohabit with or have sexual intercourse with such other so-related person, knowing him or her to be within said degree of relationship, the person so offending shall be deemed guilty of incest"); Ind. Code Ann. § 35–46–1–3 (2013) ("A person eighteen [18] years of age or older who engages in sexual intercourse or deviate sexual conduct with another person, when the person knows that the other person is related to the person biologically . . . commits incest); Kan. Stat. Ann. § 21–5604 (2013) ("Incest is marriage to or engaging in otherwise lawful sexual intercourse or sodomy . . . with a person who is 18 or more years of age and who is known to the offender to be related to the offender as any of the following biological relatives").

144. See "Inbred Obscurity" 2006; Kitrosser 1996, 333–34. A 2006 *Harvard Law Review* Note proposes that incest laws should prohibit sex in relations of familial dependence rather than consanguineous sex ("Inbred Obscurity" 2006, 2475). However, the editors argue that the distinction between familial dependence and consanguinity perfectly tracks the "consent/nonconsent distinction" (2466)—precisely the wedge this chapter hopes to open up.

145. See Schulhofer 1998, 196.

146. See, for example, Franke 2001; Gallop 1997; Vance 1992.

147. Wertheimer 2003, 163–92.

148. In Wertheimer's example (2003, 167–68), a lifeguard is required to rescue a drowning person. If the lifeguard offers to rescue the person only in exchange for his money, the agreement is void and the person should not be expected to pay.

149. Wertheimer 2003, 175.

150. See also Archard 1997, 67.

151. Wertheimer 2003, 180.

152. Schulhofer 1998, 135–36, 143–44, 174, 178, 197–98. Schulhofer also discussed Wertheimer's *Lower Grade* and *Higher Grade* scenarios at the University of Chicago "Law and Philosophy" seminar on coercion, spring 2008.

153. Wertheimer 2003, 180.

154. Schulhofer 1998, 206–26, 253.

155. Famously, MacKinnon posits (1983, 647), "perhaps the wrong of rape has proven so difficult to articulate because the unquestionable starting point has been that rape is definable as distinct from intercourse, when for women it is difficult to distinguish them under conditions of male dominance." Archard (1997, 90), like many a skeptical law student, writes that MacKinnon claims all heterosexual sex is indistinguishable from rape, and then dismisses her argument as such. This strategic misreading allows Archard and others to contain feminist critiques of rape law as

paranoid and excessive; Oberman (2001, 823–24) observes how other critics of MacKinnon have made the same mistaken conclusion. For a normative reclamation of status-based statutes to protect sexual autonomy (rather than penalize various forms of nonprocreative sex outside marriage), see Eskridge 1995, 66–67. I should also note that regulating sexual relations of trust and authority is one of two ways to mitigate the effects of structural dependence on sexual autonomy. The other is to revolutionize social conditions so that these relations of dependence dissolve, say, by abolishing the nuclear family and wage labor and securing children's financial independence. Until the revolution, I hesitantly endorse regulation. See Millett 1992, 217–24.

156. Nutting 2013, 108–9.

157. See Caringella 2009, 14–15, 65–70; Chamallas 1987–88, 796–813. See also Freedman (2013, 278–88) for a review of antirape legal and institutional reforms from the 1970s onward.

158. See Schulhofer 1998, 30–31.

159. Many states require some proof of resistance as an element in a crime of rape or sexual assault, while some have abolished the resistance requirement altogether, centralizing nonconsent instead. See Caringella 2009, 14–15.

160. See Buchhandler-Raphael 2011, 157–60; Caringella 2009, 106–7; Schulhofer 1998, 10.

161. New Jersey, Wisconsin, and Washington all require affirmative consent for exculpation; see Caringella 2009, 75–78. In Wisconsin, "consent" is "words or overt actions by a person who is competent to give informed consent indicating a freely given agreement to have sexual intercourse or sexual contact." Wis. Stat. § 940.225(4) (2010).

162. See, for example, Chamallas 1987–88; MacKinnon 2007a; Pineau 1996; Remick 1993.

163. See, for example, Bryden 2000, 402–11; Caringella 2009, 78–82; Schulhofer 1998, 43–46.

164. See Bussel 2008; Millar 2008.

165. See, for example, Estrich 1992, 10–11; Fineman 2004, 42–43. As Ehrlich evidences (2009, 325), nineteenth-century reformers wryly argued that if Congress could act quickly to pass a bill rebuilding the burned down stables for President Grant's horses, surely Congress could act as speedily to protect girls.

166. As Pateman warns (1988, 15), "that individual freedom, through contract, can be exemplified in slavery should give socialists and feminists pause when they make use of the idea of contract and the individual as owner."

167. For a thorough, trenchant treatment of the codification of child (a)sexuality and (sexual) abuse, and the consequent disciplinary encroachments the legal child requires from the state and its professional institutions, see Harkins 2009, 26–68.

168. See Harkins 2009, 197; Kincaid 1998.

169. See Berlant 1997, 66–67. In his study of thirty men convicted of sex offenses against children, sociology professor Douglas Pryor finds, "one [erotic] contingency

was the perceived vulnerability of the child. . . . Many men noted that they had picked a particular child they believed to be an easy or willing mark. . . . Erotic desire seemed to flourish for men when they were in control of their victims. . . . *The men felt that the victims began to use sex and their knowledge of what had been occurring to gain leverage. . . . Other men admitted that they lost power when the victim started to initiate sex back. . . . In these instances, erotic interest dissipated, sexual momentum essentially stopped, and offenders began to search for ways out of the situation"* (1996, 266–67, emphasis added). Surmises Ost (2009, 185–86), "our construction and objectification of children as innocent may cause us to *reduce* them simply to objects of innocence, the one aspect of childhood that may be of greatest attraction to the child sexual abuser." Yuill and Durber (2008, 266) cite studies finding that a presumed innocence and a presumed need-of-guidance were reported factors of attraction for self-identified "boylovers" and "pedophiles."

170. Schulhofer 1998, 280.

171. Wash. Rev. Code § 9A.44.010(7) (2003).

172. See Humphreys 2004; Kitrosser 1996, 324–26.

173. See MacKinnon 2001, 217.

174. The parallels here are the invalidity of coerced contracts and the absolution of criminal culpability under conditions of duress. Of course, what counts (morally, legally) as coercion to invalidate contract, and what counts (morally, legally) as duress to exonerate criminal behavior are questions as complicated as determining when and under what circumstances affirmative consent to sex is transformative. For a jurisprudential and philosophical account of coercion and a proposal to revise its meaning and scope, see Wertheimer 1987. For an analysis of duress and a proposal to revise its meaning and scope, see Carr 1991; Dan-Cohen 1992, 997–99; Gómez 2008.

175. *Meritor Savings Bank v. Vinson,* 477 U.S. 57 (1986).

176. See Fitzgerald 2004; Gregory 2004, 35–47.

177. In *State v. Grunke,* 752 N.W.2d 769 (Wis. 2008), the Wisconsin Supreme Court reversed lower court rulings and held defendants in violation of the state's sexual assault laws for attempting to have sex with a corpse. Importantly, the finding in part hinged on Wisconsin's statutory definition of consent as "indicating a freely given agreement to have sexual intercourse or sexual contact." Wis. Stat. § 940.225(4) (2006). The state, the court concluded, need not prove the corpse withheld consent, but simply that she did not affirmatively provide it (which she did not, as she was dead). At least in Wisconsin, Catharine MacKinnon's and Andrea Dworkin's grievance that under U.S. law dead women can consent to sex is allayed by this statutory affirmative standard. However, Caringella (2009, 80–82, 112–13) observes that judges in jurisdictions with affirmative consent requirements often interpret acquiescence or submission as voluntariness.

178. See Fitzgerald 2004, 94.

179. For similar critiques, see Dressler 1998; Dripps 1992, 1792–93.

180. Estrich 1987, 70–71.

181. MacKinnon (1991, 1300) observes, "The notion of consent here, the law's line between intercourse and rape, is so passive that a dead body could satisfy it." She cites A. Dworkin (1987, 129), who amps it up: "Consent in this world of fear is so passive that the woman consenting could be dead and sometimes is." But see note 177 above (a dead woman cannot consent to sex in Wisconsin).

182. See, for example, Berger 1988, 75–76; Caringella 2009, 78–85; Klein 2008, 1053. However, Berger (2000) has since attenuated her criticism of an affirmative standard while nonetheless remaining cautious that rape law reforms may patronize women.

183. Kitrosser 1996, 309.

184. See, for example, Caringella 2009, 79–80.

185. See Archard 1997, 37.

186. See "Ask First" 1993; Caringella 2009, 79.

187. Estrich 1992, 10–11; Oberman 2000, 718–28; Schulhofer 1998, 47–55.

188. Bryden 2000, 400, 403.

189. Ibid., 403. Archard (1997, 23) argues that only a particularly caricatured account of securing consent would render it so deflating for erotic spontaneity.

190. Bryden 2000, 400.

191. See Cocca 2004, 16–24.

192. See Fine and McClelland 2006. Fields finds the following in her investigation of safer-sex education in three politically and socially diverse North Carolina secondary schools: "Liberals promoted comprehensive sex education as a means to prepare young people—and, again, young women in particular—to navigate a sexually dangerous world.... Conservatives, however, argued that sexual knowledge introduces youth to a sexual terrain that is too treacherous for them to navigate successfully.... Neither argument acknowledged the pleasure that might await a person in sexual expression or relationships.... Unable to find any good reason for a middle school student to know about a range of pleasurable experiences, including clitoral orgasms, adults' impulse became to shut down learning and critical inquiry. For too many students, sex education becomes an effort to do no more than help young people survive sexual danger" (2008, 140). Levine (2002, 90–116) tracks and mourns the trajectory of safer-sex education in U.S. public schools from the 1970s until the beginning of the twenty-first century. As a result of religious and conservative political organizing, the more comprehensive safer-sex programs of the 1970s almost entirely surrendered to abstinence and abstinence-plus models by the 1990s and early 2000s. Cathy Cohen draws attention to the effects of scaling back comprehensive sex education for black youth: "The retreat from comprehensive sex education in the public schools may be one of the most significant attacks on challenging HIV and AIDS in black communities as well [as] protecting the sexual rights [of] people of color. Public schools are one of the few places—other than prisons—where we have the chance to intervene in the lives of significant numbers of black and Latino children, challenging and changing how they think about sex; how they think about themselves; and how they think about HIV and AIDS" (2009, 123).

193. Bryden 2000, 409.

194. For discussions of the distinctions between stranger and date rape, see, for example, Caringella 2009, 87; Schulhofer 1992, 57. Estrich (1987, 8–26) argues that a hard and fast distinction minimizes the harms and disqualifies the prosecutions of acquaintance rape cases, while Lynne Henderson (1988, 224–29) suggests that collapsing this distinction trivializes more violent, nonacquaintance sexual assaults (although Henderson concludes that both "simple" and "stranger" rapes should be criminal).

195. Schulhofer 1998, 281–84.

196. Beginning in the 1970s, some gay rights activists called for the abolition of age of consent laws for this reason (see, for example, Foucault, Hocquenghem, and Danet 1988; Tsang 1981), a position advanced by some later writings as well (see, for example, Schaffner 2005). Objections to age of consent laws were also objections to selective, homophobic, and racist enforcement patterns (see, for example, Delgado 1996; Rubin 1993; Schaffner 2005).

197. Foucault, Hocquenghem, and Danet 1988, 271, 284.

198. Alcoff 1996.

199. Ibid., 111.

200. Bell 1993, 154.

201. To historicize sexuality as an emergent juridical and scientific discourse of the nineteenth century, Foucault (1990, 31) offers the allegory of a "simple-minded" farmhand who "had obtained a few caresses from a little girl, just as he had done before and seen done by the village urchins around him." The girl's parents disclose his actions to the police, and the farmhand is then analyzed by an array of professionals. His features are measured and body investigated, until ultimately he is "shut away till the end of his life." "What is the significant thing about this story?" Foucault asks, and answers: "The pettiness of it all; the fact that this everyday occurrence in the life of village sexuality, these inconsequential bucolic pleasures, could become, from a certain time, the object not only of a collective intolerance but of a judicial action, a medical intervention, a careful clinical examination, and an entire theoretical elaboration." Foucault does not consider what this inconsequential, bucolic pleasure might have meant for the girl, or why her body was her best and most expected form of currency. Like Alcoff, Butler (1990, 97) argues that Foucault momentarily forgets the Foucauldian contribution that there is no sexuality prior to discourse when he appears to discover unadulterated pleasure in this sexual exchange.

202. Wertheimer 2003, 86.

203. In Oberman's "Regulating Consensual Sex" (2000, 775), "boys" appear near the conclusion, placed in parentheses, in a sentence really about securing girls' safety: "All of these [prior] proposals fall somewhat short of the promise that I believe underlies statutory rape laws: that girls (and boys) must be permitted to explore their incipient sexuality in an environment that is free from coercion, exploitation, and nonvoluntary sexual encounters."

204. MacKinnon 1989, 141–42, 248. Janet Halley (2006, 54–59) objects to MacKinnon's assimilation of same-sex harassment as male domination over women.

205. Studies cataloging sexual abuse against boys are cited in Phipps 2003, 425–26. Despite Phipps's protest against Oberman's gender-specific approach, his own citations (2003, 395–96) of the literature reflect that sexual abuse of or against girls is extremely frequent. I want to take a middle path between Oberman and Phipps: we can recognize the problem of child sexual abuse as gender-differentiated, but not entirely so, and still advocate a gender-neutral legal response.

206. Wertheimer 2003, 217.

207. See, for example, Stanley, Bartholomew, and Oram 2004; Tsang 1981. In the discussion of their findings, Stanley, Bartholomew, and Oram hypothesize: "These [age discrepant] sexual experiences may provide these adolescents with the opportunity to explore their sexuality and feel affirmed by the gay community. Gay youth often speak of feeling different from their childhood peers and unaccepted by the dominant culture. It may be less threatening for young gay males to seek out an older gay male than to risk rejection and possible humiliation from making sexual advances toward a peer . . . the assumptions of the heterosexual community may not apply to gay youth when it is that very community which does not allow gay youth an outlet to explore their sexuality" (2004, 388, internal citations omitted).

208. Alcoff 1996, 99–135; but see also Nelson and Oliver 1998. In Nelson and Oliver's study sample, "man–boy contact is more likely to involve older man and younger children than the other forms, but this relationship cannot be accorded any certainty" (564). The women in their study reported incestuous "episodes" as younger children much more frequently than the men (563).

209. See studies cited in Waites 2005, 26–27.

210. See Leahy 1992; Rind and Tromovitch 1997; Sandfort 1983. Sandfort concludes that pedophilic relationships may be beneficial for "children" and younger adolescents, momentarily ignoring the gender specificity of his own research. Despite the title of Leahy's report, "Positively Experienced Man/Boy Sex: The Discourse of Seduction and the Social Construction of Masculinity," the author never seriously engages how male adolescents' conceptions of "male political rights" and "masculine adulthood as citizenship" materialize through conceptions of sexual difference (1992, 86).

211. See Rind 2001.

212. Nelson and Oliver 1998, 565–66.

213. On the "female sex offender," see the subsection "The (Elusive) Female Sex Offender" in the Introduction; see also Angelides 2007; Nelson and Oliver 1998. On lesbian intergenerational (not necessarily child–adult) sex as pastoral, politicizing, polyvalent, subjectivizing, feminist, and/or fun, see, for example, L. Feinberg 2003, 68–73; Gallop 1997; Lorde 1982, 161–76. For a thoughtfully measured account of Simone de Beauvoir's profound, erotic relations with teenage girls, see Simons 1992; for a dubiously speculative assessment of power and intimacy dynamics that might

arise in intergenerational lesbian relations, see Bruns 2008. Scholarly literature and media attention on child sexual abuse focus almost entirely on relations between men (or male predators) and girls, men (or gay pedophiles) and boys, and occasionally women (or deluded, emotionally stunted temptresses) and boys. For an account of these media narratives and their rhetorical force, see Cocca 2004, 63–92.

214. See Martin 1994.

215. See, for example, Bell 1993, 150–60. In assessing the validity of consent in pedophilic relations, Alcoff (1996, 117) writes, "perhaps the most crucial distinction besides age that needs to be made is that between homosexual and heterosexual practices," but then disregards the distinction in her proposals. Jeffreys (1990, 208) brushes aside the possibility that "man–boy" relations may be distinct from those between men and girls. She argues by assertion only that "gay male sexuality is not different in kind from heterosexual male sexuality . . . they develop a ruling-class sexuality in which power and dominance are eroticized."

216. See, for example, Brongersma 1990; Gay Left Collective 1981; Thorstad 1990. The Gay Left Collective (1981, 56–57) states that it "feels that male heterosexual and homosexual pedophilia raise different questions." Unfortunately, the article reduces those questions to culturally diagnostic ones about the social construction of homosexual predators and the erasure of female sexuality, rather than the potential of distinct power and sexual dynamics in these different relations. Brongersma (1990) also provides research showing that relations between men and boys and men and girls are characterized by different experiences, mostly to the disadvantage of girls. He does not, however, apply his findings to explain the political fault lines between some feminists and some gay activists in the 1980s and 1990s.

217. Yuill and Durber 2008, 262–63. Rind (2001) argues that his data challenge the "victimological model" of child sexual interaction that presumes a uniform experience of trauma across gender and sexuality. However, rather than suppose that gender and age difference may compound each other to produce the effects experienced by young girls, he instead implies that homophobia and a generalized panic around child sexuality forecloses contrasting research like his own. This is right, but it supplants a more nuanced critique for recourse to victimization that grants him scientific authority against an allegedly duped research community. Commenting on another (more infamous, controversial, and congressionally censured) study conducted by Rind and his colleagues (1998) that questioned the presumptive effects of child sexual abuse, Gillian Harkins notes: "One of the main questions raised by the study then is how to interpret such 'empirical' measures of gender identity as the grounds for meaningful willingness and the rationale for psychological harm. . . . To put it in my own words, the Rind study's careful navigation of citational sources suggests that although girls more often experience sex in the context of force or dysfunctional families, in those cases there is no empirically solid evidence that the *sexual* experience and not the force and dysfunction cause harm. The family emerges as the culprit, but only to the degree that it is radically divorced from conditions of sexual activity, desire, or

willingness. . . . Sexuality is liberated from the family, a specifically gendered conduct released from its once constraining context. Willingness in this account produces the boy as a protoliberal individual. . . . Girls' potential sexuality is determined (once again) by the family and enclosed within its circuits as gender identity. And, when sexual abuse appears within the family, it may be the result of genetic inheritance and community dysfunction. Thus even as the family appears to be the only empirically verifiable source of harmful child sexual abuse, the harm of that experience is unintelligible as anything other than dysfunctional sociobiological gender identity. . . . In their own interpretation of their study, Rind et al. suggest that incestuous trauma is most likely a false positive, a form of 'secondary victimization' and 'iatrogenesis' fostered by feminist antisex moralism. If girls think that sexual abuse caused harm, it is sex panic" (2009, 206–7).

218. Marlowe 1997, 142.

219. Ibid., 141.

220. See Butler 1993b.

221. See, for example, Fields 2008, 113–36; Fine and McClelland 2006; Levine 2002, 128–30, 155–77. Fine and McClelland argue that although the past twenty-five years have witnessed a flourishing of desirous girls in media and advertising, girls' desire is contained, normalized, or extinguished through the administration of social services and the lessons of abstinence-only sex education; such programs disproportionately impact girls who are further marginalized on other axes of inequality, such as race, class, and disability. That desire is socially and pedagogically attributed and afforded to boys qua boys does not in any way presuppose that social and sexual life is easily managed for queer boys, that expectations of sexual expression and aggression are not often taxing on all boys, or that same-sex sexual desire is acknowledged or tolerated in sex education programs.

222. Roger Levesque (2000, 338–48) suggests that the United States "recognize adolescents as legal subjects," giving them greater rights over their medical, sexual, financial, and social decisions, and Allender (2009, 1845–52) tracks the development of young people's privacy rights in federal and state court cases involving abortion, contraception, and sexual activity.

223. Thanks to Lauren Berlant for this insight. Writes Kathryn Bond Stockton: "Just as children are deemed more vulnerable by their guardians in the 1900s (and thus are deemed more in need of protections, many in the form of laws), they are constructed as more problematic, as presenting adults with more and newer problems, even dangers to face. A second paradox that shows up in [childhood studies] . . . is the observation that the century of the child turns out to be the century in which the state of childhood is itself shrinking. . . . Sexual precocity . . . is high on scholars' lists of factors causing children to 'grow up fast' and thus disappear" (2009, 37, citation omitted).

224. See Franke 2001.

225. See, for example, Brown and Halley 2002; Jakobsen and Kennedy 2005.

226. Halley 2006, 20–22.

227. See, for example, W. Brown 1995, 3–29, 52–76; W. Brown 2002, 420; Warner 1999, 39–40, 45–50.

228. For similar but elaborated critique of feminist antistatism, see Hirschmann 2002, 234–45; Nedelsky 2011, 334–61.

229. MacKinnon (2007b, 828–29) queries, "Do statutory rape laws target girls for forced sex by defining girls as off limits, making it sexy to violate them as 'jail bait'? . . . Are statutory rape laws necessary or are they both perverse and ineffective?" She argues elsewhere that obscenity law eroticizes obscenity (1989, 167–68). MacKinnon's suppositions are intriguing, since feminists have long charged that her antipornography polemics and her legal reforms sexualize and symbolically strengthen pornography (see, for example, W. Brown 1995, 77–95).

230. See Adler 2001.

231. See Dean 2009. On the gap between court order and social/administrative uptake, see Horowitz 1977; Rosenberg 1991.

232. Reducing the moral problem of underage sex to a yes-or-no, legal-or-illegal question distracts from the "unsexy" project of querying the socioeconomic constraints on sexual choices (see Nussbaum 1998). Predating and paralleling Nussbaum, Youth Liberation (1981, 50) asserts, "The problem here is not so much that young women are becoming prostitutes—the problem is that this society has so little respect for the young that it provides no decent jobs or alternatives for kids in oppressive home situations."

233. See, for example, Cowan 2007, 68–69; Fields 2008; Hollenberg 1999, 277; Levine 2002; Oberman 2001, 825–82.

4. GROWING SOMEWHERE?

The title of the chapter and many of its ideas are inspired by Kathryn Bond Stockton's *The Queer Child, or Growing Sideways in the Twentieth Century* (2009).

1. The language and normative valence of "becoming" are loosely appropriated from Deleuze and Guattari (1987), for whom the political retrieval of becoming lies in its antiteleology and nonlinearity. Becoming need not be a stopover to some final destination of being (say, mature adulthood), but a description/prescription of subjectivity as processive, extending outward, and (to the extent that it is perceptible against the social grain) collective and rupturing. See also Massumi 1992, 102–7; Renold and Ringrose 2011, 294. James (2011, 177) and Lesko (2012, 11, 180–81) caution against "becoming" as the idiom for children's and adolescent's rights, insofar as "becoming" associates with individual, psychological incompleteness best attended by supervising adults and experts. This concern is partially quelled if becoming is repurposed in the way Deleuze and Guattari advise. For a critique of the containing effects of "becoming" theories of sexual identity formation on adolescents, see Savin-Williams 2005, 74–82.

2. For historicist accounts of adolescence, see Baxter 2008; Lesko 2012, 16–40. G. Stanley Hall (1904) is commonly credited for creating "adolescence" as a discrete,

turbulent episode of human development and for popularizing adolescence as an object of scientific inquiry.

3. See Baxter 2008; Giroux 2012. In contrast to the criminalization of racial minority youth as the United States' preferred policy fix to an eviscerated welfare state, a series of Supreme Court decisions have ruled capital punishment and life imprisonment without the possibility of parole unconstitutional as applied to minors, in violation of the Eighth Amendment. In these cases, the comparative neurological underdevelopment, impulsivity, and inexperience of young people are marshaled as evidence to protect them against, rather than sanction, state violence. The counterpropulsion of these rulings is promising, of course, but we should be cautious. They firmly entrench the notion of criminal behavior as a function of errant persons and corrupt (adults) or corruptible (youth) minds. Thus, having evacuated factors like poverty, joblessness, homelessness, and education from the scene of the crime, these decisions double down on capital punishment and life imprisonment as not only justified but also necessary for "adults" who are rendered the exclusive locus of culpability. See *Roper v. Simmons,* 543 U.S. 551 (2005) (holding capital punishment for juvenile offenders unconstitutional); *Graham v. Florida,* 560 U.S. ___ (2010) (holding life imprisonment without the possibility of parole for juveniles convicted of nonhomicidal crimes unconstitutional); *Miller v. Alabama,* 567 U.S. ___ (2012) (holding life imprisonment without the possibility of parole for juveniles convicted of homicide unconstitutional). Consider *Miller*'s implicit reconstitution of adult criminality: "To recap: Mandatory life without parole for a juvenile precludes consideration of his chronological age and its hallmark features—among them, immaturity, impetuosity, and failure to appreciate risks and consequences. It prevents taking into account the family and home environment that surrounds him—and from which he cannot usually extricate himself—no matter how brutal or dysfunctional" (at 15). On the one hand, Justice Kagan's summary is a brief for what I am calling peremption and the ways in which young people's life options are disqualified, funneled, or contained. On the other hand, this juridical permission slip is brokered on an authorizing fiction of the unencumbered, deliberative, and ultimately bad adult male.

4. See Giroux 2012. The other stock figure of dangerous adolescence from the 1990s until the present, of course, is the high school shooter: in his late teens or early twenties, usually white, and presumably crazy. See also Lesko 2012, 164–77.

5. For a queer-theoretic version of this critique, see A. Gordon 1999. For clinical psychological versions of this critique see, for example, Diamond 2009; Savin-Williams 2005. Savin-Williams's concerns regarding the "creation of gay youth" are many (71), only one of which is the incongruence between identitarian taxonomy and varieties of same-sex sex and intimacy (207). He argues that researchers' preoccupation with the "suffering gay adolescent" (68) functionally attaches meaningfulness, discreteness, and misery to young same-sex sexuality that belies both its complexity (76–78) and ordinariness (22, 216). He wonders if social ascription and self-labeling may contribute to the very sequelae (depression, alienation, etc.) these processes are

thought to mitigate (204). His critique of the construction of the "gay teenager" is two-pronged: first, that the gayness of gay teenagers is not as important to them as it is to the researchers who study them; and second, that adolescent sexuality is poorly captured by identitarian taxonomy, especially regarding women, U.S. cultural minorities, and some non-U.S. populations (214–16; see also Diamond 2009).

6. Pettit 2012, 60.

7. Lesko 2012, 11. Lesko explains in a similar fashion why her book on the cultural formation of adolescence concentrates more on expert and popular discourses than on the testimony of teenagers.

8. See Bulman 2005, 8. For Bulman, high school films of all stripes (in inner urban, suburban, and elite settings) ultimately value up middle-class moral values while neutralizing fears of middle-class conformism (166). Bulman's analysis of class antagonisms and bourgeois reification in different forms of the high school film is an illuminating contribution. His silence around sexual difference in the films he investigates is somewhat bizarre, if only because it likely blunts his interpretations on the representation and revalorization of middle-class value.

9. Stockton 2009, 8–9. Stockton chronicles the career of the child in modern and contemporary literature and film, noticing the sorts of "sideways growth" that the child initiates or endures since "growing up" is eternally deferred by a dominant sociolegal vision of childhood as a frozen space-time of blankness, innocence, and nonadultness. Movements and motives of children in the holding pattern that is childhood thus yield them "queer," while "actual" queer children, or protogay children, negotiate the burden of discovering and expressing messy desires that are demanded to be unidirectional, heterosexual but also nonexistent.

10. Halberstam 2011, 119; but see note 82, below.

11. Nussbaum 2006a, 13, 184–85.

12. McCloud 1993.

13. Ibid., 36.

14. I adapt the heading of this section from the first chapter of Lee Edelman's *No Future: Queer Theory and the Death Drive* (2004), titled "The Future Is Kid Stuff" (1–32). It may well be that the extent to which the political is calibrated to the futurity of the child measures the extent to which the political undermines the social and sexual welfare of children. See also Kincaid 1998, 292; the section "Toward an Adolescent Queerness," in the Conclusion.

15. "peremption, *n.*" 2014.

16. "peremptory, *adj., adv.,* and *n.*" 2014.

17. Ibid.

18. Ibid.

19. Laing 1965, 199–200.

20. "pre-emption, *n.*" 2014.

21. "perempt, *v.*" 2014.

22. Pettit 2012.

23. Ibid., 60.

24. Ibid., 82–88.

25. Pettit 1997, 55.

26. Pettit 2012, 58–59.

27. Ibid., 58, 55.

28. See Fine and McClelland 2006; on the relationship between unfreedom and noninvolvement more generally, see Markell 2008.

29. See Nedelsky 2011.

30. I adapt the subheading of this section from Markell's "The Insufficiency of Non-Domination" (2008). For an appreciative critique of usurpation, see the subsection "From Free Adults to Freeish Adolescents," in this chapter.

31. Hayward 2011; Hirschmann 2002; Krause 2013.

32. As Pettit (1997, 63) clarifies, "what is required for non-arbitrariness in the exercise of a certain power is not actual consent to that sort of power but the permanent possibility of effectively contesting it."

33. See Hirschmann 2002, 204; Nussbaum 2001, 111–66.

34. See Krause 2013, 193, 196.

35. Pettit 1997, 52.

36. Hirschmann 2002, 38.

37. Ibid., 39.

38. Ibid., 231.

39. Pettit 2012, 39–40.

40. Ibid., 43.

41. Hayward 2011, 470.

42. Ibid., 473, emphasis added; Krause (2013) distinguishes domination modeled on the form of first person activity (or inactivity) from "domination in the middle voice" (195), which captures the ways attitudes and unconscious or unintentional behaviors collude to disproportionately diminish "life-chances" for some minoritized groups (188). On oppression as perpetuated by systemic patterns and not only by malevolent perpetrators, see also W. Brown 1995, 52–76; Spade 2011, 79–100; Young 1990, 39–65.

43. Hirschmann 2002, 35; see also Krause 2013, 201.

44. Hirschmann 2002, 204. Or more precisely, this feminist "double vision" necessitates recognizing the social construction of political life while "acknowedg[ing] that some groups of people . . . have more power to participate in the constructing than do others."

45. Ibid., 135–37. See also chapter 3, note 68.

46. Krause 2013, 194.

47. Ibid., 199, emphasis added.

48. In this regard, it is indefensible to prioritize predation over peremption in the way Pettit prioritizes invasion over vitiation. Invasion is only of more serious political

concern than vitiation if the fiction of the otherwise unencumbered (male) adult is the referent and beneficiary of our critique.

49. M. Friedman 2008, 259–60.

50. Ibid., 260–61.

51. Ibid., 264, 267.

52. Ibid., 264.

53. Ibid., 265.

54. Pettit 2012, 98–99. I have substituted "republican approach" for Pettit's "eyeball test," a somewhat undetailed heuristic for determining which choices will be secured by political authority and to what degree.

55. On ethical intervention as dialogic, see O'Connell 2014; see also Markell 2008.

56. J. Feinberg 1987, 36.

57. See Downing 2004.

58. Krause (2013, 191) notes that for Pettit interference denotes intentional "worsening" (citing Pettit 1997, 55). In Pettit's *On the People's Terms* this sort of interference becomes "invasion" (2012, 43).

59. Krause 2013, 201, emphasis added. Krause is distinguishing the injustice of "oppression" from "domination."

60. J. Feinberg 1987, 37.

61. Markell 2008, 11, 26.

62. Ibid., 11, emphasis added and internal citations omitted.

63. Ibid., 27.

64. Pettit 2001b, 16, 103.

65. See Dixon and Nussbaum 2012, 562; see also Appell 2013, 726–30; Brewer 2005.

66. Pettit 2001b, 88–90.

67. Rasmussen (2011, 23–59) describes how modern political theories and contemporary U.S. public policy alike figure the adolescent as "almost autonomous" (34) or "a little bit autonomous" (35), but such characterizations are more often warrants for, rather than checks against, highly gendered, intensified regulations. In Western political thought and practice, boys' sexual desire and behavior have been rendered the greatest threat to their eventual self-governance (29), necessitating physical and moral education that redirects or disciplines their impulses. Boys' management of their sexuality then functions as proof positive of their autonomous subjectivity. But because, historically, girls have been understood as incapable of self-governance in the first place, their sexuality endangers not only themselves, but also citizen subjects (men) and thus society outright (46).

68. Pettit 1997, 119–20.

69. See also Costa 2013, 929.

70. Pettit 2001b, 14, 16; see also Markell 2008, 18.

71. Pettit 2012, 78.

72. Pettit 2001b, 65–103. See also Markell 2008, 17–23, for a concise but more elaborative rehearsal of Pettit's taxonomy of freedoms.

73. Pettit 2001b, 98.

74. If I track a consequentialist problem of Pettit's resolution, Markell (2008, 22–23) tracks an immanent one. Freedom as discursive control admits the intersubjective, developmental nature of human agency, but "nondomination" as a political corrective cannot attend to ways the subject is involved or not involved in the coconstitution of formative social relations.

75. See Pettit 2001a, 17–19.

76. Nussbaum 2011, 33, 26. However, Dixon and Nussbaum (2012) offer more generous, scaled provisions across the age spectrum. For them, the guarantee or withholding of rights should be keyed to children's dignity, rather than to their (non) capacities as party to the social contract. Still, Dixon and Nussbaum argue that restrictions on voting and jury participation, and compulsory education, may be justified to secure children's dignity. But this leaves several important questions unanswered: Which children are subject to these impositions, and how should these impositions be conducted? Appell (2013, 764–65), for example, argues that if political societies compel education, children should be paid for their attendance, and curricula should be organized around training children to enter labor markets and participate in political governance as soon as possible.

77. Costa 2013, 928–29.

78. See Appell 2013, 736–40.

79. See, for example, James 2011.

80. See, for example, Appell 2013; Herring 2012; Woodhouse 2009.

81. Gilbert 2007, 50.

82. For Halberstam (2011), childhood "failure" promises or amounts to counterhegemony: "Failure preserves some of the wondrous anarchy of childhood and disturbs the supposedly clean boundary between adults and children, winners and losers" (3). Halberstam locates in teen comedies and CGI films a "utopian alternative" (30–31). Failure here is a ticket out of a disciplinary and disciplining adulthood that is cut to the requirements of capitalism and compulsory heterosexuality. Despite the appeal of youth as the counterforce to "family and . . . lineage and . . . tradition" (70), I am reluctant to assign in advance transformative possibility to the child, the childlike, and teen wilding. Such a maneuver risks romanticism, obscuring those circumstances that can be navigated but not overcome by young people. The filmic adolescents I engage with later in this chapter do not manifest or even point toward a "utopian alternative" or refusal of dominant social, sexual, and economic arrangements. Rather, they embody relational experiments in surviving and possibly thriving askew of those arrangements, inhabiting them without being fully determined by them. Moreover, a character like *Thirteen's* Tracy Freeland cannot abandon or forget the functioning normative family, since she never had one. For a fuller discussion, see part 2 of this chapter and the section "Toward an Adolescent Queerness" in the Conclusion.

83. *Doubt* 2008; my transcriptions.

84. Shanley 2005. In the play version, Donald's last name is the more contemplative-sounding "Muller," not "Miller."

85. This may be one reason why Shanley sets the stage in 1964, nearly four decades before the revelations of sex abuse and cover-ups in the Catholic Church. See Dargis 2008.

86. See Stockton 2009, 62.

87. See also Cullingford 2010, 255.

88. Cullingford (2010, 260) points out that that omission of Donald from the play bypasses the emotive, experiential primacy of victim testimony. Other readings of intergenerational sex are more available when victim testimony is neither the affective nor empirical lynchpin. On the other hand, the removal of Donald's testimony requires the removal of Donald and synonymizes Donald's voice with the voice of the victim. This is a conflicted strategy for recovering multiple meanings of the intergenerational encounter—silencing the young subject for the sake of interpretive and ethical complexity.

89. See Jordan 2000, cited in Cullingford 2010, 248.

90. *Doubt* 2008.

91. For a similar but less sanguine reading of feminized black masculinity in visual culture, see hooks 1996, 214–17.

92. See Stockton 2009, 228–38.

93. Cullingford 2010, 246, 255; see also Place 2010, 21, 187.

94. Cumming-Bruce and Goodstein 2014: "But the [U.N.] committee expressed concern over numerous reports that church authorities had transferred priests accused of abuse to other dioceses, helping them to escape investigation and prosecution, allowing them to remain in contact with children and, in some cases, leading to further abuse."

95. Cullingford 2010, 260.

96. See Kincaid 1998, 280–83; Lancaster 2011, 82–84; see also Kipnis 2010, 5 ("Here is the scandal psychodynamic in a nutshell: scandalizers screw things up in showy, provocative ways and the rest of us throw stones, luxuriating in the warm glow of imaginary imperviousness that other people's life-destroying stupidities invariably provide").

97. Shanley 2005, 39.

98. Mrs. Miller's line, "Sometimes things aren't black and white," was struck from the film version, perhaps because it makes sexual matters uncomfortably gray (Shanley 2005, 49). The black mother cautions the white nun against facile moral analogues: the impermissibility of racial segregation and racial bullying, evidently "black and white," might not carry over to the intergenerational, interracial sexual encounter as seamlessly as Sister Aloysius would like.

99. *Doubt* 2008.

100. "Expensive Home Rich with Potential Predators" 2007.

101. See chapter 3, notes 207–12; see also Cullingford 2010, 259–60, 262; Stockton 2009, 62.

102. *Doubt* 2008.

103. Shanley 2005, 12.

104. See Cullingford 2010, 260.

105. Foucault, Hocquenghem, and Danet 1988, 273.

106. Dargis 2008; see also Cullingford 2010, 261.

107. *Doubt* 2008.

108. Ohi 2000, 101, 204, cited in Cullingford 2010, 250.

109. Angelides (2007) criticizes the scholarly, popular, and legal superimposition of victimhood and trauma onto adolescent boys who described their cross-generational sexual encounters in positive terms: "It seems a little odd to me that we uncritically accept the subjective perceptions of those young people who indeed have felt manipulated, coerced, victimized, and sexually abused by adults, yet we trivialize or discount the subjective perceptions of those that not only did not feel abused but felt their experiences were wholeheartedly consensual and positive" (357).

110. Chapter 3, notes 198–200.

111. Foucault, Hocquenghem, and Danet 1988, 273.

112. M. Friedman 2008, 259–60.

113. "peremptory, *adj., adv.,* and *n.*" 2014.

114. *Doubt* 2008.

115. Rousseau 1997, 53. See also Rasmussen 2011, 24 ("'Kids' may not practice self-determination because of their inability to adequately control themselves; they must be forced to be free, to learn autonomy through submission to external authority").

116. *Doubt* 2008.

117. Cullingford 2010, 262, 257–58, n. 60.

118. On imitation as elemental to gendered subjectivity (and subjection), see, for example (and famously), Butler 1993b; Butler 1997b. For a contiguous but positivist account of imitation, see American Psychological Association 2010; Lamb and Peterson 2012, 708. The APA finds: "Girls develop their identities as teenagers and as women, and they learn the socially acceptable ways to engage in intimate relationships by modeling what they see older girls and young women doing and by imitating the ways in which women are represented in the media" (2010, 3, internal citations omitted).

119. Pettit 1997, 139.

120. Adler 2001, 256.

121. Shanley 2005, 57.

122. Cullingford 2010, 257–58.

123. Savage and Miller 2011. For a (polemic) critique of the "It Gets Better" campaign's inattention to the less spectacular, more attritional forms of violence (more

commonly endured by girls), see Puar 2012. On delay as a central motif in the visual and literary representation of children, see Stockton 2009.

124. Cullingford 2010, 258.

125. See also Krause 2013, 199.

126. For an ethical retrieval of the "crowd" in youth films, see Halberstam 2011, 175–76. Halberstam sees *A Bug's Life* (1998) as a celebration of collective enterprise, countering the more typical Disney story of individual and individualistic heroism. Halberstam's is an important corrective, lest my *peremption* be understood as promoting an individualistic normative framework that codes any deferral of desire to the general will as harmful conformism. At the same time, *A Bug's Life* is not a call for everyone (every ant) to dedifferentiate himself to be a cog in the colony. Flik, its main character, is quirky, inventive, and lovelorn. Collaboration is made more effective by and in turn cultivates Flik's creativity. The "crowd" is also the necessary condition of possibility for the graceless Flik to win over his love object.

127. See also Huffer 2013, 113–17.

128. In a laundry list of films that purportedly degrade teen sex, Shary (2010, 65) decries that in *Thirteen* sex leads to drug abuse, which is incorrect—the film presents no such etiology.

129. Siegel's (2010) foregone intention was to value up the productive, defamiliarizing quality of "French feminism" by critiquing what she sees as the victimological current of "American feminism," a preconceived argument that disfigures her reading of one French film and one American film—each one featuring a young girl's attempt to expunge the toxicity of everyday life from her burgeoning identity. Siegel, I believe, wants the films to prove what she thinks about these feminisms, so then they do.

130. Siegel 2010, 245.

131. Karlyn 2006, 463.

132. See Davies 2007, 370–71, 376–77. Linda Williams (2008, 25–67) tracks how the "kiss" was synecdochal for the sex that could not be screened during the Production Code era, but between adults. In her aptly titled chapter, "Of Kisses and Ellipses: The Long Adolescence on American Movies (1896–1963)," she chronicles the overdetermined career of the kiss—as anticipatory to sex, synechdochal for it, or a perverse (in the Freudian sense) substitution. Williams explores how enforcement of Code dictates produced an interplay between concealment and exposure, hinging on the coupled kiss, that was not simply censorious but also pedagogic in its iterations. The lifting of the Code in the late 1960s made moot the kiss's polysemy. Child pornography laws have replaced the Production Code as the heavy censorial hand that generates through artistic remediation new dialectics of screening sex and sexuality. Certainly, in *Thirteen* and *Superbad,* the "kiss" is both a synecdoche for and allusive to the sex that cannot be screened. Child pornography prohibitions may contribute to both films' verbalized sex: Tracy tells Evie that Javi's semen tastes strange; in *Superbad* (2007), Seth graphically describes his favored pornography and preferred sex acts. The character McLovin cannot stop discoursing midcoitus.

133. Or rather, male predatory desire is easily rebuffed when it almost appears. When an unkempt, white friend of Evie's whispers to a drugged Tracy, "Wanna suck my cock, baby?" Tracy shoots him down, "Uch, no!"

134. Linda Williams, citing Richard Dyer, observes how white women in "the couple about to kiss" are lit to "glow," in Hollywood Production Code era films, which "works to purify the darker lusts their kisses may evoke" (2008, 37). Tracy's glow, here postfellatio, reflects serenity with purity's *loss*, or her inaugural accomplishment of something like intimacy.

135. As for the deadening nowhereness of this fantasy, see Berlant 1997, 59–60, 62, and the subsection "Navigating Peremption, Growing Nowhere: Racial Appropriation and Cutting," in this chapter.

136. Karlyn 2006, 462.

137. Siegel 2010, 247.

138. Similarly, Ellis Hanson (1999, 191) wonders why lesbian and feminist film critics prematurely code filmic lesbians and lesbian sex as the screening of visual pleasure for the male gaze. He answers, "in lesbian film criticism . . . aesthetic and visual pleasure is often cause for ideological pain. . . . We are loath to enjoy ourselves, as long as there is a straight man somewhere who delights over the same images."

139. MacKinnon 1982, 541.

140. Kincaid 2004, 12–13.

141. Ibid., 15.

142. See Karlyn 2006, 462; Zacharek 2003.

143. According to Karlyn: "*Thirteen* asks how girls can be supported in exploring their sexuality in a culture that continues to teach them that their primary value is as sexual objects for men. *At what age* are girls mature enough to wear panties with 'I "heart" cock' and T-shirts that read 'Porn Star' as affirmations of their own desire, rather than as signs of their unthinking acceptance of sexual ideologies based on female objectification?" (2006, 463, emphasis added). But "at what age" is not the right question. The film is not asking that question, but asking us to ask about the imprecision of that question. There is no age, ever, when girls' or women's sartorial or tactile displays of desire can be uncritically read as self-actualizing affirmation, even if that is what they in part are. There is not an age at which impressionability stops, or becomes moot, because these girls become women through imitation, and by accommodating and sometimes resisting others' appraisal. Our desires are never "our own," regardless of age, gender, or sexuality; but how, to what degree, and in the service of whom our desires are not our own is fractured by social division.

144. A report by a task force of the American Psychological Association (2010) found widespread and increasing "sexualization" of girls and women across the spectrum of U.S. cultural representations and social relations (18). "Sexualization" is defined by the authors, inter alia, as cultural practices and belief systems that value persons by their sexual "appeal": "Sexualization occurs when . . . a person is . . . made into a thing for others' sexual use, rather than seen as a person with the capacity for

independent action and decision making" (1)—that is, when availability is priori-tized over agency. Reviewing literature on "media sexuality," Lamb and Peterson find: "There is also a problematic lack of diversity of sexual expression and of models of 'sexiness' in mainstream and explicit pornographic media.... Thus while these media images of sexuality may be empowering to some extent, they are also incredibly restrictive and shape desire and subjectivity into forms that are more mainstream" (2012, 708, internal citations omitted).

145. See Dowling 2001, 52–58; Wolf 2002. Wolf acknowledges that American beauty standards have widened (in both senses) since she first wrote *The Beauty Myth* in 1991 and that there is more cultural self-consciousness regarding damaging gender norms. Still, she argues that media images of girlhood are increasingly sexualized (see also American Psychological Association 2010), that eating disorders are more perva-sive, and that boys and men are increasingly susceptible to violent beauty myths (Wolf 2002, 5–8). The emotional analogue to the premium placed on women's constricted motility is the asymmetric responsibility women bear to be deferential, affirming of others, and "nice." Hochschild 2003, 165–70.

146. This does not mean objectification always and everywhere cancels out female (or feminist) subjectivity. See Nussbaum 1995; but see also Tolman 2002, 19 ("girls and women are entitled to have sexual subjectivity, rather than simply to be sexual objects").

147. See Durham 2008. Although Durham's analysis is not immune to alarmism, she casts "sexual harm" primarily as a function of cultural tropes and media messages valorizing youth, thinness, and violence (22), rather than as a function of individual, predatory men (whom she nonetheless invokes for their rhetorical allure).

148. *Thirteen* 2003. The actors discuss these restrictions on the DVD's commentaries.

149. See Stockton 2009, 126.

150. Law circumambulates other scenes, like when Tracy and Evie shoplift or when Luke worries about violating age of consent law, but law is largely a shadowy absence. Transgressions of the law pleasure the girls, but it is not pleasure's wellspring, and that matters. Tracy and Evie shoplift not only to break the law, but also to obtain what they want but cannot afford. Their attempt to seduce Luke is eroticized by its secretiveness, but they also find him attractive. If we overestimate the erotics of trans-gression we may underestimate the erotics of their contact or their consumption. Meanwhile, the valence of law's unaware unknowingness here is far different than its aware unknowingness in *Superbad* (2007).

151. See Karlyn 2006, 464.

152. Subjection and subjectivity are not oppositional, but the postmodern insight that subjection is elemental to subjectivity has never meant that the latter is fully "determined" by the former (Butler 1995, 46). See also Butler 1997b; Foucault 1995, 326–48; Hirschmann 2002.

153. *Thirteen* 2003. See Siegel 2010, 247. On Nabokov's similar "Hispanicizing" of *Lolita*, see Freedman 1998, 870–71.

154. Edelman 2004.

155. *Thirteen* 2003.

156. Berlant and Warner 1998, 548–50.

157. Ibid., 549.

158. See Tolman 2002, 5 ("We have effectively desexualized girls' sexuality, substituting the desire for relationship and emotional connection for sexual feelings in their bodies"). In her influential ethnographic study of teenage girls from urban and suburban high schools, Tolman (2002) finds that girls tend to dissociate from their desires, resist them, or suture them to monogamous, heterosexual relations, where young female sexuality appears most respectable and least dangerous (50–165). Tolman argues that the discursive delimitation of young female sexuality (rarely culturally sanctioned, and mostly in its commoditized form) is what prefigures the "it just happened" reply typical of her subjects, whose desires remain largely unrecognized or disavowed (1–19).

159. See Sax 2010b; but see also Laye-Gindhu and Schonert-Reichl 2005, 455.

160. See Adler and Adler 2007, 553; Sax 2010b. The other long-standing incorrect assumption among researchers was that only girls and women self-injure. Most studies report comparable rates of nonsuicidal self-injury (NSSI) among men and women, although the methods differ between the sexes: women are more likely to cut themselves; men are more likely to burn themselves or "self-hit" (Andover et al. 2010, 85).

161. Adler and Adler 2007, 540, 555.

162. According to Laye-Gindhu and Schonert-Reichl: "Previous research findings that girls are more likely to internalize whereas boys are more likely to externalize suggest that girls may be more likely to hurt themselves intentionally when turning emotions inward. Feminist contributions to understanding self-harm have focused on the sociocultural construction of behavior and psychopathology in a western society that limits opportunities and does not encourage girls and women to maintain 'voice'" (2005, 448, citations omitted). As Charles Taylor writes, "we find the sense of life through articulating it" (1989, 18). For Taylor, articulation is necessary for humans to sustain themselves in moral and physical space, as is the facility to locate one's self in a telic narrative (47, 97). Articulacy and narrative-belonging, as avenues to meaning, make human life inhabitable as such. Taylor is speaking to confusions in modern philosophy (obscuring its own valuations of the "good," trumping up the proceduralist "right") that trouble humans' ability to articulate and therefore find meaning. But one might immediately ask the subsequent questions: Are all social groups equally impacted, or frustrated, by the fact of inarticulacy? Who, or what type of subject, is entitled or enabled to narrate a meaningful life course for himself? The problem of inarticulacy around the good may be a universal problem, but not one equally borne. If "articulacy is open to us," it may "bring us out of the cramped postures of suppression" (C. Taylor 1989, 107), but some of us, like Tracy, are more cramped than others—although the difference is not just of degree.

163. On the confirmation of girls' social status through heteronormative competition, see Duncan 2004, 148; E. Payne 2007, 61; Renold and Ringrose 2011, 395. Like

the "girl power" 1990s films that prefigure it, *Thirteen* shifts attention away from heterosexual romance and toward same-sex friendship as pivotal for its young female protagonist. Still, the film "pit[s] friends against each other in battles over control, power, and boys, leaving girls estranged from, rather than supported by, one another" (Kearney 2002, 133).

164. See Karlyn 2006, 455.

165. Although Chaplin and Aldao's meta-analysis (2013) finds "that by adolescence, girls, rather than boys, had a tendency to express more externalizing emotions" (757), the authors nonetheless confirm that girls have a greater tendency to internalize negative emotions like sadness and anxiety. They hypothesize that observed gender differences in emotional expression prior to adolescence may lead to girls' increased likelihood of depression in adolescence (755–57). But see also Garbarino 2006 on the "changing nature of physical aggression in American girls" and "the recent dramatic increase in violence by troubled girls" (15).

166. *Thirteen* 2003. This observation is made by director Catherine Hardwicke on the DVD's commentaries.

167. See Tolman 2002, 4.

168. See Berlant 2006, 23. On filmic girls' anger as "a weapon against gender crimes," see K. Roberts 2002, 217. Unlike other working-class "angry girls" of 1990s and 2000s cinema, Tracy's rage is targeted not at predatory men, but mostly at her family members, who are sites of condensation and displacement.

169. *Thirteen* 2003.

170. See Karlyn 2006, 465.

171. See Driscoll 2002, 216–26. Referring to both their consumerism in romance comedies and their oft-domesticized capacity for violence in horror movies, Driscoll writes, "girls in teen films have exactly this kind of comprised, enclosed agency" (230).

172. See notes 49–55, above. For a smart brief in favor of "coercive paternalism" in light of humans' tendency toward bad decision making, see Conly 2013.

173. Pettit 1997, 119–20; Mill 1998, 63.

174. I concur with Ramachandran (2009, 40): "We may legitimately fear that an individual will become unable to form their own opinions, thoughts, make their own decisions, and consider a wide variety of cultural affiliations if another controls their body, even if they consented to that control." I would argue that our legitimate fear extends to one's conduct over one's own body, like Tracy's cutting. However, Ramachandran sharply distinguishes what she defends as rights "connected to cultural and political expression and identity development" (40) from dignitarian rights of the body or autonomous rights to choice. But insofar as feminist reconstructions of autonomy emphasize the securing and fostering of relations and relational possibilities (and not exclusively "choice" in the first person present tense), it seems to me like autonomy so reconceived is compatible with Ramachandran's "principle of promoting cultural velocity" (32), especially when the principle grounds a right to identity formation and

adaptation (43, 53–54), but less so when the principle is meant to arbitrate what is "good for society" (40). See also Nedelsky 2011.

175. See chapter 3, notes 209–12.

176. See Angelides 2007, 355–57; Nelson and Oliver 1998, 572–73.

177. See Bulman 2005, 8.

178. The Guess Who, "These Eyes," *Wheatfield Soul,* RCA, 1969. Evan's intimate and sexual inexperience is at once marked and minimized by the chorus he squeaks through: "These eyes have seen a lot of loves / But they're never gonna see another one like I / had with you."

179. See Oberman 2000; Rahimi and Liston 2012, 170.

180. See Berlant 2011, 24–25. Of the main characters in Mary Gaitskill's *Two Girls, Fat and Thin,* Berlant writes: "What's stunning therefore is that each woman gets exactly what she wants out of consensual sex. She gets to be other than her default pattern. She gets to be impersonal by virtue of the imitative quality of the sex, its conventionality or formalism. *At the same time she can identify with that impersonality and see it as an opening up of something that may or may not lead somewhere*" (151–52, emphasis added).

181. Halberstam 2011, 58, 65 ("Male stupidity films... provide a pretty accurate map of the social webs that tie male unknowing to new forms of power.... *Dude* [*Where's My Car?*] tells the story of white male stupidity in a way that solicits laughter at the dudes, and as we laugh we disarm the dude and we know, finally, that he is clueless").

182. *Superbad* 2007.

183. Read unsympathetically, this and other moments representationally confirm a feminist maxim: of course prosecutorial enforcement is selective, of course it sanctions everyday boys' and men's criminal sexual behavior (see, for example, Corrigan 2006; MacKinnon 1983, 649). But McLovin is no rapist, just an unsteady aspirant to the phallic order.

184. Except McLovin's cock is blocked. This blockage allows *Superbad* to push up against sexual convention but not too hard. Sex for this young subject (and for all the young subjects of *Superbad*) is deferred until a time more normatively proper: precollege summer, or college, or anytime after the audience views the film. Like *Thirteen,* sex presented a problem for production. Christopher Mintz-Plasse, "McLovin," was under eighteen at the time of filming. According to Mintz-Plasse and director Greg Mottola, the production studio's legal department disallowed Mintz-Plasse from viewing the pictures of penises that Seth draws as a child. In Mintz-Plasse's sex scene, most of the camera shots are point-of-view because the actors were prohibited from being in bed together positioned for intercourse. When they were shot together, the legal department restricted Mintz-Plasse's movement, lest the action simulated sex too realistically.

185. Stockton 2009, 146.

186. Ibid., 142.

187. U.S. law is anything but lubricating for black and brown boys and young men. On racially disparate arrest, conviction, and sentencing rates, see, for example, The Sentencing Project 2013.

188. M. Henderson 2005.

189. Anachronistic but nevertheless appropriate usage.

190. See Way 2011, 226 ("White boys... often seek the bold and heterosexual masculinity that is attributed to Black men").

191. James Brown, "Super Bad," *Super Bad Part 1 & Part 2*, King, 1970.

192. Four Tops, "Are You Man Enough?" *Shaft in Africa*, ABC Records, 1973.

193. The scene pointedly does not include another lyric of the song: "I'm a young, black, heterosexual male / Don't drink no drank, don't smoke, don't sale / That's the real reason they want me up in jail." The Coup, "Pork and Beef," *Party Music*, 75 Ark, 2001.

194. See Troyer and Marchiselli 2005, 266; see also Spelman and Minow 1996. "If the child is to become an adult," writes Winnicott (1971, 145), "then this move is achieved over the dead body of an adult." Or, it appears, a car.

195. See Way 2011, 220.

196. This indiscernibility arises not least because homosexuality and homophobia "are likely to concern themselves intensely with each other and to assume interlocking or mirroring shapes, because the theater of their struggle is likely to be intrapsychic or intra-institutional as well as public" (Sedgwick 1985, 20).

197. These are the more typical psychoanalytic interpretations for repetition compulsion, which for Freud (1990) provided speculative evidence for his theory of the death drive. Alberti (2013, 39) describes Seth's "childhood obsession with drawing anthropomorphized penises" as "enacting an attraction to/shame over entering the Symbolic Order."

198. As Troyer and Marchiselli recount, other "dude films" recalibrate their scenes of homosociality with hetero or homophobic correctives. In *Bill & Ted's Excellent Adventure* (1989), Bill and Ted's momentary, intimate-looking concern for one another is neutralized by gay jokes and heterosexual conquests (Troyer and Marchiselli 2005, 270). For Troyer and Marchiselli, *Dude, Where's My Car?* (2000) is a more promising dude film, because the male protagonists make out without any homophobic or misogynistic rejoinders (Troyer and Marchiselli 2005, 273–74; for a queerer reading, see Halberstam 2011, 66–67). Yet these critics may understate that the audience is expected to laugh at the men making out, not with them. Seth and Evan's intimacy is more careful although still tentative, and while girls, "pussies," and "fags" still get trafficked in the promotion of young male sexual subjectivity, one senses it is because these boys (along with the cops) are fluent in no other vocabulary, but want to be. On American teenage boys' relational constitution of masculinity via everyday degradations and disavowals of femininity, see Pascoe 2007, 52–114.

199. *Superbad* 2007.

200. A main contribution of Eve Kosofsky Sedgwick's pioneering work on homosocial desire in English literature (1985) is her account of its historical adaptability, its reconfigurations that respond to and influence shifts in class structure and political authority. "Garden variety" subjugation of women in homosocial desire, therefore, should be understood not as static and unchanging, but as circumstantially mediated yet persistent. Sedgwick insists that while "homosexual" desire need not premise itself on gender asymmetry, "homophobic" practices, she hypothesizes, are elementally antifeminist and misogynist (1985, 216). On my reading, she is more ambivalent about the organizing position of women in relation to "homosocial desire" between men, in part because "homosocial" is at times placed on a continuum of male–male attachment along with homosexuality, but at other times inclusive of homosexuality itself (this semantic slipperiness is not a confusion). In any case, in the literature she samples, it seems to be the case that nonhomosexual homosocial attachments between men triangulate around women as objects of exchange, contempt, desire, or disavowal, although Sedgwick is quick to concede that "this conception of women's role may be an unwarrantably flat and ahistorical one, however, even within the limits of a study of *male* homosocial desire" (1985, 134).

201. As Way (2011, 212) puts it, "Americans' emphasis on individualism" code intimacy, connectedness, and expressions of vulnerability "with a sex (female), a sexuality (gay), and an age (childhood)."

202. Freeman 2010. Halberstam (2005, 152–53), in fact, conceives "queer temporality" as a "stretched-out adolescence" that "challenges the conventional binary formulation of a life narrative divided by a clear break between youth and adulthood; this life narrative charts an obvious transition out of childish dependency through marriage and into adult responsibility through reproduction." See also Stockton 2009, 11–17. Stockton "explor[es] the many kinds of sideways growth depicted by twentieth-century texts" (11) in order to "spell out the versions of children that both histories and childhood studies have underrecognized, oddly conceptualized, or not even seen" (17).

203. Way 2011, 263. In *Deep Secrets: Boys, Friendships, and the Crisis of Conversation* (2011), Way argues that late adolescent boys' disconnection from each other is a relatively recent and growing national epidemic (26–33). She finds that adolescent boys of all socioeconomic strata lose their same-sex friendships (34), despite the emotional and psychological importance of the relationships (91–92, 268). She doubts the reasons her teen subjects proffer for disconnection—busy schedules, too much homework—as "thin" explanations (212–28) and provides instead a "thick" analysis, linked to conditions of neoliberal late modernity: the increasing valorization of individuality, the increasing reliance on the couple form to provide all emotional meaningfulness (212), the consequent cultural equation of vulnerability with femininity, and the "backlash to women's and gay rights" that associates emotional expression with gayness (26). Likewise, Way argues that the national idealization of "autonomy" deprives boys of emotional connections as they age into manhood (268). But what the boys

of *Superbad* demonstrate is that autonomy and relationality need not be mutually opposed, that go-it-alone autonomy is not the same thing as the autonomy imperfectly secured through institutions and norms that promote or at least dignify a wider range of intimate relations. Evan and Seth are disqualified from relational autonomy by the masculinist valorization of autonomy *as* self-sufficiency.

204. Alberti 2013, 32. Alberti describes *Superbad* as an "exemplary" "bromance" film in its "obsession with gay sexuality and [its] mixture of homophobia and homophilia" (39), but he too hurriedly reads the "sleeping bag scene" as, summarily, a mechanism for making Seth and Evan "more amenable to heterosexual desire, more available and less frightening as 'straight' sexual partners" (40). Were that the case, we would not be solicited to mourn a loss, even if that loss remains mostly illegible.

205. Berlant 2010.

206. Bulman and McCants 2008, 68.

207. Ibid., 69.

208. Ibid.

209. Although as Nancy Chodorow points out in her foreword to Freud's *Three Essays on the Theory of Sexuality* (2000, x), while polymorphous perversity (not possibility) refers to the many ways the child may achieve sexual gratification, the "object choice is singular and relatively fixed, especially during the oedipal phase." See also Butler 1997b, 132–50.

210. Way (2011, 220) is mostly concerned that nominally straight boys are shutting out other boys for fear of being seen as gay. But the other concern is that the cultural codification of male–male intimacies as "gay" quashes other kinds of erotic relations or experiments. Might a fear of "gayness" and all of its associated cultural implications prevent relations that might be "not straight"? Might, as Savin-Williams worries (2005, 192–93), a "problem-obsessed orientation toward gay adolescence" generate the very suffering, self-destruction, and suicide its promoters seek to dispel? See also note 5, above. In his review of *Superbad*, Corliss (2007) upbraids producer Judd Apatow and cowriter Seth Rogen for not outing Evan and Seth as gay. Corliss, who outs himself as a "liberal New York heterosexual," wants to assuage his own phobic discomfort under the banner of gay rights: Evan and Seth's "gayness" would restore men's intimacies as containable, binary, and unthreatening.

211. Way 2011, 66, 227, 267.

212. Ibid., 220–24.

213. Berlant 2011, 33.

214. See, for example, Tolman 2002, 55 ("Psychologically, socialization into and internalization of norms of femininity associated with the female body create pressures for girls and women to 'disconnect' from their bodies"); Way 2011, 178 ("[Boys] succumb to cultural pressures of manhood and maturity out of fear that if they don't, they will be victimized and isolated. The irony is, of course, that accommodating to such pressures is precisely what makes them feel ultimately so alone").

CONCLUSION

1. Kincaid 2004, 13–15.

2. In July 2014, CNN premiered its show *The Hunt*, hosted by the indefatigable John Walsh, father of Adam Walsh. In this *To Catch a Predator 2.0*, Walsh, a self-described "manhunter," leads the charge to find ten men and two women charged with or suspected of horrifying, mostly sexually violent, and utterly statistically insignificant crimes. *The Hunt with John Walsh*, CNN, http://www.cnn.com/interactive/2014/06/us/the-hunt/. In that same month, the *New York Times* reported on a New York City preschool teacher alleged to have fondled his students. The sketchiness and strangeness of the accusations, the lying and bullying police used to secure the quasi-confession, and the rapid-fire alarm among parents and community members rehearses all the trappings of the McMartin preschool scandal of the 1980s. See Hernández 2014.

3. See, for example, Bogdanich 2014; Flanagan 2014; Gray 2014; Hess 2014; Pérez-Peña and Taylor 2014.

4. "Dear Colleague Letter" 2011.

5. Ibid., 1.

6. Ibid., 1–3. Several lower court and Supreme Court opinions since 1980 have substantiated that sexual harassment may be a form of sex discrimination actionable under Title IX and that sexual assault (teacher-on-student or peer-on-peer) can likewise be a form of sexual harassment (thereby also actionable). Landmark cases include *Alexander v. Yale University*, 631 F.2d 178 (1980); *Franklin v. Gwinnett County Public Schools*, 503 U.S. 60 (1992); *Davis v. Monroe County Board of Education*, 526 U.S. 629 (1999); *Kelly v. Yale University*, Civ. A. 3:01-CV-1591, 2003 WL 1563424 (D. Conn. 2003).

7. "Dear Colleague Letter" 2011, 16. As activists point out, the Department of Education has (as of this writing) never withdrawn federal funding from schools for sexual violence–based violations of Title IX. See "ED ACT NOW" 2013. U.S. legislators, led by Sen. Claire McCaskill, are currently considering equipping the Department of Education with the power to fine schools found in violation of Title IX. See M. Taylor 2014.

8. "Title IX Complaint" 2011.

9. See White House Task Force 2014, 16–20; Pérez-Peña 2013.

10. For a discussion of the Center for Public Integrity study confirming as much, see Lombardi 2010.

11. CNN correspondent Poppy Harlow, now infamously, mourned the "promising futures" of the two Steubenville boys convicted of rape. See "Guilty Verdict in Steubenville Rape Trial" 2013; Introduction, notes 12–14. For a similar eulogy of young men's futures (a Yale football player whose withdrawal of his Rhodes Scholarship application may have been influenced by allegations of sexual assault; men of the Duke lacrosse team accused and cleared of rape), see Parker 2012.

12. See Bogdanich 2014.

13. For a thoughtful discussion of the pros and cons of expulsion as the default sanction against students found guilty of sexual misconduct by their school's disciplinary board, see Kitchener 2013.

14. See Goldstein 2013; Potter 2013; Potter 2014. Potter is rightly concerned that colleges and universities prioritize their interests over victims' rights, which can lead to mishandling and cover-ups of sexual assault allegations. Nonetheless, there are several compelling reasons universities ought to be involved in adjudication. The first and foremost is sex equality. Also, the threshold for violating college sexual misconduct codes is far lower, both de jure and de facto, than for violating state sex laws.

15. "U.S. Department of Education Releases List" 2014. The list initially included fifty-five schools under investigation when it was first published in May, but that number has since grown. See also K. Taylor 2014.

16. See, for example, Douthat 2014 ("colleges could embrace a more limited version of the old 'parietal' system, in which they separated the sexes and supervised social life"); Harden 2012.

17. See Berlant 1995.

18. For a meta-analysis demonstrating decreasing rates of child sexual abuse, see Finkelhor and Jones 2012; see also studies cited in Goode 2012.

19. Goode 2012.

20. See Krebs et al. 2007; Krebs et al. 2009.

21. Yung 2015, 38–42.

22. For more ecological approaches to combating sexual violence, see, for example, *University of Michigan Sexual Assault Prevention & Awareness Center*, http://sapac .umich.edu; *University of New Hampshire Sexual Harassment & Rape Prevention Program (SHARPP)*, http://www.unh.edu/sharpp/; *Yale CCE Program*, http://cce.yale college.yale.edu/; see also note 34, below.

23. See note 13, above; but see also note 10. See "Why Schools Handle Sexual Violence Reports" 2013; see also Bolger 2013.

24. *Know Your IX*, knowyourix.org.

25. White House Task Force 2014, 7.

26. Ibid.; see also "ED ACT NOW" 2013.

27. White House Task Force 2014, 10, although the public service announcement video the task force released enlisting male celebrities to condemn sexual violence appeals more to chivalry than solidarity. See "1 Is 2 Many PSA: 60 Second" 2014.

28. White House Task Force 2014, 19, citing "Dear Colleague Letter" 2011.

29. White House Task Force 2014, 9–10, 14–16, 20.

30. Rep. Sheila Jackson Lee, quoted in Filler 2001, 343; "President Signs H.R. 4472" 2006.

31. See, for example, Lauerman 2014; White House Task Force 2014, 3; Woodford 2011; see also *Consent Is Sexy*, http://www.consentissexy.net/; *Only with Consent*, http://onlywithconsent.org/.

32. See, for example, White House Task Force 2014, 13.

33. *Consent Is Sexy,* http://www.consentissexy.net/. The tagline for the Consent Is Sexy poster campaign is "Sex with consent is sexy. Sex without consent is rape. Respect yourself. Respect your partner." Despite my respect for the ethical impulse of the campaign, it saddles consent with more normativity than it can or should bear. Sex with consent is not always sexy—sometimes it is unpleasant, mediocre, or only slightly better than the nonsexual alternatives of the moment. Sex without consent, legally defined, is not always rape. Consent might be necessary for mutual sexual respect, but certainly not sufficient. It might also be the case that mutually respectful sex dissolves consent as a salient feature of the exchange. BDSM and prostitution contracts aside, the goodness of good sex might be measured by the very degree to which consent is *not* tokenized or detectable as a singular moment of concession or acquiescence. In any case, I believe *Consent Is Sexy* and other student campaigns against sexual violence adopted the legal language of consent because it is popular, magnetizing, and liberal-sounding, but thereby forewent greater opportunities to engender new vocabularies and abstractions for transforming sexual culture.

34. In response to criticism of its (mis)handling of sexual misconduct, Yale University released six hypothetical scenarios demonstrating what would and would not count as consent under the school's sexual misconduct policy. But the pained efforts to gender neutralize the fictional characters, as well as the odd combination of explicitness and opacity ("Alexis continues to touch Riley in an intimate way. Riley willingly agrees to some contact, but mostly sets boundaries"), ultimately made the initiative distracting and prone to parody. See "Sexual Misconduct Scenarios" 2013; for a parody, see Nolan 2013. On the other hand, Yale's Communication and Consent Educators (CCE) program is innovative, unique among other university sexual violence prevention organizations. Rather than emphasizing injury, violence, and "no means no," CCE resists the impulse to censure and fear-monger, instead creating programs that "focus on ideals and positive practices, knowing that it's more effective to offer people better choices than to talk about how bad the negative choices are." See *Yale CCE Program,* http://cce.yalecollege.yale.edu/.

35. Thanks to Melanie Boyd for conversations on this point.

36. See W. Brown 1995, 52–76.

37. For an unforgiving criticism of Take Back the Night, see Roiphe 1993, 29–50; see also W. Brown 2005, 83–97.

38. See North 2011.

39. See Executive Directors 2011; Sex Week 2012. Olivarius was a plaintiff in and key organizer behind *Alexander v. Yale University.* See note 6, above. As she said in her address at Sex Week 2012, "When I was at Yale, the University wasn't just lacking a sexual harassment grievance procedure. . . . It was also lacking any mechanism for talking about the fun parts of sexuality. . . . Good sex makes you feel empowered, centered, happy and able to be a more effective person and professional" (quoted in Gould 2012).

40. For a defense of sex positivity, frank sexual discussion, and comprehensive sex education as bulwarks against sexual violence, sexism, and other forms of social injustice, see, for example, J. Friedman 2011.

41. Potter 2011. Harden (2012) lumps, rather than links, the Penn State scandal and campus sexual assault and does so, it seems, mainly to condemn both as symptoms of the public casualization of sex.

42. *United States v. Windsor*, 570 U.S. ____ (2013); *United States v. Kebodeaux*, 570 U.S. ____ (2013). Of course, *Obergefell v. Hodges*, 576 U.S. ____ (2015) will henceforth be recognized as the landmark marriage equality decision.

43. *Windsor*, at 25.

44. *Kebodeaux*, at 12.

45. On the rhetorical and doctrinal appeal of the consenting adult, see, for example, *Bostic v. Schaefer*, No. 14–1167 (4th Cir. 2014): "The Supreme Court's unwillingness to constrain the right to marry to certain subspecies of marriage meshes with its conclusion that the right to marry is a matter of 'freedom of choice' that 'resides with the individual.' If courts limited the right to marry to certain couplings, they would effectively create a list of legally preferred spouses, rendering the choice of whom to marry a hollow choice indeed. . . . *Lawrence* and *Windsor* indicate that the choices that individuals make in the context of same-sex relationships enjoy the same constitutional protection as the choices accompanying opposite-sex relationships. We therefore have no reason to suspect that the Supreme Court would accord the choice to marry someone of the same sex any less respect than the choice to marry an opposite-sex individual who is of a different race, owes child support, or is imprisoned" (43–44, internal citations omitted). On the ever-extending scope and inanity of sex offender regulations, see, for example, Gershman 2013; Hitz 2014, 1334–41; Wilson 2012.

46. *Bostic*, at 8–9; *Kebodeaux*, at 3, Roberts, C. J., concurring ("Public safety benefits are neither necessary nor sufficient to a proper exercise of the power to regulate the military").

47. *Kebodeaux*, at 8–9, emphasis added.

48. See chapter 2, note 75. Like the *Smith* court, the *Kebodeaux* court misreads the BJS report to conclude that "recidivism rates among sex offenders are higher than the average for other types of criminals," even while it acknowledges, in the next sentence, that the BJS study finds that sex offenders are more likely to commit *sex* crimes than non–sex offenders (*Kebodeaux*, at 8). Meanwhile, according to the report, the percentage of "statutory rapists"—which is how Kebodeaux would be categorized—rearrested for a "sex crime against a child within three years" is 2.5 percent, which cannot plausibly demonstrate high recidivism in any comparative analysis (Langan, Schmitt, and Durose 2003, 32).

49. *Kebodeaux*, at 4; *Kebodeaux*, at 1, Roberts, C. J., concurring.

50. *Kebodeaux*, at 2, Thomas, J., dissenting.

51. *Windsor*, at 13–15, Alito, J., dissenting, emphasis added.

52. Ibid., at 13.

53. Ibid.

54. Ibid., at 14–15.

55. Ibid., at 19. Justice Kennedy cites himself to this effect: "The States' interest in defining and regulating the marital relation, subject to constitutional guarantees, stems from the understanding that marriage is more than a routine classification for purposes of certain statutory benefits. Private, consensual sexual intimacy between two adult persons of the same sex may not be punished by the State, and it can form 'but one element in a personal bond that is more enduring.' *Lawrence v. Texas,* 539 U.S. 558, 567 (2003). By its recognition of the validity of same-sex marriages performed in other jurisdictions and then by authorizing same-sex unions and same-sex marriages, New York sought to give further protection and dignity to that bond."

56. The national marriage-equality movement Freedom to Marry delineates several reasons why "marriage matters" for gay and lesbian couples: it sanctions love, publicizes commitment, offers legal protections, and confers equal treatment. All of these reasons presuppose the consent of the marrying parties, and none disqualifies polygamy or incestuous marriage. See "Why Marriage?" 2014.

57. Fischel 2013a, 60, 66–67, 74–75; see also C. Cohen 1997.

58. *Windsor,* at 15.

59. See Sunstein 2005, 2100–2103; but see also Den Otter 2015; *Obergefell,* at 20–21, Roberts, C.J., dissenting.

60. Rubenfeld 2013a, 392; Rubenfeld 2013b, 1421; Spindelman 2013, 189.

61. Rubenfeld 2013b, 1394–95; Spindelman 2013, 187–88.

62. Rubenfeld 2013b, 1378. Yung (2015, 7–8, 17–18) argues that while "sexual autonomy" may be an organizing, normative principle for legal liberal and feminist scholars, it is hardly central to or consistently applied across U.S. sex law.

63. Rubenfeld 2013b, 1379.

64. Rubenfeld 2013b, 1416–17; Dougherty 2013, 333. Rubenfeld argues in favor of a separate statute for "concealing a sexually transmittable disease." In my opinion, singling out STIs is remarkably misguided, given how manageable and treatable most STIs are (or should be), given the complexities of STI transmission and preventive precautions, and given how emotionally, physically devastating other forms of deception might be. Defending his alma mater (and thereby himself) to his girlfriend, Criss says to Liz Lemon, "Wesleyan is the Harvard of central Connecticut." Liz: "Yale is the Harvard of central Connecticut." "Idiots Are People Three!" *30 Rock,* NBC, season 6, episode 3; aired January 26, 2012.

65. Rubenfeld 2013b, 1425; Rubenfeld 2013a, 398.

66. Yung (2015, 20–27) counters that there is not much of a riddle, since U.S. rape law has never been tethered primarily to the principle of sexual autonomy. He identifies three additional justifications animating modern rape law: harm (by which he means sequelae), gender (by which he means sex-based inequality), and terror (by which he means systemic enforcement of sex-based inequality).

67. The *Yale Law Journal* solicited four responses to Rubenfeld's initial article, as well as a reply from Rubenfeld himself. See Dougherty 2013; Falk 2013; Ramachandran 2013; Rubenfeld 2013a; Tuerkheimer 2013, 345; see also Yung 2015.

68. Tuerkheimer 2013, 336–57. This is not exactly how Tuerkheimer puts it. She focuses on the way gendered subordination complicates the procurement and granting of consent.

69. Ibid., 345 ("Sex does not become rape because one of the consenting parties is incompletely informed … [but] a wide enough gap between what a party consents to and what actually transpires may mean there is no consent to what actually transpires. *This* is sex without consent. This is rape"); see also Rubenfeld 2013b, 1416 ("And love? A vast engine of deception").

70. Tuerkheimer 2013, 338, citing Abrams 1999.

71. Tuerkheimer 2013, 339.

72. Ibid., 344.

73. Tuerkheimer 2013, 345. See also Dougherty 2013, 326; Falk 2013, 368 ("not all lies are sufficient to trigger prosecution … materiality is an important component of this analysis"); Ramachandran 2013, 387; Yung 2015, 12 ("Materiality of a deception differentiates an ordinary lie from actual criminal fraud").

74. Argues Falk: "The real-life victims of rape-by-fraud experience multiple physical, psychological, and emotional harms. The physical consequences of victimization include unwanted pregnancy, sexually transmitted diseases, and exposure to HIV and AIDS, possibly shortening or ending life. The psychological consequences of rape-by-fraud can be equally severe" (2013, 361, internal citations omitted). But what if one does not experience such harms? Should there be no remedy? If Amanda asks Ben to wear a condom, indeed makes sex conditional on condom-wearing, then Ben's not wearing a condom is itself sexual misconduct, violative of sexual autonomy. It should be immaterial, for the purposes of adjudicating sexual misconduct, whether or not Amanda becomes pregnant (except as proof). See also Gross 2009, 197–98 ("Suppose … in the American context, someone who is black or Latino and can pass as white. Are they obliged to reveal these details to the people they date? … Does a rule that allows a man who suspected his ethnic origin to be relevant to his female partner to be convicted of rape legitimize prejudice and racism?").

75. See Dougherty 2013, 322, 333.

76. Rubenfeld 2013b, 1377, citing, inter alia, *Theofel v. Farey-Jones,* 359 F.3d 1066, 1073 (9th Cir. 2004).

77. Dougherty 2013, 331.

78. See Gross 2009; see also *McNally v. R.,* EWCA Crim 1051 (2013).

79. See Gross 2009, 207; on the trans- and homophobia that underwrite the *McNally* ruling, see Sharpe 2014. Sharpe suggests that gender history disclosure, under limited circumstances, could conceivably be componential of a sexual autonomy right. But because such a right, to be exercised, requires demonstrable "harm suffered by cisgender people," and because the right assumes gender, in the final instance, to be a

knowable thing, I disagree with the analysis (14). As Sharpe acknowledges but does not fully resolve, subjectively felt harm can result from the internalization of social prejudice.

80. See also Yung 2015, 27–29.

81. See Nedelsky 2011.

82. Rubenfeld 2013b, 1414.

83. Rubenfeld 2013a, 391–92.

84. Ibid., 402.

85. Ibid.

86. Rubenfeld 2013b, 1435, citing *State v. Thompson,* 792 P.2d 1103 (Mont. 1990).

87. Ibid., 1435.

88. Ibid., 1412.

89. Ibid., 1436, citing *Commonwealth v. Mlinarich,* 542 A.2d 1335 (Pa. 1988).

90. In reply to his critics (2013a, 399), Rubenfeld insists that his proposed reforms would simply redefine *rape.* "States are free to . . . criminalize many sex acts that aren't rape." As evidence, he states that he is "in favor" of "a statute making it sexual assault in the third degree for prison guards to have sex with inmates, *regardless of proof of nonconsent or force*" (399, emphasis added, internal citations omitted). But what would be *sexual* about this infraction, if the right to sexual autonomy is a myth, and if the only right we retain against sexual violence is the right to bodily self-possession? Indeed, this is why Rubenfeld argues that sex with an unconscious person should be codified as battery but not *sexual* assault (2013b, 1440–41). If Rubenfeld wishes to be consistent, then the prison guard could only be conceivably convicted for some form of professional misconduct. In my opinion, only the principle of sexual autonomy (and not even consent) is capable of rendering the prison guard's behavior as sexual misconduct.

91. Wertheimer 2003, 163–93. See also chapter 3, notes 147–49.

92. See subsection, "Regulating Relations of Dependence and Trust," in chapter 3.

93. For a theoretic delineation of peremption, see "From Domination to Peremption, or the Future Is Adult Stuff," in chapter 4.

94. Rubenfeld 2013b, 1441–42. This seventeen-year-old is formally gender-neutral, but given the gender asymmetries throughout the rest of Rubenfeld's article, we can safely assume the teen is female.

95. Ibid., 1441.

96. Ibid., 1437. Dougherty (2013, 326) wonders if, according to Rubenfeld's own logic—in which consent is legally transformative for violence but not for sex—sadomasochistic sex becomes rape if one partner lies about attending Yale (if such attendance were conditional for the other partner). Rubenfeld (2013a, 393) responds that he never supposed consent was immaterial to a rape inquiry, only that force should be a requisite element of rape. This does not resolve the problem: SM sex is rape if consent is to whatever degree manipulated; vanilla sex, no matter how unconsented, is not rape unless there is force. This position is not contradictory, but it is bizarre.

97. Rubenfeld 2013b, 1441.

98. Ibid.

99. Ibid., 1442.

100. Ibid., 1409, 1443.

101. See Yung 2015, 30–31.

102. See Rubenfeld 2013b, 1422.

103. See "Sex Offenders in the Judicial Imaginary, or Why the Court Does Things with Sex Offenders," in chapter 2.

104. Spindelman 2013, 87–88.

105. Ibid., 98–212.

106. Ibid., 102.

107. Ibid., 102–21.

108. Ibid., 117, 112.

109. Ibid., 139–40, 184–85, 207–8, 214–15.

110. Ibid., 157–92.

111. Ibid., 172–73, 187–88, 192.

112. Ibid., 189.

113. Ibid., 185.

114. Ibid., 186.

115. Ibid., 88.

116. Ibid., 209, 176.

117. Ibid., 179.

118. Ibid., 184–85.

119. Ibid., 223–27.

120. Ibid., 227.

121. Ibid., 91–92.

122. Ibid., 138.

123. Ibid., 208–10.

124. Ibid., 129–33, 138–39.

125. See Hoppe 2014, 140; Lehman et al. 2014, 1000.

126. See Hoppe 2014, 145–47; Lehman et al. 2014, 999, 1003.

127. See Buchanan 2015, 1304–20; Lazzarini and Klitzman 2002, 537–40. Buchanan (2015) argues that the state's singling out HIV for compelled disclosure is both discriminatory and violates HIV-positive persons' sexual autonomy.

128. See Lehman et al. 2014, 998–99, 1004. Spindelman (2013, 96–98), true to form, argues that the laws are ineffective because gay men underutilize them.

129. "Serosorting" is "a practice some gay, bisexual and other men who have sex with men (MSM) use in an effort to reduce their HIV risk. This means they try to limit unprotected anal sex to partners with the same HIV status as their own" ("Serosorting among Gay, Bisexual and Other Men" 2011). The CDC discourages serosorting as a safer-sex method, but the advisory seems to assume that only HIV-negative persons will participate in the practice. Preexposure prophylaxis is "a way for people

who do not have HIV . . . to *prevent* HIV infection by taking a pill every day. The pill (brand name Truvada) contains two medicines . . . that are used in combination with other medicines to treat HIV . . . these medicines can work to keep the virus from establishing a permanent infection" ("Pre-Exposure Prophylaxis (PrEP)" 2014).

130. See, for example, Mairena 2012; Strub 2011; UNAIDS 2013.

131. Spindelman 2013, 186, n. 439.

132. Ibid.

133. Ibid., 226.

134. Ibid., 98, 221–23.

135. Nedelsky 2011, 46; Ramachandran 2009, 40, 32. See also chapter 4, note 174.

136. Ramachandran 2013, 387.

137. On the gender asymmetric "harms of consensual sex," see West 2008; but for a qualified defense and critical analysis of "autassassinophilia," see Downing 2004. Conly (2013) also advocates state intervention against (some) injury-inducing decisions, but as a contravention rather than endorsement of autonomy.

138. *R. v. Brown*, 1 A.C. 212 (1994).

139. *R. v. Wilson*, 2 Cr. App. 241 (1996); see also Khan 2009b.

140. "Amputee devotees" refer to "people who have a strong sexual preference for people with amputations" (McCruer and Mollow 2012, 28). For a careful, feminist analysis of amputee devoteeism, see Kafer 2012. Apotemnophilia, coined by John Money and colleagues in 1977, designates "an attraction to the idea of being an amputee" (Elliot 2000). Raising questions about the risks and harms of gender-confirming elective surgery is, to say the least, politically uncomfortable, but such questions deserve careful, unpresumptuous consideration. Jeffreys's (2014) assessment of such gender-related surgeries and treatments is, unfortunately, tendentious, mean-spirited, and wrong. She concludes, with impressive disregard for the data she collects, that all such surgeries and treatments, all the time, are "harmful"—"quackery" motivated by corporate profit and duped, mentally ill "transgenders." Medical experts, argues Jeffreys (again, without any distinctions whatsoever), commit "professional misconduct" when they assist their trans patients with "physical treatments" (79).

141. Foucault 1990, 104.

142. For other accounts of the child's career in queer theory, see Cobb 2005; Kidd 2011.

143. Edelman 2004, 21, 66.

144. Ibid., 53, 11.

145. Ibid., 2, 11, 29, 3.

146. Ibid., 27.

147. Ibid., 21, 41–44.

148. Muñoz 2009, 14, 11.

149. Ibid., 22, 94.

150. Ibid., 95.

151. Ibid., 96.

152. Halberstam 2011, 106–11, 118–21.

153. Ibid., 120.

154. Ibid., 31.

155. Ibid., 120.

156. Ibid., 119–20, 173–87.

157. Halberstam 2012, 10, xii–xv, xxv, 5.

158. Ibid., xx.

159. Ibid., 149.

160. Halberstam 2005, 161. In *In a Queer Time and Place* (2005), Halberstam stakes a normative claim for the "stretched-out adolescences of queer culture makers," which seems to align with my revaluation of adolescence here and in chapter 4. But insofar as what queerness, adolescence, and queerness-as-adolescence portend for Halberstam is *"the refusal of adulthood"* (74) that "challenge[s] our notions of adulthood as reproductive maturity" (162), there is ultimately no symbolic difference between children and teens, as both are identically burdened as bearers of social transgression. This conflation appears more clearly in later work. See, for example, Halberstam 2011, 30–31 ("A cynical critic might find this narrative [in CGI films] to be a blueprint for the normative rites of passage in the human life cycle, showing the child viewer the journey from childhood captivity to adolescent escape and adult freedom. A more radical reading allows the narrative to be utopian, to tell of the real change that children may still believe is possible and desirable"); Halberstam 2012, xxi ("While we currently train teenagers to think of sex in terms of all the bad things . . . many children are more wily and more canny than their parents think, and it is this generation of kids . . . who will probably recognize, name, and embrace new modes of gender and sexuality within a social environment that has changed their meaning forever"). Despite earlier gestures toward collapsing the adult/child binary, Halberstam's juxtaposition between revolutionary children and reactionary adults leads to the inexorable conclusion that "children are different from adults in all kinds of meaningful ways" (2012, xxiii). And between revolution and reaction, there is no conceptual space or distinction for the adolescent as surviving and navigating, rather than upending or discarding, normative order.

161. Muñoz 2009, 94; see also Edelman 2004, 41.

162. See, for example, E. Bernstein 2010; R. Bernstein 2011; Fields 2005; Fischel 2013b.

163. As Muñoz (2009, 2–3) elaborates Ernst Bloch's distinction: "Abstract utopias . . . are untethered from any historical consciousness. Concrete utopias are relational to historically situated struggles, a collectivity that is actualized or potential."

164. Halberstam 2011, 73.

165. Ibid., 71; see also chapter 4, note 82.

166. Edelman 2004, 27.

167. Ibid., 67.

168. Ibid., 11.

169. Ibid., 29, 2, 17, 26.

170. Ibid., 31.

171. Ibid., 21.

172. See, for example, A. Gordon 1999. Mark Jordan's *Recruiting Young Love: How Christians Talk about Homosexuality* (2011) is a magisterial defense of the "inventive uncertainties of adolescence" (196). In syncopation with this project, Jordan describes adolescence as a figure for sexuality as something-to-be-settled (xiii) and charts how the Christian church, in the modern and late modern United States, has varyingly appropriated psychological, sexological, and political discourses to construct, contain, and (rarely) promote young people's sexuality. Likewise, he demonstrates how "secular" institutions of the modern and late modern United States adopt church practices as blueprints for coming-of-age and coming-out rituals. He argues that we should more carefully analyze religion as elemental to adolescent identity formation and, inversely, that we should advocate for religious rites, myths, and characters that model modes of sexuality and relationality other than taxonomic identity and marriage, respectively (193–214). In church discourse (as in, it seems, some political theory, legal theory, and queer theory), evidences Jordan, adolescents are either "read up into married adulthood" or "read back into passive childhood," as corruptible by queerness (197–98).

Bibliography

"1 Is 2 Many PSA: 60 Second." 2014. YouTube video, posted by "The White House." April 29. https://www.youtube.com/watch?v=xLdElcv5qqc.

48 Hours. 2011. "Notorious Teacher Sex Scandals." *CBS News.* Accessed April 14. Multimedia. http://www.cbsnews.com/pictures/notorious-teacher-sex-scandals/.

Abrams, Kathryn. 1999. "From Autonomy to Agency: Feminist Perspectives on Self-Direction." *William and Mary Law Review* 40: 805–46.

Adler, Amy. 2001. "The Perverse Law of Child Pornography." *Columbia Law Review* 101 (2): 209–73.

———. 2012. "To Catch a Predator." *Columbia Journal of Gender and Law* 21 (2): 130–58.

Adler, Patricia A., and Peter Adler. 2007. "The Demedicalization of Self-Injury: From Psychopathology to Sociological Deviance." *Journal of Contemporary Ethnography* 36 (5): 537–70.

Agan, Amanda Y. 2011. "Sex Offender Registries: Fear without Function?" *Journal of Law and Economics* 54 (1): 207–39.

Agudo, Sarah E. 2008. "Irregular Passion: The Unconstitutionality and Inefficacy of Sex Offender Residency Laws." *Northwestern University Law Review* 102: 307–42.

Alberti, John. 2013. *Masculinity in the Contemporary Romantic Comedy: Gender as Genre.* New York: Routledge.

Alcoff, Linda Martín. 1996. "Dangerous Pleasures: Foucault and the Politics of Pedophilia." In *Feminist Interpretations of Michel Foucault,* edited by Susan Hekman, 99–135. University Park: Pennsylvania State University Press.

Allender, Daniel. 2009. "Applying *Lawrence*: Teenagers and the Crime Against Nature." *Duke Law Journal* 58: 1825–58.

Althusser, Louis. 2001. "Ideology and Ideological State Apparatuses." In *Lenin and Philosophy and Other Essays,* translated by Ben Brewster, 85–126. New York: Monthly Review Press.

American Psychological Association. 2010. "Report of the APA Task Force on the Sexualization of Girls." http://www.apa.org/pi/women/programs/girls/report -full.pdf.

———. 2015. "Understanding and Preventing Child Abuse and Neglect." http:// www.apa.org/pi/families/resources/understanding-child-abuse.aspx.

Anderson, Scott. 2002. "Prostitution and Sexual Autonomy: Making Sense of the Prohibition on Prostitution." *Ethics* 112 (4): 748–80.

Andover, Margaret S., et al. 2010. "An Examination of Non-Suicidal Self-Injury in Men: Do Men Differ from Women in Basic NSSI Characteristics?" *Archives of Suicide Research* 14 (1): 79–88.

Andre-Clark, Alice Susan. 1992. "Whither Statutory Rape Laws? Of *Michael M.,* the Fourteenth Amendment, and Protecting Women from Sexual Aggression." *Southern California Law Review* 65: 1933–92.

Angelides, Steven. 2004. "Feminism, Child Sexual Abuse, and the Erasure of Child Sexuality." *GLQ* 10 (2): 141–77.

———. 2007. "Subjectivity under Erasure: Adolescent Sexuality, Gender, and Teacher-Student Sex." *Journal of Men's Studies* 15 (3): 347–60.

Appell, Annette Ruth. 2013. "Accommodating Childhood." *Cardozo Journal of Law and Gender* 19 (3): 715–79.

Archard, David. 1997. *Sexual Consent.* Oxford: Westview Press.

———. 2004. *Children: Rights and Childhood.* New York: Routledge.

"'Ask First' at Antioch." 1993. *New York Times,* October 11. http://www.nytimes .com/1993/10/11/opinion/ask-first-at-antioch.html.

Atmore, Chris. 1999. "Towards Rethinking Moral Panic: Child Sexual Abuse Conflicts and Social Constructionist Responses." In *Child Sexual Abuse and Adult Offenders: New Theory and Research,* edited by Christopher Bagley and Kanka Mallick, 11–26. Aldershot: Ashgate.

Austin, J. L. 1975. *How to Do Things with Words.* 2nd ed. Cambridge, Mass.: Harvard University Press.

Baldwin, Gabriel. 2004. *"Connecticut Department of Public Safety v. Doe:* The Supreme Court's Clarification of Whether Sex Offender Registration and Notification Laws Violate Convicted Sex Offenders' Right to Procedural Due Process." *Journal of the National Association of Administrative Law Judges* 24: 383–403.

Barthes, Roland. 1972. *Mythologies.* Translated by Annette Lavers. New York: Hill and Wang.

Baxter, Kent. 2008. *The Modern Age: Turn-of-the-Century American Culture and the Invention of Adolescence.* Tuscaloosa: University of Alabama Press.

Bechara, Stephanie. 2013. "Red Signs Will Identify Sexual Predators in Bradford County." WCJB TV-20. April 10. Video. http://www.wcjb.com/local-news/2013/ 04/red-signs-will-identify-sexual-predators-bradford-county.

Beck, Laura. 2013. "Here's What CNN Should Have Said about the Steubenville Rape Case." *Jezebel.* March 18. http://jezebel.com/5991018/heres-what-cnn-shouldve -said-about-the-steubenville-rape-case.

Bedarf, Abril R. 1995. "Examining Sex Offender Community Notification Laws." *California Law Review* 83 (3): 885–939.

Bell, Vikki. 1993. *Interrogating Incest: Feminism, Foucault, and the Law*. London: Routledge.

Benhabib, Seyla. 1992. *Situating the Self: Gender, Community, and Postmodernism in Contemporary Ethics*. New York: Routledge.

Berger, Vivian. 1988. "Not So Simple Rape." *Criminal Justice Ethics* 7 (1): 69–81.

———. 2000. "Rape Law Reform at the Millennium: Remarks on Professor Bryden's Non-Millennial Approach." *Buffalo Criminal Law Review* 3: 513–25.

Berlant, Lauren. 1995. "Live Sex Acts (Parental Advisory: Explicit Material)." *Feminist Studies* 21 (2): 379–404.

———. 1997. *The Queen of America Goes to Washington City: Essays on Sex and Citizenship*. Durham, N.C.: Duke University Press.

———. 1999. "The Subject of True Feeling: Pain, Privacy, and Politics." In *Cultural Pluralism, Identity Politics, and the Law*, edited by Austin Sarat and Thomas R. Kearns, 49–84. Ann Arbor: University of Michigan Press.

———. 2006. "Cruel Optimism." *differences: A Journal of Feminist Cultural Studies* 17 (3): 20–36.

———. 2007. "Slow Death (Sovereignty, Obesity, Lateral Agency)." *Critical Inquiry* 33 (4): 754–80.

———. 2010. "Sitting on an Airplane, a Mule." *Supervalent Thought*. September 18. http://supervalentthought.com/2010/09/18/sitting-on-an-airplane-a-mule/.

———. 2011. *Cruel Optimism*. Durham, N.C.: Duke University Press.

Berlant, Lauren, and Michael Warner. 1998. "Sex in Public." *Critical Inquiry* 24 (2): 547–66.

Bernstein, Elizabeth. 2010. "Militarized Humanitarianism Meets Carceral Feminism: The Politics of Sex, Rights, and Freedom in Contemporary Antitrafficking Campaigns." *Signs* 36 (1): 45–71.

Bernstein, Robin. 2011. *Racial Innocence: Performing American Childhood from Slavery to Civil Rights*. New York: New York University Press.

Bersani, Leo. 1987. "Is the Rectum a Grave?" *AIDS: Cultural Analysis/Cultural Activism* 43: 197–222.

Best, Joel. 1990. *Threatened Children: Rhetoric and Concern about Child-Victims*. Chicago: University of Chicago Press.

Bienen, Leigh B. 1998. "Defining Incest." *Northwestern University Law Review* 92: 1501–1640.

Bishop, Donna M. 2000. "Juvenile Offenders in the Adult Criminal Justice System." *Crime and Justice* 27: 81–167.

Bogdanich, Walt. 2014. "Reporting Rape, and Wishing She Hadn't: How One College Handled a Sexual Assault Complaint." *New York Times*. July 12. http://www.nytimes.com/2014/07/13/us/how-one-college-handled-a-sexual-assault-complaint.html.

Boland, Ryan A. 1995. "Sex Offender Registration and Community Notification: Protection, Not Punishment." *New England Law Review* 30: 183–226.

Bolger, Dana. 2013. "Colleges Help Rape Survivors Where Courts Fail." *New York Times.* March 12. http://www.nytimes.com/roomfordebate/2013/03/12/why-should -colleges-judge-rape-accusations/colleges-help-rape-survivors-where-courts-fail.

Bornstein, Kate. 2006. "Gender Terror, Gender Rage." In *The Transgender Studies Reader,* edited by Susan Stryker and Stephen Whittle, 236–43. New York: Routledge.

Boyd, Justin H. 2007. "How to Stop a Predator: The Rush to Enact Mandatory Sex Offender Residency Restrictions and Why States Should Abstain." *Oregon Law Review* 86 (1): 219–48.

Brewer, Holly. 2005. *By Birth or Consent: Children, Law, and the Anglo-American Revolution in Authority.* Chapel Hill: University of North Carolina Press.

Brongersma, Edward. 1990. "Boy-Lovers and Their Influence on Boys: Distorted Research and Anecdotal Evidence." *Journal of Homosexuality* 20 (1/2): 145–73.

Brown, Trent. 2004. "Flynt and Black Each Make One Last Response in Debate on Obscenity." *Adult Video News.* April 15. http://business.avn.com/articles/video/ Flynt-and-Black-Each-Make-One-Last-Response-in-Debate-on-Obscenity-38282 .html.

Brown, Wendy. 1995. *States of Injury: Power and Freedom in Late Modernity.* Princeton, N.J.: Princeton University Press.

———. 2001. *Politics Out of History.* Princeton, N.J.: Princeton University Press.

———. 2002. "Suffering the Paradoxes of Rights." In *Left Legalism/Left Critique,* edited by Wendy Brown and Janet Halley, 420–34. Durham, N.C.: Duke University Press.

———. 2005. *Edgework: Critical Essays on Knowledge and Politics.* Princeton, N.J.: Princeton University Press.

Brown, Wendy, and Janet Halley, eds. 2002. *Left Legalism/Left Critique.* Durham, N.C.: Duke University Press.

Bruhm, Steven, and Natasha Hurley. 2004. "On the Queerness of Children." In *Curiouser: On the Queerness of Children,* edited by Steven Bruhm and Natasha Hurley, ix–xxxviii. Minneapolis: University of Minnesota Press.

Bruns, Cindy M. 2008. "May-December Lesbian Relationships: Power Storms or Blue Skies?" *Journal of Lesbian Studies* 12 (2–3): 265–81.

Bryant, Anita. 1977. *The Anita Bryant Story: The Survival of Our Nation's Families and the Threat of Militant Homosexuality.* Old Tappan, N.J.: Fleming H. Revell.

Bryden, David P. 2000. "Redefining Rape." *Buffalo Criminal Law Review* 3: 317–512.

Buchanan, Kim Shayo. 2015. "When Is HIV a Crime? Sexuality, Gender and Consent." *Minnesota Law Review* 99 (4): 1231–1342.

Buchhandler-Raphael, Michal. 2011. "The Failure of Consent: Re-Conceptualizing Rape as Sexual Abuse of Power." *Michigan Journal of Gender and Law* 18 (1): 147–228.

Bulman, Robert C. 2005. *Hollywood Goes to High School.* New York: Worth Publishers.

Bulman, Robert C., and Nicole S. McCants. 2008. "Enlightened Teenage Masculinity." *Contexts* 7 (3): 68–69.

Burgess, Susan. 2006. "Queer (Theory) Eye for the Straight (Legal) Guy: *Lawrence v. Texas'* Makeover of *Bowers v. Hardwick.*" *Political Research Quarterly* 59 (3): 401–14.

Burgett, Bruce. 2009. "Sex, Panic, Nation." *American Literary History* 21 (1): 67–86.

Bussel, Rachel Kramer. 2008. "Beyond Yes or No: Consent as Sexual Process." In *Yes Means Yes: Visions of Female Sexual Power and a World Without Rape,* edited by Jaclyn Friedman and Jessica Valenti, 43–52. Berkeley: Seal Press.

Butler, Judith. 1990. *Gender Trouble: Feminism and the Subversion of Identity.* New York: Routledge.

———. 1993a. *Bodies That Matter: On the Discursive Limits of "Sex."* New York: Routledge.

———. 1993b. "Imitation and Gender Subordination." In *The Lesbian and Gay Studies Reader,* edited by Henry Abelove, Michèle Aina Barale, and David M. Halperin, 307–20. New York: Routledge.

———. 1995. "Contingent Foundations." In *Feminist Contentions: A Philosophical Exchange,* edited by Seyla Benhabib et al., 35–58. New York: Routledge.

———. 1997a. *Excitable Speech: A Politics of the Performative.* New York: Routledge.

———. 1997b. *The Psychic Life of Power: Theories in Subjection.* Stanford: Stanford University Press.

———. 2006. *Precarious Life: The Powers of Mourning and Violence.* New York: Verso.

———. 2011. "Sexual Consent: Some Thoughts on Psychoanalysis and Law." *Columbia Journal of Gender and Law* 21 (2): 3–27.

Califia, Pat. 2000. *Public Sex: The Radical Culture of Radical Sex.* 2nd ed. San Francisco: Cleis Press.

Canaday, Margot. 2012. *The Straight State: Sexuality and Citizenship in Twentieth-Century America.* Princeton, N.J.: Princeton University Press.

Caringella, Susan. 2009. *Addressing Rape Reform in Law and Practice.* New York: Columbia University Press.

Carmon, Irin. 2013. "Steubenville Rapists Can Be Saved." *Salon.* March 21. http://www.salon.com/2013/03/21/how_to_save_a_teenage_rapist/.

Carpenter, Catherine L. 2006. "The Constitutionality of Strict Liability in Sex Offender Registration Laws." *Boston University Law Review* 86: 295–370.

Carpenter, Dale. 2012. *Flagrant Conduct: The Story of Lawrence v. Texas.* New York: W. W. Norton.

Carr, Craig L. 1991. "Duress and Criminal Responsibility." *Law and Philosophy* 10 (2): 161–88.

Case, Mary Anne. 2003. "Of 'This' and 'That' in *Lawrence v. Texas.*" *Supreme Court Review* 74: 75–142.

Casper, Monica J., and Lisa Jean Moore. 2009. *Missing Bodies: The Politics of Visibility.* New York: New York University Press.

Cave, Damien. 2009. "Roadside Camp for Miami Sex Offenders Leads to Lawsuit." *New York Times.* July 9. http://www.nytimes.com/2009/07/10/us/10offender.html.

Cavender, Gray. 1998. "In the 'Shadow of Shadows': Television Reality Crime Programming." In *Entertaining Crime: Television Reality Programs,* edited by Mark Fishman and Gray Cavender, 79–94. New York: Aldine De Gruyer.

Center for Sex Offender Management. 2000. "Myths and Facts about Sex Offenders." Office of Justice Programs, U.S. Department of Justice. http://www.csom.org/pubs/mythsfacts.pdf.

———. 2007. "Female Sex Offenders." Office of Justice Programs, U.S. Department of Justice. http://www.csom.org/pubs/female_sex_offenders_brief.pdf.

Chamallas, Martha. 1987–88. "Consent, Equality, and the Legal Control of Sexual Conduct." *California Law Review* 61: 777–862.

Chaplin, Tara M., and Amelia Aldao. 2013. "Gender Difference in Emotion Expression in Children: A Meta-Analytic Revew." *Psychological Bulletin* 139 (4) 735–65.

Chauncey, George, Jr. 1993. "The Postwar Sex Crime Panic." In *True Stories from the American Past,* edited by William Graebner, 167–78. New York: McGraw-Hill.

———. 2004. "'What Gay Studies Taught the Court': The Historians' Amicus Brief in *Lawrence v. Texas.*" *GLQ* 10 (3): 509–38.

Chen, Stephanie. 2009. "After Prison, Few Places for Sex Offenders to Live." *Wall Street Journal.* February 19. http://online.wsj.com/article/SB123500941182818821.html.

Chodorow, Nancy. 2010. "Foreword." In Sigmund Freud, *Three Essays on the Theory of Sexuality,* edited and translated by James Strachey, vii–xix. New York: Basic Books.

Cobb, Michael. 2005. "Childlike: Queer Theory and Its Children." *Criticism* 47 (1): 119–30.

Cocca, Carolyn E. 2002. "From 'Welfare Queen' to 'Exploited Teen': Welfare Dependency, Statutory Rape, and Moral Panic." *NWSA Journal* 56 (2): 56–79.

———. 2004. *Jailbait: The Politics of Statutory Rape Laws in the United States.* New York: State University of New York Press.

Cohen, Cathy J. 1997. "Punks, Bulldaggers, and Welfare Queens: The Radical Potential of Queer Politics?" *GLQ* 3 (4): 437–65.

———. 1999. *Boundaries of Blackness: AIDS and the Breakdown of Black Politics.* Chicago: University of Chicago Press.

———. 2009. "Black Sexuality, Indigenous Moral Panics, and Respectability: From Bill Cosby to the Down Low." In *Moral Panics, Sex Panics: The Fight Over Sexual Rights,* edited by Gilbert Herdt, 104–29. New York: New York University Press.

Cohen, Meredith. 2008. "No Child Left Behind Bars: The Need to Combat Cruel and Unusual Punishment of State Statutory Rape Laws." *Journal of Law and Policy* 16 (1): 717–56.

Cohen, Stanley. 2002. *Folk Devils and Moral Panics: The Creation of the Mods and Rockers.* 3rd ed. New York: Routledge.

Conly, Sarah. 2013. *Against Autonomy: Justifying Coercive Paternalism.* Cambridge: Cambridge University Press.

Connell, R. W., and James W. Messershmidt. 2005. "Hegemonic Masculinity: Rethinking the Concept." *Gender and Society* 19 (6): 829–59.

Corliss, Richard. 2007. "*Superbad*: A Fine Bromance." *Time*. August 17. http://con
tent.time.com/time/arts/article/0,8599,1653918,00.html.

Corrigan, Rose. 2006. "Making Meaning of Megan's Law." *Law and Social Inquiry* 31
(2): 267–312.

Cossman, Brenda. 2007. *Sexual Citizens: The Legal and Cultural Regulation of Sex and
Belonging*. Stanford: Stanford University Press.

Costa, M. Victoria. 2013. "Is Neo-Republicanism Bad for Women?" *Hypatia* 28 (4):
921–36.

Cover, Robert M. 1986. "Violence and the Word." *Yale Law Journal* 95: 1601–29.

Cowan, Sharon. 2007. "'Freedom and Capacity to Make a Choice': A Feminist Analy-
sis of Consent in the Criminal Law of Rape." In *Sexuality and the Law: Feminist
Engagements*, edited by Vanessa E. Munro and Carl F. Stychin, 51–72. New York:
Routledge-Cavendish.

Critcher, Cras. 2002. "Media, Government and Moral Panic: The Politics of Paedophilia in Britain 2000–1." *Journalism Studies* 3 (4): 521–35.

Cullingford, Elizabeth. 2010. "Evil, Sin, or Doubt? The Dramas of Clerical Child
Abuse." *Theatre Journal* 62 (2): 245–63.

Cumming-Bruce, Nick, and Laurie Goodstein. 2014. "U.N. Panel Says Vatican Is
Lax over Abusive Priests." *New York Times*. May 23. http://www.nytimes.com/
2014/05/24/world/europe/vatican-fails-to-act-against-abusive-priests-panel-says
.html.

Dalton, Derek. 2001. "The Deviant Gaze: Imagining the Homosexual as Criminal
through Cinematic and Legal Discourses." In *Law and Sexuality: The Global Arena*,
edited by Carl Stychin and Didi Herman, 69–83. Minneapolis: University of Minnesota Press.

Dan-Cohen, Meir. 1992. "Responsibilities and the Boundaries of the Self." *Harvard
Law Review* 105: 959–1003.

Dargis, Manohla. 2008. "Between Heaven and Earth, Room for Ambiguity." *New
York Times*. December 11. http://www.nytimes.com/2008/12/12/movies/12doub
.html?_r=0.

Davey, Monica. 2006. "Iowa's Residency Rules Drive Sex Offenders Underground."
New York Times. March 15. http://www.nytimes.com/2006/03/15/national/15
offenders.html.

Davies, Jon. 2007. "Imagining Intergenerationality: Representation and Rhetoric in
the Pedophile Movie." *GLQ* 13 (2–3): 369–85.

Davis, Linda. 2007. "Wolin Court Date Postponed Again." *Contra Costa Times*. June
20. http://www.contracostatimes.com/search/ci_6189137?nclick_check=1.

Dean, Tim. 2009. *Unlimited Intimacy: Reflections on the Subculture of Barebacking*. Chicago: University of Chicago Press.

"Dear Colleague Letter: Sexual Violence." 2011. The Assistant Secretary, Office for
Civil Rights, United States Department of Education. April 4, 1–19. http://www2
.ed.gov/about/offices/list/ocr/letters/colleague-201104.pdf.

de Beauvoir, Simone. 1989 (1953). *The Second Sex*. Translated by H. M. Parshley. New York: Vintage.

Decker, John F., and Peter G. Baroni. 2011. "'No' Still Means 'Yes': The Failure of the 'Non-Consent' Reform Movement in American Rape and Sexual Assault Law." *Journal of Criminal Law and Criminology* 101 (4): 1081–1169.

Deleuze, Gilles, and Félix Guattari. 1987. *A Thousand Plateaus: Capitalism and Schizophrenia*. Translated by Brian Massumi. London: Athlone Press.

Delgado, Richard. 1996. "No: Selective Enforcement Targets Unpopular Men." *ABA Journal* 82: 87.

D'Emilio, John. 2007. "Will the Courts Set Us Free? Reflections on the Campaign for Same-Sex Marriage." In *The Politics of Same-Sex Marriage*, edited by Craig A. Rimmerman and Clyde Wilcox, 39–64. Chicago: University of Chicago Press.

D'Emilio, John, and Estelle B. Freedman. 1997. *Intimate Matters: A History of Sexuality in America*. 2nd ed. Chicago: University of Chicago Press.

Denno, Deborah W. 1998. "Life Before the Modern Sex Offender Statutes." *Northwestern University Law Review* 92: 1317–1414.

Den Otter, Ronald C. 2015. *In Defense of Plural Marriage*. Cambridge: Cambridge University Press.

Denov, Myriam S. 2003. "The Myth of Innocence: Sexual Scripts and the Recognition of Child Sexual Abuse by Female Perpetrators." *Journal of Sex Research* 40 (3): 303–14.

Dewan, Shaila. 2007. "Duke Prosecutor Jailed: Student Seeks Settlement." *New York Times*. September 8. http://www.nytimes.com/2007/09/08/us/08duke.html.

De Young, Mary. 2006. "Another Look at Moral Panics: The Case of Satanic Day Care Centers." In *Critical Readings: Moral Panics and the Media*, edited by Chas Critcher, 277–90. Maidenhead: Open University Press.

Diamond, Lisa M. 2009. *Sexual Fluidity: Understanding Women's Love and Desire*. Cambridge, Mass.: Harvard University Press.

Dixon, Rosalind, and Martha C. Nussbaum. 2012. "Children's Rights and a Capabilities Approach." *Cornell Law Review* 97 (3): 549–83.

Douard, John. 2008–9. "Sex Offender as Scapegoat: The Monstrous Other Within." *New York Law School Law Review* 53: 31–52.

Doubt. 2008. DVD. Directed by John Patrick Shanley. Santa Monica: Lionsgate.

Dougherty, Tom. 2013. "No Way Around Consent: A Reply to Rubenfeld on 'Rape-by-Deception.'" *Yale Law Journal Online* 123: 321–34. http://www.yalelawjournal .org/forum/no-way-around-consent-a-reply-to-rubenfeld-on-rape-by-deception.

Douthat, Ross. 2014. "Stopping Campus Rape." *New York Times*. June 28. http:// www.nytimes.com/2014/06/29/opinion/sunday/ross-douthat-stopping-campus -rape.html.

Dowd, Maureen. 2010. "Rome Fiddles, We Burn." *New York Times*. July 17. http:// www.nytimes.com/2010/07/18/opinion/18dowd.html.

Dowling, Colette. 2001. *The Frailty Myth: Redefining the Physical Potential of Women and Girls.* New York: Random House.

Downing, Lisa. 2004. "On the Limits of Sexual Ethics: The Phenomenology of Autassassinophilia." *Sexuality and Culture* 8 (1): 3–17.

Doyle, Aaron. 1998. "'Cops': Television Policing as Policing Reality." In *Entertaining Crime: Television Reality Programs,* edited by Mark Fishman and Gray Cavender, 95–116. New York: Aldine De Gruyer.

Doyle, Vincent. 2008. "How to Make 'Kiddie Porn' in Canada: Law Enforcement, the Media, and Moral Panic in the Age of AIDS." In *Moral Panics over Contemporary Children and Youth,* edited by Charles Krinsky, 77–94. Surrey: Ashgate.

Dressler, Joshua. 1998. "Where We Have Been, and Where We Might Be Going? Some Cautionary Reflections on Rape Law Reform." *Cleveland State Law Review* 46: 409–42.

Dripps, Donald A. 1992. "Beyond Rape: An Essay on the Difference Between the Presence of Force and the Absence of Consent." *Columbia Law Review* 92 (7): 1780–1809.

Driscoll, Catherine. 2002. *Girls: Feminine Adolescence in Popular Culture and Cultural History.* New York: Columbia University Press.

Duggan, Lisa. 1994. "Queering the State." *Social Text* 39: 1–14.

———. 2004. "Holy Matrimony!" *The Nation,* February 26. http://www.thenation.com/article/holy-matrimony.

Duncan, Neil. 2004. "It's Important to Be Nice, but Nicer to Be Important: Girls, Popularity and Sexual Competition." *Sex Education* 4 (2): 137–52.

Dunn, Karen, and Bill Dobilas. 2013. "Public Notice: Sexual Predator Lives Here." *HLN on Air.* April 19. Video. http://www.hlntv.com/video/2013/04/19/sex-predators-signs-posted-lawn-florida.

Durham, M. Gigi. 2008. *The Lolita Effect: The Media Sexualization of Young Girls and What We Can Do About It.* Woodstock: Overlook Press.

Duwe, Grant, William Donnay, and Richard Tewksbury. 2008. "Does Residential Proximity Matter? A Geographic Analysis of Sex Offense Recidivism." *Criminal Justice and Behavior* 35 (4): 484–504.

Dworkin, Andrea. 1987. *Intercourse.* New York: Free Press.

Dworkin, Ronald. 2006. *Justice in Robes.* Cambridge, Mass.: Belknap Press.

"ED ACT NOW." 2013. *Know Your IX.* http://knowyourix.org/i-want-to/take-national-action/.

Edelman, Lee. 2004. *No Future: Queer Theory and the Death Drive.* Durham, N.C.: Duke University Press.

Ehrlich, J. Shoshanna. 2009. "You Can Steal Her Virginity but Not Her Doll: The Nineteenth Century Campaign to Raise the Legal Age of Sexual Consent." *Cardozo Journal of Law and Gender* 15: 229–45.

Einhorn, Catrin. 2008. "Judge Blocks Rules Limiting Sex Offenders on Halloween." *New York Times.* October 27. http://www.nytimes.com/2008/10/28/us/28halloween.html.

Elliot, Carl. 2000. "A New Way to Be Mad." *Atlantic Monthly.* December 1. http://
www.theatlantic.com/magazine/archive/2000/12/a-new-way-to-be-mad/304
671/.

Elstein, Sharon G., and Noy Davis. 1997. *Sexual Relationships between Adult Males and
Young Teenage Girls: Exploring the Legal and Social Responses.* Washington, D.C.:
American Bar Association Center on Children and the Law.

Ely, John Hart. 1980. *Democracy and Distrust: A Theory of Judicial Review.* Cambridge,
Mass.: Harvard University Press.

English, Kim. 2009. "The Containment Approach to Managing Sex Offenders." In *Sex
Offender Laws: Failed Policies, New Directions,* edited by Richard G. Wright, 427–48.
New York: Springer.

Eskridge, William N., Jr. 1995. "The Many Faces of Sexual Consent." *William and Mary
Law Review* 37 (1): 47–68.

———. 2008. *Dishonorable Passions: Sodomy Laws in America, 1861–2003.* New York:
Viking Adult.

Estes, Adam Clark. 2013. "CNN's Not the Only One Peddling Sympathy for the Steubenville Rapists." *The Atlantic Wire.* March 17. http://www.theatlanticwire.com/
national/2013/03/cnns-not-only-one-peddling-sympathy-steubenville-rapists/
63204.

Estrich, Susan. 1987. *Real Rape.* Cambridge, Mass.: Harvard University Press.

———.1992. "Palm Beach Stories." *Law and Philosophy* 11 (1/2): 5–33.

"Expensive Home Rich with Potential Predators." 2007. *Dateline NBC.* July 25. Video.
http://www.msnbc.msn.com/id/19961209/ns/dateline_nbc-to_catch_a_preda
tor/.

Ezard, Nadine. 2001. "Public Health, Human Rights and the Harm Reduction Paradigm: From Risk Reduction to Vulnerability Reduction." *International Journal of
Drug Policy* 12: 207–19.

Falk, Patricia J. 1998. "Rape by Fraud and Rape by Coercion." *Brooklyn Law Review*
64: 39–180.

———. 2013. "Not Logic, but Experience: Drawing on Lessons from the Real World
in Thinking about the Riddle of Rape-by-Fraud." *Yale Law Journal Online* 123: 353–
70. http://www.yalelawjournal.org/forum/not-logic-but-experience-drawing-on
-lessons-from-the-real-world-in-thinking-about-the-riddle-of-rape-by-fraud.

Family Research Council. 2014. "Ten Arguments from Social Science against Same-
Sex Marriage." *Family Research Council.* http://www.frc.org/get.cfm?i=if04g01.

Farley, Lara Geer. 2008. "The Adam Walsh Act: The Scarlet Letter of the Twenty-First
Century." *Washburn Law Journal* 47: 471–503.

Feinberg, Joel. 1987. *Harm to Others: The Moral Limits of the Criminal Law.* New York:
Oxford University Press.

Feinberg, Leslie. 2003. *Stone Butch Blues.* Los Angeles: Alyson Publications.

Fields, Jessica. 2005. "'Children Having Children': Race, Innocence, and Sexuality
Education." *Social Problems* 52 (4): 549–71.

———. 2008. *Risky Lessons: Sex Education and Social Inequality.* New Brunswick, N.J.: Rutgers University Press.

Filler, Daniel M. 2001. "Making the Case for Megan's Law: A Study in Legislative Rhetoric." *Indiana Law Journal* 76: 315–66.

Fine, Michelle, and Sara I. McClelland. 2006. "Sexuality Education and Desire: Still Missing After All These Years." *Harvard Educational Review* 76 (3): 297–338.

Fineman, Martha Albertson. 2004. *The Autonomy Myth: A Theory of Dependence.* New York: New Press.

———. 2008. "The Vulnerable Subject: Anchoring Equality in the Human Condition." *Yale Journal of Law and Feminism* 20 (1): 1–24.

Finkelhor, David, and Lisa Jones. 2012. "Have Sexual Abuse and Physical Abuse Declined Since the 1990s?" Crimes Against Children Research Center, University of New Hampshire. 6 pages. http://www.unh.edu/ccrc/pdf/CV267_Have%20SA%20%20PA%20Decline_FACT%20SHEET_11-7-12.pdf.

Fischel, Joseph J. 2010a. "*Per Se* or Power? Age and Sexual Consent." *Yale Journal of Law and Feminism* 22 (2): 279–341.

———. 2010b. "Transcendent Homosexuals and Dangerous Sex Offenders: Sexual Harm and Freedom in the Judicial Imaginary." *Duke Journal of Gender Law and Policy* 17 (2): 277–312.

———. 2013a. "Against Nature, against Consent: A Sexual Politics of Debility." *differences: a Journal of Feminist Cultural Studies* 24 (1): 55–103.

———. 2013b. "Pornographic Protections: Itineraries of Childhood Innocence." *Law, Culture and the Humanities.* doi: 10.1177/1743872113492396.

Fitzgerald, Louise F. 2004. "Who Says? Legal and Psychological Constructions of Women's Resistance to Sexual Harassment." In *Directions in Sexual Harassment Law,* edited by Catharine A. MacKinnon and Reva B. Siegel, 94–110. New Haven: Yale University Press.

Flanagan, Caitlin. 2014. "The Dark Power of Fraternities." *Atlantic Monthly.* March. http://www.theatlantic.com/features/archive/2014/02/the-dark-power-of-fraternities/357580/.

"The Florida County Where Police Post 'Sexual Predator' Road Signs Outside Homes of Convicted Rapists and Child Molesters." 2013. *Daily Mail Online.* April 18. http://www.dailymail.co.uk/news/article-2310843/The-Florida-county-police-post-sexual-predator-road-signs-outside-homes-convicted-rapists-child-molesters.html.

Foucault, Michel. 1980. *Power/Knowledge: Selected Interviews and Other Writings 1972–77.* Edited and translated by Colin Gordon et al. Brighton: Harvester Press.

———. 1990. *The History of Sexuality: An Introduction.* Translated by Robert Hurley. New York: Vintage Books.

———. 1995. *Discipline and Punish.* 2nd ed. Translated by Alan Sheridan. New York: Random House.

———. 2003. *Society Must Be Defended: Lectures at the Collège de France, 1975–1976.* Edited by Mauro Bertani and Alessandro Fontana. Translated by David Macey. New York: Picador.

————. 2007. *Security, Territory, Population: Lectures at the Collège de France 1977–1978*. Edited by Michel Senellart. Translated by Graham Burchell. New York: Palgrave Macmillan.

Foucault, Michel, Guy Hocquenghem, and Jean Danet. 1988. "Sexual Morality and the Law." In *Politics, Philosophy, Culture: Interviews and Other Writings, 1977–1984*, edited by Lawrence D. Kritzman, 271–85. New York: Routledge.

Franke, Katherine. 2001. "Theorizing Yes: An Essay on Feminism, Law, and Desire." *Columbia Law Review* 101 (1): 181–208.

————. 2004. "The Domesticated Liberty of *Lawrence v. Texas*." *Columbia Law Review* 104 (5): 1399–1426.

Freedman, Estelle B. 1987. "'Uncontrolled Desires': The Response to the Sexual Psychopath, 1920–1960." *Journal of American History* 74 (1): 83–106.

————. 2013. *Redefining Rape: Sexual Violence in the Era of Suffrage and Segregation*. Cambridge, Mass.: Harvard University Press.

Freeman, Elizabeth. 1998. "Honeymoon with a Stranger: Pedophiliac Picaresques from Poe to Nabokov." *American Literature* 70 (4): 863–97.

————. 2010. *Time Binds: Queer Temporalities, Queer Histories*. Durham, N.C.: Duke University Press.

Freud, Sigmund. 1990 (1920). *Beyond the Pleasure Principle*. Edited and translated by James Strachey. New York: W. W. Norton.

————. 2000. *Three Essays on the Theory of Sexuality*. Edited and translated by James Strachey. New York: Basic Books.

Friedman, Jaclyn. 2011. *What You Really Really Want: The Smart Girl's Shame-Free Guide to Sex and Safety*. Berkeley: Seal Press.

Friedman, Marilyn. 2003. *Autonomy, Gender, Politics*. New York: New York University Press.

————. 2008. "Pettit's Civic Republicanism and Male Domination." In *Republicanism and Political Theory*, edited by Cecil Laborde and John Maynor, 246–68. New York: Springer; Malden, Mass.: Blackwell.

Gagnon, John. 2003. "Changing Times, Changing Crimes." *Sexualities* 6 (1): 41–45.

Gallop, Jane. 1997. *Feminist Accused of Sexual Harassment*. Durham, N.C.: Duke University Press.

Gamson, Joshua. 1995. "Must Identity Movements Self-Destruct? A Queer Dilemma." *Social Problems* 42 (3): 390–407.

————. 1998. *Freaks Talk Back: Tabloid Talk Shows and Sexual Nonconformity*. Chicago: University of Chicago Press.

————. 2001. "Normal Sins: Sex Scandal Narratives as Institutional Morality Tales." *Social Problems* 48 (2): 185–205.

Garbarino, James. 2006. *See Jane Hit: Why Girls Are Growing More Violent and What Can Be Done about It*. New York: Penguin Press.

Garfinkle, Elizabeth. 2003. "Coming of Age in America: The Misapplication of Sex-Offender Registration and Community-Notification Laws to Juveniles." *California Law Review* 91 (1): 163–208.

Gavey, Nicola. 2005. *Just Sex? The Cultural Scaffolding of Rape*. London: Routledge.

Gay Left Collective. 1981. "Happy Families? Pedophilia Examined." In *The Age Taboo: Gay Male Sexuality, Power and Consent,* edited by Daniel Tsang, 53–64. Boston: Alyston Publications.

Gershman, Jacob. 2013. "Sex Offenders May Be Banned from Social Media, N.J. Court Rules." *Wall Street Journal.* November 27. http://blogs.wsj.com/law/2013/11/27/sex-offenders-may-be-banned-from-social-media-n-j-court-rules/.

Gilbert, Jen. 2007. "Risking a Relation: Sex Education and Adolescent Development." *Sex Education* 7 (1): 47–61.

Giroux, Henry A. 2012. *Disposable Youth: Racialized Memory and the Culture of Cruelty.* New York: Routledge.

Goddard, Alexandria. 2012. "Big Red Players Accused of Rape & Kidnapping." *prinniefield.com.* August 23. http://prinniefied.com/wp/steubenville-high-school-gang-rape-case-firs/.

Goldstein, Adam. 2013. "Rape Is a Crime, Treat It as Such." *New York Times.* March 12. http://www.nytimes.com/roomfordebate/2013/03/12/why-should-colleges-judge-rape-accusations/rape-is-a-crime-treat-it-as-such.

Golladay, Michelle. 2013. "Legislation Would Close 'Gap' in Sex Assault Law Involving Disabled." *Connecticut Law Tribune.* March 29. http://www.ctlawtribune.com/PubArticleCT.jsp?id=1202594133927.

Gómez, Daniel Varona. 2008. "Duress and the Antcolony's Ethic: Reflections of the Foundations of the Defense and Its Limits." *New Criminal Law Review* 11 (4): 615–44.

Goode, Erica. 2012. "Researchers See Decline in Child Sexual Abuse Rate." *New York Times.* June 28. http://www.nytimes.com/2012/06/29/us/rate-of-child-sexual-abuse-on-the-decline.html.

Goodman, Brenda. 2007. "Georgia Court Frees Man Convicted in Sex Case." *New York Times.* October 27. http://www.nytimes.com/2007/10/27/us/27georgia.html?_r=1&ref=genarlowwilson.

Goodnough, Abby, and Monica Davey. 2009. "Effort to Track Sex Offenders Draws Resistance." *New York Times.* February 8. http://www.nytimes.com/2009/02/09/us/09offender.html.

Gordon, Angus. 1999. "Turning Back: Adolescence, Narrative, and Queer Theory." *GLQ* 5 (1): 1–24.

Gordon, Jane. 2003. "Ruling Opens Door to List Sex Offenders." *New York Times.* March 9. http://www.nytimes.com/2003/03/09/nyregion/ruling-opens-door-to-list-sex-offenders.html.

Gordon, Linda. 1988. "The Politics of Child Sexual Abuse: Notes from American History." *Feminist Review* 28: 56–64.

Gorrell, Paul J. 2006. "The Roman Catholic Pedophilia Crisis and the Call to Erotic Conversion." *Theology and Sexuality* 12 (3): 251–62.

Gould, Sophie. 2012. "Olivarius Discusses Sexuality." *Yale Daily News*. February 6. http://yaledailynews.com/blog/2012/02/06/olivarius-discusses-sexuality/.

Gramsci, Antonio. 1971. *Selections from the Prison Notebooks of Antonio Gramsci*. Edited and translated by Quintin Hoare and Geoffrey Nowell Smith. London: Lawrence & Wishart.

Grant, Judith. 1996. "Morality and Liberal Legal Culture: Woody Allen's *Crimes and Misdemeanors*." In *Legal Reelism: Movies as Legal Texts*, edited by John Denvir, 154–71. Urbana: University of Illinois Press.

Gray, Eliza. 2014. "Colleges Are Breaking the Laws on Sex Crimes, Report Says." *Time*. July 9. http://time.com/2969580/claire-mccaskill-campus-sexual-assault-rape/.

Greenfeld, Lawrence A. 1997. "Sex Offenses and Offenders: An Analysis of Data on Rape and Sexual Assault." Bureau of Justice Statistics, Office of Justice Programs, U.S. Department of Justice. vi + 39 pages. http://bjs.ojp.usdoj.gov/content/pub/pdf/SOO.PDF.

Gregory, Raymond F. 2004. *Unwelcome and Unlawful: Sexual Harassment in the American Workplace*. Ithaca, NY: Cornell University Press.

Grigoriadis, Vanessa. 2007. "'To Catch a Predator': The New American Witch Hunt for Dangerous Pedophiles." *Rolling Stone*, July 30, 64–71.

Gross, Aeyal. 2009. "Gender Outlaws before the Law: The Courts of the Borderland." *Harvard Journal of Gender and Law* 32: 165–231.

"Guilty Verdict in Steubenville Rape Trial." 2013. *CNN Transcripts*. March 17. http://transcripts.cnn.com/TRANSCRIPTS/1303/17/rs.01.html.

Guttmacher Institute. 2006. "Facts on American Teens' Sexual and Reproductive Health." September. https://www.guttmacher.org/pubs/fb_ATSRH.pdf.

———. 2014. "American Teens' Sexual and Reproductive Health." May. http://www.guttmacher.org/pubs/FB-ATSRH.html.

Hacking, Ian. 1991. "The Making and Molding of Child Abuse." *Critical Inquiry* 17 (2): 253–88.

Halberstam, J. Jack. 2012. *Gaga Feminism: Sex, Gender, and the End of Normal*. Boston: Beacon Press.

Halberstam, Judith. 2005. *In a Queer Time and Place: Transgender Bodies, Subcultural Lives*. New York: New York University Press.

———. 2011. *The Queer Art of Failure*. Durham, N.C.: Duke University Press.

Hall, G. Stanley. 1904. *Adolescence: Its Psychology and Its Relation to Physiology, Anthropology, Sociology, Sex, Crime, Religion and Education*. New York: A. Appleton.

Hall, Stuart M., et al. 1978. *Mugging, the State, and Law and Order*. London: Macmillan.

Halley, Janet E. 1993. "Reasoning About Sodomy: Act and Identity in and after *Bowers v. Hardwick*." *Virginia Law Review* 79 (7): 1721–80.

———. 2006. *Split Decisions: How and Why to Take a Break from Feminism*. Princeton, N.J.: Princeton University Press.

Halperin, David M. 1995. *Saint Foucault: Towards a Gay Hagiography*. New York: Oxford University Press.

Halwani, Raja. 2010. *Philosophy of Love, Sex and Marriage: An Introduction.* New York: Routledge.

Hansen, Chris. 2007. *To Catch a Predator: Protecting Your Kids from Online Predators Already in Your Home.* New York: Dutton.

Hansen, Chris, et al. 2007. "Ethics of NBC's Sting Show 'To Catch a Predator.'" Interview with Neal Conan, *Talk of the Nation,* National Public Radio, January 16. http://www.npr.org/templates/story/story.php?storyId=6870926.

Hanson, Ellis. 1999. "Lesbians Who Bite." In *Out Takes: Essays on Queer Theory and Film,* edited by Ellis Hanson, 183–222. Durham, N.C.: Duke University Press.

Harcourt, Bernard E. 1999. "The Collapse of the Harm Principle." *Journal of Criminal Law and Criminology* 90 (1): 109–94.

———. 2001. *The Illusion of Order: The False Promise of Broken Windows Policing.* Cambridge, Mass.: Harvard University Press.

———. 2004. "'You Are Entering a Gay and Lesbian Free Zone': On the Radical Dissents of Justice Scalia and Other (Post-) Queers." *Journal of Criminal Law and Criminology* 94 (3): 503–50.

———. 2007. *Against Prediction: Profiling, Policing, and Punishing in an Actuarial Age.* Chicago: University of Chicago Press.

Harden, Nathan. 2012. "For Yale Women, Equality Remains Out of Reach." *Huffington Post.* July 18. http://www.huffingtonpost.com/nathan-harden/yale-sexual-assault -case-_b_1681135.html.

Harkins, Gillian. 2009. *Everybody's Family Romance: Reading Incest in Neoliberal America.* Minneapolis: University of Minneapolis Press.

Hawkes, Gail, and R. Danielle Egan. 2008. "Landscapes of Erotophobia: The Sexual(ized) Child in the Postmodern Anglophone West." *Sexuality and Culture* 12: 193–203.

Hayward, Clarissa Rile. 2011. "What Can Political Freedom Mean in a Multicultural Democracy? On Deliberation, Difference, and Democratic Governance." *Political Theory* 39 (4): 469–97.

Henderson, Lynne N. 1988. "What Makes Rape a Crime?" *Berkeley Women's Law Journal* 3: 193–229.

Henderson, Mae G. 2005. "James Baldwin's *Giovanni's Room:* Expatriation, 'Racial Drag,' and Homosexual Panic." In *Black Queer Studies: A Critical Anthology,* edited by E. Patrick Johnson and Mae G. Henderson, 298–322. Durham, N.C.: Duke University Press.

Herald, Marybeth. 2004. "A Bedroom of One's Own: Morality and Sexual Privacy after *Lawrence v. Texas.*" *Yale Journal of Law and Feminism* 16: 1–40.

Herdt, Gilbert, ed. 2009a. *Moral Panics, Sex Panics: The Fight over Sexual Rights.* New York: New York University Press.

———. 2009b. "Moral Panics, Sexual Rights, and Cultural Anger." In *Moral Panics, Sex Panics: The Fight over Sexual Rights,* edited by Gilbert Herdt, 1–46. New York: New York University Press.

Hernández, Javier C. 2014. "At Manhattan Preschool, Accounts of Sex Abuse Case Differ." *New York Times.* July 23. http://www.nytimes.com/2014/07/24/nyregion /anger-at-a-manhattan-preschool-over-sexual-abuse-accusations-.html.

Herring, Jonathan. 2012. "Vulnerability, Children, and the Law." In *Law and Childhood Studies,* edited by Michael Freeman, 243–63. Oxford: Oxford University Press.

Hess, Amanda. 2014. "Harvard, Dartmouth, Princeton: Why Are So Many Elite Schools Being Investigated for Mishandling Sexual Assault?" *Slate.* May 5. http:// www.slate.com/blogs/xx_factor/2014/05/05/campus_sexual_assault_why_are _so_many_elite_universities_being_investigated.html.

Higdon, Michael J. 2008. "Queer Teens and Legislative Bullies: The Cruel and Invidious Discrimination Behind Heterosexist Statutory Rape Laws." *U.C. Davis Law Review* 42: 195–253.

Hirschmann, Nancy J. 2002. *The Subject of Liberty: Toward a Feminist Theory of Freedom.* Princeton, N.J.: Princeton University Press.

Hitz, John. 2014. "Removing Disfavored Faces from Facebook: The Freedom of Speech Implications of Banning Sex Offenders from Social Media." *Indiana Law Journal* 89: 1327–63.

Hobson, Bret R. 2006. "Banishing Acts: How Far May States Go to Keep Convicted Sex Offenders Away from Children?" *Georgia Law Review* 40 (3): 961–94.

Hochschild, Arlie Russell. 2003. *The Managed Heart: Commercialization of Human Feeling.* Berkeley: University of California Press.

Holland, Patricia. 2004. *Picturing Childhood: The Myth of the Child in Popular Imagery.* New York: I. B. Tauris.

Hollenberg, Elizabeth. 1999. "The Criminalization of Teenage Sex: Statutory Rape and the Politics of Teenage Motherhood." *Stanford Law and Policy Review* 10: 267–78.

hooks, bell. 1996. *Reel to Real: Race, Sex, and Class at the Movies.* New York: Routledge.

Hopbell, Maureen S. 2004. "Balancing the Protection of Children against the Protection of Constitutional Rights: The Past, Present and Future of Megan's Law." *Duquette Law Review* 42: 331–53.

Hoppe, Trevor. 2014. "From Sickness to Badness: The Criminalization of HIV in Michigan." *Social Science and Medicine* 101: 139–47.

Horowitz, Donald L. 1977. *The Courts and Social Policy.* Washington, D.C.: Brookings Institution.

Howe, Adrian. 2001. "Homosexual Advances in Law: Murderous Excuse, Pluralized Ignorance and the Privilege of Unknowing." In *Law and Sexuality: The Global Arena,* edited by Carl Stychin and Didi Herman, 84–99. Minneapolis: University of Minnesota Press.

Huffer, Lynne. 2013. *Are the Lips a Grave? A Queer Feminist on the Ethics of Sex.* New York: Columbia University Press.

Human Rights Campaign. 2010. "HRC Refutes Vatican Official's Statement on Pedophilia and Sexual Orientation." April 13. http://www.hrc.org/press-releases/entry/ hrc-refutes-vatican-officials-statement-on-pedophilia-and-sexual-orientatio.

Human Rights Watch. 2007. "No Easy Answers: Sex Offender Laws in the US." *Human Rights Watch* 19 (4): 1–141. http://www.hrw.org/en/reports/2007/09/11/no-easy-answers.

Humphreys, Terry P. 2004. "Understanding Sexual Consent: An Empirical Investigation of the Normative Script for Young Heterosexual Adults." In *Making Sense of Sexual Consent,* edited by Mark Cowley and Paul Reynolds, 209–26. Aldershot: Ashgate.

"Inaugural Address by President Barack Obama." 2013. The White House, Office of the Press Secretary. January 21. http://www.whitehouse.gov/the-press-office/2013/01/21/inaugural-address-president-barack-obama.

"Inbred Obscurity: Improving Incest Laws in the Shadow of the 'Sexual Family.'" 2006. *Harvard Law Review* 119: 2464–85.

Irvine, Janice M. 2006. "Emotional Scripts of Sex Panics." *Sexuality Research and Social Policy* 3 (3): 82–94.

Jackson, Stevi, and Sue Scott. 1999. "Risk Anxiety and the Social Construction of Childhood." In *Risk and Sociocultural Theory: New Directions and Perspectives,* edited by Deborah Lupton, 86–107. Cambridge: Cambridge University Press.

Jain, Sarah S. Lochlann. 2006. *The Politics of Product Design and Safety Law in the United States.* Princeton, N.J.: Princeton University Press.

Jakobsen, Janet R., and Elizabeth Lapovksy Kennedy. 2005. "Sex and Freedom." In *Regulating Sex: The Politics of Intimacy and Identity,* edited by Laurie Schaffner and Elizabeth Bernstein, 247–70. New York: Routledge.

James, Allison. 2011. "To Be (Come) or Not to Be (Come): Understanding Children's Citizenship." *The ANNALS of the American Academy of Political and Social Science* 633 (1): 167–79.

Janus, Eric S. 2006. *Failure to Protect: America's Sexual Predator Laws and the Rise of the Preventive State.* Ithaca, N.Y.: Cornell University Press.

Janus, Eric S., and Emily A. Polacheck. 2009. "A Crooked Picture: Re-Framing the Problem of Child Sexual Abuse." *William Mitchell Law Review* 36 (1): 142–68.

Jeffreys, Sheila. 1990. *Anticlimax: A Feminist Perspective on the Sexual Revolution.* London: Women's Press.

———. 2014. *Gender Hurts: A Feminist Analysis of the Politics of Transgenderism.* London: Routledge.

Jenkins, Phillip. 1998. *Moral Panic: Changing Concepts of the Child Molester in Modern America.* New Haven: Yale University Press.

———. 2001. *Pedophiles and Priests: Anatomy of a Contemporary Crisis.* 2nd ed. New York: Oxford University Press.

Johnson, Luke. 2013. "Ken Cuccinelli Appeals to Defend Virginia's Anti-Sodomy Law at Supreme Court." *Huffington Post.* June 25. http://www.huffingtonpost.com/2013/06/25/ken-cuccinelli-sodomy-supreme-court_n_3498444.html.

Jordan, Mark D. 2000. *The Silence of Sodom: Homosexuality in Modern Catholicism.* Chicago: University of Chicago Press.

————. 2011. *Recruiting Young Love: How Christians Talk about Homosexuality*. Chicago: University of Chicago Press.

Kafer, Allison. 2012. "Desire and Disgust: My Ambivalent Adventures in Devotee-ism." In *Sex and Disability*, edited by Robert McCruer and Anna Mollow, 331–54. Durham, N.C.: Duke University Press.

Kamir, Orit. 2005. "Cinematic Judgment and Jurisprudence: A Woman's Memory, Recovery, and Justice in a Post-Traumatic Society (a Study of Polanski's *Death and the Maiden*)." In *Law on the Screen*, edited by Austin Sarat, Lawrence Douglas, and Martha Merrill Umphrey, 27–81. Stanford: Stanford University Press.

Kaplan, Meg S., and Arthur Green. 1995. "Incarcerated Female Sexual Offenders: A Comparison of Sexual Histories with Eleven Female Nonsexual Offenders." *Sexual Abuse: A Journal of Research and Treatment* 7 (4): 287–300.

Karlyn, Kathleen Rowe. 2006. "*Thirteen* and the Maternal Melodrama." *Feminist Media Studies* 6 (4): 453–68.

Katz, Jonathan Ned. 1995. *The Invention of Heterosexuality*. New York: Dutton.

Kearney, Mary Celeste. 2002. "Girlfriends and Girl Power: Female Adolescence in Contemporary Cinema." In *Sugar, Spice, and Everything Nice: Cinemas of Girlhood*, edited by Frances Gateward and Murray Pomerance, 125–43. Detroit: Wayne State University Press.

"KEEP VIRGINIA KIDS SAFE!" 2013. *Ken Cuccinelli for Governor*. http://www.va childpredators.com/ (no longer active).

Kelleher, Paul. 2004. "How to Do Things with Perversion: Psychoanalysis and the 'Child in Danger.'" In *Curiouser: On the Queerness of Children*, edited by Steven Bruhm and Natasha Hurley, 151–71. Minneapolis: University of Minnesota Press.

Keller, Bill. 2012. "Predators on Pedestals." *New York Times*. October 14. http://www .nytimes.com/2012/10/15/opinion/keller-predators-on-pedestals.html.

Khan, Ummni. 2009a. "Having Your Porn and Condemning It Too: A Case Study of a 'Kiddie Porn' Expose." *Law, Culture and the Humanities* 5: 391–424.

————. 2009b. "A Woman's Right to Be Spanked: Testing the Limits of Tolerance of SM in the Socio-Legal Imaginary." *Law and Sexuality Review* 18: 79–119.

Kidd, Kenneth. 2011. "Queer Theory's Child and Children's Literature Studies." *PMLA* 126 (1): 182–88.

Kincaid, James R. 1998. *Erotic Innocence: The Culture of Child Molesting*. Durham, N.C.: Duke University Press.

————. 2004. "Producing Erotic Children." In *Curiouser: On the Queerness of Children*, edited by Steven Bruhm and Natasha Hurley, 3–16. Minneapolis: University of Minnesota Press.

Kipnis, Laura. 1999. *Bound and Gagged: Pornography and the Politics of Fantasy in America*. Durham, N.C.: Duke University Press.

————. 2010. *How to Become a Scandal: Adventures in Bad Behavior*. New York: Metropolitan Books.

Kitchener, Caroline. 2013. "How to Encourage More College Sexual Assault Victims to Speak Up." *Atlantic Monthly.* August 23. http://www.theatlantic.com/national/archive/2013/08/how-to-encourage-more-college-sexual-assault-victims-to-speak-up/278972/.

Kitrosser, Heidi. 1996. "Meaningful Consent: Toward a New Generation of Statutory Rape Laws." *Virginia Journal of Social Policy and Law* 4: 287–338.

Kitzinger, Jennifer. 1988. "Defending Innocence: Ideologies of Childhood." *Feminist Review* 28: 77–87.

———. 2004. *Framing Abuse: Media Influence and Public Understanding of Sexual Violence Against Children.* London: Pluto Press.

———. 2006. "The Ultimate Neighbor from Hell? Stranger Danger and the Media Framing of Paedophilia." In *Critical Readings: Moral Panics and the Media,* edited by Chas Critcher, 135–47. Maidenhead: Open University Press.

Klein, Richard. 2008. "An Analysis of Thirty-Five Years of Rape Reform: A Frustrating Search for Fundamental Fairness." *Akron Law Review* 41 (4): 981–1054.

Kleinhans, Chuck. 2004. "Virtual Child Porn: The Law and the Semiotics of the Image." *Journal of Visual Culture* 3 (1): 17–34.

Kohm, Steven A. 2009. "Naming, Shaming, and Criminal Justice: Mass-Mediated Humiliation as Entertainment and Punishment." *Crime Media Culture* 5: 188–205.

Krause, Sharon R. 2013. "Beyond Non-Domination: Agency, Inequality, and the Meaning of Freedom." *Philosophy and Social Criticism* 39 (2): 187–208.

Krebs, Christopher P., et al. 2007. "The Campus Sexual Assault (CSA) Study." National Institute of Justice, U.S. Department of Justice. https://www.ncjrs.gov/pdffiles1/nij/grants/221153.pdf.

———. 2009. "College Women's Experiences with Physically Forced, Alcohol- or Other Drug-Enabled, and Drug-Facilitated Sexual Assault before and since Entering College." *Journal of American College Health* 57 (6): 639–49.

Krinsky, Charles, ed. 2008. *Moral Panics over Contemporary Children and Youth.* Surrey: Ashgate.

Kunz, Carol L. 1997. "Toward Dispassionate, Effective Control of Sex Offenders." *American University Law Review* 47: 453–85.

Laing, R. D. 1965. *The Divided Self: An Existential Study in Sanity and Madness.* New York: Penguin Books.

Lamb, Sharon. 2002. *The Secret Lives of Girls: What Good Girls Really Do—Sex Play, Aggression, and Their Guilt.* New York: Free Press.

Lamb, Sharon, and Zoë D. Peterson. 2012. "Adolescent Girls' Sexual Empowerment: Two Feminists Explore the Concept." *Sex Roles* 66 (11–12): 703–12.

Lancaster. Roger N. 2011. *Sex Panic and the Punitive State.* Berkeley: University of California Press.

Landau, Elizabeth. 2009. "Gaps Found in Young People's Sexual Knowledge." CNN. December 15. http://www.cnn.com/2009/HEALTH/12/15/sex.report/index.html.

Langan, Patrick A., Erica L. Schmitt, and Matthew Durose. 2003. "Recidivism of Sex Offenders Released from Prison in 1994." Bureau of Justice Statistics, Office of Justice Programs, U.S. Department of Justice. iv + 40 pages. http://bjs.ojp.usdoj.gov/content/pub/pdf/rsorp94.pdf.

Larson, Jane E. 1997. "'Even a Worm Will Turn at Last': Rape Reform in Late Nineteenth-Century America." *Yale Journal of Law and Humanities* 9: 1–71.

Lauerman, John. 2014. "Harvard Reviews Sexual Assault Policy as Students Push Change." *Bloomberg News.* January 30. http://www.bloomberg.com/news/articles/2014-01-30/harvard-reviews-sexual-assault-policy-as-students-push-change.

Laye-Gindhu, Aviva, and Kimberly A. Schonert-Reichl. 2005. "Nonsuicidal Self-Harm among Community Adolescents: Understanding the 'Whats' and 'Whys' of Self-Harm." *Journal of Youth and Adolescence* 34 (5): 447–57.

Lazzarini, Zita, and Robert Klitzman. 2002. "HIV and the Law: Integrating Law, Policy, and Social Epidemiology." *Journal of Law, Medicine and Ethics* 30: 533–47.

Leahy, Terry. 1992. "Positively Experienced Man/Boy Sex: The Discourse of Seduction and the Social Construction of Masculinity." *Journal of Sociology* 28 (1): 71–88.

Lehman, J. Stan, et al. 2014. "Prevalence and Public Health Implications of State Laws that Criminalize Potential HIV Exposure in the United States." *AIDS Behavior* 18: 997–1006.

Lesko, Nancy. 2012. *Act Your Age! A Cultural Construction of Adolescence.* New York: Routledge.

Levenson, Jill S., and Leo P. Cotter. 2005. "The Effect of Megan's Law on Sex Offender Reintegration." *Journal of Contemporary Criminal Justice* 21 (1): 49–66.

Levesque, Roger J. R. 2000. *Adolescents, Sex, and the Law: Preparing Adolescents for Responsible Citizenship.* Washington, D.C.: American Psychological Association.

———. 2007. *Adolescents, Media, and the Law: What Developmental Science Reveals and Free Speech Requires.* Oxford: Oxford University Press.

Levine, Judith. 2002. *Harmful to Minors: The Perils of Protecting Children from Sex.* New York: Thunder's Mouth Press.

Lloyd-Richardson, Elizabeth, et al. 2007. "Characteristics and Functions of Non-Suicidal Self-Injury in a Community Sample of Adolescents." *Psychological Medicine* 37: 1183–92.

Locke, John. 2003. *Two Treatises of Government and a Letter Concerning Toleration.* Edited by Ian Shapiro. New Haven: Yale University Press.

Logan, Wayne A. 1999. "Liberty Interests in the Preventive State: Procedural Due Process and Sex Offender Community Notification Laws." *Journal of Criminal Law and Criminology* 89 (4): 1167–1232.

Lombardi, Kristen. 2010. "A Lack of Consequences for Sexual Assault." Center for Public Integrity. February 24. http://www.publicintegrity.org/2010/02/24/4360/lack-consequences-sexual-assault-0.

Lorde, Audre. 1982. *Zami: A New Spelling of My Name.* Berkeley: Crossing Press.

Loseke, Donileen R. 2003. "'We Hold These Truths to Be Self-evident': Problems in Pondering the Pedophile Priest Problem." *Sexualities* 6 (1): 6–14.

Loudon-Brown, Mark. 2007. "'They Set Him on a Path Where He's Bound to Get Ill': Why Sex Offender Residency Restrictions Should Be Abandoned." *N.Y.U. Annual Survey of American Law* 62: 795–846.

Lynch, Mona. 2002. "Pedophiles and Cyber-predators as Contaminating Forces: The Language of Disgust, Pollution, and Boundary Invasions in Federal Debates on Sex Offender Legislation." *Law and Social Inquiry* 27 (3): 529–57.

———. 2004. "Punishing Images: Jail Cam and the Changing Penal Enterprise." *Punishment and Society* 6 (3): 255–70.

MacKinnon, Catharine A. 1982. "Feminism, Marxism, Method, and the State: An Agenda for Theory." *Signs* 7 (3): 515–44.

———. 1983. "Feminism, Marxism, Method, and the State: Toward Feminist Jurisprudence." *Signs* 8 (4): 635–58.

———. 1989. *Toward a Feminist Theory of the State.* Cambridge, Mass.: Harvard University Press.

———. 1991. "Reflections on Sex Equality Under Law." *Yale Law Journal* 100: 1281–1328.

———. 2001. *Sex Equality: Rape Law.* New York: Foundation Press.

———. 2007a. *Women's Lives, Men's Laws.* Cambridge, Mass.: Belknap Press.

———. 2007b. *Sex Equality.* 2nd ed. New York: Foundation Press.

Mairena, Oscar. 2012. "Public Health and the Criminalization of HIV Transmission, Exposure & Non-Disclosure." *National Alliance of State and Territorial Directors.* December 4. https://www.nastad.org/sites/default/files/Presentation-HIV-Criminalization-UNDP-NASTAD-Meeting-12-04-12.pdf.

"Making Outcasts Out of Outlaws: The Unconstitutionality of Sex Offender Registration and Criminal Alien Detention." 2004. *Harvard Law Review* 117: 2731–52.

Marcotte, Amanda. 2013. "A Movie about Steubenville from a Male Perspective Is a Great Idea." *Slate.* April 14. http://www.slate.com/blogs/xx_factor/2014/04/04/brad_pitt_s_plan_b_buys_the_rights_to_anonymous_vs_steubenville_a_male_centric.html.

Marcus, Sharon. 1992. "Fighting Bodies, Fighting Words: A Theory and Politics of Rape Prevention." In *Feminists Theorize the Political,* edited by Judith Butler and Joan W. Scott, 385–403. New York: Routledge.

Markell, Patchen. 2008. "The Insufficiency of Non-Domination." *Political Theory* 36 (1): 9–36.

Marlowe, Julian. 1997. "It's Different for Boys." In *Whores and Other Feminists,* edited by Jill Nagle, 141–44. New York: Routledge.

Martin, Biddy. 1994. "Extraordinary Homosexuals and the Fear of Being Ordinary." *differences: A Journal of Feminist Cultural Studies* 6 (2–3): 100–125.

Marx, Karl, and Friedrich Engels. 1998 (1845). *The German Ideology.* Amherst, N.Y.: Prometheus Books.

Massumi, Brian. 1992. *A User's Guide to Capitalism: Deviations from Deleuze and Guattari.* Cambridge, Mass.: MIT Press.

McBride, Kelly. 2013. "Why Railing against CNN for the Steubenville Coverage Is a Waste of Time." *Poynter.* March 19. http://www.poynter.org/latest-news/top-stories/207647/why-railing-against-cnn-for-the-steubenville-coverage-is-a-waste-of-time.

McCloud, Scott. 1993. *Understanding Comics: The Invisible Art.* Northampton, Mass.: Kitchen Sink Press.

McCollam, Douglas. 2007. "The Shame Game." *Columbia Journalism Review* 45 (5): 28–33.

McCreery, Patrick. 2001. "Beyond Gay: 'Deviant' Sex and the Politics of the ENDA Workplace." In *Out at Work: Building a Gay-Labor Alliance,* edited by Kitty Krupat and Patrick McCreery, 31–51. Minneapolis: University of Minnesota Press.

———. 2008. "Save Our Children/Let Us Marry: Gay Activists Appropriate the Rhetoric of Child Protectionism." *Radical History Review* 2008 (100): 186–207.

McCruer, Robert, and Anna Mollow, eds. 2012. *Sex and Disability.* Durham, N.C.: Duke University Press.

McKenzie, Mia. 2013. "On Rape, Cages, and the Steubenville Verdict." *Black Girl Dangerous.* March 18. http://www.blackgirldangerous.org/2013/03/20133171g5wckiks8gpaoiahe4zc46go4awsu/.

McRobbie, Angela, and Sarah L. Thornton. 1995. "Rethinking 'Moral Panic' for Multi-Mediated Social Worlds." *British Journal of Sociology* 46 (4): 559–74.

Meiners, Erica R. 2009. "Never Innocent: Feminist Troubles with Sex Offender Registries in a Prison State." *Meridians: feminism, race, transnationalism* 9 (2): 31–62.

———. 2015. "Offending Children, Registering Sex." *WSQ: Women's Studies Quarterly* 43 (1 & 2): 246–63.

Michels, Scott. 2012. "Thirteen and Locked Up for Life?" *Salon.* October 2. http://www.salon.com/2012/10/02/thirteen_and_locked_up_for_life.

Mill, J. S. 1998. *On Liberty and Other Essays.* 2nd ed. Edited by John Gray. Oxford: Oxford University Press.

Millar, Thomas Macaulay. 2008. "Toward a Performance Model of Sex." In *Yes Means Yes: Visions of Female Sexual Power and a World Without Rape,* edited by Jaclyn Friedman and Jessica Valenti, 29–42. Berkeley: Seal Press.

Millett, Kate. 1992. "Beyond Politics: Children and Sexuality." In *Pleasure and Danger: Exploring Female Sexuality,* edited by Carol S. Vance, 217–24. London: Pandora, 1992.

Minow, Martha. 1986. "Rights for the Next Generation: A Feminist Approach to Children's Rights." *Harvard Women's Law Journal* 9 (1): 1–24.

Minow, Martha, and Mary Lyndon Shanley. 1996. "Relational Rights and Responsibilities: Revisioning the Family in Liberal Political Theory and Law." *Hypatia* 11 (1): 4–29.

Mohr, Richard D. 1988. *Gays/Justice: A Study of Ethics, Society, and Law.* New York: Columbia University Press.

———. 2004. "The Shag-A-Delic Supreme Court: 'Anal Sex,' 'Mystery,' 'Destiny,' and the 'Transcendent' in *Lawrence v. Texas*." *Cardozo Women's Law Journal* 10: 365–95.

Muñoz, José Esteban. 2009. *Cruising Utopia: The Then and There of Queer Futurity*. New York: New York University Press.

Munro, Vanessa E. 2007. "Dev'l-in Disguise? Harm, Privacy, and the Sexual Offences Act 2003." In *Sexuality and the Law: Feminist Engagements*, edited by Vanessa E. Munro and Carl F. Stychin, 1–18. New York: Routledge-Cavendish.

Murtha, Tara. 2013. "Steubenville: How the Media Promotes Rape Culture." *AlterNet*. March 19. http://www.alternet.org/media/steubenville-how-media-promotes-rape -culture.

Nedelsky, Jennifer. 2011. *Law's Relations: A Relational Theory of Self, Autonomy, and Law*. Oxford: Oxford University Press.

Nelson, Andrea, and Pamela Oliver. 1998. "Gender and the Construction of Consent in Child-Adult Sexual Contact: Beyond Gender Neutrality and Male Monopoly," *Gender and Society* 12 (5): 554–77.

Nobles, Matt R., Jill S. Levenson, and Tasha J. Youstin. 2012. "Effectiveness of Residence Restrictions in Preventing Sex Offense Recidivism." *Crime and Delinquency* 58 (4): 491–513.

Nolan, Hamilton. 2013. "How to Have Sex at Yale." *Gawker*. September 13. http://gawker.com/how-to-have-sex-at-yale-1307498752.

North, Anna. 2011. "The Real Reason Yale Banned 'Sex Week.'" *Jezebel*. November 11. http://jezebel.com/5858643/why-yale-really-banned-sex-week.

Nussbaum, Martha C. 1995. "Objectification." *Philosophy and Public Affairs* 24 (4): 249–91.

———. 1998. "'Whether from Reason or Prejudice': Taking Money for Bodily Services." *Journal of Legal Studies* 27 (2): 693–734.

———. 2001. *Women and Human Development: The Capabilities Approach*. Cambridge: Cambridge University Press.

———. 2006a. *The Fragility of Goodness: Luck and Ethics in Greek Tragedy and Philosophy*. Cambridge: Cambridge University Press.

———. 2006b. *Frontiers of Justice: Disability, Nationality, Species Membership*. Cambridge, Mass.: Belknap Press.

———. 2011. *Creating Capabilities: The Human Development Approach*. Cambridge, Mass.: Belknap Press.

Nutting, Alissa. 2013. *Tampa*. New York: HarperCollins.

Oberman, Michelle. 1994. "Turning Girls into Women: Re-Evaluating Modern Statutory Rape Law." *Journal of Criminal Law and Criminology* 85 (1): 15–79.

———. 2000. "Regulating Consensual Sex with Minors: Defining a Role for Statutory Rape." *Buffalo Law Review* 48: 703–84.

———. 2001. "Girls in the Master's House: Of Protection, Patriarchy, and the Potential for Using the Master's Tools to Reconfigure Statutory Rape Law." *DePaul Law Review* 50: 799–826.

O'Connell, Hilary. 2014. "Public Health for Public Bodies: Harm Reduction, Sex Work, and the Politics of Intervention." BA thesis, Yale University.

Odem, Mary E. 1995. *Delinquent Daughters: Protecting and Policing Adolescent Female Sexuality in the United States, 1885–1920*. Chapel Hill: University of North Carolina Press.

Ohi, Kevin. 2000. "Molestation 101: Child Abuse, Homophobia, and the Boys of St. Vincent." *GLQ* 6 (2): 195–248.

Oliveri, Rigel. 2000. "Statutory Rape Law and Enforcement in the Wake of Welfare Reform." *Stanford Law Review* 52 (2): 463–508.

Olsen, Frances. 1984. "Statutory Rape: A Feminist Critique of Rights Analysis." *Texas Law Review* 63 (3): 387–432.

Oppel, Richard A., Jr. 2013. "Ohio Teenagers Guilty in Rape that Social Media Brought to Light." *New York Times*. March 17. http://www.nytimes.com/2013/03/18/us/teenagers-found-guilty-in-rape-in-steubenville-ohio.html.

Orben, Jessica Ann. 2005. "*Connecticut Department of Public Safety v. Doe:* Sex Offenders' Due Process Under 'Megan's Law' and the Effectiveness of Sex Offender Registration." *University of Toledo Law Review* 36: 789–812.

Ortberg, Mallory. 2013. "CNN Reports on the 'Promising Future' of the Steubenville Rapists, Who Are 'Very Good Students.'" *Gawker*. March 17. http://gawker.com/5991003/cnn-reports-on-the-promising-future-of-the-steubenville-rapists-who-are-very-good-students.

Oshana, Marina A. L. 1998. "Personal Autonomy and Society." *Journal of Social Philosophy* 29 (1): 81–102.

Ost, Suzanne. 2009. *Child Pornography and Sexual Grooming: Legal and Societal Responses*. New York: Cambridge University Press.

Parker, Kathleen. 2012. "The Yale QB and the New York Times: All the News That's Unfit to Print." *Washington Post*. January 27. http://www.washingtonpost.com/opinions/the-yale-qb-and-the-new-york-times-all-the-news-thats-unfit-to-print/2012/01/27/gIQAFxKPWQ_story.html.

Pascoe, C. J. 2007. *Dude You're a Fag: Masculinity and Sexuality in High School*. Berkeley: University of California Press.

Pateman, Carole. 1980. "Women and Consent." *Political Theory* 8 (2): 149–68.

———. 1988. *The Sexual Contract*. Stanford: Stanford University Press.

———. 2007. "On Critics and Contract." In *Contract and Domination*, edited by Carole Pateman and Charles Mills, 200–229. Cambridge: Polity.

Payne, Elizabeth C. 2007. "Heterosexism, Perfection, and Popularity: Young Lesbians' Experiences of the High School Social Scene." *Educational Studies* 41 (7): 60–79.

Payne, Robert. 2008. "Virtual Panic: Children Online and the Transmission of Harm." In *Moral Panics over Contemporary Children and Youth*, edited by Charles Krinsky, 31–46. Surrey: Ashgate.

"perempt, *v.*" 2014. *OED Online*. Oxford University Press. http://www.oed.com/view/Entry/140674?redirectedFrom=perempt.

"peremption, *n.*" 2014. *OED Online.* Oxford University Press. http://www.oed.com/view/Entry/237386?redirectedFrom=peremption.

"peremptory, *adj., adv.,* and *n.*" 2014. *OED Online.* Oxford University Press. http://www.oed.com/view/Entry/140680?rskey=yodzMs&result=2&isAdvanced=false.

Pérez-Peña, Richard. 2013. "College Groups Connect to Fight Sexual Assault." *New York Times.* March 19. http://www.nytimes.com/2013/03/20/education/activists-at-colleges-network-to-fight-sexual-assault.html?pagewanted=all.

Pérez-Peña, Richard, and Kate Taylor. 2014. "Fight against Sexual Assaults Hold Colleges to Account." *New York Times.* May 3. http://www.nytimes.com/2014/05/04/us/fight-against-sex-crimes-holds-colleges-to-account.html?hpw&rref=us.

Periman, Deborah. 2008. "Revisiting Alaska's Sex Offender Registration and Notification Statute." *Alaska Justice Forum* 25 (1/2): 2–5. http://justice.uaa.alaska.edu/forum/25/1-2springsummer2008/c_asora.html.

Pesta, Abigail. 2012. "Laws Gone Wild: As Teen Sweethearts Go to Prison for Sex, Mothers Rebel." *The Daily Beast.* January 25. http://www.thedailybeast.com/articles/2012/01/25/should-teens-be-jailed-for-sex-offenses-a-growing-parental-rebellion-says-no.html.

Peterson, Latoya. 2008. "The Not-Rape Epidemic." In *Yes Means Yes: Visions of Female Sexual Power and a World Without Rape,* edited by Jaclyn Friedman and Jessica Valenti, 209–20. Berkeley: Seal Press.

Pettit, Philip. 1997. *Republicanism: A Theory of Freedom and Government.* New York: Oxford University Press.

———. 2001a. "Capability and Freedom: A Defense of Sen." *Economics and Philosophy* 17: 1–20.

———. 2001b. *A Theory of Freedom: From the Psychology to the Politics of Agency.* Cambridge: Polity Press.

———. 2012. *On the People's Terms: A Republican Theory and Model of Democracy.* Cambridge: Cambridge University Press.

Phelan, Shane. 2001. *Sexual Strangers: Gays, Lesbians, and Dilemmas of Citizenship.* Philadelphia: Temple University Press.

Phillips, Lynn M. 1999. "Recasting Consent: Agency and Victimization in Adult–Teen Relationships." In *New Versions of Victims: Feminists Struggle with the Concept,* edited by Sharon Lamb, 82–107. New York: New York University Press.

Phipps, Charles A. 1997. "Children, Adults, Sex, and the Criminal Law: In Search of Reason." *Seton Hall Legislative Journal* 22: 1–66.

———. 2003. "Misdirected Reform: On Regulating Consensual Activity Between Teenagers." *Cornell Journal of Law and Public Policy* 12 (2): 373–445.

Pineau, Lois. 1996. "Date Rape: A Feminist Analysis." In *Date Rape: Feminism, Philosophy, and the Law,* edited by Leslie Francis, 1–26. University Park: Pennsylvania State University Press.

Pittman, Nicole. 2013. "Sex Offenders Aren't All Monsters." *The Daily Beast.* May 7. http://www.thedailybeast.com/articles/2013/05/07/sex-offenders-aren-t-all-monsters.html.

Place, Vanessa. 2010. *The Guilt Project: Rape, Morality, and Law.* New York: Other Press.

Posner, Richard A., and Katharine B. Silbaugh. 1996. *A Guide to America's Sex Laws.* Chicago: University of Chicago Press.

"Potential Predators Go South in Kentucky." 2007. *Dateline NBC.* December 28 [Updated by Chris Hansen, January 9, 2008]. Transcript. http://www.msnbc.msn .com/id/22423433/page/3/.

Potter, Claire. 2011. "The Penn State Scandal: Connect the Dots between Child Abuse and the Sexual Assault of Women on Campus." *Tenured Radical, Chronicle of Higher Education.* November 10. http://chronicle.com/blognetwork/tenuredradi cal/2011/11/1401/.

———. 2013. "The Five Big Lies about Campus Rape." *Tenured Radical, Chronicle of Higher Education.* August 13. http://chronicle.com/blognetwork/tenuredradical/ 2013/08/the-five-big-lies-about-campus-rape/.

———. 2014. "Inside the Red Zone: The College Rape Season." *Tenured Radical, Chronicle of Higher Education.* July 13. http://chronicle.com/blognetwork/tenured radical/2014/07/inside-the-red-zone-the-college-rape-season-begins-soon/.

Potter, Roberto Hugh, and Lyndy A. Potter. 2001. "The Internet, Cyberporn, and Sexual Exploitation of Children: Media Moral Panics and Urban Myths for Middle-Class Parents?" *Sexuality and Culture* 5 (3): 31–48.

Pratt, John. 2000. "Emotive and Ostentatious Punishment." *Punishment and Society* 2 (4): 417–39.

"pre-emption, *n.*" 2014. *OED Online.* Oxford University Press. http://www.oed.com/ view/Entry/149931?redirectedFrom=preemption.

"Pre-Exposure Prophylaxis (PrEP)." 2014. *Centers for Disease Control and Prevention.* May 19. http://www.cdc.gov/hiv/prevention/research/prep/.

Prescott, J. J., and Jonah E. Rockoff. 2011. "Do Sex Offender Registration and Notification Laws Affect Criminal Behavior?" *Journal of Law and Economics* 54 (1): 161–206.

"President Signs H.R. 4472, the Adam Walsh Child Protection and Safety Act of 2006." 2006. White House Archives. July 27. http://georgewbush-whitehouse.archives .gov/news/releases/2006/07/text/20060727-6.html.

"Prevention Versus Punishment: Toward a Principled Distinction in the Restraint of Released Sex Offenders." 1996. *Harvard Law Review* 109: 1711–28.

Pryor, Douglas W. 1996. *Unspeakable Acts: Why Men Sexually Abuse Children.* New York: New York University Press.

Puar, Jasbir K. 2007. *Terrorist Assemblages: Homonationalism in Queer Times.* Durham, N.C.: Duke University Press.

———. 2012. "The Cost of Getting Better: Suicide, Sensation, Switchpoints." *GLQ* 18 (1): 149–58.

Purdum, Todd S. 1998. "Death of Sex Offender Is Tied to Megan's Law." *New York Times.* July 9. http://www.nytimes.com/1998/07/09/us/death-of-sex-offender-is-tied-to -megan-s-law.html.

Quinn, Mae C. 2014. "From Turkey Trot to Twitter: Policing Puberty, Purity and Sex-Positivity." *N.Y.U. Review of Law and Social Change* 38: 51–98.

Rahimi, Regina, and Delores D. Liston. 2012. *Pervasive Vulnerabilities: Sexual Harassment in School.* New York: Peter Lang.

Ramachandran, Gowri. 2009. "Against the Right to Bodily Integrity: Of Cyborgs and Human Rights." *Denver Law Review* 87 (1): 1–57.

———. 2013. "Delineating the Heinous: Rape, Sex, and Self-Possession." *Yale Law Journal Online* 123: 371–88. http://www.yalelawjournal.org/forum/delineating-the -heinous-rape-sex-and-self-possession.

Rasmussen, Claire E. 2011. *The Autonomous Animal: Self-Governance and the Modern Subject.* Minneapolis: University of Minnesota Press.

Remick, Lani Anne. 1993. "Read Her Lips: An Argument for a Verbal Consent Standard in Rape." *University of Pennsylvania Law Review* 141 (3): 1103–51.

Renold, Emma, and Jessica Ringrose. 2011. "Schizoid Subjectivities? Re-theorizing Teen Girls' Sexual Culture in an Era of 'Sexualization.'" *Journal of Sociology* 47 (4): 389–409.

Rind, Bruce. 2001. "Gay and Bisexual Adolescent Boys' Sexual Experiences with Men: An Empirical Examination of Psychological Correlates in a Nonclinical Sample." *Archives of Sexual Behavior* 30 (4): 345–68.

Rind, Bruce, and Philip Tromovitch. 1997. "A Meta-Analytic Review of Findings from National Samples on Psychological Correlates of Child Sexual Abuse." *Journal of Sex Research* 34 (3): 237–55.

Rind, Bruce, Philip Tromovitch, and Robert Bauserman. 1998. "A Meta-Analytic Examination of Assumed Properties of Child Sexual Abuse Using College Samples." *Psychological Bulletin* 124 (1): 22–53.

Roberts, Dorothy E. 1997. *Killing the Black Body: Race, Reproduction, and the Meaning of Liberty.* New York: Pantheon Books.

Roberts, Kimberley. 2002. "Pleasure and Problems of the 'Angry Girl.'" In *Sugar, Spice, and Everything Nice: Cinemas of Girlhood,* edited by Frances Gateward and Murray Pomerance, 217–34. Detroit: Wayne State University Press.

Robertson, Stephen. 2005. *Crimes against Children: Sexual Violence and Legal Culture in New York City, 1880–1960.* Chapel Hill: University of North Carolina Press.

Roiphe, Katie. 1993. *The Morning After: Sex, Fear, and Feminism on Campus.* Boston: Little, Brown.

Rose, Sonya O. 1999. "Cultural Analysis and Moral Discourses: Episodes, Continuities, and Transformations." In *Beyond the Cultural Turn: New Directions in the Study of Society and Culture,* edited by Victoria E. Bonnell and Lynn Hunt, 217–40. Berkeley: University of California Press.

Rosenberg, Gerald N. 1991. *Hollow Hope: Can the Courts Bring about Social Change?* Chicago: University of Chicago Press.

Rousseau, Jean-Jacques. 1997. *Rousseau: The Social Contract and Other Later Political Writings.* Edited and translated by Victor Gourevitch. Cambridge: Cambridge University Press.

Rubenfeld, Jed. 2013a. "Rape-by-Deception—A Response." *Yale Law Journal Online* 123: 389–406. http://www.yalelawjournal.org/forum/rape-by-deceptiona-response.

———. 2013b. "The Riddle of Rape-by-Deception and the Myth of Sexual Autonomy." *Yale Law Journal* 122: 1372–1443.

Rubin, Gayle S. 1981. "Sexual Politics, the New Right, and the Sexual Fringe." In *The Age Taboo: Gay Male Sexuality, Power and Consent*, edited by Daniel Tsang, 108–15. Boston: Alyston Publications.

———. 1993. "Thinking Sex: Notes for a Radical Theory of the Politics of Sexuality." In *The Lesbian and Gay Studies Reader*, edited by Henry Abelove, Michèle Aina Barale, and David M. Halperin, 3–37. New York: Routledge.

———. 2011a. "Blood under the Bridge: Reflections on 'Thinking Sex.'" *GLQ* 17 (1): 15–48.

———. 2011b. "The Leather Menace: Comments and Politics on S/M." In *Deviations: A Gayle Rubin Reader*, 109–36. Durham, N.C.: Duke University Press.

Sandel, Michael J. 1982. *Liberalism and the Limits of Justice*. Cambridge: Cambridge University Press.

Sanders, Lynn M. 1997. "Against Deliberation." *Political Theory* 25 (3): 347–76.

Sandfort, Theo. 1983. "Pedophile Relationships in the Netherlands: Alternative Lifestyle for Children?" *Alternative Lifestyles* 5 (3): 164–83.

Sarat, Austin. 2009. "Remorse, Responsibility, and Criminal Punishment: An Analysis of Popular Culture." In *The Passions of Law*, edited by Susan A. Bandes, 168–90. New York: New York University Press.

Sarat, Austin, Lawrence Douglas, and Martha Merrill Umphrey. 2005. "On Film and Law: Broadening the Focus." In *Law on the Screen*, edited by Austin Sarat, Lawrence Douglas, and Martha Merrill Umphrey, 1–26. Stanford: Stanford University Press.

Satz, Ani B. 2008. "Disability, Vulnerability, and the Limits of Antidiscrimination." *Washington Law Review* 83: 513–68.

Savage, Dan, and Terry Miller, eds. 2011. *It Gets Better: Coming Out, Overcoming Bullying, and Creating a Life Worth Living*. New York: Dutton.

Savin-Williams, Rich C. 2005. *The New Gay Teenager*. Cambridge, Mass.: Harvard University Press.

Sax, Leonard. 2010a. *Girls on the Edge: The Four Factors Driving the New Crisis for Girls*. New York: Basic Books.

———. 2010b. "Why Are So Many Girls Cutting Themselves?" *Psychology Today*. March 14. http://www.psychologytoday.com/blog/sax-sex/201003/why-are-so-many-girls-cutting-themselves.

Saxer, Shelley Ross. 2009. "Banishment of Sex Offenders: Liberty, Protectionism, Justice, and Alternatives." *Washington University Law Review* 86: 1397–1453.

Schaffner, Laurie. 2005. "Capacity, Consent, and the Construction of Adulthood." In *Regulating Sex: The Politics of Intimacy and Identity*, edited by Laurie Schaffner and Elizabeth Bernstein, 189–208. New York: Routledge.

Schissel, Bernard. 2008. "Justice Undone: Public Panic and the Condemnation of Children and Youth." In *Moral Panics over Contemporary Children and Youth,* edited by Charles Krinsky, 15–30. Surrey: Ashgate.

Schulhofer, Stephen J. 1992. "Taking Sexual Autonomy Seriously: Rape Law and Beyond." *Law and Philosophy* 11 (1/2): 35–94.

———. 1998. *Unwanted Sex: The Culture of Intimidation and the Failure of Law.* Cambridge, Mass.: Harvard University Press.

Schultz, Pamela D. 2008. "Naming, Blaming, and Framing: Moral Panic over Child Molesters and Its Implications for Public Policy." In *Moral Panics over Contemporary Children and Youth,* edited by Charles Krinsky, 95–110. Surrey: Ashgate.

Searcey, Dionne. 2009. "A Lawyer, Some Teens, and a Fight over 'Sexting.'" *Wall Street Journal.* April 21. http://online.wsj.com/article/SB124026115528336397.html.

Sedgwick, Eve Kosofsky. 1985. *Between Men: English Literature and Male Homosocial Desire.* New York: Columbia University Press.

———. 1992. "Epidemics of the Will." In *Incorporations,* edited by Jonathan Crary and Sanford Kwinter, 582–95. New York: Zone.

———. 2008. *Epistemology of the Closet.* Berkeley: University of California Press.

The Sentencing Project. 2013. "Report of the Sentencing Project to the United Nations Human Rights Committee Regarding Racial Disparities in the United States Criminal Justice System." http://sentencingproject.org/doc/publications/rd_ICCPR%20Race%20and%20Justice%20Shadow%20Report.pdf.

"Serosorting among Gay, Bisexual and Other Men Who Have Sex with Men." 2011. Centers for Disease Control and Prevention. October 24. http://www.cdc.gov/msm health/serosorting.htm.

"Sex Predators Will See Signs at Their Homes." 2013. *First Coast News.* April 8. Video. http://www.firstcoastnews.com/news/article/307905/3/Sex-predators-in-Brad ford-County-will-see-signs-at-their-homes.

Sex Week 2012 Executive Directors. 2011. "SW 2012 Directors to Student Body: Sex Week Is Coming." *Broad Recognition.* November 4. http://broadrecognition.com/opinion/sway-directors-to-student-body-sex-week-is-coming/.

"Sexual Misconduct Scenarios." 2013. *Sexual Misconduct Response at Yale.* September 9. http://smr.yale.edu/sites/default/files/files/Sexual-Misconduct-Scenarios.pdf /.

Shanley, John Patrick. 2005. *Doubt: A Parable.* New York: Theatre Communications Group.

Shapiro, Rebecca. 2013. "Poppy Harlow, CNN Reporter, 'Outraged' over Steubenville Rape Coverage Criticism: Report." *Huffington Post.* March 20. http://www.huffing tonpost.com/2013/03/20/poppy-harlow-cnn-steubenville-rape-coverage-criti cism_n_2914853.html.

Sharpe, Alex. 2014. "Criminalising Sexual Intimacy: Transgender Defendants and the Legal Construction of Non-Consent." *Criminal Law Review* 3: 207–23.

Shary, Timothy. 2010. "Virgin Springs: A Survey of Teen Films' Quest for Sexcess." In *Virgin Territory: Representing Sexual Inexperience in Film,* edited by Tamar Jeffers McDonald, 54–67. Detroit: Wayne State University Press.

Shepard, Benjamin. 2003. "In Search of a Winning Script: Moral Panic vs Institutional Denial." *Sexualities* 6 (1): 54–59.

Sherwin, Richard K. 2005. "Anti-Oedipus, Lynch: Initiatory Rites and the Ideal of Justice." In *Law on the Screen*, edited by Austin Sarat, Lawrence Douglas, and Martha Merrill Umphrey, 106–52. Stanford: Stanford University Press.

Siegel, Carol. 2010. "Irreconcilable Feminisms and the Construction of a Cultural Memory of Virginity's Loss: *À ma soeur!* and *Thirteen.*" In *Virgin Territory: Representing Sexual Inexperience in Film*, edited by Tamar Jeffers McDonald, 238–54. Detroit: Wayne State University Press.

Simon, Jonathan. 2000. "Megan's Law: Crime and Democracy in Late Modern America." *Law and Social Inquiry* 25 (4): 1111–50.

Simons, Margaret A. 1992. "Lesbian Connections: Simone de Beauvoir and Feminism." *Signs* 18 (1): 136–31.

Singer, Mathew. 2008. ". . . And Procedure for All: Rehearings for 'Dangerous' Offenders." *University of Cincinnati Law Review* 76: 1067–91.

Small, Jamie L. 2015. "Classing Sex Offenders: How Prosecutors and Defense Attorneys Differentiate Men Accused of Sexual Assault." *Law and Society Review* 49 (1): 109–41.

SMART. 2010. "SORNA Applicability." *Office of Justice Programs.* U.S. Dept. of Justice. http://www.ojp.usdoj.gov/smart/sorna.htm.

Smith, Anna Marie. 2001. "The Politicization of Marriage in Contemporary American Public Policy: The Defense of Marriage Act and the Personal Responsibility Act." *Citizenship Studies* 5 (3): 303–20.

Snyder, Howard. 2000. "Sexual Assault of Young Children as Reported to Law Enforcement: Victim, Incident, and Offender Characteristics." Bureau of Justice and Statistics, Office of Justice Programs, U.S. Department of Justice. July. http://www.bjs.gov/index.cfm?ty=pbdetail&iid=1147. 14 pages.

Spade, Dean. 2011. *Normal Life: Administrative Violence, Critical Trans Politics, and the Limits of Law.* New York: South End Press.

Spelman, Elizabeth V., and Martha Minow. 1996. "Outlaw Women: *Thelma and Louise.*" In *Legal Reelism: Movies as Legal Texts*, edited by John Denvir, 261–79. Urbana: University of Illinois Press.

Spindelman, Marc. 2013. "Sexuality's Law." *Columbia Journal of Gender and Law* 24 (2): 87–252.

Stanley, Alessandra. 2006. "Gotcha! 'Dateline' Paves a Walk of Shame for Online Predators." *New York Times.* May 17. http://www.nytimes.com/2006/05/17/arts/television/17stan.html.

Stanley, Jessica L., Kim Bartholomew, and Doug Oram. 2004. "Gay and Bisexual Men's Age-Discrepant Childhood Sexual Experiences." *Journal of Sex Research* 41 (4): 381–89.

"State Supreme Court Releases Dangerous Decision in Sexual Assault Case." 2012. Connecticut Sexual Assault Crisis Services, Inc. http://www.connsacs.org.

Stockton, Kathryn Bond. 2009. *The Queer Child, or Growing Sideways in the Twentieth Century.* Durham, N.C.: Duke University Press.

Strub, Sean. 2011. "Prevention vs. Prosecution: Creating a Viral Underclass." *POZ Blogs.* October 18. http://blogs.poz.com/sean/archives/2011/10/prevention_vs _prosec.html.

Stychin, Carl F. 1995. *Law's Desire: Sexuality and the Limits of Justice.* New York: Routledge.

——. 1998. *A Nation by Rights: National Cultures, Sexual Identity Politics, and the Discourse of Rights.* Philadelphia: Temple University Press.

——. 2003. *Governing Sexuality: The Changing Politics of Citizenship and Law Reform.* Portland: Hart Publishing.

Sunstein, Cass R. 2004. "The Right to Marry." *Cardozo Law Review* 26 (5): 2081–2120.

——. 2008. "Due-Process Traditionalism." *Michigan Law Review* 106: 1543–70.

Superbad. 2007. DVD. Directed by Greg Mottola. USA: Columbia Pictures.

Sutherland, Edwin H. 1950. "The Diffusion of Sexual Psychopath Laws." *American Journal of Sociology* 56 (2): 142–48.

Sutherland, Kate. 2003. "From Jailbird to Jailbait: Age of Consent Laws and the Construction of Teenage Sexualities." *William and Mary Journal of Women and Law* 9: 313–50.

Szymialis, Jordan J. 2010. "Sexting: A Response to Prosecuting Those Growing Up with a Growing Trend." *Indiana Law Review* 44 (1): 301–39.

Taylor, Charles. 1989. *Sources of the Self: The Making of Modern Identity.* Cambridge, Mass.: Harvard University Press.

Taylor, Kate. 2014. "List of Names in Sex Assaults Roils Columbia." *New York Times.* May 13. http://www.nytimes.com/2014/05/14/nyregion/list-of-names-in-sex -assaults-roils-columbia.html.

Taylor, Marisa. 2014. "Lawmakers, Activists Mull Title IX and Campus Sexual Assault." *Al Jazeera America.* June 3. http://america.aljazeera.com/articles/2014/6/ 3/campus-sexual-assaultmccaskill.html.

Terry, Karen J., and Alissa R. Ackerman. 2009. "A Brief History of Major Sex Offender Laws." In *Sex Offender Laws: Failed Policies, New Directions,* edited by Richard G. Wright, 397–426. New York: Springer.

Thirteen. 2003. DVD. Directed by Catherine Hardwicke. USA: Fox Searchlight Pictures.

Thorstad, David. 1990. "Man/Boy Love and the American Gay Movement." *Journal of Homosexuality* 20 (1/2): 251–74.

"Title IX Complaint Press Release." 2011. *Yale Herald.* March 31. http://yaleherald .com/uncategorized/title-ix-complaint-press-release/.

"To Catch a Predator—Bowling Green, Kentucky." 2015. *Daily Motion,* January 21. http://www.dailymotion.com/video/x2f62fh.

"To Catch a Predator—Ocean County, New Jersey—2 of 2." 2015. *Daily Motion,* January 21. http://www.dailymotion.com/video/x2f61xv.

Today. 2011. "Mary Kay Letourneau: Fallout of Case Was Tragic." *NBC News,* January 28. Video. http://www.nbcnews.com/id/21134540/vp/41310512#41310512 (no longer available).

Tolman, Deborah L. 2002. *Dilemmas of Desire: Teenage Girls Talk about Sexuality.* Cambridge, Mass.: Harvard University Press.

Tribe, Laurence H. 1980. "The Puzzling Persistence of Process-Based Constitutional Theories." *Yale Law Journal* 89: 1063–80.

———. 2004. "*Lawrence v. Texas*: The 'Fundamental Right' that Dare Not Speak Its Name." *Harvard Law Review* 117: 1893–1955.

Tronto, Joan C. 2013. *Caring Democracy: Markets, Equality, and Justice.* New York: New York University Press.

Troyer, John, and Chani Marchiselli. 2005. "Slack, Slacker, Slackest: Homosocial Bonding Practices in Contemporary Dude Cinema." In *Where the Boys Are: Cinemas of Masculinity and Youth,* edited by Murray Pomerance and Frances Gateward, 264–78. Detroit: Wayne State University Press.

Tsang, Daniel, ed. 1981. *The Age Taboo: Gay Male Sexuality, Power and Consent.* Boston: Alyston Publications.

Tuerkheimer, Deborah. 2013. "Sex Without Consent." *Yale Law Journal Online* 123: 335–52. http://www.yalelawjournal.org/forum/sex-without-consent.

Turner, Bryan. 2006. *Vulnerability and Human Rights.* University Park: Penn State University Press.

UNAIDS. 2013. "Ending Overly Broad Criminalisation of HIV Non-Disclosure, Exposure, and Transmission: Critical Scientific, Medical, and Legal Considerations." http://www.unaids.org/sites/default/files/media_asset/20130530_Guidance_Ending_Criminalisation_0.pdf?}

"U.S. Department of Education Releases List of Higher Education Institutions with Open Title IX Sexual Violence Investigations." 2014. U.S. Department of Education. May 1. http://www.ed.gov/news/press-releases/us-department-education-releases-list-higher-education-institutions-open-title-i.

Valentine, David. 2006. "'I Went to Bed with My Own Kind Once': The Erasure of Desire in the Name of Identity." In *The Transgender Studies Reader,* edited by Susan Stryker and Stephen Whittle, 407–19. New York: Routledge.

Valier, Claire. 2004. "Introduction: The Power to Punish and the Power of the Image." *Punishment and Society* 6 (3): 251–54.

Vance, Carole S., ed. 1992. *Pleasure and Danger: Exploring Female Sexuality.* London: Pandora.

Vandiver, Donna M., and Glen Kercher. 2004. "Offender and Victim Characteristics of Registered Female Sexual Offenders in Texas: A Proposed Typology of Female Sexual Offenders." *Sexual Abuse: A Journal of Research and Treatment* 16 (2): 121–37.

Vásquez, Bob Edward, et al. 2008. "The Influence of Sex Offender Registration and Notification Laws in the United States: A Time-Series Analysis." *Crime and Delinquency* 54 (2): 175–92.

Wacquant, Loic. 2009. *Punishing the Poor: The Neoliberal Government of Social Insecurity.* Durham, N.C.: Duke University Press.

Waites, Matthew. 2005. *The Age of Consent: Young People, Sexuality and Citizenship.* Basingstoke: Palgrave MacMillan.

Walton, Jean. 1999. "White Neurotics, Black Primitive, and the Queer Matrix of *Borderline.*" In *Out Takes: Essays on Queer Theory and Film,* edited by Ellis Hanson, 243–70. Durham, N.C.: Duke University Press.

Wardenski, Joseph J. 2005. "A Minor Exception? The Impact of *Lawrence v. Texas* on LGBT Youth." *Journal of Criminal Law and Criminology* 95 (4): 1363–1410.

Wark, McKenzie. 1995. "Fresh Maimed Babies: The Uses of Innocence." *Transitions* 65: 36–47.

Warner, Michael. 1999. *The Trouble with Normal: Sex, Politics, and the Ethics of Queer Life.* New York: Free Press.

Watney, Simon. 1996. *Policing Desire: Pornography, AIDS and the Media.* 3rd ed. Minneapolis: University of Minnesota Press.

Way, Niobe. 2011. *Deep Secrets: Boys, Friendships, and the Crisis of Conversation.* Cambridge, Mass.: Harvard University Press.

Welsh-Huggins, Andrew. 2013. "Steubenville Sex Offender Hearing: Trent Mays, Ma'Lik Richmond May Be Moved to Rehabilitation Center." *Huffington Post.* June 14. http://www.huffingtonpost.com/2013/06/14/steubenville-rape-sex-offender-hearing-trent-mays-malik-richmond_n_3441067.html.

Wertheimer, Alan. 1987. *Coercion.* Princeton, N.J.: Princeton University Press.

———. 2003. *Consent to Sexual Relations.* New York: Cambridge University Press.

West, Robin. 2008. "The Harms of Consensual Sex." In *The Philosophy of Sex: Contemporary Readings,* edited by Alan Soble and Nicholas Power, 317–24. Lanham, Md.: Rowman & Littlefield.

White House Task Force to Protect Students from Sexual Assault. 2014. "Not Alone: The First Report of the White House Task Force to Protect Students from Sexual Assault." Not Alone: Together Against Sexual Assault. April. https://www.notalone.gov/assets/report.pdf.

"Why Marriage?" 2014. *Freedom to Marry.* http://www.whymarriagematters.org/pages/why-marriage.

"Why Schools Handle Sexual Violence Reports." 2013. Know Your IX. http://knowyourix.org/why-schools-handle-sexual-violence-reports/.

Williams, Francis N. 2009. "The Problem of Sexual Assault." In *Sex Offender Laws: Failed Policies, New Directions,* edited by Richard G. Wright, 17–64. New York: Springer.

Williams, Linda. 1999. *Hard Core: Power, Pleasure, and the "Frenzy of the Visible."* 2nd ed. Berkeley: University of California Press.

———. 2008. *Screening Sex.* Durham, N.C.: Duke University Press.

Williams, Wendy W. 1997. "The Equality Crisis: Some Reflections on Culture, Court, and Feminism." In *The Second Wave: A Reader in Feminist Theory,* edited by Linda Nicholson, 71–92. New York: Routledge.

Wilson, Charles. 2012. "Federal Judge Bans Sex Offenders from Social Networking." *Washington Post.* June 25. http://www.washingtonpost.com/politics/federal-judge -bans-sex-offenders-from-social-networking/2012/06/24/gJQAkGRa1V_story .html.

Winnicott, D.W. 1971. *Playing and Reality.* New York: Basic Books.

Wolak, Janis, et al. 2008. "Online 'Predators' and Victims: Myths, Realities, and Implications for Prevention and Treatment." *American Psychologist* 63: 111–28.

Wolf, Naomi. 2002. *The Beauty Myth: How Images of Beauty are Used Against Women.* New York: Perennial.

Wood, Helen, and Beverly Skeggs. 2004. "Notes on Ethical Scenarios of Self on British Reality TV." *Feminist Media Studies* 4 (1): 205–8.

Woodford, Antonia. 2011. "Schools Revise Sexual Misconduct Policies." *Yale Daily News.* October 7. http://yaledailynews.com/blog/2011/10/07/schools-revise-sex ual-misconduct-policies/.

Woodhouse, Barbara Bennet. 2009. "A World Fit for Children Is a World Fit for Everyone: Ecogenerism, Feminism, and Vulnerability." *Houston Law Review* 46 (3): 817–65.

Wright, Richard G. 2009a. "Internet Sex Stings." In *Sex Offender Laws: Failed Policies, New Directions,* edited by Richard G. Wright, 115–58. New York: Springer.

———, ed. 2009b. *Sex Offender Laws: Failed Policies, New Directions.* New York: Springer.

"Yes on 8 TV Ad: Everything to Do with Schools." 2008. YouTube video, posted by "VoteYesonProp8." October 20. http://www.youtube.com/watch?v=7352ZVMKB QM.

"Yes on 8 TV Ad: It's Already Happened." 2008. YouTube video, posted by "VoteYes onProp8." October 7. http://www.youtube.com/watch?v=oPgjcgqFYP4.

Young, Iris Marion. 1990. *Justice and the Politics of Difference.* Princeton, N.J.: Princeton University Press.

Youth Liberation. 1981. "Children and Sex." In *The Age Taboo: Gay Male Sexuality, Power and Consent,* edited by Daniel Tsang, 46–52. Boston: Alyston Publications.

Yuill, Richard, and Dean Durber. 2008. "'Querying' the Limits of Queering Boys through the Contested Discourses on Sexuality." *Sexuality and Culture* 12: 257–74.

Yung, Corey Rayburn. 2015. "Rape Law Fundamentals." *Yale Journal of Law and Feminism* 27: 1–46.

Zacharek, Stephanie. 2003. "Thirteen." *Salon.* August 20. http://www.salon.com/ 2003/08/20/thirteen_2/.

Zerilli, Linda M. G. 2005. *Feminism and the Abyss of Freedom.* Chicago: University of Chicago Press.

Index

Rehnquist, Chief Justice William. *See
Connecticut Department of Public
Safety v. Doe*
relations of dependence. *See
dependence*
Rind, Bruce, 261n217
Robertson, Stephen, 247n12, 248n20
Roe v. Wade, 73, 75, 240n92, 241n104
Rose, Sonya O., 228n26
Rubenfeld, Jed, 203–9, 214, 284n64,
285n67, 285n69, 286n90, 286n94,
286n96
Rubin, Gayle, 11, 38–47, 48, 49, 55,
229n46, 231n66

sadomasochistic sex, 11, 36, 38, 124,
208, 212, 213, 234n6, 286n96
same-sex marriage. *See* marriage
Sandusky, Jerry, 15, 26, 57, 193, 199–200
Savile, Jimmy, 15, 26, 57, 193
Savin-Williams, Rich, 264n5, 279n10
Scalia, Justice Antonin: on competency,
66. *See also Connecticut Department of
Public Safety v. Doe; Lawrence v. Texas*
Schulhofer, Stephen, 11, 13, 94–98,
113–14, 115, 117, 122, 213, 252n98
Sedgwick, Eve Kosofsky, 277n196,
278n200
sex between minors, 10, 57, 116, 119,
121, 244n138, 244n140, 246n3,
249n46, 250n63; consent and, 86,
105, 115–27, 234n6; criminalization
of, 77, 101; decriminalization of,
18, 86, 99–108, 127, 131; queer,
244n139
sex education, 14, 105, 107, 147, 179,
199, 223n29, 254n124, 283n40; abstinence, 9, 138, 262n221; safer-sex, 48,
103, 129, 212, 258n192
sex offender registration and notification (SORN), 1, 3–4, 5, 17–18, 56,
59, 72, 78, 195–202, 207, 221n3,

222n7, 223n20, 240n88, 245n152;
online registries, 1, 2, 3, 4, 59, 60, 61,
62, 72, 79, 236n32, 240n101. *See also
Adam Walsh Child Protection and
Safety Act; Connecticut Department of
Public Safety v. Doe; Doe v. Moore; Doe
v. Tandeske; Jacob Wetterling Crimes
Against Children and Sexually Violent Offender Registration Act;
Megan's Law; United States of America
v. Madera*
Sex Offender Registration and Notification Act. *See Adam Walsh Child
Protection and Safety Act*
sex offenders: female, 21–22, 221n1,
226n62; GPS tracking of, 3, 4,
236n18; as the new queers, 3, 7, 9,
19–21, 57–58, 74–75, 225n53; police
response to, 1–3, 8, 22, 221n3, 234n8,
245n152, 280n2; and residency
restrictions, 4, 59, 60–62, 221n2;
young people as, 3–4, 245n148. *See
also Adam Walsh Child Protection
and Safety Act; homosexuality:
equation with pedophilia; Jacob
Wetterling Crimes Against Children
and Sexually Violent Offender
Registration Act; Megan's Law;
recidivism; sex offender registration
and notification*
sex panics. *See panics*
sexting, 5, 9, 15, 25
sexual abuse within the family, 57, 67,
74, 111, 230n53, 234n9, 237n40,
239n70, 261n217
sexual ethics, 3, 45, 47, 56–57, 247n9
sexual orientation, 15, 38, 87, 132, 133,
198
sexual predators, 1–6, 9, 15, 20, 221n3;
Internet, 8, 28, 32, 39–41, 71, 193,
230n53, 230n56, 230n58, 232n93.
See also To Catch a Predator

JOSEPH J. FISCHEL is assistant professor of women's, gender, and sexuality studies at Yale University.